Black Jack
A Drama of Magic,
Mystery and Legerdemain

The story of a young woman who
overcame unimaginable obstacles to
obtain the object of her desires.

THE WORLD'S GREATEST MAGICIAN
BLACK HERMAN

POWER

EUROPE

NORTH AMERICA

AFRICA

THE MISSING KEY   THE KEY to SUCCESS

SOUTH THAT

COVERS the WORLD   THE KEY To HAPPINESS

SECRETS OF
MAGIC-MYSTERY & LEGERDERMAIN
The Missing Key to Success, Health and Happiness

BLACK JACK

by

GEORGE PATTON

iUniverse, Inc.
New York   Bloomington

iUniverse books may be ordered through booksellers or by contacting:

iUniverse
1663 Liberty Drive
Bloomington, IN 47403
www.iuniverse.com
1-800-Authors (1-800-288-4677)

Because of the dynamic nature of the Internet, any Web addresses or links contained in this book may have changed since publication and may no longer be valid. The views expressed in this work are solely those of the author and do not necessarily reflect the views of the publisher, and the publisher hereby disclaims any responsibility for them.

ISBN: 978-1-4401-3666-5 (sc)
ISBN: 978-1-4401-3667-2 (ebook)
ISBN: 978-1-4401-6878-9 (hc)

Library of Congress Control Number: 2009925857

Printed in the United States of America

iUniverse rev. date: 8/14/2009

For Eva

Table of Contents

Preface

Scene opens on a nurse's station in a retirement home. Balloons, half a dozen or more, brightly colored float in a bunch above the countertop. They are tethered by long white ribbons. The camera pans onto a large sheet cake sitting on the counter. It too is brightly adorned with white icing and red and yellow confectionary roses. The camera records the message on top of the cake placed in the middle among a dozen candles. It reads: 'Happy 107th Birthday Miss Eva'.

Two nurses approach the desk. They greet the orderlies behind the counter with a question. "What's going on?"

The excited reply from the nurse's aide, "It's Miss Eva's birthday today. She is one hundred and seven years old."

'Miss Eva' is the oldest living resident in the nursing home and quite a celebrity. The newspapers will be there to take her picture, TV reporters as well. She is now the oldest living woman in Cleveland.

Blessed with a clear mind, she puts on a performance. "Honey, if you think I'm something now, you should have seen me in my heyday, when I had great legs," she says from her wheelchair. The reporter and the audience surrounding them in the alcove next to the nursing station laugh. She continues to regale them with stories of her youth until she loses her train of thought about five minutes later. She stops, puts a feeble hand to her head and starts again, "Now, what was I saying?"

"That's alright, sweetheart. I believe we have enough. Happy Birthday." He gives the cut sign to his cameraman after his sign off to the viewing public. They pack up their gear and excuse themselves from the remaining partygoers. The cameraman juggles a large slice of birthday cake with his gear.

Within the half hour, the party ends as Miss Eva grows tired and is wheeled back to her room for a nap. There would be another small party for her in the dining room at dinner.

As the orderly puts her into the bed, he notices she looks sad. "What's wrong, Miss Eva? Didn't you like your party?"

"No, it's not that, Lou," she remembered his name. "I was just thinking. If I could do my life over. You know I've really married some stinkers."

"Oh, it couldn't be that bad," Lou chided, sitting down next to her bed.

"Yes, it could." She was insistent. Now reinvigorated and warming to her task. "Did you know I was married to one of the greatest magicians of all time?"

"No, really? Do tell, Miss Eva."

"It's a fact. I was young and had great legs. He was tall and fearsome. They called him Black Jack. Black Jack Herman."

Thus she begins the tale of the greatest story of her life.

Over the next several days, remembrances would pour forth. On this one subject, she became completely lucid. It was as if a dam had broken somewhere in the deep recesses of her subconscious. The information, nee memories, flowed copiously. Her life's blood from the fountainhead of her soul.

Eva remembered dates, details, subtle nuances of expression as if they had happened yesterday instead of eighty-odd years ago. Her face was radiant-'yes it had been, hadn't it?' hair dark, shiny and long gorgeous legs. Men loved her legs. They would drool over them, especially in those outfits that Black Jack would buy for her. 'Black Jack', her mind focused on him. His face, the hard lines of the jaw, the high cheek bones, and the proud nose jutting out from his granite mask. Both fearsome and alluring at the same time. Women would fall under his spell instantly-do anything for him after just one look into his eyes. Those eyes, rich brown with a hint of ruby red. Haunting eyes, compelling eyes. Vibrant orbs that bespoke of chaos and terror, they seemed to have seen all the suffering of the world. Yet powerful enough to remake the universe in their own design. Those haunting eyes that carried the secret of the power of illusion. The power to make women see paradise and ecstasy. To make men see fear and despair.

Eva recalled how men acted around him, always on guard, somewhat disturbed, abashed. Never completely comfortable. Old acquaintances having become familiar with his demeanor, his style, would share a drink, a story, a joke. Underneath, they never were completely at ease. Upon exiting, they would leave hurriedly, sometimes with shoulders slumped. Hastily removing themselves from an uncomfortable presence. Perhaps they sensed his dark aura as it exuded from the corners of his smile. As it extruded from around the corners of the smile in his eyes. Those haunting eyes.

Women hated to leave his presence, even for a minute. The servant girls would leave with remorse if they had to walk into the next room. Upon re-entering his presence, they would glow like fireflies on a hot summer night. It was his darkness, his hardness, the hint of dastardly derring-do. That element of the unexpected that was always present. He cultivated this image, relished it, and refined it. His mastery of the unexpected was unsurpassed. Moreover, he knew how to please women with those subtle nuances. Gestures of the hand. Eyes posturing. He could invade a woman's private space from across the room with the promise of passion. Then quickly withdraw, leaving them feeling violated, unsure, alone. As if the sun, having warmed the earth, denied its grace and left the cold lonely planet longing for a return to paradise. Eva recalled how at parties she had actually watched women fight just to be in his presence. For his part, he denied any part in the drama. As she recalled, his take on things was simply, "Everybody wants something. They are all losers whether they know it or not. I have only so much to give. They take too much."

Above all, he had his secrets. Secrets of mind control taught to him from ancient tombs. Secrets of magic and legerdemain taught to him by mentor and former partner 'The Prince' who raised him from a young lad. Most of all the secrets of women that he had cultivated from varied teachings in the ancient texts. Women were the key. Where women flocked and were enthralled, men would follow. This was the secret to his showmanship, and he was the consummate showman.

The show was preeminent; magic was his ultimate expression. Only on stage performing did he feel fully alive, blood flowing through his veins, extremities coursing electricity. The power and majesty of his performance. This is what the crowds wanted, felt vicariously through him. Drained from him, loved him, hated him.

While Eva was not his only assistant, she was by far the most fetching. She held the men's attention center stage. Some of the women were enticed by her beauty as well. This allowed Black Jack to work his magic with less scrutiny.

As he changed his act, replacing card tricks with feats of magic and then mental prowess, Eva remained the constant. A vision of loveliness at center stage, in a variety of outfits each more garish than the last. She was the lynchpin, the focal point, the pearl in the oyster.

After the shows, when they circulated with friends and clientele, Eva was the ultimate garnish. Herman had chosen well and he knew it. When they were together, he beamed almost like a teenager. Eva was simply radiant in any one of the many gowns in her wardrobe.

As her confidence grew, the surety of her position, she blossomed into a master of circumstance, second only to Black Jack. Eva made the perfect partner.

Eva learned some of his secrets, basic magic and misdirection, how to read people and subtly influence their behavior. Enough to become the perfect companion. She assiduously avoided his 'mental' powers. The secret of his mind control. These deeper secrets, she dare not approach; they terrified her. In her mind, she recalled the classical Greek tragedy of Icarius-flying too close to the sun, the source. He was destroyed for his insolence. She would choose to be wiser and not inquire too closely.

The men. The men were the key to his empire. He would court the powerful people of the black elite. Deacons, businessmen, promising politicians. To these he would propose the Garvey Doctrinaire, "I've seen how the mafia controls the people in Chicago. Their day is fading and ours is dawning. We can be self sufficient if we control the means of production and finance its growth internally. Most importantly, we must stop the in-fighting. Unite!"

The women were the lure-just bait to attract the rich and powerful in the major metropolis' he traveled. Once he had won the hearts and minds of the power elite, he could subtly influence their actions. Mold them and move them in the direction that he desired. This was his grand design, to shape the course of society for his own purposes. The details of which were known to no one.

Eva glimpsed images perused from his patterns of behavior with the patrons. He was alternatingly stern, then accommodative in his private dealings with these powerful people. Keeping them off guard-guessing, unsure of themselves. He once bragged to her, Their tiny minds, so pedantic and predictable were open before him. "I can strum them like an instrument. Orchestrate them like a chorus." Eva was his ultimate audience. He cherished performing for her, reveled in her adoration. She was the only witness to these private performances, snatched glimpses into his soul. She had no choice but to keep his secrets and of course, she could never leave. Compelled as she was, to stay with him forever.

As she became less fearful, she could readily see how he courted a constant state of anxiety and uncertainty among those surrounding him. People around him cavorted in a sort of dance, a Machiavellian dance, and Black Jack called the tune. Eva was sure no one else could see it; they were too wrapped up in their lives. Their petty wants and desires, petty jealousies. Eva alone was witness to his manipulations.

Take the poker games, for example. Having taken the name 'Black Jack' and being a master of illusion and legerdemain, you would think the average individual would be hesitant to play poker with him. Just the opposite. Everyone wanted to test their skill against him. Everyone dreamed of being the braggart who beat the great Black Jack. It would never happen. He would remove his jacket before a game, a good will gesture to prove he was not hiding anything. Still the lambs balked at being led to the slaughter. Many times the bouncers had to intercede. Next, he played shirtless to prove there was "nothing up my sleeve." Still the ensuing commotion courted disaster as the losers either claimed cheating or, denied a rematch, became raucous. Finally, he would pick someone from the audience, always a woman, have them deal the cards onto a table facedown, then instruct her to turn the cards over one at a time, from across the room, same result.

Once accosted in public and challenged to a game of cards, Black Jack took a deck out of his pocked and coined the phrase '52 pick-up.' As he sprayed the deck into the man's face, two bodyguards stepped in front to intercede and prevent any further interaction as Black Jack and Eva turned and went on their way.

Still the cries of collusion and chicanery came from the rubes, who despite their initial enthusiasm for the challenge, detested being fleeced and made to look foolish in front of friends and neighbors. Of little consequence to them was their part in the drama. The hubris, in imagining that they could actually beat the master of magic in a fair game. Eventually, the public card games were discontinued. Even shunned at the suggestion. Black Jack had tired of outwitting the rubes at cards. Their belligerent response bordered on tedium and denigrated his whole performance. Leaving him looking more like a bar room brawler and hustler than a magician. The real power he soon realized lay in men's minds; their wants and desires, hopes and fears. Harness those and you control the crowd. Mesmerize them. Keep them awestruck with wonder, and they would always come back for more. This rule applied doubly to the elite, the intelligentsia. The more you had to lose, the greater anxiety.

Where the card games disappeared in public, they magically appeared in private in the circles of the power elite. Here the object was not to humiliate, but to influence. In these circles of games, Black Jack was rarely the big winner. Unless there was the need to punish or exact a penance for some misdeed on the part of one of his regular patrons. Usually money would pass from one player to another, whoever was 'lucky' that night. Rewarding the faithful perhaps or initiating a newcomer. Black Jack always orchestrated the flow of cards and conversation while subtly influencing the minds of his patrons. Keeping their senses so occupied with liquor, women and card play, they never realized the depth of his influence over them. This was the dance, and only Eva could see it.

She was there too, of course. Looking incredible in a long gown or a short bejeweled beige skintight dress with beaded entrails that hung down to her knees, but did nothing to hide those luxurious legs that mesmerized men. Bewitching them while Black Jack worked his spells. The beads sparkling and knocking together as she walked, created continual kaleidoscopic patterns. She looked the epitome of a queen of the king's court in this outfit. Accessorized as it was by hanging diamond earrings and a lattice-work diamond necklace that hung from her neck and covered the space between her breasts down the cleavage. She once admitted that this was her favorite outfit.

Eva had become, was becoming, like her master. Relishing the spotlight, reveling in the attention of men, and the envy of women. Just the opposite of Black Jack, the envy of men and the lustful object of women. Together they were the closed circle.

Her job at the card games was to entertain, to disarm with flattery, to distract, to look beautiful. Black Jack believed that all of life was the power of the mind and misdirection. These card games were a microcosm. Eva misdirected the patrons while he worked his mental prowess. Meanwhile, the servants swirled around with food, fresh drinks and cigars. The conversation flowed, the money changed hands, and the waltz continued late into the night.

This intelligentsia, they would remain his steadfast and highest paying clientele. They were not just cash cows, however.

He tried exhaustively to mold their minds to the concept of black self-sufficiency. 'Separate but... better' was a slogan that worked. Touched a responsive chord among his neighbors in Harlem. That is, as long as the overall economy remained solid. Until the stock market crash ushered in economic collapse creating the Great Depression.

Then suddenly, the slogan became-'Separate but equal isn't equal enough!'

1
The Wiser For Wear

Eva slumped into her hotel bed, too tired to undress. Her body ached from the long arduous rehearsal. Long fingers rubbed aching thighs and buttocks, calves, arches. She hurt there, of course. Ached deeply in private places. Her psyche similarly scourged.

The lavender wallpaper of the rented room, thick and matted, bubbled and cracked in places where the cockroaches made their appearance. They scurried, beating hasty retreat upon her entrance. Eva lay on the covers feigning sleep, her mind overworking the evening's practice.

This was their last chance to get it right. Black Jack was very clear on that point. "Tomorrow is opening night. If we fail, if *you* fail, the show will be a flop. There will be no going back."

How he exhorted her. She had never seen this dark hardness before- at least, not directed at her. And how he chastised, repeatedly, punishingly, oblivious to her will, her fears. Crudely, Herman had demonstrated that she was just an object- like the trained bear who performs upon command or faces the lash. Black Jack had lashed her good- right there on stage. Instilled the fear of God into her. The fear of Black Jack Herman.

Tears leaked through closed eyes as she pondered this new

direction her life was taking. Eva couldn't return home disgraced, soiled. 'Her father' she shuddered, 'Oh the impetuousness of youth,' his voice in her ears. Eva cursed the day she decided to attend that magic show many months ago. Her mind slipped into reverie.

Once upon a time, outside Tupelo, Mississippi, two teenage sisters, almost identical in appearance and close enough in age to be twins, disobeyed their parents and skipped school to see a magic show. Traveling the short bus ride to the big city, they arrived very early in the morning and waited all day so that they could be among the first in line when the doors opened for the evening's performance.

Their temerity was handsomely rewarded with seats third row center aisle. From there the young women, barely eighteen, could have an unobstructed view of the whole stage. They giggled in anticipation and delight, reveling in their good fortune; they would get to see the legendary Black Jack Herman up close. They never considered that he would get to see them as well.

Indeed, Black Jack saw them during the opening of his act, 'How lovely to look at.' There they were, 'two peas in a pod,' sitting in the third row on the aisle. He caught their eyes. He smiled at them with his eyes, beckoning. They giggled, nervous energy expressed as mirth. The sisters watched the show awestruck with fascination and wonder as the illusions were revealed one at a time.

Every so often, Black Jack would regard them to ensure that he had their rapt attention. He needn't fear, they were entranced with his persona, never having seen anyone so dapper and debonair before.

The performance concluded. The young women remained in a state of heightened titillation. Their emotions were rekindled anew when a page delivered a message to their seats from the great magician himself. They had been invited backstage; there was no thought of not accepting. Once behind the curtain, they were quickly whisked away to a reception; an after-show party thrown by Black Jack for his friends and associates.

The great man himself showed up late, looking like a sultan

dressed in a flowing golden robe and a turban. The girls were dumbstruck by their incredible luck to be this close to him. After performing a few parlor tricks for his guests, he turned his complete attention to the young ladies. "Good evening, ladies. Did you like the show?" The juveniles, beside themselves with joy, just giggled.

'They were so beautiful and so alike. Close enough in age to be twins.' He knew he must have them for the show. 'Always to go on. Something fresh and new. For the show.' Never a man to hold back when he saw something he wanted, he pressed his gambit. "How would you young ladies like to accompany me on the rest of the tour?"

They twittered and looked at one another. The oldest said, "Oh no, we couldn't. I'd be too afraid."

"Nonsense," he retorted. "Just name your fear and you conquer it. When I am about to go on stage, I name my fear 'Oh Omanagomikonga, you will not cause me to fail or harm me in any way.' Then I go out and do my show."

Again, nervous laughter from the girls who clung together for support.

"I will be leaving for my next performance in a couple of days. Be assured I will show you riches beyond your wildest imagination." Reaching behind both girls' ear at the same time, Herman produced rubies, one for each. He had made the pitch. The girls were receptive. Let the offer sink in. Let them stew a while. Someone else caught his attention. "Excuse me, ladies. Enjoy the party."

Herman saw them again two days later. The sisters had gone shopping for the family at a local grocery. As they emerged laden with packages, a shining black limousine ground to the curb. The chauffeur, arising from the driver's side, addressed the duo. "Good afternoon, ladies. Master Herman has instructed me to convey you back to your home. Here let me help you with those."

Before they could protest, the packages were removed and placed in the front seat. That task completed, he opened the door to the limo's luxury cabin. The women gasped in surprised. Black Jack was there looking to die for, dressed as he was, black suit with blood red tie and black top hat. "Please get in, ladies," came the honey sweet command from the semi-darkness of the coach. The young ladies felt their limbs moving without conscious effort toward the vehicle. Before they knew what was happening, they were in the backseat with Herman sipping champagne. "Once around the park, Carl, then to the girls' home."

"Very good, sir." It would be hours before they arrived home, slightly the worse for wear. The two sisters were falling under the spell of this master manipulator. One slightly more than the other.

The siblings had always been very competitive, with Eva, the younger sister, a trace resentful that her older sister always seemed to get everything first. Got to do everything first. Thus when the opportunity presented itself for her to experience something first, she quickly seized the chance to usurp her older sis.

The following evening, a young woman knocked on her front door. A letter was delivered from Black Jack. It was addressed to the two women. Eva accepted the letter and read it alone, throwing it into the fireplace when she was finished. Before the paper had completely crumbled into ashes, she knew what she would do. Soon thereafter, within days, she left. Never to return.

Eva caught up to the traveling magic show in New Orleans, the next destination. When Black Jack arrived for the evening's performance, there she was standing outside the stage entrance, looking wide-eyed and wondrous. Her hands, clasped together before her, covered her lap. A floral satchel in her grasp held her worldly belongings.

Herman immediately took her into his arms, hugging and kissing her for long minutes. He took her into his dressing room away from his entourage, lowered the lighting and put some jazz records on a player. "I just bought these in town. Do you like jazz?" he asked, handing her a glass of champagne.

"Yes, very much. Thanks," Eva said first accepting, then sipping her drink. They sat there sipping drinks and talking until it was time for Herman's performance. Eva passed out on his couch, exhausted from her trip.

The next day he took her shopping. Herman purchased a lot of fancy and revealing outfits. Eva was delighted, but somewhat dismayed. She questioned his extravagance.

"If you are going to be my assistant, you will have to look the part. You will have to look dazzling," he advised.

"But you already have a lovely assistant," she queried.

Black Jack looked directly into her eyes and said, "Girl, I am going to teach you things the others dare not dream. The mind can open dimensions unseen and unimagined. Finely trained, its power cannot be denied or repelled." Eva was a bit overwhelmed at this candor and taken aback by his close proximity. She was fearful, yet exhilarated.

The tour was on the final leg of the journey when Eva joined the troupe. After a week in New Orleans, it was up the Mississippi to Memphis, St. Louis and then home to Chicago.

Life on the road was fascinating to the young lady from the small Mississippi town. The hotels they stayed in were the finest that money could buy in the south. The many faces of the varied locales danced around her in a dizzying array. The whole scenario of the troupe moving from one venue to another reminded her of a story she had read about caravans moving across the desert. She fantasized that she was in the company of an Arab sultan and his court. She was the princess. She was Sharazade. Once back in his palatial apartment in Chicago with the maids and other servants at her beck and call, she felt completely like that fantasy princess.

While on the road, Herman had begun to slowly indoctrinate the girl into the world of magic. His world. As it became evident that she had some talent for showmanship, he quickened the pace of her instruction.

He continued his lessons upon their arrival back in Chicago. However, she did not stay in his apartment for long. On her third day, she overheard the servants' gossip.

"I wonder what Wanda will say about this one," the cook said to the chambermaid. The two were in the kitchen preparing potatoes for the evening's meal.

Eva had awoken from a mid-afternoon nap. She and Herman had been keeping late nights since they arrived. Eva awoke parched, threw on a housecoat, one of the many gifts she had received, and hurried downstairs to quench her thirst.

When she neared the kitchen, she could hear the women's

voices drifting down the hall. Eva heard "Wanda" and guessed they were talking about Herman's wife. While he had not mentioned her by name, he told her about his wife and kids when they arrived in town. Discretion and curiosity caused her to stop in her tracks and listen quietly to the continued conversation emanating from the kitchen.

"When will she be back?" asked the maid with more than idle curiosity. She had yet to clean the children's rooms.

"In just a couple of days," said the cook dumping the batch of cleaned potatoes into a pot to boil. "And won't she just love that cute young thing he's got up in the guest room this time? It's too much I tell you."

"But he hasn't touched her, at least not in the house," the chambermaid argued, self appointed attorney for Herman's defense. "Look at the poor young thing. She's probably still a virgin." Secretly, the maid, like most women, had a thing for Black Jack.

"Fiddlesticks," snorted the cook, attacking a stalk of celery with unnecessary malice. "Who knows what happened while they were on the road." Truer words were never spoken. Eva slipped back upstairs unnoticed.

By the time Herman arrived home in the early evening, Eva had dressed and was downstairs in the parlor listening to records on his Victrola. She had seen one once in the window of a store back home. However, until now she did not know of anyone who was rich enough to afford one. Eva was becoming particularly fond of a gritty voiced trumpet player by the name of Louis Armstrong. She had discovered that she liked jazz, jazz clubs, and also gin. They seemed to go together, jazz and gin.

"So, how was your afternoon, little lady?" His commanding voice filled the room, as did his presence.

"Oh just fine, sir," Eva's voice was more timid than usual. Also, she was more formal than usual, given the intimacies of their life on the road. This was a conscious effort on her part. Mindful of the afternoon's conversation that she had overheard, she did not want to give the servants anymore fodder for gossip.

This change did not go unnoticed by Black Jack, as attested to by the quizzical look on his face. However before he could explore the matter further, the maid arrived with the evening's first martini.

"Good evening, sir. Dinner will be ready in about half an hour. Cook is just taking the steaks out of the icebox now. I hope you enjoy your drink. A fresh supply of gin arrived this afternoon. The man assured me it was top shelf."

"It had better be for the prices he charges," Herman smirked and sipped. Then savored and appeared satisfied. "It will do. Thank you, Harriet. Tell Cook to chill a bottle of the French champagne for dinner."

"Very good, sir," the attractive woman curtsied and backed out of the room carrying the empty martini tray. "This gin is okay, but the champagne is really something. Extra-bubbly and so sweet. They import it from France and send it by rail from New York." He stopped suddenly aware that Eva seemed self absorbed. "What's the matter, Eva? Aren't you listening to me?"

"Oh, huh? Yes, I heard you," she said somewhat distractedly as she turned down the volume to a point just above a whisper.

"Is there anything wrong?" He wanted to use one of those tender endearments like 'honey', but he knew all too well that the walls had ears. While he was most certainly the king of his castle, he realized that 'no man is an island' as is the saying. And that if he wished to maintain domestic bliss, a certain decorum must be maintained in the presence of the domestics.

"No, I'm fine. Really." Eva was unconvincing in her protests. Suddenly she resembled a petulant teenager. Really, she was just a small town girl who, all at once, realized she was lost in the big city. A fish out of water.

Herman surmised the problem. After all, he had dealt with a young woman's pangs of homesickness before. Eva was not the first pretty face that he had snatched from the crowd in some small town.

"Come on, its okay, you can tell me," his voice softened, dripping charm.

"Nothing, really. It's just a little overwhelming, all of this." She gestured with both hands. "I guess I'm just unsure where I fit in."

He pounced on that last. "What do you mean? Has someone

been saying things to you?" That was said loudly enough for anyone outside the room to overhear, if they had a mind to.

"No," a timid little voice responded. "But where will I stay?"

"Is that all?" exasperated. "Honey," he didn't care if anyone heard him now. "You will stay with my assistant. She has an extra bedroom in her flat." The next he said loudly for popular consumption. "Darling, remember I see great potential in you. You are going to be a hit with the audience. My show stopper."

'There. That ought to do it,' he thought. He knew he had one supporter among the female staff. That would be enough to satisfy his wife upon her return. Whatever the cook thought, be damned. Having to play such games in one's own household. Imagine! "Harriet," he shouted. "I need another drink."

By the time Wanda arrived from her mother's with the kids three days later, Eva was safely tucked away with the other assistant.

Black Jack was able to play off the whole happenstance with his usual deftness and aplomb. "Honey, baby doll, you should've seen these two sisters. They could've been twins."

"But you only got the one," Wanda cross-examined. She was getting a little tired of this line of questioning. This was hardly the first time this sort of thing had happened. She was resigned to her husband's peccadilloes on the road. But for cryin' out loud, did he have to bring them home with him? Her home? Truth be told, she had had a couple indiscretions of her own while Herman was on the road. She did not wish to parade around her trysts. Even in the modern era of jazz and gin.

"Baby, I told you," a certain exasperation in his voice at having to rehash the tale. "I could only get one. I sent a note inviting the both of them, promising employment and 'riches untold and undreamed of' at least to small town girls," he added wryly. "Eva was the only one to show before we left New Orleans. She said her sister wouldn't go along. But, honey, I got the best one. She's got a real talent for this game. I have a feeling after she is fully trained, she will be the best assistant I've ever had."

'That's what I'm afraid of,' thought Wanda, coming down with a sudden case of foresight. "She had better be. According to cook, you have wined and dined her every night since you've been back."

Herman rankled he knew he was right about cook. "And look how she's mixed up my records." Wanda was furiously straightening the collection. Now she was looking for excuses to berate the girl whom she had not yet met. 'That's enough,' thought Black Jack. He knew how to settle an argument with his blushing bride of many years. He put down his empty brandy snifter and walked slowly over to his somewhat perturbed spouse. Looking down at her with those dark brown soulful eyes, he said in a low voice, "I know what I'm doing. You'll see I'm right. Don't worry your pretty little head about it." Then a smile, that Black Jack smile, the one usually reserved for the paying customers. That, combined with a swift pat on the rump, did the trick. Disarmed her, becalmed her. Ignited the fires of her subterranean desires. "Come on, time for your wifely duties. Wifey, let's go upstairs now." A gentle command yet not one to be ignored or disobeyed. She left the records and headed for the stairs. Back Jack was in hot pursuit. He would calm her concerns with the prowess of his passion.

Wanda though had the last word on the subject. She stopped halfway up the curved banister, turned to her approaching husband and said, "Let's have her over for dinner. Soon."

"This table looks lovely, ma'am," said Eva coquettish in both voice and demeanor. Yet, she was stunningly dressed in a fashionable black suit with wide lapels and a double row of white buttons. The outfit came with a wide-brimmed black hat, trimmed in white. The ensemble had been a gift from Herman two days previous.

Her attire and demeanor presented the most incongruous contradiction. She was either a small town girl playing big city belle, or a fashionable vamp playing country bumpkin. Wanda realized right away that either was a dangerous combination in her home. With her husband and his long history of bewitching small town girls, she felt justified in remaining on her guard. Still this was her house, and she was the mistress of the manor. The bearer of his children. 'Why this girl is little more than a child,' Wanda realized. She could afford to be magnanimous, play the part of the gracious hostess. Still, deep within there was a part of her that hated this girl. Hated her as the winter hates the spring. Envied her youth and inexperience. The same qualities that she, Wanda, had possessed not so many years ago. But were now lost forever. The qualities that all men desired. Yes, this girl would do well on the stage. Secretly, Wanda hoped not too well.

"Thank you very much, my dear," Wanda responded politely with cool aloofness. They were all seated now with cocktails before them. Herman at one head of the mahogany table, with Wanda on the other side. Eva sat on his right.

Wanda continued with her pleasant line of inquiry, "Do you have anything like this at home?" She gestured with both hands indicating the ornate and intricately carved wooden dining set, which included a mahogany highboy with glass doors displaying row after row of crystal glassware.

"Why, gosh no," exclaimed Eva. There was that country bumpkin again. "I don't think anyone in town has anything this grand."

"And where did you say that was?" Wanda's fangs were beginning to show.

In response, Eva became all the more bashful. "Why it's a small town in Mississippi. I'm sure you never heard of it."

At that point, Herman interjected. "She comes from a small town near the state college. You'll remember I told you already Eva and her sister were in the audience."

"And you just happened to see her from the stage." Wanda appeared to be emboldened by her cocktail, which she had downed rapidly.

Black Jack's recreation of events continued. "Dear, you know I have an eye for talent." He delivered the well worn line with silky smooth precision, born of practice. Why, he was almost smiling as he delivered the next, "My dear, isn't it about time for the first course? Ring for cook, will you?"

Dinner went well even if Eva's presence was only coolly tolerated by Wanda. At least she had ceased her cross-examinations, preferring to remain the coldly aloof matron. Wanda decided to treat this young woman as exactly what she was, an inexperienced fish out of water. A plaything of her husband, one of many. He would soon tire of her and drop her on the road somewhere, as was his habit. Even if she did have some modicum of talent, what of it?

Eva presented no threat. After all, she was just a poor pawn in her husband's grand scheme.

Wanda realized that her battle was actually with him. She also knew from years of experience that there was nothing she could do on that score. She had tried every trick in the book from threats and tantrums to playing the loving seductress or the vampy flirt, in attempt to inspire a reaction from her husband. Nothing worked more than once or twice. Black Jack remained inscrutable, unflappable in public, as if he could see right through his wife's games. He would treat her as if she were a misbehaving child, ignoring her antics in public, and complete sexual domination of her when they were in private. However fulfilling their nights together, they had dwindled in the last few years. As his roving eye increased, so she became relegated to more of a side show and less the 'main attraction.' Wanda comforted herself with the thought that powerful men must have their passions. Wanda satisfied herself with the knowledge that at least she had everything that was his, his children, his apartment, his servants. If not always his bed.

After a dinner which Eva just fawned over, they retired to the parlor to hear some of the latest recordings. Wanda crossed the room to the record player and selected one of her favorite pieces, a Scott Joplin rag. Not facing the girl, she inquired curtly, "Eva, I see that you are quite fond of music."

Eva blushed. "Oh, yes ma'am." The girl caught herself. "Yes, Mrs. Herman," she finished politely. Then suddenly she seemed to intuit the meaning behind the question. "Oh, I'm sorry. I guess I made quite a mess of your record collection when I was here the other day." She apologized profusely and quite genuinely. Wanda found herself failing to hate her, this small town ingénue. "I don't suppose you have many record players back home."

"No, no one that I know," Eva replied politely.

"What's your favorite type of music?" genuine curiosity.

"Why jazz," came the quick reply. "There's a lot of it come out of 'N'Awlins.' The record shop will play new recordings over their loudspeaker to the crowds standing outside. But ours is a town of sharecroppers, not too many can afford to buy Victrolas. Certainly nothing as nice as you have here." She paused for a moment to catch her breath. Then realizing that she hadn't explicitly answered the perceived question, she added, "There is this new fella out of N'Awlins that I really like. He sings and plays a mean trumpet?" Wanda burst in, "I know who you mean, Louis Armstrong."

"Yes, that's him." Eva was beaming. She was about to say that Black Jack had promised to take her to see him at the club if and when he came to Chicago, but she thought better. Discretion being the better part of valor.

When the 'rag' finished, Wanda asked Eva if she wished to hear a Louis Armstrong record.

"Oh, yes, please," responded Eva wide-eyed and genuious. She knew from her previous experience that the collection held two Armstrong titles. She was in luck. Wanda had put on her favorite. She sat up pertly on their luxurious loveseat, thoroughly enjoying the music.

Herman sat in the back of the room in the semi-darkness smoking his cigar. He was pleasantly involved in his thoughts as he watched the women interact. His women.

Later, after a suitable time had elapsed, it was time to have Eva chauffeured back to her new apartment. Her roommate would be expecting her. "My dear, I'm going to walk Eva down to the car. I'll be right back to tuck you into bed. In the meantime, better see that the maid has put the children to sleep." With that, he and the girl left the parlor and walked into the foyer where Herman placed a wrap around Eva's shoulders. "It's cold tonight. I want you to stay warm," he said softly as he touched her tenderly.

"Here comes Carl with the limo now. We'd better go." Together they bounded out the front door and down the steps to the waiting vehicle. Carl opened the rear door at their approach. Herman whispered in her ear, "I'm going to be busy for the next couple of days." He looked back toward the house. "You work with Lilly. She will drill you on the tricks you saw her perform on stage. You be a good girl, okay?" Black Jack moved close to the young girl to whisper instructions. She could smell tobacco mixing with his cologne and remnants of brandy. It excited her. Her hand trembled as she grasped the open door.

"Of course, I will" She did not dare look up into his eyes.

Suddenly she was flushed and weak. It had been a long day and perhaps the wine at dinner had gone to her head. She daren't admit, especially to herself, that she had fallen in love with the married man. Something that everyone else knew, all those sophisticated socialites. If she were to succumb to that realization, she would have to consider that all of her dreams were naught but the silly imaginings of a moonstruck teenager who was totally out of her league. Still, she could not shake the feeling that she and Herman were somehow meant to be together. No matter that she had now met the wife, quite an imposing creature indeed. Eva knew she and Black Jack were destined for each other.

Finally getting a grasp on her emotions, she looked back at him, turning her head slightly to meet his gaze. "Don't worry; I will learn my lessons well. I won't disappoint you."

Black Jack looked her dead in the eye and said earnestly, "You could never disappoint me. Now get going." A slight pat on her rear.

There was no conversation as Carl drove Eva back to her new home and waiting roommate. Eva was off in a dream world.

Carl had seen this part of the picture many times. He knew his part. Moreover, he knew better than to offer advice unless requested, or to interfere inadvertently. He knew a good job was hard to find, and this was one of the best. It had its perks. Thus without a word between them, Carl deposited Eva at her apartment house and waited until she gained entry. Lilly was waiting for her inside.

Lilly was a somewhat voluptuous woman of charitable nature and gregarious spirit. At the ripe old age of twenty four, she was a ten year veteran of the show biz game. Herman was by far her best employer; she would do anything for him. Like most people who knew him. He just had that effect on people. At first, you were in awe of him and then you couldn't help but like him. It was part of his charm. Of course, when the occasion called for it, he could be the embodiment of terror, part of his inscrutability. Lilly had seen both sides in her tenure with him. She remembered all too well the night in Chattanooga when Black Jack had caught a man trying to cheat at cards. Where the dagger had come from so quickly, who could say. Anyway, after Black Jack had plunged the short dagger through the man's hand that hid the palmed card, there was blood everywhere. As she recalled, they had to get out of town real fast that night. That cheating bastard had friends, as bastards often do. They arrived armed and out for vengeance. Luckily, Carl had packed up early since it was their last night in town. Black Jack, having seen the gang coming, played a trick on them. He went out to greet them and then disappeared in a cloud of smoke. By the time those suckers knew what was going on, 'we were on our way out of town.' She smiled at the memory. Of course they lost the tent when the mob burned it to the ground.

The limousine pulled up outside the building. Lilly had been watching from the front window, expecting the girl. She would gladly teach Black Jack's latest protégée, not that it would matter. She'd wind up like all the rest. Discarded. Meanwhile, while Black Jack was outside saying goodnight, the two Louis Armstrong records had mysteriously broken. The maid was in the parlor sweeping up the pieces when Herman re-entered his abode. Wanda had retired to the upstairs bathroom.

Eva settled in very nicely with her new roommate. They were hardly strangers, having bunked together on the road. Herman had deposited her several days ago, when apprised of Wanda's imminent return. It was one thing for the staff to wag their tongues after-the-fact. Altogether another for the mother of his children to find this beautiful young thing under her roof.

Lilly had come home one afternoon to the sight of Herman's limo parked outside her building. Thus, she knew something was afoot. Arriving at her apartment door, Lilly found it ajar. She entered. There they were, Herman and Eva setting up house. "Oh, hey babe, you're back. I knew you had this extra room, so I brought you a boarder." A broad grin marked his face forcing the half-chewed, unlit cigar to one side.

Lilly was not phased in the least. She had anticipated this eventuality. He couldn't keep his star pupil at his place and to leave a country girl, pretty as she was, alone in the big city was unthinkable. What better recourse than to stash her here, where he could visit when he wanted, and still keep her safe from outside influences.

After all, Lilly reasoned, her place, while not fashionable, was far enough away from Wanda's residence. Out of sight, out of mind as the saying goes. Lilly didn't even question his unauthorized entry of her locked apartment. That was just his style. When he wanted something, he just took it.

Besides, caring for Herman's little love interest would have its perks. Already it was paying off. She could see Carl in the kitchenette stocking the ice box and cabinets with groceries.

"Sure, Black Jack, anything you say," Lilly cooed, relieving herself of her coat and the meager packages that she brought from the shops. "I kinda figured that she would stay here. After we got along so well on the road." She smiled at Eva, who had emerged from her new bedroom to stand in the doorway. Eva smiled back.

Lilly continued, "Why we'll be just like sisters. I can teach her the act when you're not around," anticipating his next request. She had been with him long enough. He expected her to be nursemaid, teacher, chaperone and whatever else was necessary.

"Great." Black Jack stood in the middle of the apartment with his hands on hips, one woman on either side of the large room. You could see his mind calculating, head held high, assessing the big picture. "Her bedroom set will come tomorrow. They couldn't get it here today. Something about a broken axle on the delivery truck. Eva, I guess you'll have to sleep on the couch tonight."

"That's alright, Daddy," came the coquettish reply from across the room. "I will manage."

Lilly concurred, "No problem. I will put some sheets on the couch. It can be very comfortable. Besides, it doesn't get very cold this time of year."

Eva crossed the room to stand with Herman. He addressed her in low tones. "Baby, did you finish putting away all of your new clothes?"

"Not yet." She looked up at him, regarding the large man with something between adoration and worship.

"Well, you had better finish. We don't want them to wrinkle, do we? Besides, I want to have a few words with 'Lil'."

Obediently, Eva returned to the bedroom to finish her tasks.

Black Jack removed the cigar from his lips and strode over

toward Lilly so that they might have discussions of a more confidential nature.

"Now, listen 'Lil.' I want you to take good care of her. She is going to be very important to the act. She's got natural talent. Once we get her trained, develop that poise, personality, she is going to be a real show stopper. Take us to the next level. I've been thinking of taking the show in a new direction, more upscale. You know, a real classy magical act. So don't let anything happen to her. I'm counting on you." With that, he clutched her, his hands on her upper arms, facing her.

For an instant his grand vision swept over her, caught her up in his dream. She felt abashed, yet exhilarated, then exhausted in the wake of that emotional tide. So this one was really different, the genuine article. She stuttered, "S,Sure baby, don't worry. I'll take good care of her."

As promised, the two women got along like sisters. Compared to bunking on the road, the two bedroom apartment was huge. The large living room slash kitchenette looked out onto the street below and facing east, in the mornings, the room was flooded with sunlight, casting a golden glow throughout. Each woman had a room to which to retire when privacy was desired, and Herman kept the larder stocked so there was no fighting over food.

A couple of hours five days a week, Lilly would demonstrate card tricks, a ring trick or any of the other popular tricks that magicians purveyed. Eva would watch attentively and spend much of the afternoon practicing that day's lesson, adding each new illusion to her repertoire. In the evenings on those occasions when Herman was not expected and Lilly did not have a date, the two girls would attend a movie together and stop for a bite to eat.

This was more the exception however, rather than the rule. For while the two women were not that far apart in age, they were leagues apart in sophistication. After all, it was the age of gin, jazz and highlife. The roaring twenties were being invented all around them. Chicago was the epicenter, and the southside was the mecca of it all. Now while Herman paid well enough to tide her over when the show was on hiatus. She was also a young woman. A very pretty young woman, in fact. And well, every girl needs a few sugar daddy's to bring excitement into one's life. Lilly was not sure that Eva could really understand the needs and desires of a sophisticated modern woman in the big city. The women's independence movement was gaining momentum in both spirit and deed. Lilly was determined that she was going to get hers. She got hers several nights a week. While she was discriminating, she didn't inquire too closely the pedigree of her paramours. All she asked was that they were clean, fun and spent freely on her.

After the first week, Eva had the routine down. When Lilly came back to the apartment, her apartment, with a beau after dinner or a show, Eva would make herself scarce until she heard them move into the bedroom. Not that every date ended in the bedroom. "A girl's got to have her standards," Lilly joked one time. But Eva could usually tell owing to the type of noise they made in the outer room. If it was unusually boisterous, there would soon be noise of another kind in the bedroom. Sometimes, they would go at it for hours. Between the creaking of the bedsprings and the loud verbalizations, Eva would have to put the pillows over her head to muffle the sounds of lovemaking wafting through the rooms until late into the night.

Consequently, Eva became preoccupied with thoughts of sex and relationships. She had been a virgin when she left home. Although her parents had a typically large family for the agrarian south, she had never thought of them as having sex. Let alone overhear them consummating their feelings for one another. In church school they were taught the difference between lust and love. Love was the expression of caring between a man and a woman, with the intention of providing a family to share the life of toil on God's green earth.

Lust was the wanton coupling of animals, like beasts in the field, designed to satisfy some passing carnal urge. It was this fornication between unmarrieds or worse, the covetous adulterer. That was the path to damnation. God had scourged the earth at least twice on this account. The church school teachers were very clear on the point. Wanton lust was the road to hell.

Yet, here she was having fallen for the charms of a married man. Seduced by the excitement he generated and the promise of 'riches undreamed of.' She felt very alone, curled up in her bed, pillow pulled over her head. Cringing from the sounds of fornication emanating from the next room. Felicitous congress inextremis.

Herman had been very good to her that first time when he found out that she was a virgin. They had kissed for a while in her hotel bedroom, the one she shared with Lilly on the road. Then he gave her something to drink, 'corn liquor' mixed with fruit juice he said. It warmed her, relaxed her. They petted some more. She was becoming overwhelmingly excited. She had never gone this far with a boy before, and here she was with a grown man who knew exactly what to do, where to touch a woman. 'Oh my, his hands,' how they excited her. She concentrated on her memories of excitation in order to drown out the carnal cacophony permeating the walls of her little bedroom.

Expertly he undressed her, peeled her like a grape or more appropriately, a banana. Husked her like an ear of corn. She trembled from fear with the knowledge that he was about to enter her. That she was embarking on a journey of discovery from which there could be no return. Sensing her trepidation, he mumbled something into her ear. She relaxed perceptibly and lay down contentedly. Her anxiety had magically vanished; a sense of rightness now possessed her.

Herman undressed in the dim light peeking underneath the locked door. He gently lifted legs and placed a towel underneath her behind, before covering her body with his and mounting her. Try as she might, she couldn't remember more than that. Except to recall in amazement how powerful he was. He took her breath away.

In the morning, when she came around, she was glad that there was a towel covering the bedsheet. Upon close inspection, that wetness she felt was blood. At first, she thought her period had begun early. Within the day she realized her mistake. That had been her first time and so far, her only time. What a gentleman Black Jack had been. He even had roses delivered to her the very next afternoon before the evening's performance.

As she lay cringing in her empty bed, she could feel her body longing for him. The pleasure of his touch. Her body ached for him to touch her again. Right then and there, she decided that she would endure anything to be near him. To be by his side, in his presence, was what she desired. Above all else, Eva knew there and then that she loved him, would always love him. Rightly or wrongly, it was a feeling too powerful for her to fight.

II
Thoroughly Moderns

A few weeks thereafter, Herman began rehearsing a new show for his summers' swing through the Midwest. The circuit would start with Milwaukee and then the tour would continue with other northern industrial towns.

Henry Ford had invented the automated assembly line and begat the industrial boom that was beginning to blossom, fostering the end of the Great War. Major metropolitan areas had burgeoning populations with ready cash to spend on entertainment. It was the best of times.

As it says in the Bible, 'to everything there is a season.' So it was to putting on a road show, better to tour the south during the winter when it was no so dreadfully hot. In fact, you could pitch a tent in places a hall of suitable size was unavailable. This was desirable for several reasons, chief among them you didn't have to pay exorbitant rents. Some halls raised their rates when they heard his revue was in the area. Instead, just pay a peanuts farmer for the use of an already harvested field. It was found money for him. Besides, holding the show outside of town kept the prying eyes of the local constabulary to a minimum, less palms to grease. Also, in a tent you could put 'em in without worry of violating state fire codes. The weather was passable in the south during the winter months. There were no afternoon thunderstorms to pop up and disturb the tent or dampen the evening's turnout.

Herman had been touring the south for over a decade, beginning when he was only sixteen under the tutelage of his mentor, the Great Prince Herman. By now, he knew how to read the evening's crowd. How to know the town upon entering. To sense when conditions were right for a good show and, rarely, to cancel a performance, moving on before unpacking. He always trusted his sixth sense; all the good magicians had this quality. You would not last in this business otherwise. Just like the feeling he had when he saw Eva and her sister, he had to have them. He was meant to have them. That's what he put in his letter to them. No matter that only the one sister showed. That would be enough. That is how it was meant to be. She would transform his act. He embodied a surprising amount of fatalism for one who believed in his own manifest destiny.

When he performed in the northern industrial circuit, those venues where more structured. No tents, only performance halls. All the proper permits were appropriated weeks in advance. All fire codes were observed. No extemporaneous acts were contemplated or tolerated. No rowdy patrons spilling out into the streets. And above all, no high stakes, late night poker games with the patrons. While the north was all about rules and regulations, Herman much preferred the rigidity. The performances were more refined, dignified. Not the haphazard rough and tumble of performing in a bawdy atmosphere. There you had to be quick with your wits and even quicker on your feet.

Yes, all in all, he much preferred touring the northern cities on those cool summer eves. Of course, the biggest reason had to be that he could perform before mixed crowds. In the south, because of the Jim Crow laws, he was not allowed to perform before Caucasian audiences.

The show he was working on now would be his best show ever. It would propel him to new heights of stardom within the magical community. The stars were all aligned. The war was almost over; the economy was booming and there was a new energy in the air. That new music, jazz, with its truncated rhythms, was sweeping the cities. Replacing the refined predictable rhythms of ragtime. People were opening up to new experiences and desires. 'Hell, women were marching in the street. How crazy was that.'

Yes, the stars were all aligned to usher in a new age of enlightenment and prosperity. Black Jack would seize the opportunities offered and ride the crest of that wave. Yes, he would be there to get his, and Eva would be his star. He was sure of that, his sixth sense confirmed they were star-crossed. Their destinies intertwined. 'Yes,' he thought. 'I will train her; teach her the secrets of magic. She has no idea how powerful she can become.' The stars willed it.

About a week after she had moved into her Chicago digs, Black Jack showed up one afternoon bearing a special gift. Lilly was out getting her hair done, a preparation for the evening's tryst. Eva had wondered out loud one day, "Why do you spend so much time getting your hair done in the afternoon when you only get it messed up that night?" "Why, my dear, it's all part of the game," came the cool response. "Besides, you have to look good for your man. Any man. Also, it makes me tingle with anticipation thinking about all the fun we are going to have that night. It's a ritual thing. Didn't somebody say that 'All the world's a stage' and that we're all just performing?"

Eva, upon reflection, thought that maybe Lilly had protested too much. Anyway, she opened the door and there was Herman standing there with this big portable record player complete with megaphone. She squealed with delight and wrapped her arms around him. "Oh Daddy, that's just what I wanted."

"I thought it might be getting a little bit lonely around here without me," he crooned in a deep husky voice. "I've got some records down in the car."

"Come on in. I've got the perfect place for it, here in the living room." She was as giddy as a ten year old girl who had just been given a pony for her birthday.

Black Jack placed the victrola on the indicated table by the fireplace. When he turned around, he was nearly floored by the biggest kiss. The young woman had literally attacked him. Their mouths meshed, her wrists locked around his neck, standing on her tippy toes. While the earth shook, neither breathed nor moved observably. They resembled a stone statue that could be entitled 'A Lover's Kiss.'

"Wow." Herman was genuinely taken aback when his lips finally disengaged from hers. "I guess I had better come by more often. Let me call down to Carl and have him bring up the records so that we can try out your new toy."

"No, don't. Not yet." There was a devilish look in her eyes. The passion play produced the previous evening from the adjoining bedroom still played on her mind. Better engage in a little petting while she had the apartment to herself. There would be time later to engage in the more public passions.

After a half hour or so, they called down to Carl to bring up the records and champagne. While Louis Armstrong played his trumpet, they giggled and made plans for dinner. For the first time, she felt at home. A sense of rightness possessed her. She belonged with him.

"Let's do it again." Black Jack's exasperated voice could be heard all through the warehouse. The stockyard district offered some privacy from the prying eyes of the public and jealous competitors. While there was a general camaraderie among the magical community, tricks were passed along only with the consent of the owner. Foreknowledge of a spectacular new trick for an upcoming tour might give a competitor the advantage of reworking his act. Utilizing advance bookings, one could steal the thunder, usurping the novelty factor of a fellow magician's act. 'Stealing the show' it was called. It was not the first magician to come up with the trick; it was the first to perform that trick or a similar one onstage. As the saying goes, 'Knowledge is power.'

The stockyards provided some security in that outsiders tended to stand out during the day. Nobody would be caught dead there during the night. That in fact was much more than just a saying. You did not want to run afoul of the meatpackers, people had a nasty way of disappearing. The modern rustlers drove trucks, as it is a lot easier to steal cattle when they are already cut into little pieces. The meatpackers used the Pinkertons to watch the yards at night. They and the gangs would nightly play a deadly game of cat and mouse. Anyone prowling around down there would just get in the way, with disastrous consequences. To steal a magic trick just wasn't worth it.

So Black Jack practiced in relative solitude and security. Drilling his protégée for up to twelve hours a day. While off the stage he was her 'sugar daddy', on that platform, he was a hard taskmaster. At first, the transformation terrified the young girl. She would look to Lilly for cues and reassurance. But Eva received little consolation from the other woman. It was do or die.

Timing is everything in magic. Timing and acting. You had to sell the trick. Your face and bodily movements had to persuade the audience. First nervous and frightened, this part Eva had no trouble with. Then feigning pain or extreme discomfort on cue.

This was the problem, the girl couldn't act. As a 'virgin' actor from a small town, she had stage fright. Eva was awkward, plodding, either rushing the trick or bumbling her way through the illusion. Black Jack was not a man blessed with patience. He would yell at her constantly, causing her to burst into tears, makeup running down her pretty face. On occasion, he even slapped her or struck her with his cane when she did not move fast enough or wound up in the wrong place. This was very disconcerting and disheartening to the young girl who loved the man so deeply. She dreaded his sharp looks or disdaining, derisive comments. Eva pleaded for patience with promised improved performance. She sighed. "This magic stuff is harder than it looks," she said to no one.

From the very first moment of planning, Black Jack and Lil', the veterans, decided that Eva, the stage show 'virgin', would play the role of victim. Black Jack had decided to upgrade the act, no longer would he have card tricks as the mainstay. The act would be graduated to the more traditional and sophisticated fare of the magicians from across Europe.

'The Perils of Pauline' had been for years one of the most popular movie series with audiences everywhere. Black Jack wanted to draw upon that success and at the same time, utilize the natural talents that Eva had to offer. She looked good on stage; the audience would empathize with her plight if she were put into a position of distress. All she had to do was pretend to be in peril. But even this was proving difficult.

Take the box, for example. It was the simplest thing for the unwilling victim to be crammed into a three foot cube where only her head stuck out. Then while Black Jack ministered over her with magical words and a wave of his cane, the "Lovely Assistant Lilly" would thrust swords into the box in a pre-arranged pattern. The 'victim' would have to feign fear, not burst out in laughter. "Stop. Let's do it again," roared the disgruntled tyrant.

"Oh, Daddy. I'm sorry. I'll try harder. Really, I will," came the sweet sincere cries of a young woman clearly out of her element. She desperately wanted his approval.

"Again." Herman would not even look at her.

A mock struggle between Lilly and her intended victim, while Black Jack amused the supposed audience with tales of sultans and harem girls in deepest India. Describing that these tortures were designed to discipline the unruly ones, break their spirit. Also, to amaze and dismay neighboring potentates with demonstrated mastery of the supernatural.

This time Eva seemed to be getting the act down. She squealed with just a tinge of fear as the blade was thrust into the box, supposedly into her abdomen. She cried in real agony as another blade thrust into the side of the box and reappeared out the other side, her underwear attached. Finally, a smaller empty box was placed over her pleading contorted face. Audience members would be tempted to yell "Stop!" to protect this precious Pygmalion from the final presented perils. Those pleading eyes, that helpless expression on her pursed lips, as that box covered her face. You could imagine that you were viewing her whole and alive for the last time.

Black Jack himself seized the last blade displayed by his assistant over her head. He moved to the front of the stage and walked the circumference showing off the sword to the phantom audience. "This is the sultan's blade," he would shout. "Notice the broad bladehead, good for loping off the ears or head of a disobedient disciple." He held the blade by both ends up to the light so that the shiny metal would reveal its' prowess to the crowd. "See the finely crafted Japanese steel, folded seven times. The finest in the land." After the supposed 'Oohs and aahs,' he would return to stand behind the box with the sword held in a downward position dangling precariously over the small box containing the victim's head. This procedure was known in the business as the 'Sword of Damocles' after the Greek legend. "And now without further hesitation, the sultan will end the misery of the unruly slave girl. Sacrificing her for the appeasement of the Gods, despite pleas from the harem to spare her life. If the gods are appeased, they may restore her life. If I don't screw up this trick, I won't have to find another victim." The phantom crowd rumbled with laughter.

Deftly, Black Jack plunged the sword into the little box. Immediately, the steel blade met with resistance. Herman thrust it, with great difficulty, deeper and deeper, until the broad bladehead disappeared to the hilt. The initial screams of the victim collapsed into silence as the blade supposedly did her in.

Walking in front of the box again, the magician looking exhausted waved his wand and advised the audience that if the gods were truly to be pleased, that they would have to join him in the recitation of these magic words. He spoke the words gravely over the box and intimated that the audience should repeat the incantation. A pause on his part, while the faux audience repeated the charm. 'O wha ta goo siam.' "Again, faster." 'O wha ta goo siam.'

"Lilly, remove the blades from the box."

Lilly, who had been standing to one side, moved back to center stage, shaking her shapely assets for the men in the front rows. The beaded chains hanging from her Victorian corset swung to her undulating movements.

Lilly started slowly removing the swords on the side of the box first, some with great difficulty. The blades from the front followed. Each sword was removed in its turn, a reverse order of their placement. Finally, when all swords but one, the broadsword plunged down from the top, had been removed, Herman peered into the box.

Turning to the audience again, he grimaced, "Oh, this doesn't look good. The gods are not entirely satisfied. I'll try my magic wand once again while you cheer loudly." Herman moved to the table, holding the box and turned it around three times reciting his mumbo jumbo. Then he rapped loudly on the top of the box with his cane and said something like, "Girl into pieces, come back to meses." Afterward he removed the 'Sultan's blade' in one long powerful movement.

Lilly joined him on the other side of the box and together they lifted the main unit off of the container, into which the young victim had been stuffed.

There she was presto-chango, alive and unhurt, smiling and waving. The two illusionists helped her out of the container and down onto the floor where they all stood with clasped hands, arms outstretched over their heads. Finishing with a triple bow and salutation to the throngs of cheering men and women in the audience, who were now standing and providing the trio with thunderous applause.

"That was much better Eva," barked Herman breaking character. "See that you remember how to do that when we have a live audience. Alright Lil'. Let's wrap it up. That's enough for today."

"Sure thing, boss. I'll go tell Carl we're almost ready to go."

"Don't let him see you in that outfit, or we will be here all night," Herman joked.

Eva's lessons in magic and legerdemain did not end with the setting of the sun. After the girls were ferried to their flat for cleaning and primping, Carl would swing the limousine back and pick them up for a night on the town. After the usual half an hour of honkings and pleading from the street for them to hurry along, they would finally present themselves. Perfumed and prettied in rouge and shiny satin, the girls were transported to the Herman household to pick up Black Jack for a night's extravaganza.

Waiting outside for the man of the hour to make his appearance, "He's worse than a woman," Lilly would snort. The girls giggled nervously as if they were waiting for dates to the prom. To Lilly, a creature of the night, this was an everyday occurrence, a ritual of the modern life. Nevertheless, she looked eagerly toward each evening.

Eva was in a magical wonderland of her own, chauffeurs and limos, party dresses and primping. To be with a tall, darkly handsome man who totally dominated her, thrilled her down to the very depths of her being. She was glad that Lilly usually went her own way. Lilly was Herman's beard. The story was that the two of them were trying to 'sophisticate' this country girl. Immerse her in social situations so that she could become accustomed to comporting herself with certain flair and air of distinction in the elite circles that Black Jack frequented. All of this was true; it was just that Herman was the only tutor required for the job. Of course, it was better that Wanda did not find this fact out.

There he was at the top of the stoop to the brownstone looking dapper in white tie and top hat. Wanda trailing behind was still engaging him in conversation. "But baby, we have to teach her how to act around men. How to pick them up and hold their interest. She needs to become more comfortable around men and women in social situations. When she can master that nonchalance and appear sincerely bewitching, we can perform our illusions with greater effect. Remember a magician is only as good as his assistants. They sell the show. Lilly's job is to show her the ropes, show her how it's done."

"You two are pretty proud of your pampered princess. Why can't I come and observe your teaching methods?" decried Wanda sounding cynical.

"Honey," said an exasperated husband. "You know magic is like a con game. Everything revolves around timing and acting. While she is in training, we don't want too many influences around. It throws us off of our game to have non-professionals around." This was the old excuse, one that Wanda had no defense against. It was Black Jack's ultimate trump card.

"When will you be back?" asked Wanda, changing the subject. Herman had won the argument again. Was there ever any doubt?

"It won't be too late," he promised vaguely. "We have another hard day of practice ahead of us tomorrow."

"I just hope it's all worth the effort," coaxed his wife.

"It will be, baby. You'll see this show will be the best yet, and the tour this summer will make more money than ever before. Now, let me go. The girls put in a long day, and they must be terribly hungry."

He kissed her on the cheek and proceeded to saunter down the steps to the waiting limo. Carl seized this as his cue and stepped out of the driver's side to open the door to the luxury cabin and the waiting women. When the vehicle had turned the corner and they were safely away from the familial abode, Herman addressed Lilly, who was sitting across from the couple. "Lil' where are we dropping you tonight?"

Later, sipping aperitifs at the French restaurant, Herman turned his softer side to the young girl. "I'm glad that you are beginning to learn your place in the act. How you act on stage is different than real life. You must also learn how to entice and allure men and women in social situations. Remember, all of life is a game, and you must be able to identify what game a person is playing at any given moment. Anticipate how you can get them to play the game you want them to. That part is relatively simple. In advanced sessions, you will learn to identify types of individuals; you will instantly know to which routine they will be most susceptible.

"You mean which game to run on them?" asked Eva, desperately straining to understand her tutor and comprehend the logic behind this behavioral science.

"Crudely put, but yes. Don't think of it in terms of a con game. It's not like we are hurting or stealing from people. Most people live a rather boring, mundane life. We are just providing a little mystery, magic. A little entertainment to satisfy their souls. It is an unspoken, unconscious contract between magician and client from time immemorial. In the dark ages, the magician provided certainty that there was something more to life other than drudgery and suffering. They also teased a short cut to riches and power. Also for those impotent, weakling rulers, magicians provided a means to hold onto power. To legitimize their illegitimate rule. In these modern times of science, magic provides a pleasant distraction to most. To a few it tantalizes the intellect; there just might be something more out there. Some greater power as yet unseen. You see, honey, people need magic. Do you understand?"

"Well, I suppose I do. Just like when those men long ago claimed to turn lead into gold."

"Oh, so you know about that? One of the greatest tricks in Black Magic. It has always wrought terrible consequences. In those medieval times, the very suggestion of such a shortcut to riches was enough to get many a woman, and man too, burned at the stake as witches. A practice they continued for hundreds of years. Right here in this country less than two hundred years ago, the first Europeans killed many women as witches."

"My goodness," sighed the young woman, wide-eyed. "In Sunday school they told us that all of that stuff- witches, magic and the like-were the domain of the Devil."

Herman laughed softly, "That's just what the preachers would have you believe to keep you backward, uneducated. You have seen our tricks. There isn't anything devilish about them, is there?"

"No," she said thoughtfully, dragging the word out of her mouth.

"See there," Herman was satisfied. "It's a good thing we live in these educated modern times. Still people need the illusion that there is something more. They come to the shows for that emotional excitement. In other words, they come to experience the possibility of mystery and magic. Understand?"

"I guess so," still sounding unsure. The petite protégée decided to take his word for it.

"Good," the father figure applauded. "Now, pick up your glass. The waiter is coming with our entrees."

"But how about that man whose wallet you stole?" She referred to an incident earlier in the evening in the lounge while they were waiting to be seated.

"Lifted, honey. The correct term is lifted. We gave it back to him right away, didn't we?"

"Yes," agreed Eva, in the voice of a small girl being reprimanded.

"And we didn't take any of the money. So there was no harm, no foul. In fact, the man was so happy to have his wallet returned that he bought us each a drink."

"But why did we do; have to do that again," the princess puzzled.

"Baby doll, that was your tutorial in misdirection and legerdemain." Black Jack sighed. He would have to explain it to her once again. He began patiently. "You distracted him with your question, and while he was standing there looking at your pretty body," she blushed. "I was able to liberate the wallet from his rear pocket. We then provided him with the 'illusion' that he had dropped his wallet. He was so grateful for our performance, that he paid us for the privilege of playing the part of the audience. This is all part of your lessons in acting, learning to read people and manipulate them."

"I suppose," and then with enthusiasm, "Anything you say, Daddy. She was smiling at him, a schoolgirl again.

Later after the sumptuous meal, after Black Jack had introduced his apprentice to some important acquaintances, they left the restaurant for the limo. Herman gave Carl his cues upon entry. "Give us an hour, Carl." The chauffeur understood perfectly and faded into the night.

Eva, tipsy from bubbly and brandy, tired from a long day of practice found the comfortable rear seat doubled very well as a bed. She entered the vehicle and sprawled horizontally across the cushion. Herman knew the limo was perfect for bedding, but he had no intention of sleeping. He sat down next to his lounging lovely and gathered her up in his arms.

"Your performance today, my dear, was fantastic. I think it's time for your reward." His head moved toward hers. Her lips sought out his eagerly. Their embrace continued for long minutes before his hands sought out the zipper on the back of her dress. His hands, chilled by the night air, soon warmed as they explored her hot, young flesh.

"Oh Daddy," she moaned as his lips caressed the nape of her neck and underside of her protruding chin. His hands swept the dress from her upper torso; she shivered in her sudden nakedness. Quickly, he removed his jacket and wrapped her in it, in the process, removing her dress entirely. Their bodies close together now; the young girl was transported off to a cloud where passions play.

Afterward, the young woman, now fully belonging to him, clung tightly to her 'sugar daddy', her mentor, her only lover. Herman disengaged slowly, but deliberately. Helping Eva retrieve her clothing from the floor where he had discarded the garments in the heat of passion, he waited patiently for the girl to dress before reclaiming his jacket.

Emerging from the vehicle, he lit a cigar both for the satisfaction the tobacco would provide, and to cover the scent of their lovemaking on his clothing. He knew he could not return home in this condition. Wanda would be waiting for him. He knew from experience that if there was one thing a wife could spot, it was the scent of another woman on her man.

When Black Jack spied Carl returning, he quickly kissed Eva on the cheek and went to meet his man. "Carl, take her home. She's had a hard day. Then you can take off. I have some business to take care of. I'll take a taxi home later."

"Very good, sir. Good evening, sir." With that, Carl raised his hand to his cap in salute and entered the limousine. Herman grabbed a cab to one of the numerous jazz joints that dotted the south side. By the time he arrived home, all one could scent was whiskey and cigars. Wanda, who had given up waiting for her husband, had gone to sleep hours earlier.

III
Welcome to the Show

After several more weeks of contemplation and planning, the acts for the new show were beginning to take shape. At least, on paper. In practice, they needed a lot more work. Lilly was a consummate professional when it came to prestidigitation. Show her the trick once or twice and she could pick it up. Even personalize it with a little flair or something extra of her own.

Eva was proving to be a lummox, her performances were inconsistent. Best presentations, she was still tentative and awkward. As if she was unconsciously holding back. Herman, who was by this time, thoroughly enchanted by her beauty, chalked it up to 'stage fright' and figured she would grow out of it. Anyway, she was pleasant to look at. Maybe he and Lilly could work Eva's awkwardness into the act.

As he saw it in his mind's eye, his new act for the summer tour of 1918 would begin thusly: He would appear in white tie, top hat and tails in an explosion of white smoke, center stage. To warm the crowds, he would perform a few standard tricks; his cane turns into a bouquet of flowers, the endless handkerchief routine, followed by the endless deck of cards. Each time he finished a trick, one of his lovely assistants would appear to remove the props that were overwhelming the magician. After the card trick ended, with Black

Jack holding a deck displayed spread along each arm, Lilly would wheel a table on stage whereupon Herman would rest his top hat upside down for the trick 'conjuring gone wrong.'

He was supposed to pull out a rabbit, but everything else came out instead, including a bowl of goldfish. Afterward, the new wand also turned into a bouquet of flowers. Herman would exasperatedly pick up the wayward hat and place it back on his head in disgust.

Moments later, he would feel something up there. Lifting the hat, there would be a full grown chicken sitting on his head. Flabbergasted, he would order the 'Lovely Lilly' to take the table away hat, chicken and all. Only after she had pushed the table slowly off stage, wiggling the 'hitch in her git-along', Herman would suddenly sense something alive in his tuxedo. Reaching one hand in around the other side, he finally produced that wayward rabbit. He could see the audience now wailing with laughter.

Next, while the girls were setting up the stage for his history of magic demonstrations, Black Jack would walk into the audience and look for a few female volunteers to assist in simple card tricks. 'No men,' he reminded himself and, 'No deviations from the script,' i.e. no challenges from the crowd. This is how he had gotten into trouble in the past. After that, he would return to the stage to have the attractive assistants and ladies from the audience put him into chains.

While they immobilized him, he would talk to the audience about the magic of the Zulu tribe and why they were practically undefeatable. "The Zulu's have learned the powers of the mind. Before going into battle, they will psyche themselves up, drinking a special magical elixir which gives them boundless energy and mental acuity." He would make the pitch for the wonder tonic. Then, continuing the act in his mind, "Even in captivity, they had learned the ability to quickly slip out of any chains and overpower an unsuspecting enemy. Like this!" He would then escape to the amazement of the audience. Eva would appear to drag off the heavy chains, exit stage left. Lilly, about the same time, would appear with his golden turban. Now for the main part of the show.

"The maharajas of India have been plying the secrets of the dark arts for untold thousands of years. Some of these ancient controls were bestowed upon me after my chance acquaintanceship with the mahatma of a powerful northern cabal. One of the greatest of these is the magic sword trick used to discipline naughty slave girls or to impress a visiting potentate with the powers under your province. "Husbands don't try this at home," Black Jack clapped.

Entering stage right, the two assistants would begin the play. Eva, her hands tethered, would be led on stage in a mock struggle with Lilly, her disciplinarian. Led by outstretched arms to a set of movable steps, the 'slave girl Eva' would be forced to climb up and enter the container. Herman and Lilly would lift the top of the box, sitting on the floor, over the poor girl's head and into place. Leaving just a terrified head exposed, the trick would be performed to its ultimate conclusion, and then the two lovely ladies would remove that apparatus from the stage. (In latter years, a cabinet would be devised to incarcerate the terrified victim.)

Next, Black Jack would begin the preamble for the 'Hindu Rope Trick.' This trick, being the epitome of East Indian magic and having been performed in America in one variation or another for many years, was expected by the audience. Herman pictured Lilly performing this trick. It required a certain timing and stage presence that Eva did not yet possess. Better that she stood to one side of the stage and looked amazed. It would help sell the trick. He hoped that once on the road, Eva would pick it up. What a great ending if they were, all three, to escape up the rope and disappear!

After Lilly performed the rope trick, the duo would again terrify the luscious Eva by sawing her in half and putting her back together again. The look of distress on the poor girl's face as the saw tore into her, 'Well that would be worth the price of admission,' Herman chuckled to himself. The one aspect of the show he had yet to decipher was the ending.

Herman, the consummate showman for over a decade, trained by the best, knew he needed a showstopper for the finale. Something that no one else was currently performing.

The idea came to him a couple weeks later, after hours in one of the jazz clubs he frequented after he sent Eva home. The horns were set to wail and really blowing up a storm. One of the patrons at an adjoining table turned to his companion and said, "Man, them cats is so hot. They gonna raise the roof."

Then it hit him, 'Why not raise one of the girls into mid air?' It would have to be Eva, of course. She was the designated victim. Right then he realized that he and Lil' were in for a lot of work. Black Jack worked tirelessly over the next several weeks designing and choreographing the sensational illusion. No small feat in itself. When he presented the trick, the girls were dubious. To train their darling neophyte in less than a month would be daunting, but it could be done. It would have to be done. This is the trick that would put their act over the top. A feat of levitation extraordinaire. Not hesitating once he made up his mind, as was his custom, Herman began booking engagements for the following month in cities across the Midwest.

Now with their plans set, they trained even harder with emphasis on the 'Amazing Feat of Levitation' as marquee advertisements would describe the showstopper.

However, try as they might, the young apprentice just couldn't stay still long enough to convincingly sell the illusion. Moreover, she was clumsy on the switch. Her inexperience caused herky jerky movements which belied the suggestion that she was supposed to be entranced and floating through the air.

Herman refused to give up on Eva, but his patience was slipping, and it showed.

"Can't you stay any more still than that? You are supposed to be in a trance," he exploded after four hours of practice.

"I'm sorry. My foot fell asleep and it was tingling something awful. I guess that it was from all the time I spent in that box," Eva complained, nearly in tears.

Lilly had taken on the role of peacemaker in the now frequent fights between the couple. "Go easy on her, hon. On show day she only has to perform each trick once. The whole show is less than two hours." Then she walked over to the couch where Eva was still lying prone and said, "In between stage appearances you can jump around off stage. Even stick pins in your feet, but for this illusion to work you must be able to lie perfectly still after he hypnotizes you and covers you with the blanket. Then lying completely still," Lilly repeated this procedural point for emphasis, "You are to listen for Herman's verbal cue. Then you know what to do next."

"Okay," came the sheepish reply from the voice on the couch.

"Fine," Lilly, now assuming the role of ringmaster. "Let's do it again from the top."

That night they dropped exhausted, tortured Eva off at the apartment. Herman and Lilly went out for dinner, drinks. After cigar and whiskeys, Herman confided his fears. "I don't know Lil'. I don't think she's ready."

"Nonsense. She will do fine. She has ninety percent of it under control. With repetition, she will improve even more. It's just a case of 'stage willies,'" soothed Lilly, downing her drink. That woman could drink with the best of men.

"But the big trick, our showstopper, if she blows that, it will ruin everything."

"Too bad you couldn't really hypnotize her," Lil' shot back with a wry smile. "Seriously though, she will get the hang of the trick. It takes time and she's still green. Remember how it was for you being the neophyte?"

"I guess you are right." Herman chewed on his cigar, then removed it from his mouth and examined it, trying to divine the future from its entrails. "It's too bad I can't put her under a spell."

"I think you're both under a spell, each others. It's a good thing your wife hasn't found out about the extent of your relationship." The whisky and the shank of the evening had combined to produce a truth serum. Words poured unabashedly from the woman's lips. It was then she realized she was either too drunk or not drunk enough. After thoroughly examining the ice cubes in her glass, she raised her voice, "Hey, bartender." Her outstretched arm held up the empty glass, ice clinking, "Another round over here."

The week before the magic troupe was to leave Chicago for their first engagement; there came the surprising announcement of a dinner party being thrown in their honor by Mrs. Herman. The chauffeur deposited the young ladies, dressed in their summer finery, at the front door of Black Jack's residence. The chambermaid met them at the door and escorted them into the parlor where Black Jack was mixing martinis with a dubious expression.

"Here, I think you'll need these," he said slightly under his breath, as if afraid of being overheard. "It may be a long night."

"In that case, you had better make mine a double," quipped Lilly, quickly downing the gin splashed with vermouth, presenting the empty vessel back to her host. "I'd like the other half of this please."

Eva had taken her glass demurely and seated herself quietly on the sofa. Relations between she and her 'sugar daddy' had been strained lately owing to the constant practice and her continued misperformance. Everyone's nerves had been strained of late. Lilly just put it down to pre-tour jitters. But anyone who was familiar with the situation could tell that the honeymoon between Black Jack and Eva was over.

Wanda needed to confirm this fact for herself before her man and this young vamp spent months together in close quarters on the road. She would be perfectly happy if the girl fell flat on her face and ran home crying to 'what-ya-ma-callit' Mississippi. No matter how much it cost in lost bookings. She would not be disappointed after this dinner.

"So, how are you making out in this big city, dear?" Everyone knew this address was meant for Eva. Wanda's voice wafted into the room from the hall as she made her entrance descending the stairs.

"Oh, I'm alright, messus." The young woman barely looked up from the drink in her lap.

"Good. Good. Glad to hear it. We haven't seen much of you lately, and I was afraid that you might be feeling lost in the big city. Many young girls like yourself, on your own for the first time, often become homesick for small town life."

Wanda had made her entrance as she spoke, dressed in a floor length purple evening gown complete with sparkling diamond necklace and earrings. Sporting a new hairdo for the occasion, she draped herself around her husband, her arms adorned with golden bangles shimmering in the artificial room light illuminating the early summer's evening. She looked completely dazzling as the queen of her castle and her possessions.

"Darling, where's my drink?" she veritably cooed into her husband's ear.

"Right here, my love," the perfunctory response as he fulfilled her anticipated request, martini already in hand. Now fully satisfied with her complete dominance of the proceedings, Wanda purred, "Either of you ladies need a refill? Dinner's not for a little while yet." Eva unmoving demurred. However, Lilly unimpressed, rose to the occasion, "I'm already on my seconds. Wanda, you'll have to catch up."

"This isn't a contest, my dear. There's no competition here." There was just the slightest touch of vanity in her voice as she clung to her man.

Moments later, Black Jack extricated himself from her clutches, tiring of this petty posturing. "Ladies, ladies. There's enough for everyone. Here, let me freshen your drinks." He circulated with the pitcher among his guests. Completing this duty, he replaced the nearly empty pitcher on the liquor trolley where his wife remained. 'Now to start the evening's fun,' he thought.

"Lilly, Wanda says she would like to see our show." A devilish glint in his eye was caught by the addressee.

"Let her buy a ticket like anyone else," quipped Lilly, devouring her olive.

"Now, now. Don't be like that," Herman protested.

"You know better than anyone its bad luck to bring spouses around before a big show, especially someone who's not in the business." Lilly was adamant in her recitation of showbiz folklore and superstition.

Wanda broke in, warming to the argument. "But I could be a pair of fresh eyes. An objective audience of one. Of course, I wouldn't get in the way. You would hardly know I was there."

"We would never be able to forget," objected Herman, finding a convenient avenue of attack against his spouse's request. "You know how you become when we go to the theatre, always criticizing the actors."

Wanda, not put off by this opening salvo against her perfectly reasonable request, refilled her glass from the rapidly emptying pitcher and fired her query. "Is there perhaps some reason that you are afraid of my criticism? Maybe if there is a problem with the show, better to bring it into the open now and not out on the road in front of live audiences. If there is something that needs to be fixed, better to take the time now and cancel those bookings while we can and save that unnecessary expense. After all, if the show just needs a little re-working, then maybe part of the tour can be salvaged when you're ready."

Herman's temperature was rising, his voice responded with similar change in amplitude. "I don't know who's been telling you things," he rebuked his errant wife. "But there are no problems with the show."

"Oh, really? Then why all the long practices? Why all the glum faces? I've noticed the change in attitudes around here. I'm not blind, you know."

The alcohol from the strong gin drinks having gone to her head, Eva exploded from her bump-on-a-log position on the sofa. "There is something wrong with the show all right. It's me. It's me. I'm not ready for the stage, and everybody knows it. I'm screwing up the act." The nearly hysterical girl rose from her seated position abruptly dropping the glass in the process. It broke into pieces upon contact with the floor. Tears streaming down her face, she ran out of the room and locked herself in the hall bathroom.

After her abrupt exit, Lilly walked over to the martini pitcher, draining the last of its contents into her glass. "Great party, bro." She patted Herman on the shoulder and returned to her position near the window.

Black Jack turned to Wanda. There were daggers in his eyes. "Now look what you've done," he said and stormed out to console his protégée.

Just then the chambermaid entered to announce dinner. She was momentarily startled at seeing the discord in progress. Then she noticed the broken glass.

Vehemently, Wanda instructed her to "go get a dustpan and clean that up."

"Yes, ma'am. Right away, ma'am." The maid curtsied and left.

The two remaining women ignored each other. Black Jack spent the next twenty minutes at the bathroom door pleading with his young apprentice.

"My dear, it's alright. Please come out. She doesn't know what she's talking about. You're going to give a great performance. It's just pre-opening jitters."

"I don't know. You're always so cross with me. I just can't seem to pick up the routine. And I'm not fast enough on the switch. If I can't do it on an empty stage, how am I going to be able to perform in front of a crowd?" Her self-deprecating argument did make sense. This was the name of the fear that had been nagging in the back of Herman's mind. Usually starlets performed better in practice, not the other way. Of course, there were those rare exceptions. They usually involved people who were born to the stage, raised in show business. Now Eva did have some innate stage presence and she was beautiful. It's just that she was too self conscious. If he could break her of that, he could make her a star. He was certain of that. 'Damn Wanda. She had purposefully waited to this moment to set off her bomb in the hopes of destroying the girl's confidence. But what was her aim? Did she really want to drive the girl away and destroy the show? Destroy him? Was she actually that vain? He would have to deal with her later.' He really did love Eva, but he was not ready to admit how much, even to himself.

A hand brushed his arm. "Here, boss, I brought you a refill. Take this. How's she doin'?" It was Lilly. "I can't get her to unlock the door. Wanda really did a number on her. I didn't expect that. I guess I should..." his voice trailed off.

"Here, let me talk to her for a while. You go have a couple of drinks, and then we will be there for dinner." Lilly, replacing Black Jack at the locked door, called to Eva, "Honey, it's me. Open up, okay? He's gone."

"Is he really?" sobbed the squeaky voice from within.

"Sure, hon. I wouldn't lie to you. Now, come on."

The door cracked open and the bleary-eyed face peered forth. "I feel so awful. I wish we could get out of here." Tears had left her face streaked with mascara.

"Well, we can't. There's that old showbiz saying about the show must go on- no refunds, and all that nonsense. Well, that applies here. We need to clean you up, march you back into the dining room and show Wanda what you're made of." 'Maybe show us all,' she thought idly while reaching into her hanging purse for fresh lipstick and rouge.

A few long minutes of primping later, the two women marched into the dining room to join the host and hostess. They were seated at either end of the long table stabbing their appetizers. Taking her place at one of the middle chairs while Lilly was seated opposite, Eva once again addressed Wanda, "Good evening again, mistress. Please excuse my outburst. Just a case of pre-opening night jitters as your husband alluded. There is nothing to worry about. The show will be a great success. We have all worked very hard to make that success a reality. Thank you for having us here tonight."

Wanda, still pleased with herself, responded, "Thank you for allaying any fears on my part, my dear. That was a very nice speech. Did they teach you that in school? Down in 'Ole Miss.'"

"I guess, ma'am," Eva continued demurely, ignoring the ignoble remark. "That much of the credit belongs to the constant tutelage of your dear husband. He has extensively instructed me in the social graces that are expected, nay required, for someone circulating in your social setting."

Herman winced, biting his fork at this statement. Lilly hid behind her half-empty glass trying to suppress laughter.

"Well, at least I am glad to see that all of his time and hard earned money have produced proficiency."

"As I said, my dear. I was right; the young woman does have a certain proclivity for show business."

Lilly could not contain herself any longer and burst out laughing. Wanda was not sure what exactly the joke was, but she was sure that she bore the brunt of it. And so it went, the less than memorable evening devolved into an alcoholic haze. The remembrance of which is best left to forgetfulness' first finale.

The itinerary had been set in stone for weeks. By now, the deposit refund date, or 'required up front' money as it was sometimes called, had already passed for the first third of the venues booked. Black Jack had a lot of capital riding on this venture. More than just his reputation was riding on their successful production. The proceeds of one tour tended to fund his performances the next season. In addition, there were the continual costs of entourage payroll and the wife and kids. Wanda tended to spend quite freely.

In many respects, his business was much like that of the family farmer. The proceeds of one crop would be repartitioned to repair hearth and home, with the remainder preserved for the following season. Like those family farmers, Black Jack was just one or two bad harvests away from sacrificing the family farm. This was not a well hidden secret within the household. The wonder then at Wanda's continued recalcitrance towards his employ of Eva. Women could be so irrational.

He desperately wanted to find a way to make magic and his gift for legerdemain pay off on a continual basis. Thus, losing the dependence on the seasonality of touring. Alas, to date the solution escaped his grasp.

The tour would begin in Milwaukee for a week; proceed on to Cleveland, then Detroit and Pittsburgh. On the way back they would stop in Indianapolis for three days playing before a predominately Caucasian audience, and then swing down to St. Louis where they would play for a predominately minority audience. The tail-end of the trip came the Piece de-Resistance. Saving the best for last as it was also known-three weeks in Chicago! Performing before the home crowd. It was hoped that word of their successful road show would stimulate advance sales for their Chicago showings and herald their triumphant return to home base. The tour would conclude the second week of September. There would be just enough time for rest and relaxation. Then they would have to begin plans for the swing through the southern circuit. "The life of a performer never stops. It just pauses occasionally," Herman was heard to say more than once.

The tour began with a drive to Milwaukee, only forty miles from home base. Thereafter, they would rent a boxcar for the limo and props, and two sleeper cabins for the troupe, which for this venture consisted of the two female assistants, Herman and his chauffeur. They would use grips and stagehands provided by the theatre operators to save on expenses. Hence, they would be required to arrive at each location a few days early to practice with the crew.

Arriving for the first performance on a Tuesday morning, they had three days to practice and whip Eva into shape before a sold out opening night on Friday.

The practices with the crew went well. Lighting and curtains were fine; they were the consummate professionals. Eva performed the routines with aplomb; her 'distressed' look sold the tricks as planned. However, she was still a little stiff in the show stopping levitation finale. Rather, the point was, she wasn't stiff enough. Anyone sitting in the front rows could surmise when the switch was occurring, spoiling the illusion. These few would point it out, and that is all the audience would remember out of an otherwise flawless performance. The critics would harp; the flaw and sales would plummet. This was not a farfetched fantasy or a case of performer's angst. There were people in the press who lived to unmask magicians as frauds. Black Jack knew all too well the price of failure. He could be back working the carney circuit selling his herb tonic in a heartbeat. Moreover, the trick could not be pulled as it was proudly billed on the marquee. He decided to try the soft touch with the girl rather than scare her anymore than she already was. 'She is a little girl, after all. Still a teenager in many ways.' Although she grew up in the south, she grew up in a happy family environment, not on the road grappling with fame and fortune, singing for her supper as it were.

His thoughts were good intentioned. But as the saying goes the road paved with good intentions is often fraught with tumult and peril. It usually leads to...well, it usually leads to places you would rather not go. The Wednesday evening rehearsal was just about to wind to conclusion. The young apprentice had just lain down on the couch and was lying very still, having been 'entranced' by the Great Black Jack.

Lilly finished laying the linen cloth over the prone body and then it happened.

"Ach, Ach-choo! Ach-choo!" Two distinct high pitched sneezes emanated from under the cloth covering containing the neophyte, purportedly catatonic.

"That's it. Cut!" shouted Herman. "That's it. You've ruined the illusion. How will anyone believe you are hypnotized when you are sneezing all over the place? People in trances don't sneeze."

"I'm sorry, Daddy. The lint itched my nostrils." Eva began trying to desperately worm her way back into Herman's good graces. It was no use; his patience was at an end.

"You had better learn to act as if your life depended on getting the trick right. Imagine you are over in Europe in the trench war. The enemy is looking for you, and you are hiding in the dark, lying in the tall grass. If they catch you, they will stab you with a bayonet. No questions. No excuses. No do-overs."

Black Jack looked over glowering at the girl whose head was peeking out from under the cover. He continued his rantings, "If you can't do that, then perhaps I should have taken your sister instead of you."

After dropping that bombshell, Herman uncharacteristically stormed off the stage. His stage. The blood drained from Eva's face.

"Don't worry, darlin'. I'll go talk to him. He didn't mean that. He really loves you. Perhaps too much. He really wants you to get it right. It's just nerves. You have to learn to just do the trick. Don't think about it. Don't be afraid of failing. Just relax and let it happen."

Lilly hurried off the stage after Herman, leaving Eva alone. All alone. Feeling like she was the only one left alive in the entire world. She desperately wished that the Earth would open and swallow her.

The next afternoon when Eva arrived at the performance hall for dress rehearsal, she was advised that today's practice would be a closed session. Just she and Black Jack. In her dressing room, draped over a chair at the make-up table, was a new black satin outfit. A yellow rose on the table covered a note from Herman. She was instructed to don her new costume and meet him onstage immediately upon her entry.

Without hesitation, she removed her street clothes and under things, putting on her new outfit. The shimmery black satin adorned her torso, while the short skirt flattered her long legs. The laced backing presented quite a challenge. She had a devil of a time securing it properly.

When she appeared on stage about half an hour after her arrival, she found Herman had dismissed the stage hands. He was waiting alone dressed in white tie and tails, standing in front of a table which held several conjuring devices and other props used in the show. She walked toward him.

"Stop," he commanded. "Turn around." Immediately she began a slow pirouette under his cold gaze. Her pleated skirt rose to reveal velvety thighs.

"Faster." She spun around on high heels, the skirt flared to reveal the black satin underwear that had accompanied the dress. She continued to turn for several revolutions, with one arm crooked and the other stretched above her head to help her maintain balance. She pirouetted as well as any professional ballerina. Black Jack was pleased. "That's enough," he shouted.

Eva came to an abrupt stop barely breathing hard. Nevertheless, her bosoms heaved in the tight outfit. A small smile creased her lips at the recognition of her lover's look of approval, heightened desire.

"That was very good," a low approving tone accompanied the statement. "I can see all eyes will be on you. That is just as it should be. Allowing me to work my magic. My dear, you will be my greatest illusion. If you just concentrate on your craft. Now come here." An outstretched hand thrust in her direction. Her body responded unconsciously, languidly flowing toward him.

Her eyes grew smoky. Suddenly she was in a dream world. Everything else on the stage vanished from her comprehension. They two were alone in this magical world. His outstretched arm reached around her back and drew her close. Their lips met and embraced lovingly, lustfully, then wantonly. She was still in her trance when she felt his free hand tickling her under her skirt. Roving fingers, teased and tickled, then probed. She could hear a low moan in her throat developing in response. The magic fingers moved freely about underneath the satin material and then plunged deeply into her womanhood. Eva widened her thighs in response and thrust her pelvis towards the pronged intruder. She kissed his lips harder, mouth now fully upturned to meet his, an open receptacle for his thrusting tongue.

She wilted in his arms, now fully comfortable in her position as one of his possessions. Her dreamlike state of blissful surrender continued until his hand freed itself from her and pulled down her satin panties upon departure. Eva regained partial hold on reality as she heard him running down the fly on his trousers.

"No, not here," she whispered, her lips disengaging from his mouth.

"Of course here. And now," a husky command. He tightened his grip on the girl. She shrieked as the hot shaft of a branding iron lashed into her. Searing her with its fire, and in its turn, fueling her own desire.

"But we are on stage," she cried, trying to reason with him even as her body responded to his savage thrusts with undulations of her own.

"You must learn to free yourself of your inhibitions. When you are on stage, you must give your all to the audience. Stand naked before them, perform for them, command them. Only then can you obtain the power they have to give. The adoration. Feel the power, live your life on the stage." He had guided her onto the table, knocking some of the props onto the stage floor in the process. They clanged uselessly onto the stage, echoing in the empty theatre.

Her body betrayed her better senses, her sense of caution, propriety. She raised her legs and wrapped them around his hips. The moans escaping her throat in tempo to his thrusts. Still her mind cried out through kiss swollen lips. "No, not here. Not this. Please." He ignored her pleas. Between pants she continued, "Stop, oh stop. Someone will see us."

Abruptly, he stopped and withdrew from her. His quick movement had left her dazed momentarily, her legs dangling in midair. Relishing her confusion, he grabbed her by the left forearm and turned her around so that she fell belly down onto the table. Before she knew what was happening, he had thrust his engorged manhood into her again.

She shrieked protests at this final defilement. However, crushed under his weight she could offer little resistance. She cried in resignation at her predicament. Herman continued his tutorial, "Feel the power of the stage. Feel the energy. You must learn to open yourself to the fullest extent. The stage is your life. Don't hold anything back." She continued to struggle futilely underneath him sobbing softly. Black Jack was relentless in his exhortation.

"Open yourself, your soul, to me girl. Open your soul to me." Herman finished roughly and withdrew, leaving the girl sobbing and exposed, bent over the table. Sternly, he admonished her, "Okay, straighten your clothing. It's time we begin today's rehearsal. I trust your performance will improve over last night's abysmal showing."

Eva's transcendental transformation from that moment on was nothing short of miraculous. Her fervid movements on stage bespoke of a new passion for her craft and belied the nonchalance with which she had comported herself previously.

Lilly was not only puzzled, she was completely mystified by this remarkable overnight change in the young apprentice. She surmised that something extraordinary must have occurred, but what? Her common sense prevailed and she never inquired as to the source of this unequivocal metamorphosis.

The opening performance the following night was a complete success. Eva and Lilly received bouquets of roses, one pink, one yellow. They stood center stage holding their flowers sharing the thunderous ovation with Black Jack. It truly was his night.

IV
Once Every Seven Years!

After a successful showing in Milwaukee, the tour moved on to the next venue. In Cleveland, they soon learned their new found fame had preceded them. Their week of bookings was completely sold out. Eva and Lilly hugged each other, jumping up and down on the train platform as Black Jack read the telegram from his booking agent. "The show's a hit. Ladies, we have arrived," he shouted, grabbing the two in loving embrace. "Let's go out and paint the town red. Carl, make sure the props are delivered to the theatre under lock and key, and see that our bags get to the hotel." Turning back to his harem, "Let's go, ladies. Time's a-wasting." They locked arms one woman on each side and strode into the station in search of a taxi stand. Destination, a well deserved evening of entertainment and relaxation.

Cleveland was a big success, as was Detroit. One evening, at a cocktail party after a performance in Pittsburgh, they met a man who was introduced as the son of the Turkish ambassador to the United States. "A wonderful show with superb illusions." Herman bowed deeply, "Thank you for your kindness, sir. It is a pleasure to make your acquaintance."

"And such lovely assistants. You are truly a lucky man to be blessed with such riches," the ambassador's son continued in sincere flattery.

Herman, trying to intuit the others meaning in the compliment, gambled, "Yes, they are the secrets of my success. For, you see, they are so beautiful that the audience barely regards me with any attention at all."

"Ha, Ha." The son laughed with a wave of his arm. "The magician gives away his most valuable secret."

"Alas, if I could only give away my greatest treasure as well to a consummate man of the world such as yourself. But this is not to be the case. The heart is a fierce warrior that puts restrictions on us all." Herman continued gravely in confidential tones.

"You misunderstand my meaning, sir. It is natural for any man to retain the most cherished prize for himself. Besides, anyone with eyes can see how she looks at you. You are her alpha and omega. I can tell you from personal experience that such a gift, when given freely can be the most joyous prize in the entire world."

Herman relaxed his posture almost imperceptibly as the young man with the thick mustache continued, "I was only admiring and wished to congratulate you on your magnificent accomplishment. You know, my father was a student of magic when he was a young man. He would love to meet you and see your show."

Herman looked doubtful. "While I would certainly like to accommodate you, and it is an intriguing idea, we had not planned to play Washington D.C. on this trip. Besides, if we did, because of local laws, I don't think we could play before a mixed audience." Black Jack was trying to be tactful and not offend the guest, but technically the nation's capital was in the south.

The other man frowned, but continued undaunted, "Then we will call it a 'Command Performance.' You shall perform inside our embassy. After all, when we are on Turkish soil, we can do whatever we wish. And we wish for you and your delicious assistants to entertain us. We will invite the other ambassadors and we will bill it as 'A Night of Magic.'"

"And legerdemain," added Black Jack thinking quickly. They could swing by the capital after their performances here in Pittsburg. They would have to cancel or at least postpone their performances in Indianapolis, but it would be well worth their while. Imagine performing for the representatives of the Crown Heads of Europe. Wait until he told the girls.

The ambassador was less than delighted, "I send you for steel, and you come back with a magic act. What a clever son you are."

"Father, wait until you see this show and the women." He placed his forefingers and thumb to pursed lips. "They are to kill for. Wait, you will see."

The embassy was more than opulent. It was extravagant on a grand scale with its gold painted, hand designed, metal ceilings, crystal chandeliers and hanging tapestries. The women were overwhelmed by their bed chambers. The pink satin sheets on the large canopied beds. The finely detailed crown molding bordering frescoed ceilings enchanted with old world charm. Eva now knew what it was like to be a fairy princess. Even Lilly, who had stayed in elegant hotels in her travels, was awestruck by the level of grandeur. The women romped through each other's rooms like little girls until late in the night.

Black Jack could hear faint giggling as he smoked his cigar on the balcony of his room, contemplating the city of presidents. The trail of smoke left his being and wafted up into the humid Washingtonian night. It was early August, and there was the scent of rain in the air. Black Jack's thoughts hovered much like the cigar smoke, uncertain of purpose and direction.

Here he was in one of the most powerful cities in the world and he, a successful businessman, could not walk down the street freely enter any restaurant, sit down and have a drink. Yet he could sit here as the guest of a foreign government and rub elbows with some of the most powerful people in the world. What a glaring inconsistency. As Herman looked out over the city of Jefferson and Lincoln, he could sense change in the air. It was as palpable as the moisture laden currents streaming in from the mountains of West Virginia.

America had stepped in and ended the Great War, taken its place among the foremost nations of the world. There was even some talk about forming a League of Nations with the United States in preeminence. Certainly such a rising star, a great nation, would have to provide a shining example to the rest of the world. America had graduated from adolescence to adulthood. There was the general feeling that this was going to be the American Century. That we were about to inherit some sort of manifest destiny. Hell, women were marching in the street demanding the right to vote. Black Jack smiled to himself, 'Yes, sir. Change was in the air. If women got the right to vote, then anything was possible.'

An idea was germinating in the back of his head. Once you had achieved fortune and fame, the next destination was to use these tools in the effective exercise of power. The power to influence men's minds and change public policy. It was a numbers game, of course, but it could be done slowly and subtly. Without drawing ire and retribution from the power elite. The powers that be had a vested interest in maintaining the status quo. Everyone knew that dirty little fact. Just look here at the nation's capital, south of the Mason-Dixon Line. What lesson did this send to foreign dignitaries? Do as I say, but pay no attention to what I do.

The south had risen again alright. More powerful and pervasive in its' perverted practices than ever before. The big monied politicians all cast a blind eye and held an upturned hand out behind their backs. Graft was king. Meanwhile they uttered publicly pleasing platitudes on social progress, or often, more privately uttered banalities of benign neglect. 'They always appear to be such a happy people.' Yes, change was in the air. It was festering in shanty towns and the tar-paper shacks of the south. But, it needed leaders. Leaders needed a consistent source of funds. If only he could find a way to turn his 'overnight success' into a constant cash generating machine. Black Jack smoked his cigar into extinction late into the night. Near dawn, a fierce rainstorm moved down from the mountains to wash the dirt out of the streets. Flushing the flotsam and jetsam into the Potomac and out to the Atlantic.

The embassy's grand ballroom was transformed into a theatre for the occasion. A stage was erected complete with curtains and lighting courtesy of the Turkish government. Stagehands and grips were persuaded to accompany them from Pittsburgh on the promise of substantial payment. They simply called in sick after Herman's last performance.

The women, dazzling in their black satin costumes, were consummate professionals. Eva, no longer predisposed to bouts of anxiety and self consciousness, stole the show with her beauty. She was a prestigitator's dream, bejeweled and ravishing. Eva, the focus of everyone's attention, allowed Black Jack to weave his illusions flawlessly. Herman even invited the Turkish ambassador on stage during the sword trick to plunge swords into the box where Eva was imperiled. To everyone's delight, he ad-libbed, performing his task with great savagery. Eva counterbalanced his performance with a heightened dramatic flair.

However, the show stopper was indeed Herman's levitation of his prone assistant, during which he invited the wife of one of the ambassadors on stage to help him verify that the young woman was indeed suspended in mid-air. Most of the assembled crowd had never seen such a trick before and were left fascinated with the clever conundrum. There was considerable, "Marvelous performance, Mr. Herman. So real. So convincing. And the performance of your assistants, how theatrical." The Turkish ambassador was patting him on the shoulders in the middle of the reception hall. They were surrounded by a multitude of drink-wielding guests, the crème de la crème of Washingtonian society.

"Thank you so much for allowing us to entertain for you. Please call me Black Jack. And you were not so bad onstage yourself. I understand from your son that you used to be a magician."

"Dabble is the correct phrase. Since a young man, I have been fascinated with the shows provided by the traveling gypsies of my country. Also, certain Hindu fakirs of whom I have had the pleasure. But, dear sir, I must say that, unequivocally, your performance here tonight was extraordinary."

"Thank you so much, Your Excellency. You must remember to thank your son. It is due to his insight and ingenuity that we are here tonight."

"Yes, yes," agreed the ambassador, looking around over the heads of dignitaries for his prodigal offspring. "Where is that boy? Oh, over there with the women, of course."

The Secretary of State braved the throngs of diplomats crowded around Herman in order to offer congratulations. "Mr. Herman, congratulations on a most magical performance. I must admit I've not seen any better."

"Thank you very much, sir. That means a lot coming from a fellow American," replied Black Jack as he stretched his hand out in response to the other's gesture.

The Turkish ambassador seized the opportunity as it was presented.

"Gentlemen," he began, embracing the two of them in outstretched arms, pulling them closer. "I'm very glad I had the opportunity to bring these two great Americans together." The largess of his actions was not lost on others of the diplomatic community. They crowded closer, sensing another show about to take place.

"Speaking of magic, Mr. Secretary. Is it not amazing that inside these 'Walls of Magic' we could put together this little performance in just a few short days? I don't believe you could say the same say, outside in the city." The ambassador had sprung his trap.

The Secretary, who was not completely unprepared for the assault, still stammered, "Well, of course in a city as big as D.C., with all of its attendant bureaucracy, filling out the proper forms and allowing time for the requests to be analyzed is a prerequisite."

"Still, you would allow this man to perform for us," the Turk pressed his advantage. "There are no laws that would hinder or restrict the performance of this good American."

"Of course, laws can be bypassed or ignored. The laws you refer to are antiquated. They have little bearing today," the secretary countered.

"Sir, one of your highest laws, ideals, is the concept of the 'inalienable rights of all men' is it not?" A rhetorical question. The ambassador did not wait for an answer. "But, when I travel about in your city, I see that while you profess 'all men are created equal' you practice a separate equality for different classes of citizens."

The Secretary, now clearly irked at this ambush, responded, "Clearly sir, as I have stated, there are still remnants of an antiquated culture present. Shadows from our past. As likewise, your country still reels from those pogroms against Turkish citizens presumed descendant of Armenian or gypsy lineage."

"Yes, yes," dismissed the ambassador with the wave of his hand. "We still hear hundreds of complaints about the Armenian question, but where is the proof? More to the point, here in America a great amount of lip service is given to support your assertations of high moral values, of 'equality and justice for all.' Intimating that you are so much better than the rest of the world," crowed the Turkish ambassador, gesturing grandly with his arms for the audience.

"Ideas and ideals worth striving toward are never obtained easily. Our individual freedoms and democratic process are our strength. Unlike your system, when the majority of the populace agrees on a change, we will make it happen and enact it into law. Now if you will excuse me, I wish to congratulate those two young women on their fine performance."

Herman had observed the drama with keen interest. He now realized that in politics it was hard to tell one's enemies from one's friends. He also began to realize just how hard a struggle the 'fight for equality' would be. Perhaps for the first time. He was more certain than ever that it would be achieved. Soon thereafter, he excused himself from the ambassador and rejoined his girls. It was time to prepare to return to his world.

When all the gear was stowed safely aboard and he was seated in his stateroom watching the westbound railcar chase the setting sun, Herman had a chance to be alone with his thoughts. After his experiences at the Turkish embassy, Black Jack realized that everyone had an agenda, priorities. His agenda now was to get his wayward show back on schedule. His priority, a successful presentation in front of a hometown audience. This accomplishment would provide him with the stepping stones needed to consolidate his power base and standing within his community. The logical first step in his conquest of political power. He still needed a vehicle to reach the masses, but he assured himself that this would appear in time. In the meantime, there would be the luxury of basking in the limelight of his unequivocal success, his triumphant homecoming and to bask in the adoration of this young woman who loved him completely and without reservation.

Eva was the pearl in his oyster. How she had transformed from that scared little girl-that first rehearsal in Milwaukee. He smiled remembering how roughly he had taken her on the stage. Completely dominating her, oblivious to her will, her fears. After that event, she ceased being a spoiled child and became a grown woman-his woman, who knew what was expected of her and responded accordingly. This was his greatest feat of magic, her instantaneous transformation.

Herman congratulated his intuition that had picked her out of a crowd three quarters of a year ago. He knew she could be a star. Perhaps better than Lilly-one day.

Of course, that was years in the future. Right now, he and Lilly were a team; Eva was their pretty protégée and his lover. The woman who shared his bed and satiated his desires. As the train hit a bump and hiccupped the passengers slightly, it refocused his attentions on the end of the road. The light at the end of the tunnel, if you will.

Soon as St. Louis was finished, they would be re-entering Chicago. Their love affair would have to be tempered with discretion. They had taken many liberalities on the road that could not be afforded in the hometown. Moreover, the excuse of his tutorial could no longer apply. After returning from her first tour as a successful professional, Eva would be expected to forge a life of her own. Wanda, a jealous person by nature, was overly suspicious of their relationship already.

He would have to explain to Eva that they couldn't spend as much time together. That they must be clever about their assignations if the charade was to continue undiscovered. He would assure Eva that he would find excuses to be with her, practices, parties and the like. Unfortunately, they could not be together every night as it was on tour. He sincerely hoped she would understand and take it well. He was continually surprised at the depth of his affection for her. He really loved her deeply.

He decided to sit her down and explain the facts of life to her on their last night in St. Louis. Sitting her on his lap in private, he explained how things must be. "Its okay, Daddy. I understand." Her tone was reassuring.

And that's another thing; you can't call me 'Daddy' in mixed company once we get back to Chicago. People will jump to conclusions and gossip spreads like wildfire. There are a lot of important businessmen whose favor I am trying to cultivate. Cavorting around with my mistress openly in public would send them the wrong impression. That I am not capable of handling my household business discreetly. After all, no one minds what you do. Just don't flaunt your affairs. It is bad policy."

"Is that all I am then? Just an affair?" the young woman pouted.

"No. No, much more than that. You are my partner, my performer extraordinaire. The love of my life. It's just that things are complicated. Now is not the time for any dramatic rearrangements. We will be together as often as possible the next couple of months. It will be okay, you'll see. I promise. Soon we will begin to practice for our winter tour through the south. Then we can be together most days and many nights. Won't that be fun?"

"Yes, I guess so. It just seems that two or three months is so far away. Won't you miss me? Won't you miss your little 'Pookie Bear'? She cuddled closer, ingratiating her hips into his lap.

"Of course I will, my darling. I will be with you as often as possible without drawing the suspicions of Wanda. You know how jealous she is."

Eva bustled, "I don't think she likes me very much. She was not very nice to me before we left on the tour."

"She's afraid of you, baby. You have a tremendous talent and she can see that. She also sees the way you look at me, and this scares her even more. You will have to be mindful of that when you are around her. You are an actress now. So act."

"And do you still love me?" An index finger wheedled him along with the tone of her voice.

"You know I love you. More and more each day." Black Jack surprised himself with his candor.

The train pulled into Chicago and the wayward troupers were met with great fanfare. The publicity agent Black Jack had hired to promote his triumphant homecoming had alerted the press to the imminent arrival of the magician. ' 'Black Jack the Great'- who has recently wowed international dignitaries at the Ambassadorial Ball in Washington D.C., now appearing in Chicago after a string of sole out performances across the Midwest.' So screamed the headlines on the press release provided prior to their arrival.

There was a marching band playing on the platform as the train pulled in. A stark contrast to their departure. They had left hopefuls; they had returned heroes. Herman, standing in the doorway of the railcar as it berthed in front of the crowd, was glad to see his money was being well spent. The reporters would eat this up and write glowing accounts that would virtually ensure that the Chicago shows would be sold out. If they performed as expected, they would become the toast of the town. Black Jack would be the envy of his friends and enemies alike. As he learned recently, sometimes it is hard to distinguish between the two.

As he stepped off of the train, a young drum majorette placed a string of flowers around his neck, while the band played exuberantly. Herman raised his hands to the cheers of the crowd, many of them paid participants. Then he lowered them indicating the desire for silence. The maestro was going to speak. "Hello. Thank you all for coming to greet us. It has been a long and rewarding trip. We are glad to be back home in sweet Chicago-at last." The crowd roared its approval and as the band made jubilant noises, Black Jack continued, "As you may have heard, we have recently performed for the representatives of many great world powers. We knocked their socks off. They said they had never seen anything like our show and my lovely assistants." Herman pointed to the two lovely young ladies who were still standing in the doorway of the railcar. They curtsied; the crowd roared approval.

Black Jack continued, "I was even asked to tour Europe performing for the Crown Heads themselves. To which I replied, 'Sir if they wish to see the show, they will have to go to Chicago, my hometown. I have deprived those good people long enough.'" Herman paused several minutes as the climatic applause faded. "Well, I want you all to tell your friends that we are back in town and ready to put on a show that is so profound. It's only here in Chicago; you can't get it in Europe, even if you wear a crown. Well, that's all. Now I am going home to my wife and kids. See you all at our next performance." With that he motioned to the band to begin the finale, as he made his way through the crowd shaking hands.

Until finally, he reached Wanda and the kids who were standing in the back. They embraced and he left with them in Wanda's chauffeured limousine. Never looking back.

Eva and Lilly were left standing on the platform as Carl arranged for their limo and bags to be unloaded from the baggage car. As the gathering dissolved around them, they resembled the last reluctant guests of a New Year's Eve party. Unwilling or unable to move on and greet the new dawn.

Lilly grabbed the hand of the younger woman and soothed in pre-emptive sympathetic tones. "Don't worry, kid. It don't mean a thing. It's just show business. Remember we are the masters of illusion. Let's go get a drink while we wait for Carl to take us home."

Masters of illusion indeed! Meanwhile the greatest master of illusion was working to prove to his spouse that he still loved her. Problem was she knew all of his usual tricks. 'It would take more than sawing a woman in half to convince her,' he thought. Then he realized that it might require exactly that much sleight-of-hand to convince Wanda of his devotion. He would have to work on that.

Right now his first concern was preparing for the crowning climax of his successful tour. Opening night in Chicago. The prescription: a little rest, then perform his husbandly duties. A little rest and his petty household problems would solve themselves. At least, that is what he led himself to believe. Nevertheless, he was at that moment on top of the world, better stop and enjoy the view.

The Chicago engagement was an unmitigated success. For three weeks, Herman and his accomplices held audiences spellbound with their magical exploits. The crowds seemed to never tire of seeing Eva in peril. They oohed, aahed with every sword that ran her through and gasped as she was sawed in half. Only to clap with thunderous approval when she was revealed to be safe and sound.

Wanda was there, too, for every performance in her private box watching and waiting. No one knew how many times during the many performances she wished the young girl's peril might have a different ending.

She was also with Black Jack every night at the obligatory

receptions and parties that followed the evening's entertainment. Joined as she was to her husband as if they had always been that way.

Coincidentally, the young women were attracting much of the attention to themselves. Almost enough to rival Herman.

Lilly had completely filled out her date card after the first week. She was now able to live out the modern girls' dream of entertaining different companions for breakfast, lunch and supper after the evening's performances. The girls' apartment could have been mistaken for a flower shop, as delivery boys had beat a path to their door. Each one loaded down with more flowers and gifts than the last. It was springtime in Chicago in their too little two bedroom abode.

Eva was completely overwhelmed by the attentions of so some gentlemen of all ages. She was equally scorched by the scorning eyes of jealous wives and girlfriends who were somehow threatened by her eloquent portrayals of impending peril. What she did not understand was that her performances touched some deep secret chord in men. Watching her struggle helplessly empowered them, unconsciously they harkened back to the time when men reigned supreme and women sat docilely at their feet.

The modern woman on the march for freedom and equality resented these portrayals of helplessness at the hands of a brutal taskmaster. For in effect, that is what they were, brutal reminders of man's continual brutish domination over women. Interestingly the original 'Perils of Pauline' concept did not evoke such bitter resentment from the fairer sex. These stories were designed more as a morality play wherein the pretty young innocent Pauline was manhandled by the dastardly Snidely. Finally, to be rescued at the last moment by the dashing hero who made mad passionate love to her and cherished her forever. It was a romantic fantasy to which all women could relate. It was the stuff of which little girls' dream. The struggling and moaning were purely incidental. In the magic act, there was no white knight to come running on stage and save the pretty Eva from the capricious whims of the evil tyrant, Black Jack.

While this mistreatment of women may have been the primary

motivating mechanism for enjoyment in the minds of many paying patrons, it was not the only emotion evoked. In many of the men, especially those suitors of Eva's, there was the strong desire to protect and cherish Black Jack's pretty young protégée.

At first, Eva shied away from social contact with her many suitors until Lilly pointed out that some casual dates, perhaps a constant companion, would allay some of the lingering suspicion. Suspicions, primarily on the part of Wanda, that Eva and her husband were continuing to have an affair. An ascertion to which both parties had denied. It was reasoned that as long as she did not appear to be a little girl, star struck, clinging on to the star of the show. But instead a modern woman who was enjoying the fruits of her labor, appearances would be satisfied. She and Herman could sneak around town and see one another on occasion. That way, Eva could continue her love affair with a married man. That's just the way things were done in modern society. So Eva, the actress, learned to play a new role.

For the next several months, they played peek-a-boo lovers. Eva, while having a constant companion in public, spent most of her nights alone. Her pillows drawn over her head in attempt to drown out the sounds of lovemaking coming from the next bedroom. A continual reminder of the void in her life, now that her man had to spend most of his time with his wife.

She cursed herself silently while lying in that empty bed. Why did she fall in love with a married man and runaway to follow his star? Yes, she was star struck, seduced. She was just a silly teenager who ought to have known better. Crying in the dark, she suddenly felt all alone, friendless- lovelorn.

The months passed slowly, or rather dragged on, for an indeterminably long time. The endless parties, then there was the publicity campaign for the new book on magic that Herman had decided to write in order to capitalize on the success of the recently completed tour. This occupied much of the day for a couple of weeks. The girls, professionally attired, would pose for pictures, make public appearances. Many times performing with only a cardboard replica of the great magician. Other than the occasional publicity picture, the girls didn't see much of Herman during the two months following their tour. He was 'holed up' in seclusion writing his book.

Late fall, they all got together for a big dinner, at which time Herman announced rehearsals would soon begin for the winter tour through the south.

"We are going to do a slightly different version of the show we just performed," instructed Herman.

"Uh oh. Welcome back to the world of rough and ready, goodbye sophistication," replied Lilly, only half-mockingly. "Are we gonna hire some extra bouncers this year?"

"Now, Lil', it won't be as bad as last year and yes, we will employ local muscle. Just hear me out."

Black Jack, sitting at one end of the long dining room table, turned to Eva, "You remember the performance where we met? It will be something like that. Just with less card tricks."

"That was a nice show," agreed Eva. "But you mean you won't go into the audience anymore?"

"That's right. We will perform many of the same illusions. However, we will also emphasize the sale of my special health tonic, which will be available after the show. You see, the southern audiences are necessarily less cultured than the northern counterparts. Primarily owing to the inability of many people in the south to obtain an adequate education."

"And Black Jack here wants to capitalize on the gullibility of the unfortunate," Wanda barged into the conversation, making her presence felt for the first time.

Herman swept down on her savagely, "It hasn't bothered you at all up until now. You've enjoyed the privileges my money, hard earned money, can buy."

"I'm just saying you still play to your audience despite your high minded talk about equality and empowerment," retorted Wanda, warming to the fight.

Before Black Jack could launch a reply and escalate the argument over the dinner table, Lilly interrupted, changing the topic. "So, Black Jack, when is this book that we've heard so much about due to be released?"

Herman, who always relished talking about himself, welcomed

the redirection of discussion. "It will be out for Christmas. 'Black Jack's Pocket Book of Magic: Amaze Your Friends With Two Hours of Magic For One Hour's Worth of Work.'"

"All that's on the cover? Hon, that sure is one long title," teased Lilly. "I hope you didn't give away all of our best illusions."

"Are you kidding? I gave away some simple magic tricks. Like you know, for a teenage boy to perform to impress a young lady." He could feel Wanda's stare on him from across the room. He did not meet her gaze. "Mostly it is about my life story to date and anecdotes from life on the road. The publisher hired a co-writer to add a little color to some of the tales, not like we needed any." He winked at Lilly, who smiled back.

"It sounds wonderful, Black Jack," said Eva demurely. "I'll have to buy a copy."

"Don't be ridiculous. You'll both get a copy with your check. After all, your pictures are on the cover."

Wanda looked livid. Sitting at the far end away from the ensuing celebration, she really did resemble the skeleton invited to the feast.

"Oh, Daddy, that's wonderful news. You mean we get a share of the book?" It was Lilly, she was beside herself.

Eva was beaming at the news of this unexpected pre-Christmas present. "Oh, that is wonderful news. I'll be able to send that money home to my folks." She was almost in tears.

No other business of consequence was possible that night after the surprise announcement of their impending good fortune. Except for repeated toasts to Herman, his business sense and toasts for a salubrious winter tour.

A week later, they began rehearsals at their secluded stage hidden in the stockyards. Before they began, Herman sat the girls down and went over the new line-up. "At the beginning of the show, we will have Carl announce us. Carl, you remember your lines?"

The big man nodded. "Ladies and Gentlemen, presenting prestidigitator supreme and showman extraordinaire, the legendary magician Black Jack Herman." (Pause) "Master of illusion and magic- witness incredible feats of legerdemain performed by the master and his beautiful assistants."

"Good, Carl. Good. Next time, use a bit lower voice and more power," coached Black Jack pointing to his solar plexus.

"After the introduction, the lights will go down, and then I will appear onstage in an explosion of smoke. First, I will perform the endless handkerchiefs and produce flowers for a few ladies in the audience. After that, we will do the rabbit in the hat, where we produce everything in the world before we finally find the rabbit. That is always very funny and entertaining."

"So far, that is the same act we performed over the summer," Eva said, thinking out loud.

"You're right, honey. Here's where we begin the change, instead of engaging the audience, you and Lilly will help me perform some card tricks. Some of the old ones and a few new tricks I have been working on. Then we move on to the Zulu magic."

"Whoa. Here it comes." teased Lilly.

"Yes, Lil'. Here it comes. We tell them about the special Zulu tonic-the warrior's secret that made them invincible in battle and insatiable in bed. On sale after the show at the rear of the tent."

Lilly turned to Eva and joked, "Told you so. It will be snake oil down on the farm." They both giggled.

"Come on, girls, pay attention. After I take a swig of the stuff, we will invite some people up on the stage to tie me up first, and then put me in chains. Both times, I will escape in front of the audience using my secret Zulu knowledge.

"Don't you mean, you'll invite some women on stage, Daddy?" queried Eva with an impish glint in her eyes. It was still less than a year since they had met, and she remembered all too well, his penchant for pretty women.

"Don't fret it, baby. It's all in the act. That's all," his tone was reassuring and his eyes confirmed, smoldering with his lust for her. Eva blushed.

"Okay, after the plug for the Zulu tonic, we will move into the 'Perils of Eva' portion of the program. First, the swords in the box and then for the big finish, we will saw you in half."

Both assistants looked shocked. It was Eva who spoke first. "You mean we won't do the levitation trick?"

"No." Herman's tone was firm and final. "In most of our venues we will be pitching the big tent. The lighting and backdrops are not suitable to adequately convey the illusion. We will save it for when we perform in a proper theatrical setting. Before our close, we will do a costume change. I will dress as a sultan, you two as harem girls."

After a few quick sleights of hand, we will perform the Indian rope trick. I will send you two up the rope and then disappear in a cloud of smoke, leaving the rope hanging in midair. The lights will come up. Carl, you will come back on stage, announce the end of the evening's entertainment and inform the patrons that the tonic and my book will be on sale for one hour. Be sure to remind them to stock up because Black Jack only comes around once every seven years!

You two lovely ladies will man the booths along with your assistants. You two will be there primarily to look good and to keep an eye on the cash. I will remain aloof- appearing only on stage. By the way, you two had better learn to belly dance. It's part of the final act."

"Belly dance?" the two women spoke in unison.

"Yes, we have to give 'em something for their money." There was that finality of tone which indicated this matter was not open for discussion. Then, an aside to Carl. "Carl, you will drive the truck with all of our rigging and props. The girls will come with me in the roadster. For this trip, we will leave the limo at home."

"Very good, sir."

"Well, everybody, shall we get some rehearsal time in today? After the first of the year, we hit the road!"

True to his word and right on schedule, they hit the road in the middle of January. This tour would take them through the mid-south. The previous tour a year ago had taken them across the deep south, stopping at major cities like Savannah, Atlanta, Birmingham, and of course, Tupelo, Mississippi. There Black Jack had plucked Eva and her sister out of the audience before moving on to New Orleans.

That seminal event in her life seemed so long ago, so far away in time. She almost felt that her other life was nothing more than a dream, a memory borrowed from someone else. Some other young woman. She had always been here- on stage with him, performing. Secretly she was saddened inside that they would not be performing near her old home. Her family could come out and see her achievements. See how professional she had become. Her father and brothers would be amazed at the illusions. Her mother, how she would cringe as each knife was thrust into the box, at her screams when the saw blade supposedly tore into her flesh. Most of all, she would see the look on her older sister's face, looking up from the audience. Watching her with this man who adored her and dominated her so completely. Eva smiled contentedly as that last image danced in her mind and lingered.

Leaving the train in Cincinnati, they would perform in a rented hall for the first week, after which they would truly be on the road. Motoring to their next destination, they would pitch the tent outside Lexington and perform for the weekend. Heading east they camped just outside Charleston, West Virginia for several days before heading for Richmond.

In Virginia's capital, they would rent a hall for a full week's worth of performances. As Richmond was a major center of commerce and easily accessible, Herman expected large crowds. He was not to be disappointed.

"Welcome to Richmond, Virginia, folks. Capital of the 'Ole South. Watch your step!" Black Jack mockingly played the role of railroad conductor when they first arrived in town. He wasn't kidding. In most of these towns, the wrong deed or statement could get you locked up or worse. Black Jack always greased the palms of the local officials and the constabulary whenever they landed in a new town. "A little green goes a long way to clear up those inevitable problems that always seem to occur."

After Richmond and the first leg of the tour, they drove over to Norfolk, by the sea, for a week's rest. Master Herman knew a man who could put them up at a bungalow on the beach, 'no questions asked.' Carl had to linger in Richmond for a couple days to fix the truck, which had experienced some troubles overcoming the Virginia mountains. Herman and his assistants had the place all to themselves.

It was in Norfolk that Black Jack and Eva fell in love again, deeper than ever before. Not that Eva had ever fallen out of love with the man. Their forced separation the previous fall had taken its toll on romance. He had seemed preoccupied, distant.

Holding hands during long walks on the beach, cuddling by a roaring fire on those long winter evenings rekindled their desire. Staring into each other's eyes, they would kiss silently. Not wishing for words to disturb the magic. The lovers transcended the need for verbalization, instantly each was aware of the other's thoughts and desires. It was a magical week. Eva wished that it last forever.

It was an eternity for Lilly who was a captive audience. A prisoner to this display of unbridled affection. As it was unwise for an unescorted woman, especially one of her attractiveness and desirability to roam the town by herself, she remained a prisoner of love. Lilly would survive. Secretly, she envied the couple their happiness.

The return swing would take the illusionists through the Raleigh-Durham area, then from Winston-Salem down to Charlotte and across to Knoxville. Thus, they embarked on a series of two night performances that went under the moniker 'barnstorming.' One day to erect the tent, two nights- one show each night and then, a getaway by the following afternoon. It was a tedious timetable, but it was best not to stay in one place for too long. Many times the crew would work all night after the second show, that way they could be on the road by first light. In small towns, one could not be too careful. Once the excess cash was wired back to his accounts in Chicago, best to move on quickly. Of course, Herman and Carl were always armed, just in case trouble presented itself. The tour concluded with stops in Chattanooga, Nashville and Evansville, Indiana before retiring to the comforts of Chicago, just ahead of spring.

The winter tour proved to be a financial success despite the hardships and rigors of the road. The biggest threat to the traveling magic troupe occurred in Evansville, Indiana. After the first night of performances, the Ku Klux Klan, a hate group growing in popularity and organization, held a rally nearby and crosses were burned on an adjoining farm. Herman cancelled the second performance and was on the road before dark. Black Jack, vowing never to return to, as he put it, "that hateful place," took his girls home. True to his word, he never did.

The love affair between Herman and Eva which had rekindled in winter reached full bloom that spring. Eva asked if they couldn't always be together that way. The way they were in their bungalow by the beach. Black Jack assured her of his love, but cautioned that this was not the right time. Reasoning that while he was building his empire, he had to remain respectable in the eyes of the rich and powerful community leaders. He had to remain married to Wanda. After all, he warned, Wanda was no fool. There was only so much humiliation she would take. She could make trouble if she was pushed too far.

Also, there were the children's feelings to consider. All good reasons for hesitation, for moving slowly. Lilly, as well, offered her expert advice to Eva on men. "When reeling in a big fish, you have to pull slowly or he may jump off the line."

Meanwhile, the two lovers continued to engage in behavior that became all the more risqué. Seen in each other's company all over town and out until all hours, they became the talk. Their love affair became the worst kept secret in Chicago. For Black Jack, relations at home became even more strained, if that were possible. So much that even Wanda welcomed relief that time had come to plan the troupe's return to the road.

Not wishing to tinker unnecessarily with a winning formula, Black Jack decided not to make many changes to the entertainment they had performed the previous summer. The only major change was to replace the sword box with a cabinet into which the swords were thrust. All that remained was to fall back into the routine of regular rehearsals and to reintegrate the levitation illusion. In less than three weeks, they would be ready.

Black Jack and Eva were by now completely simpatico. They would arrive and leave together, do everything together, even finishing each other's sentences. Lilly, who had purchased her own car, came and left as she pleased. The usually patient and understanding assistant was becoming increasingly annoyed that the couple had taken over her apartment. Now it was Eva's moans that could be heard through the wall all night. Lilly was growing tired of being the camouflage for the couple's burgeoning love affair. Privately, she told herself that on their return to Chicago in the fall some changes would have to be made. In the meantime, she would smile and accept the situation, pulling the pillows over her head at night on those occasions when she slept alone.

V
Madame Deborah and Dark Magic

On the road that summer, Herman met a performer who was to have a profound affect on his life and Eva's. She was billed on the marquee outside a small club as 'Madame Deborah, Mentalist and Spiritual Advisor.' Intrigued, Herman and Eva stopped in to see the show. The woman on stage gave an impressive performance.

Dressed in a white flowing gown, she stood in the middle of the small stage and answered questions from the audience that had been submitted in advance. Herman was amazed at her competence and apparent genuine talent in this area. She was apparently working alone without the aid of 'spies,' who would circulate among the audience and communicate via secret code with the performer on stage. That is how this type of trick was usually accomplished. Herman recalled how he also had employed this scheme on various road shows in the past. Madame Deborah's act was different. She would read the question presented to her and just ask the author to stand before rendering her advice.

Eva had written a question on a slip of paper and handed it to the hostess when they first sat down at their table. She squealed with delight, the little girl in her, when Madame Deborah read the question out loud. "'Madame Deborah, will my happiness last?' Stand up, Eva." Eva sprang out of her seat and met the other woman's gaze. "Eva, after a new beginning, I foresee a long satisfying relationship with the one you love. But beware, every rose has thorns."

Herman was not as impressed with this answer as he had been with others. 'Standard boilerplate,' he thought. 'You see a pretty young woman with a man and you know what's on her mind.'

The two of them were, however, generally impressed with her act. So much so, that upon visiting Deborah's dressing room after her performance, Herman offered her a position with him upon his return to Chicago that fall. The 'new beginning' Madame Deborah had talked about was becoming a self-fulfilling prognostication.

After a string of sold out performances in Chicago marking the end of the 1919 tour, Black Jack made several surprise announcements. First and foremost, he would not be touring the south that winter. The road show would go on hiatus. Next, Madame Deborah would be officially joining 'Black Jack Herman's Magical Revue.'

Herman had brought her onto the stage with him in Chicago and she proved to be a big hit. Far from upstaging him, she actually enhanced the evening's entertainment. Many in the audience lingered long after the show hoping for a personal meeting. It was then that Herman, the consummate entrepreneur, decided to take her into his fold.

That decision would pay off in spades for Black Jack in just a few weeks when one of the general predictions made by Madame Deborah on stage apparently came to pass. It was a prediction that soon Chicago would face disaster and disgrace. Within a month, three baseball players for the Chicago White Sox were accused of fixing World Series games for money. The heinous event, called the "Black Sox Scandal," nearly ruined major league baseball. Chicagoans were devastated. Word spread like wildfire that Madame Deborah foresaw the event well in advance. Demand for her services increased exponentially, and Herman seized the opportunity.

His next change would have a profound effect on his relationship with Eva. He announced to her over dinner shortly after the

"Black Sox Scandal" erupted that he would be renting her a luxury apartment. The young woman, nearly bursting with joy, threw herself across the small table, wrapping her arms around his neck. Smothering him with kisses in response to the good news.

"Now, hold on," he tried to curb her enthusiasm. "You will live there, of course. But this will be a place of business as well. It will be a place for me to meet and greet the power elite. You know, hold poker games and the like. Also, it will be a place where Madame Deborah can hold readings. You wouldn't believe the demand we've for that. I'm thinking of hiring a secretary just to handle the appointments."

Eva was hearing nothing of this. To her, this was exactly the 'new beginnings' that she had in mind. Now she and her man would be together all of the time. In her own apartment! While Herman droned on about something, she was envisioning how the furniture should look, the draperies. The kitchen, 'it must have a big kitchen' so that she could hold dinner parties. Not like that tiny kitchen she shared with Lilly. 'Everything was going to be wonderful!'

It was mid-afternoon one late January day nineteen twenty. The first true decade of the American century had arrived. As with all momentous occasions, controversy kept company. A small group in Eva's new apartment was holding a wake of sorts for their perceived loss of innocence. The assemblage included Herman, Lilly, Madame Deborah and several close associates.

"Drink up, everybody. Here's to the democratic process. When a majority of the populace agrees on a change, they make it happen and enact it into law." Herman encouraged the revelers, raising his glass to toast.

"Yeah, so when a majority of the populace goes temporarily insane, we get an insane law. Or insane politicians or both," echoed Lilly, joining the toast.

Deborah queried in jest, "Is that what Lincoln meant about 'fooling all of the people all of the time?'"

"No, he said that it couldn't be done," answered Black Jack with mild sarcasm. "Well, it can. Drink up everybody. Here's to the good life.'"

Lilly, after draining her glass, corrected, "I think you mean here's to the high life. We won't have much of that anymore."

Eva walked in with another bottle of champagne. "Who wants some more?"

Deborah, with her penchant for succinct turns of phrase, had begun referring to Herman as BJ, the moniker caught on with his close associates, at least in private.

"Geez, BJ, how much of this stuff did you buy?"

"Didn't you hear? BJ bought out the whole bar," Eva answered, pouring refills.

"Hooray," a chorus cheered and glasses were clinked in his honor.

BJ rose to his own defense. "Well, why not? There is no law against drinking in private."

"How convenient! You just can't buy the stuff or consume it in a public place," scoffed Lilly. The many years as a magician's assistant had left her able to see only the ugly truths that illusionists, such as politicians, hide. If you couldn't get the stuff, how could you drink? "So Congress and the states didn't outlaw drinking, that would be legislating morality. Intermixing the domains of church and state. Just make public possession a crime. The rest would take care of itself, so their reasoning went."

BJ, the practical realist, ever the student of human nature, understood his assistants' argument and attempted to allay her concerns. "Don't worry, somebody will think of a way around the law. In the meantime, we've got ours!"

Eva, warming to the conversation, gave a most appropriate toast, "As they say in N'Awlins, let the good times roll!"

And so it went. All evening, the requiem continued as they commiserated the fall of modern times and the rise of Prohibition. You would think they were witnessing the fall of the Roman Empire.

Of course they were not. Civilization went on, grew and adapted. New power brokers rose to fill the void. To answer the opportunity created by the temperance totalitarians. In the interim, as BJ had so eloquently stated, they had theirs.

Inside Eva's apartment, business continued as usual and in

fact, was better than ever. Herman had his poker games where he concentrated on influencing business and civic leaders. Madame Deborah did a brisk business with her readings, and everyone enjoyed the company of alcohol.

Eva dismayed there was too much company in her place all of the time. This was definitely not what she envisioned, a luxurious love nest for her and her man. She feared she was turning into more of an innkeeper or mistress of ceremonies.

Deborah had the second bedroom turned into her 'reading room' designed to her specifications.

The room was painted black; the windows blocked out. Stars and planets, scientific notation and ancient symbols were painted on the walls and ceiling in incandescent paint.

A lone circular table draped in black cloth was located in the center of the room. Three to four chairs revolved around this epicenter, never more. Located under the table by her chair were light switches controlling lighting for various effects. She used these as required during consultations to convey the proper mood.

Sometimes up to five or six half-hourly sessions were carried out each night, six nights a week. Madame Deborah did not work Sundays. Nor for that matter did Herman entertain on Sundays. The day evolved into Eva's one day of solitude. The only day in which she felt at home in her apartment.

The rest of her week was spent in the service of the business of spiritualism; to aid her in dealing with the continuous client cacophony, Herman had hired a chambermaid to assist in the comings and goings. An extra serving girl was required for poker nights and at parties. On any given night during the week, the luxury apartment gave the appearance of a high class lounge in Union Station. The six months supply of liquor ensured that his customers would continue to gravitate back to this social center and remain under his influence.

As Herman predicted, society took care of itself. One Saturday evening in early summer, Black Jack and Eva dressed for an evening out on the town.

"What's this place called again? 'A Speak Easy'? Eva questioned, while presenting her back to him. Nimbly, his fingers ran the zipper up on the evening gown.

"That's right, baby. It is a new type of jazz joint. Actually it is a private club so they can serve liquor, but they don't charge. You have to know somebody to get invited. Also, you can't talk about it in public. Hence the term, speak easy."

Eva frowned. "Oh, how do they make money if they don't charge for drinks?"

"You pay a cover charge when you enter. That is kinda like club dues. It pays for the musicians and to rent the space. The booze is free," he explained while fixing his tie.

"That's kind of how we do it. They must have copied our method," exclaimed Eva, donning her wrap.

"A little different. We don't charge anyone to come into our place. Donations are asked for on poker nights and Deborah receives a hefty donation for her services, of which, she pays a goodly portion in rent. Enough to pay for you and your luxuries," Black Jack tweaked her on the nose as they left the apartment.

Carl deposited them on the doorstep of former Jazz Joint, now a private club. Couples dressed in the season's finery were lined up awaiting their turn to enter the steel door with the sliding panel at eye level, obviously placed there for conversation.

Eva watched in fascination as each group would approach the door and upon challenge, have to submit a 'password' to gain entry. Upon questioning, Herman offered that this was to maintain a discriminating clientele. Once they passed their challenge and gained entry, the couple was delighted to see familiar faces imbibing and engaged in conversation. They were ushered to their table close to the stage just as the evening's entertainment was preparing to commence.

"Oh, Daddy, this is great," exclaimed Eva. "It has seemed like forever since I was able to order a martini and enjoy live music."

"I know how you feel, baby," echoed Herman. "After all, what's jazz without gin?"

Later while Eva was thoroughly enjoying herself, Herman stepped away and inquired of the management. "This is a good looking set up you have got here." He leaned across the bar so that he wouldn't have to quite shout his request to the proprietor. "This gin is very good. Tastes like the genuine article. Much better than that 'bath tub' stuff that I have sampled around. I hold parties occasionally for a distinguished clientele, and my supply is running low. I was wondering if you could help me. My name is Black Jack Herman, by the way."

The owner encouraged, "Yes, Mr. Herman. Everyone knows who you are. Tell you what, leave me your phone number and if my supplier wants to do business, he will call you."

"Fair enough," came the quick reply with accompanying handshake.

Returning to his table, he whispered to Eva the contents of his previous conversation. "Someone will call you. Expect it any day. They didn't say when. But this is good quality hooch, and we need to restock our supply." He pinched her legs and said mischievously, "I don't want anything to spoil our little love nest."

Eva kissed him on the cheek, leaving a ruby marker of her love. Giggling, she dabbed the mark with her napkin until it had all but disappeared.

True to the agreement, a man called several days later and set up a meeting to discuss terms. Herman met the man, a Mr. Konetti, at the 'speak easy' the next afternoon. After introductions, they settled down to cases.

"I know you. You're that magician that saws women in half—makes 'em fly through the air."

"Yes, that's me. Have you ever seen my show?"

"Naugh, haven't had the pleasure. Hear you're pretty good though."

"I am the best," Black Jack insisted sincerely.

Terms were accepted and delivery schedules established. One of Mr. Konetti's assistants would make deliveries to Eva's apartment, discretely of course.

As they parted, Mr. Konetti said, "It's good doing business with a businessman such as you."

Upon exiting the club and before entering his limo, Herman wiped his feet deliberately several times, as if unconsciously trying to rid his shoes of a slimy substance. Catching himself, he smiled and upon examining the soles 'there was no clinging residue apparent.' Herman chalked it down to imagination. Still something nagged at him. He recognized it as uneasiness over this new acquaintance. 'A necessary evil' he concluded, part of the cost of doing business in this ever changing modern world. Nevertheless, one that would bear watching.

However, it was other evils that evinced themselves in the days and weeks to come. His martial relations had reached low ebb. Wanda was no longer satisfied to be the other woman in his ménage. To be available to him only when he deemed propitious. Truth be known, their inconstancy of relations was making her all the more combative. She had been married to him long enough to know well his fervid sexual appetite. Wanda surmised, if he was not being intimate with her, she knew with whom he fraternized and with what frequency. She had never bought this working apartment nonsense and was now of a mind to make him pay for his indiscretions.

She cornered him one summer's morning over breakfast. "If you are going to stay over there until all hours of the night, why don't you just move in with her?"

Black Jack, not wishing to spar, especially on an empty stomach, feigned ignorance. "I don't know where you get your ideas. Can't we just have some normalcy? I'm not in the mood to suffer foolish conversation."

"Why don't you go then? Have your girlfriend make your breakfast?" came Wanda's venal reply, still sparring.

"You're sounding insane, do you know that? You really have no idea how hard she works orchestrating all of the activities that we have going on there. Part of her job as hostess is to make sure things run well. I don't think you could do half the job she does," Herman retorted.

"Luckily, we won't have to try out your theory because I'm never going to go over there."

"No one's going to ask you to," Herman assured severely.

Wanda, now in tears, "You know, you defend her the way you used to defend me. You don't talk about me that way anymore. I am the mother of your children. It's not right, you falling in love with another woman." Wanda's plaintive cry bespoke an unaccustomed sincerity.

"What's right got to do with anything?" Herman's composure was slipping.

"Remember love, honor and obey, 'til death," she chided.

"That can be arranged," he said icily, rising from the table and storming out of the room.

"Don't think that you're the only one to have affairs. I'm not just sitting here pining away for you." Her words, like daggers, were thrust toward his back as he left the room. Although her hurtful words were intended to injure, the projectiles missed their mark. Black Jack was long past caring what she did and with whom. In his mind, the marriage was over. He took further steps in that direction early the same afternoon.

Later that very week, two delivery men showed up at Eva's apartment. They brought with them a large ornate mahogany armoire and highboy. When Eva questioned, the men replied that instructions were to place the items in the master bedroom. Black Jack was greeted with feverent hugs and kisses when he arrived a few hours after the movers. He responded with typical nonchalance, "Hey, I haveta put my clothes somewhere." Thus, their life together began with a somewhat understated whimper.

Demons more persistent and powerful than those orchestrating his drowning marriage began preying on his mind. Leading him down a dark path of not return, but infinite possibilities. It started when Black Jack felt the urge rising, the urge to return to the stage. Touring was in his blood and like any good magician, he needed to feel the power of the stage, the adoration of his audience.

Herman decided that he needed a new hook, something to keep the audience thrilled and on the edge of their seats. They were always entranced by Deborah and her 'parlour tricks', no matter how genuine. He would give them her act and more, a hint of black magic, thrilling and seductive.

'Books', that's what he needed. Books on the black arts. Herman began by browsing local booksellers and curio shoppes, placing orders for exotic texts. Waiting weeks until some items became available. Soon Herman began to correspond with the authors themselves. He spent much of his free time secluded in his love nest, pouring over the materials and copying notes into a little pocket notebook that became his constant companion.

By the end of that summer, he had compiled quite a collection on the occult and hypnotism. In the process, his demeanor changed. He was darker, edgier, driven with purpose. At first Eva did not notice this change. She still looked at him through honeymoon eyes. Happy to have him around full time with no pretensions, she doted on his every whim. There is after all, bliss in ignorance. Soon thereafter and almost daily, Black Jack and Deborah began holding discussions inside her temple. Lengthy conversations that would sometimes stretch deep into the afternoon or until her scheduled clients arrived. What they discussed, no one would say. However Eva, who was by this time garnering an inkling that something was amiss, feared that she would find out soon enough.

The nomenclature of Voodooism was spread about the apartment haphazardly on bookcases and shelves. Black Jack even installed an alter adorned with a human skull and draped in red velvet in Madame Deborah's sanctuary, over her most strident opposition. He insisted that it lent an air of authenticity to the room.

It was speculated, behind his back, that he was actually holding ceremonies in the room late at night when the apartment was still and all was quiet.

Dismissing such rumors out of hand when questioned, he did not however deny doing them. Lending credibility to the rumors of his fascination with the occult.

His friends even began to joke that 'Black' in Black Jack stood for Black Magic. Smiling to himself when he overheard this line of conversation at one of his usual parties, he did nothing to dissuade them of this notion. His mystique was growing. He recognized the indicators.

As a trained illusionist, he was content that he had now focused his clientele on the supernatural. People would readily believe that his powers emanated from some unworldly source. This he would use to his advantage. While they were in awe of him, feared him, he could lead them in whichever direction pleased him. Again, the power of the show! This was the true talent of the consummate showman; to hold an audience mesmerized, to take them to new heights and expose their deepest fears. Finally, to touch their collective being, the collective unconscious of the crowd with awe and wonder. Thus, tapping their latent energy and bending their will to meet his own desires.

Few people could successfully and continually exploit large crowds to do their bidding. Sway them by oratory and illusion, which were more mutually inclusive than most believed; to act in a fashion prescribed by the magician on stage, the ringmaster.

Few artists of any profession possessed such talents; the exceptional pianists, violinists, or tenor, of course, and the occasional circus high-wire act. But who with mere words, concepts and illusions could inspire a crowd to riotous emotion. Hardly anyone outside the realm of politicians and precious few of them. In recent American history, there was President 'Teddy' Roosevelt who could inspire crowds to great virtues by means of oratory alone. A great communicator, a man of the masses. There was another. A magician by the name of Houdini. In Germany there would soon come one who would inspire by sheer force of will.

Herman knew of only one African American, besides himself, who had such power to motivate the masses to his purpose. He had been corresponding with him for some time now, beginning after the incident at the Turkish Embassy two years previous. Now the time was approaching where upon they would turn the twenties to their advantage. He must be ready.

Beginning that fall Eva and Lilly were introduced to the secrets of hypnotism and indoctrinated as priestess' of Voodooism. The latter was just for show Black Jack assured them. "Remember we are showmen and women. We can't give a simple explanation when an elaborate display could better sell the act. Above all, we must be entertaining."

The girls, looking dubiously at one another, knelt in front of the voodoo altar dressed as they were in frilly under things. They said nothing as their hands were tied in front of them by Madame Deborah, who was dressed in a long flowing red gown. All were barefoot except for Herman. He was the master of ceremonies and as such, began the ritual by placing a recording of beating drums to play.

Deborah, lighting the candles on the altar, whispered to the girls that this was all for show, practice as it were. She assured that there was nothing to be afraid of, and that they must concentrate on the ceremony so that they could do the same to others.

"Don't worry. It will be over soon. Here, drink this." She handed each girl a golden chalice from which to drink. There was a red viscous liquid inside, slightly sweet tasting. Lilly wished out loud for some gin.

"Silence!" Black Jack barked, coming to stand before them holding a book of sayings. He had a woolen cloth draped across his broad shoulders. "This ceremony will be conducted with all the appropriate solemnity. Now, the two of you will stare at the skull on the altar." The women obeyed his command. "Baron Samedi, hear my plea. Take these two priestess-to serve thee." The drums on the recording increased in intensity and pitch as Black Jack repeated his chant.

The women, staring intently at the skull, were astonished and slightly frightened as fire burst forth from the eyes. Suddenly feeling lightheaded and giddy, they found themselves unable to gaze away from the glowing skull. Madame Deborah joined in the incantations at the lighting of the skull. "He hears our wants and grants our desires. He grants these two the position to which they aspire."

Herman stepped before the two acolytes who seemed entranced by their surroundings. He parleyed en Francais, "Voulez vous, couchez avec Le Baron, nes't pas? Baron Samedi vous allez, les gouverneuses." Just then, using his consummate sleight-of-hand, a white powder exploded into the face of each of the two kneeling captives.

The recording was stopped, apparently by Deborah, who also raised the lighting from the dim glimmer which had accompanied the ceremony. Magically, the skull and candles had extinguished themselves.

Black Jack, continuing his masterful performance, uttered

his final line, in English this time. "Rise now you daughters of Samedi."

Slowly rationality returned to the new apprentices in the dark arts. Regaining their senses, they struggled to their feet, hands still tied. Turning to look at each other, the girls began to giggle uncontrollably. Lilly said to Eva, "You should see your face. It's got white powder all over it."

Eva responded, "Yours is no better. Plus you've spilled red liquid down your cheek and onto your breasts." Realizing that she was as scantily clad as her counterpart, she began to blush. Modesty had returned.

Deborah rejoined the group and began the liberating of wrists with Lilly. "How did you ladies like our little performance?"

"Very realistic," exclaimed Eva. "I actually became frightened when the skull burst into flame," she added, looking over towards Herman for consolation. He, however, was backing further into the shadows of the room, looking very serious, refusing to relinquish the role he obviously relished.

"And what was in the cup? It tasted sort of like tomato juice, but sweet. It wouldn't be bad with gin," said Lilly. Then placing her freed hands to her head, "You know I think I still feel a little lightheaded. BJ, what was in there?"

"Oh, just a few herbs and minerals, mixed with tomato juice, lemon and honey. That was the sweetness you tasted. The effects are not long lasting, but they are exhilarating. Rather like the old Coca Cola. I think I will market it as Herman's Voodoo Tonic." He continued to keep character, speaking with quiet solemnity from across the room.

"All I know is I'll be glad to wash up now that it's over. It all seemed too real," ventured Eva, happy now that she too was freed of her bonds.

"You cannot wash until morning. The make-up you wear is your badge of indoctrination into our secret society. As we have done to you, so you in turn will do to others. Thus we will solidify our control over those weak-minded followers who crave an easy road to riches and power. And those superstitious amongst us who fear losing their hold on the riches they have acquired."

Madame Deborah joined in, "Don't worry. This hocus pocus is meaningless. Just trappings to confuse the mind. The real power comes from utilizing hypnosis to guide people to perform to their ultimate potential."

Black Jack interjected at this point, apparently not wishing to give away too much of the game plan too soon. Even to his most intimate of accomplices.

"You two, now, go into the kitchen and bring a bottle of champagne and some glasses. We will toast to our accomplishments of this day!"

After the two women had scurried into the kitchen to do Black Jack's bidding, Deborah addressed the mahatma. "You really had them going there with all of that mumbo jumbo. I think Eva is a little scared, Lilly too. Why didn't you let them know you were kidding? That it's all a joke?"

"We needed to put on a convincing show. If we can fool them, especially Lilly who has been with me for years, we can fool others, those not initiated in the ways of magic, with ease. Besides," he added with a twinkle in his eye, "It is not important for them to know it was a joke. It is only important for me to know."

Madame Deborah fell silent as Herman continued his sinister scowling.

The evening passed pleasantly for the two couples. The apprentices, who were ordered not to wash or dress, continued in their subservient roles to their mistress and master. The couples wined and dined in resplendent repast until retiring to their respective quarters. Eva could not remember when they made love with such reckless abandon, so heightened was his passion. Something must have gotten into him. Between sessions of their passions play, she could hear cooings and cawings coming from the outer room. She guessed that Lilly and Deborah were enraptured as well.

While the voodoo mystique was played at in private, the experiments in hypnotism were practiced in full view of the public. The public in question being the patrons and revelers that frequented the couple's swank parties. It was about this time that Herman began encouraging people to refer to him as 'professor'.

"Due to my extensive studies in the occult sciences, you will notice I do not call them arts, you must now refer to me as 'Black Jack Herman, Professor of the Secret Science of Success.' You can call me Professor Herman for short. I am professor of the secrets of power and control, versed in the practice of mental manipulation for the betterment of mankind. To some," he put his arm around Eva, sitting docilely on the floor next to his chair in the large living room of their abode, "I am still the Professor of Love." The young woman smiled demurely.

'Professor' Herman continued, "You will notice again that I do not call them occult arts. Rather these teachings represent powers of the mind and physical universe that were known to the ancients and lost over the eons of time. The people who built the pyramids possessed such powers, the power to motivate the masses to move mountains. These talents were replicated across the world, in Mexico and India. Yet the science of their techniques was lost over time. Some of these powers have lain latent in the minds of men for over two thousand years.

Buddhist monks and Chinese scholars, followers of the I Ching, have demonstrated dynamic mental powers to this day. Yes, my friends, I tell you truly that if you can develop your mental powers to the fullest, you will be able to perform superhuman feats of strength, sexual prowess and dominate any opponent in physical or mental challenges.

From my readings I have learned how to prepare your mind, through the powers of hypnotism, to receive these gifts. I postulate to you here tonight that those willing to accept my gift will become the vanguard of the new society destined to remake our world."

He had taken everyone's breath away with his brilliant oratory. The gathering remained silent. Some with fear and anticipation, others in rapt contemplation of the concept. Professor Herman, his audience on the edge of their seats, continued to lead them in his chosen direction.

"It is alright I know these are difficult concepts to grasp all at once. Let me provide a little demonstration. You all know my assistant Lilly. Come here, girl!"

The young woman rose from her seat and walked across to where Herman and Eva were seated.

"Kneel before me." The young woman responded on cue. "Now, Lilly has been hypnotized by me before. I have given her a post-hypnotic suggestion, meaning that I can re-initialize her trance with just a word or deed. Are you ready, my dear?"

"Yes, Professor." She sat hands on her knees, staring up at him.

"Relax. Now lean your head back. You are feeling exhilarated. Close your eyes and concentrate on my voice. I am your control."

"You are my control," she intoned. The group murmured.

"Quiet, please!" Herman continued. "Lilly, I know that as a little girl you wanted to dance in the ballet. Recreate for us now, my ballerina, one of the favorite dances from your youth." The woman rose rather rigidly at first, then flexing her legs, began to prance around the apartment leaping and pirouetting to music that only she could hear.

The women in the group were especially impressed. Their companions expressed reservations through dubious grimaces.

Herman seized on their skepticism. "One of the benefits of hypnotism is to enhance a dormant or latent talent. This is accomplished in part by removing fear from the equation. Fear is the mind killer, the inhibitor; it robs you of the ability to perform to your full potential. That is what you are witnessing, even a consummate showgirl like Lilly has reservations that inhibit her actions and reign in the ability to achieve her desires." He clapped his hands and shouted, "Lilly, that is enough. Well done. Now go and get the barbells behind the couch. Bring them here." In a minute, the dancer turned weightlifter was standing before him holding two twenty-five pound weights.

"This portion of the demonstration will highlight the ability of the unconscious mind to bypass the perceived physical limitations of consciousness. Lilly, lift the weights to your shoulders, one after another." The entranced woman effortlessly performed front curls until ordered to stop. "Now place them on the floor. Everyone, you may examine the weights to insure that there has been no fakery.

To assure yourselves that what you have just seen is the genuine article."

Professor Herman continued his tutorial while members of his grouping examined the authenticity of the objects now residing at the feet of the woman standing before him stoically. "I could have had her lift many times this much weight, but her muscles must be gradually prepared for such extreme departures from normal. As she is a faithful assistant and good friend, I would not risk her future well-being for a cursory demonstration. Eventually, as she is progressed properly, she will be able to demonstrate all of the fascinating performances of the Hindu 'Fakirs.' I refer, of course, to walking on hot coals, lying on a bed of nails, even slowing her heartbeat. These abilities will come after she has learned to harmonize her conscious and unconscious, raising her combined being to a higher level of spirituality. But that will take years more of training."

The professor could see that he was overwhelming his audience-providing too much information too soon. He decided it best to end with a joke and dismiss his apprentice. "Not to worry, your unconscious mind cannot be commanded to do anything that is aberrant or abhorrent to your being. For instance, you cannot be commanded to kill or rob or even to have sex with someone you find repellent." The women in the group tittered.

"You can, however, have some fun at parties. Lilly, cluck like a chicken, laying a prize winning egg," he commanded suddenly. The stationary object became at once animated, dancing around and waving her arms, mimicking a chicken obviously in great distress. After a minute or two, she squatted down on the floor and continued to cackle excitedly while delivering her masterpiece. The audience loved this comedic conclusion to the demonstration.

"Enough. Shibboleth!" Black Jack used a code word to bring his accomplice out of her trance. She was sitting before him, legs curled, looking slightly bemused. Eva smiled reassurances to her colleague.

"Hypnotic sessions designed to foster increased success in business or intellectual pursuits will be handled privately in one-on-one sessions. Madame Deborah will pass among you and arrange appointments. What we can provide here tonight is a light hypnotic affect, akin to intoxication, for entertainment purposes only. Now, don't be shy. Who wants to be hypnotized first? Come on, we're all friends." A few brave souls, all women, raised their hands.

For all intents and purposes, that was the epitome of how these parties progressed. Sometimes Eva would perform the role of hypnotee, as Lilly had done. She performed feats of unusual dexterity and strength. Performing the chicken as a finale was incorporated into both women's repertoire. Neither one remembered any of the actions performed while 'under,' they relied on their counterpart for reassurance and consolance. Herman assured his guests that this was genuine science and not an act. His offer to entrance members of the audience was his proof, designed to sell his services as 'Professor Herman Mentalist.'

The sessions in hypnotism thus added another revenue stream to his profitable practice, which now included Madame Deborah's fortune telling, Black Jack's power tonic and royalties from his pocket book on magic. Now that the enterprise was generating increasing amounts of cash, and Herman and Deborah were plotting their return to the stage, he decided it was time. Time to offer his wife a settlement she could ill afford to refuse.

Responding to his summons, Wanda arrived at the offices of Herman's solicitors ready for a fight. "I'll bury him before I let him go. I had him first, and I will have him last."

The lawyers were reassuring, if a bit terse. "Your husband has proposed a monthly sum to be placed in your accounts from which you can draw to fulfill the needs of you and the children. In addition to this monthly stipend, you will receive an amount equal to one third of his current wealth. By agreeing to this arrangement, you will recuse yourself from any claim against the future earnings of Herman's enterprises. You must sign here, here and again, over here." The lawyers indicated the appropriate lines for her to initial and sign.

Refusing any mention of a settlement, even a generous one in recognition of their years together, she remained vehement that Herman's place was with her and the children. "The years I have had to put up with this nonsense, his continual affairs, strange dealings and manipulative ways, he wants to buy me off with a fraction of his earning potential now that the gravy train is just getting started. He should realize that he's not dealing with a fool." She voiced her concerns freely.

"Besides if he expects me to give him up for that little tramp from what-ya-ma-call-it Mississippi, he's got another thought coming." Wanda stormed out of the suite of offices vowing to extricate herself from his magical world of masochism, while maintaining her standard of living and retaining custody of their children. "My lawyers will be in contact with you. Before I'm through with him, he will owe me every dime he ever makes and never see his children again. Just wait until I start telling what I know in a court of law." She left the building feeling that she had won a great victory. Holding her head up she exalted in the crisp autumn breeze. Composing herself, she returned to her chauffeured limousine for the return trip to her home. 'I'll see him bankrupt and in prison before he marries that little witch,' she smiled knowingly.

Black Jack decided to wait for the last possible moment to break the bad news to Eva. Unfortunately that meant just before the holidays. It was just the two of them, and they had just been seated at their favorite supper club. "Please provide us with a bottle of your finest French champagne." Casually, he ushered the gentle request.

"Champagne? Oh Daddy, what are we celebrating?" Eva squealed with excitement.

"Just wait."

The champagne had been delivered and dispensed into fluted glasses. Bubbles ascended the amber liquid forming columns that led to the congregation of effervescence crowning the top of the glass. Eva watched pensively as her partner raised his glass in toast. "My dear, this is a special night. It is dedicated to us. To the celebration of our journey together. Just three and a half years ago, I plucked you out of the audience. Since then, you have blossomed into the premiere performer that I foresaw that evening. More importantly, you have become my lover and constant companion. The most important person in my life."

"Oh, Herman," tears welling in her eyes.

"Up until now, you have been my paramour, my concubine, a slave to love. Originally, I had meant this occasion to announce your emancipation. But, unfortunately due to the obstinance of my bitter wife, you will have to continue to be my love slave for the foreseeable future." His voice dropped as his head slumped.

"Oh honey, that's all right. It doesn't matter. I will love you forever." Her outstretched hand pushed forward to meet his halfway.

"It does matter." Herman seemed hurt, embarrassed. He grabbed her outstretched hand with both of his. "It's just that I had this whole big thing planned and now, I don't want this little guy to grow lonely waiting for my wife to change her mind." He withdrew his hands, and Eva was left with a small box in hers.

Her eyes grew two sizes contemplating the little blue box. She squealed in hushed tones, "Honey, is this for me?" Gingerly, she opened it revealing a diamond ring centered.

"It's not really an engagement ring anymore. Now it's more of a promissory ring. The promise of better times when we can be together as man and wife."

"Yes, darling, yes. I will wait for you. Together we will wait her out. If she won't divorce you, we will still have our working relationship in town, and all the time in the world while we are on tour." Eva cooed, never taking her eyes from his auburn orbs.

He slipped the ring on her finger. "One more thing," Black Jack began gravely, "Wanda wants me to move back to her place for the holidays. You know, for the kids."

The rest of the evening was a haze of cordials, condolence and congratulations all rolled into one. Eva had lost the present, but she had gained a promissory ring. 'Yes, Yes. Forever yes. She would wait for him.'

VI
The Magic and Mystery Tours

Practice for the new show had been underway for a couple of weeks in their warehouse hideaway. The sign on the sandwich board stage right stated proudly: 'Professor Herman and Madame Deborah Present-The Magical Mysterious Tour de Force of 1921. Starring: Professor Herman 'Mentalist' and Madame Deborah 'Spiritualist Supreme'. Onstage, the troupe was practicing tirelessly to perfect the changes in their re-energized routines. Backstage, Black Jack had hired his brother Andrew as stage manager.

With all of the new routines, someone was needed to coordinate the placement of the props offstage in sequential order. Herman and Deborah had conceived a very ambitious program, and backstage was beginning to resemble an assembly line. Now Andrew and Black Jack had toured years ago in the 'bad old days' of barnstorming and brawling traveling tent shows. Due to some sibling rivalry and antagonism, they had been estranged for some years. By providing this opportunity, Black Jack was attempting to make amends to his younger brother.

The girls onstage had just completed one of the routines where they switch places unbeknownst to the audience. Suddenly there was a clapping from the front of the warehouse. A well dressed man emerged from the shadows. It was Mr. Konetti, an associate of Mr. Enttoleni the 'purveyor of spirits' (otherwise known as bootlegger).

Herman shouted brusquely, "What the hell are you doing here?"

"Oh, sorry to interrupt. Great show, by the way. Thought I saw your limo out there. Just wanted to drop by. We are moving into security now. Taking over some of the Pinkerton's clientele. We've demonstrated that we can do a better job of preventing thefts."

The dapper dandy Konetti reached in his lapel and produced an expensive cigar for Herman. "Here, have a cigar. One of Cuba's finest. Anyway, before we are done, we will control everything down here. Well, I can see you are busy. Pardon the interruption. I just wanted to say hello."

This little monologue unnerved the usually unflappable Mr. Herman. He took the news as it was intended, a harbinger of things to come. Black Jack continued to stand in the doorway after the car had driven away. Divining the future was going to be easy this particular day. Then just as suddenly, he turned and shouted at his staff, "Okay, girls. Let's get back to work. Break's over!"

Once on the road several weeks later, reality revolved only around the show. Magic became their entire world. "Places everyone." Professor Herman barks last minute instructions, "Lighting, make sure you dim the lights promptly on my cues. Andrew, keep those boxes in proper order. Keep up, girls. The changes are going to come really fast. Here we go." The music swells, the spotlight ignites and the curtain rises on a blank stage. 'Kaboom!' In smoke and noise, Herman appears!

Professor Herman: "In my travels I have seen the past, present and future. I have witnessed terrifying rituals and trials. I present to you tonight the combined wisdom of the ages. The combined wonders of the natural and spiritual worlds. Wonders of worlds seen and unseen, witness powers never dreamed or imagined.

The powers of the fully cultivated mind. Never before displayed to civilization, the mental prowess I demonstrate for your pleasure and amazement come from the teachings of Buddhist monks from high in the Himalayas, Zulu medicine men from deepest Africa, American Indian shaman and the Voodoo high priests of Haiti!

Hazah! (smoke and explosives) The two assistants appear fettered, incarcerated in their respective boxes. The professor addresses the crowd, "I know that you have all seen these tricks before, the woman sawed in half, the woman perforated with swords (Deborah demonstrates in double time on the hapless duo). Herman continues, "But can you truly believe your eyes or is it all just an illusion?" He waves his hand- more smoke. When the smoke clears a minute later, the girls have switched boxes, swords in place and cut in half.

"Can any of us ever truly believe our eyes?" More smoke, a two-handed toss this time. Hands spread wide, stretched over his head. When the smoke clears in another minute, the assistants and their restraints are no longer on the stage. Instead Herman is standing over a box with saw in hand sawing the now imprisoned Deborah in half.

He finishes the task and spreads the two halves of the box far apart. The half with the head is turned away from the audience. Walking the half with the wiggling feet across the stage, he grumbles aloud, "Never an assistant around when you need one. I wonder, where are those wayward women?" Then pretending to hear a voice from that half of the box, he raps on it with his cane. The box collapses and Eva appears. "So, that's where you were hiding," he chides. Suddenly a thought occurs to him. "Wait a minute. If you were in here, then maybe Lilly is..." Herman rushes across the stage and raps on that half of the box. It too collapses, revealing the other assistant.

Professor Herman turns to the audience. "That's the way it is around here sometimes. Never anything where you left it." Laughter abounds. Herman continuing to his girls, "Have either of you two seen Deborah?" They shake their heads, outthrust their arms in mock confusion. "Never mind. I'm sure she will turn up. Go and get the big box." The two wheel off the smaller collapsible each in a different direction. Quickly emerging together, stage right, pushing the wardrobe-sized cabinet.

Herman opens and closes the French doors on the cabinet, tapping the sides and bottom of the empty box to prove solidity. "Now for my next feat of prestidigitation," a knock from inside interrupts him. He opens the doors. "Deborah, now how did you get in there? Never mind. Lilly, join her." Herman and Eva turn the wardrobe around twice. Herman raps with his cane twice, says the magic words and presto, when opened, they have disappeared. Eva pushes the cabinet off stage. Herman says, "I hope you've enjoyed those illusions. Now, on with the rest of the show." He drops a smoke bomb and disappears!

The curtain falls, then rises again. In the interim, a few scant minutes, the women have dressed in white linens. Professor Herman, in a white linen suit, is seen presiding over a Voodoo ritual. As the unseen drums in the background increase in tempo and pitch, the kneeling women sway back and forth to the ministrations of the voodoo master. Small explosions emanate from the floor in reaction to his pointing fingers. The ceremony reaches its zenith as the women rise and dance uncontrollably around him.

Madame Deborah, dressed in blood red, enters the stage and speaks loudly to the celebrants. The short sharp commands barked in Creole, French or some dead language cause everything to stop. The girls fall down on the floor lying still. The 'professor' translates for the crowd, "The high priestess has declared the young women are ready for the trials ahead."

Two props are wheeled onto stage. One a bed of nails, the other appears to be rows of hot coals. The 'professor' continues, "The science of Voodooism is one of the most extreme of the mental sciences. It achieves a state of mind over matter by creating an other-worldly condition whereby the subject's unconscious mind is freed from the limitations imposed by normal consciousness.

Tremendous feats of strength and endurance are possible when the mind is operating to its full potential, once fear and anxiety are eliminated. Watch as Madame Deborah encourages her subjects to perform their tasks." The woman in red helps Lilly first walk across and then lie down on the bed of nails. She then leads Eva by the hand to cross the stage and stand on the reclining Lilly. Neither of the women show any emotion.

After standing on the other's stomach for nearly half a minute, Eva is helped down to the audiences thundering ovation. The two women are then led over to the hot coals. Herman drops a piece of paper onto the coals. It ignites into flame, proving that indeed the coals are hot. Deborah and Herman each take the hand of one attendant disciple and lead them over the coals. There is a resulting thunderous ovation while the four of them address the crowd.

Props are moved around by stage hands half-seen. The thunderous ovation subsides. The stage is dark except for spotlight on the foursome center stage.

"Well, while we have the girls here we might as well perform my signature illusion. Deborah, will you assist me?" The spotlight is widened to reveal two tables behind them center stage, facing end to end.

Deborah and Herman each place one 'entranced' woman on a table. The audience murmurs in anticipation of the expected levitation. This time a double levitation.

The professor begins his preamble. "The Buddhist monks of the high Himalayas perfected the secrets of mind over matter over two thousand years ago. They believed that with total concentration and prayer, one could leave the body entirely and enter the astral plane. They have demonstrated many powers that, to the ordinary man, appear to be magic. One of these is the ability to defy gravity, or cause others to do so by sheer force of will.

I have perfected the levitation of one subject at a time, but for two, I will need your help. If we all concentrate together, we can tap into the Universal World Soul for the energy we need to accomplish our task," The music playing in the background comes to a halt. The light intensifies on the tables. Professor Herman, wand in hand, turns from the audience to the tables waving his hands and chanting in the process. The fascinated audience watches as the girls slowly begin to rise from the table. Deborah takes a silver hoop and passes it around one, then both, of the women hanging in mid-air. Herman groaning, "I don't know how much longer I can keep them suspended. Audience, I need your help."

After Deborah has completed her task, the women are slowly lowered back to the tables and the stage lights come up. Herman, now yelling to be heard over the cheering audience, commands each prone woman to "Awaken now, return to us from the supernatural world." With a clap of the hands over each, they revive and sit up, eventually standing by their table.

The foursome once again turn and greet the audience and bathe in rapt exultation. Holding hands, they bow to the crowd repeatedly until the curtain rings down. Lights on stage fade to black-suddenly Black Jack in whiteface holding a flare close to expose his "caked" face appears. Running back and forth spewing hocus pocus he taunts the crowd-jubilation turning to fear. Blowing on the torch, center stage, it blazes a river of fire and extinguishes. The stage goes dark again.

Silence-Has he just blessed the crowd or cursed them? Consternation abounds neighbor talking to neighbor. Somewhere a woman shrieks and has fainted calls for the house lights go unanswered.

Now backstage the big man, laughing, addresses his compatriots.

"Great job, girls, truly superb. Now you can go change and relax. Andrew, get those props stowed. We have one more show here tomorrow. Deborah, are you ready? Better get out there before the natives get restless."

"Don't worry, BJ. I'm on top of it," soothed the spiritualist as she changed into her white robes for the final act. The finale, a solo performance, highlighted her incredible talents in soothsaying. She gathered the questions and headed for the solo chair in the middle of the stage. The curtain rose and as the spotlight graced her, the audience rose united in ovation. By now, her fame and prowess were well known. Many in the audience had come specifically to see her. Just to have her read their question and peek into their lives. Rarely did they leave disappointed.

Madame Deborah always made it a point of honor, a bond with her public, to answer every question presented to her in writing. Amazingly, while all of her answers could never be positive, they always seemed to soothe the listener. Black Jack himself marveled at this occurrence over and over, remarking more than once that her talent was a gift from God.

At the wrap party the following night, the champagne flowed until early into Sunday morning. The professor, indeed the entire troupe, was in high spirits. "Ladies and gentlemen, may I offer you a hearty congratulations on a job well done." Black Jack toasted with a raised glass of wine.

"Thank you, Daddy." Eva smiled.

"Thanks, Herman." Lilly was holding her own bottle.

"Well done yourself, BJ. You make a marvelous master of ceremonies." Madame Deborah walked in wearing a Chinese robe.

"Now it's on to Chicago where we open on Friday for three weeks at the Orpheum. Drink up, everyone. All of this champagne is to be gone by dawn." Then a quick aside to his brother, "Andrew, before you let those guys go, make sure everything is locked down and ready for the shippers on Monday morning."

"Home," Eva said, rubbing her weary feet. "It will be good to go home and sleep in my own bed."

Just then, Lilly plopped down beside her, refilling Eva's glass. "You think your feet hurt now. Just imagine how much they would blister and hurt if those coals were really hot."

"It doesn't hurt that we coat our feet with wax just before we walk across. I can never get rid of all the wax. It sticks in my toes," Eva grumbled, still rubbing her feet gingerly.

"Just think of it as a beauty treatment," Lilly jested.

"Seriously though, Lil'. I know those nails are rubber, but how do you stand it with my standing on you and all?" Eva queried with concern.

"Oh, that. It's my rock hard stomach." She lay back on the cot they shared and pounded flat end of the champagne bottle on her belly. A minor explosion burst forth to soil her costume. No one cared. "Before I worked with BJ, I used to work in the circus. They would shoot me out of a cannon twice a day. Back then, you could bounce cannon balls off of this baby," bragged the actress using her belly as a tray to refill her glass.

Eva congratulated, "I had no idea that I was in the presence of such a world renowned performer."

"Ladies, what are you two up to over here by yourselves?" It was Black Jack in unusually high spirits.

"Nothing, honey. Just girl talk," Eva batted doeful eyes.

"Hey BJ, got anymore of that phosperous paper? It would make a real hit at parties," interjected the slightly inebriated assistant.

"Not enough for you to play with. That stuff is expensive. I'll need it for Chicago. We have three weeks of shows left." Herman refilled their glasses. Lilly's bottle was officially declared a casualty of war.

"It's a good thing the rubes don't know that that paper bursts into flame on contact with air. I bet that's one trick you won't put in your next book." Lilly smiled at him, thinking that he would share in her jest. Instead, she received a stern look in response.

"There is a lot of information that will not be going into any book. Here take this bottle. I will go and find another," Black Jack said solemnly, then departed.

"Party pooper," Lilly teased under her breath after his departure.

"You know what I'm really glad of?" Eva asked rhetorically. "I'm glad he really doesn't hypnotize us." Both girls giggled.

Home, home at last. 'To rest tired body in one's own bed. A familiar pillow on which on which to lay my head.'

Eva idly tossed thoughts around in her mind. Perhaps she would be a songwriter in her next life or a poet. She was definitely growing weary of the road. Now that it was fall in Chicago and there was a chill in the air, Herman was already planning his Deep South tour of 1922. The 'Voodoo, Twenty-Two Tour', six major cities in thirty eight days. It would be good to 'leave Chicago- all that cold and snow'; the words rhymed in her mind. Starting in Florida, oh boy, Tampa this time, and traveling from Atlanta to New Orleans. Then up the Ole Mississip' to finish in St. Louis.

It would be good to see her family again. She would send them tickets for the theatre in New Orleans. That was a grand palace. Her parents were still there of course, but some of her siblings had moved on. Her brother had moved to Chicago, in search of work and her, apparently, nearly three years ago. He got married and according to his last letter, had a baby girl already one year old. She made a mental note to call him. 'She would have to get around and see them now that she had some time.'

Eva continued to luxuriate on the crisp coolness of satiny

sheets. 'Imagine my older brother married and with a baby.' It was too bad that he didn't fit into this sophisticated world of hers- she needed allies. Especially now that Black Jack's brother was back and acting as general manager. He seemed to bring out a certain dark hardness in Herman, if one could imagine him with any more solemnity.

They had grown up on the streets raising one another as it were until Ben, Black Jack's real name, took up with Magician Prince Herman and went on the road. Later, he worked with Andrew until they became estranged, something about some time done in Tallahassee? She could never get the story straight from either of them. Anyway, he was back and had performed well as road manager. Everyone said so. Now his duties would include manufacture of Herman's now renamed voodoo tonic and control of the mail order business.

They needed the help, the way business was growing and after this last tour, they were swamped with orders. It was just that his personality, well, it grated on her nerves and he seemed to be around the apartment all of the time.

Eva assured herself that things would be different if they were married. 'Finally married,' she heard herself think. Eva wondered if she should ask Black Jack to proposition his wife again.

"Well, I'll see what I can do," he said gruffly. The two had been lounging on the couch one afternoon listening to jazz.

"Let me make a few calls. See what I can do." And that was the end of that.

Nearly four months had passed, not another word from Herman.

Lying there in her bed, she rubbed the ring with her pinky, then stopped, almost as if expecting a genie to magically appear. She recalled Lil's words about reeling him in slowly. She had him hooked, maybe now it was time to pull a little harder on the line. 'Time to reel in that man of mine.' The song continued to unfold in her head. 'I know things will be different this time. 'Cause I'm gonna get that man to fall, back in line.' She smiled whimsically at her ingenuity and dozed contentedly in the mid-afternoon, fall sun streaming in to spatter the canopied bed with accents of color.

The tour arrived in New Orleans toward the end of winter, after Mardi Gras and the associated parties had ended. Incongruously, the city looked both washed clean and war weary. The delta city that had seen many a spectacle was now preparing for one more; 'Professor Herman's Voodoo Tour' was coming to town. The widely anticipated show had already generated enough enthusiasm to make tickets hard to come by. This was rare in a city that took Voodoo as its unofficial religion and was known to ride fakers out of town on a rail. The advance word was that Professor Herman was just that good, and Madame Deborah was unbelievable in the accuracy of her advice. There was no doubt that she was in touch with spirits.

The day of the third performance, Eva awoke early and stepped out onto the balcony of the French Quarter hotel to sip coffee. It was wonderful to be here in the Cajun capital where the race mixing laws were somewhat relaxed. Ironic, since it was here in Louisiana that segregation as institution was sanctioned by the Supreme Court of the land nearly twenty-five years ago. But money talks, at least in the French Quarter. It was almost like being back in Chicago. Almost.

The sun had arisen hours earlier in a blaze of glory over the gulf and kissed the weathered angles on the building tops and churches with the brilliant promise of a new day. The air was typically humid, to the point of being slightly moist. This helped carry the sounds of hustle and bustle, human commerce, to her third floor balcony.

"We were a little off timing last night. We need to pick up the pace." Herman was leaning against the railing smoking a cigar a few feet away from the table. He had been up for hours.

"Can't you even say good morning?" came the coarse reply. Eva did not regard him, instead continued sipping her coffee and looking out over the city.

"Your parents coming tonight?" he cut to the chase.

"Yes. I guess they're here in the city somewhere."

"Don't worry. You will be perfect. Show them how well you turned out." Herman peered into the future.

"It's not that. I was just thinking about them. You know, missing them a little, I guess. Also, I am hoping to make enough this trip to send my whole family to St. Louis to live. We have relatives there. It's a much better life than sharecropping in Mississippi." Eva sighed over her coffee and finished solemnly, "I would like to buy them a house."

Herman stood silently puffing his cigar, calculating.

"I guess we could arrange that. The new book still has your picture on it, and Andrew says the magic tricks by mail business is going strong. I could advance you enough for say a down payment on a modest home."

In earlier years, she would have jumped up and flung her hands around his neck, like a little girl. But she was growing weary, weary of the road and weary of his obsession with black magic. Instead she said, "Great. That's great, BJ. Thanks a lot. That will give me some good news to tell my daddy when we go to dinner tonight." The coffee cup never left the clutch of her hands. Unconsciously, her pinky had been rubbing her engagement ring.

After Herman left, she considered her actions. She could have shown a little more gratitude. After all, he didn't have to do that. It was really a grand gesture on his part. She would have to make it up to him. He couldn't help who he was, that was how he had survived and prospered. He actually believed he had a manifest destiny, and he was striving to make his dreams come true. "Don't worry," she told herself, "I'll make it up to him."

"Very realistic performance, dear. I trust that at no time you were in any actual danger." The older man sitting at one end of the table expressed the appropriate fatherly concern.

"Honey, of course not. It's all an illusion. Right, dear?" Eva's mother volunteered with just a touch of concern.

"Yes, Mother." Eva was exasperated at being treated like a little girl in a public restaurant. Couldn't they see that in a few short years she had transformed into the consummate performer and consort of this great man?

"You do look a little tired, dear. Are you getting enough rest?" More motherly meddling.

"Not on the road, Mother. We have a rigorous schedule. We

get plenty of rest in between tours," replied Eva, informative if unconvincing.

"Have you heard from your brother lately? We just got a letter from him. He says his wife is expecting another child. They've only been married two years."

"No, I hadn't heard. We don't keep in touch that much." Eva was quickly tiring of this line of questioning.

"The first one was a girl, wasn't it? What's her name?"

"I sure hope he has a boy this time," her father interjected.

"Charles, please. The girl's name is Vivian, and we don't care what it is as long as it's healthy," Eva's mother said firmly. Then turning to Eva and putting a hand over hers. Oddly, the hand covered held the diamond ring. "Imagine us, dear. We're grandparents." Her animated face clearly showed the elation.

Herman seized the opportunity. "So, these are your first grandchildren. Congratulations! I'm sure that they are only the first of many more in the years to come."

Eva blushed. Knowing her parents well, she realized that he was skating on thin ice, whether he realized it or not. People from the south had traditional notions. They did not care much for these 'modern' cohabitations. Her mother had said as much in her letters, hinting that more than once she had to dissuade her husband of the notion that 'he should go to Chicago and straighten this man out.' Secretly Eva believed that her older brother had moved to Chicago at her parents' behest, ostensibly to spy on her. She had since dismissed that thought.

Having to deal with all of this baggage, she was happy that she had this gift for them, this show stopper, the promise of a house in St. Louis. Being the consummate show woman, she would wait until the propitious moment to spring the news. Maybe it would be better if Herman dispensed the good news. You know, man to man. Yes, that would be appropriate. It would be sort of a dowry. Excellent that would kill two birds with one stone. She smiled across the table at her man, beaming radiantly, almost oblivious to her parents on either side.

After dessert, a scrumptious flambé number obviously of

French design, Eva prompted her intended. "Honey," she began demurely, "You know." She immediately had everyone's attention.

"Yes. Yes. Eva has something she would like to discuss with you," the ringmaster began awkwardly.

"No. No, honey. I think you'd better tell them- about the dowry?" she prompted.

"Um…right. The dowry," Herman cleared his throat.

"Dowry? What's this?" Eva's parents exclaimed in unison.

"Well, Eva has been working for me for almost four years now. And she has been quite an asset," Herman continued with formality.

"In fact our daughter ran away to be with you almost exactly four years ago," Eva's father interjected forcefully.

"Daddy," the little girl at the table cried. "Let him finish."

"Yes, it was four years ago in New Orleans that we met. Anyway, she had been quite an asset. Since we are planning to marry eventually, it is customary to pay a fee for the replacement of your family's asset."

"Black Jack," Eva sing-songed chidingly. "You make it all sound like such a business deal. I am not a piece of property. I am your accomplice," she concluded succinctly. She turned to her parents, realizing that only she could complete this task. "Mother, Daddy, what he is trying to say is that we would like to give you enough for a down payment on a house in St. Louis. You can go and live near Uncle William." There it was done.

"We don't want any charity," Eva's father stated flatly.

"Sir, if you knew me well, you would realize that I am not a man blessed with a charitable spirit. I've worked hard for everything I have. Your daughter has helped a great deal, perhaps immeasurably. It is a debt that I owe to you."

"We owe," Eva insisted firmly.

Her mother began to sob softly, tears of joy.

Her father reached out and shook Black Jack's hand. "In that case, sir. I accept."

Later in their bedchambers, while Eva brushed her long hair, she discussed the results of the evening. "I think that went very well, don't you?"

"Yes, after we found the proper vehicle. The right rapprochement."
As usual, Black Jack had analyzed the situation in terms of a rational
business transaction. This however was not a zero sum game. They
both came out winners. The family got money, and he got Eva. 'He
got Eva.' Herman ruminated over that realization for awhile.

"I'm serious. My father appreciated you talking to him man to
man about his property, his daughter."

"Yes, I could see that. He loves you very much. It was a brilliant
idea of yours about the dowry. You're quite a clever girl," he
congratulated earnestly.

"Then you're quite a lucky man to get such a clever girl as your
lover," Eva replied obviously quite pleased with herself.

Upon returning to Chicago that spring, the couple once again
took up their respective lives. Black Jack returned to his wife and
family pretending to be the dutiful, loving husband.

Meanwhile his mistress Eva saw to the daily routine of running
their luxury apartment. In short, nothing changed and the couple
saw each other nearly every day.

Eva, who had decided long ago to play whatever part in this
great man's life that fate provided, was nevertheless shocked at
Black Jack's suggestion.

"Honey," They were relaxing, reclined on the sofa in the late
afternoon sun before the first of Deborah's clients was scheduled
to arrive. "I know we can't be married now, and I apologize for
that, for my wife's intransigence. But nobody says we can't have a
'honeymoon.'" There was that wicked glint in his eye.

"Baby, what are you saying?"

"Well, we have some time before the summer tour, and I was
planning a business trip. Why don't I take you along?"

"You mean it? You really mean it? Daddy, that sounds wonderful."
Eva was beside herself with joy.

"Sure. We will have a big going away party. Spend a couple of
nights in a downtown hotel and then leave on our trip. Wanda will
never be any the wiser. What do you think?" He grinned smugly,
knowing the answer.

"Why you...What a wonderfully devious idea. When do we
leave?"

"In a few weeks. I'll get everything set tomorrow."

They cuddled into the early evening, oblivious to the comings and goings in the busy apartment.

A large bon voyage reception was held at their apartment, followed by a surreptitious exit. Long after the guests had departed, the couple slipped into a waiting limousine to be whisked to a clandestine destination. The bridal suite of a downtown Chicago hotel where they would 'honeymoon' for the next two days.

Eva awoke the next afternoon to the sound of Herman arguing on the phone with someone. After a minute or two, she could tell that he was talking to his brother on the other end of the line.

"I don't care what he charged-pay it. That's what those guys are all about. They want to muscle into your market. Take as much as they can while still pretending to be your friend. After that, they get ugly. Don't play with him. Give him what he wants. We will have to figure out a way to deal with it later." Hanging up the phone, Herman noticed Eva had emerged from the bedroom.

"What was that all about?" she said softly trying to displace concern.

"Oh, Andrew says Konetti's people misquoted the price of the champagne. It was up twenty percent. Some unspecified expenses involved. I told him to pay it whatever it was. It was worth it. We had a grand party last night, didn't we?"

"Yes, dear." She marched over and put her arms around his middle, holding him tight. "A memorable occasion. The most memorable of my entire life."

Eva looked up at him and added slyly, "Last night <u>and</u> this morning were awfully memorable also."

"You were pretty memorable yourself, my dear." He slapped her behind and let his hand linger lewdly. "I'll call room service and order us some breakfast. Then I bet we'll have enough time to celebrate again before the food arrives. Better get back in that bed bitch." He slapped her rump again, harder this time. Eva yelped playfully and ran back to the bedroom.

Later, after, over Belgian waffles, sausage and coffee Herman apprised her of the rest of the conversation between him and his brother. "The tour is set to start with a July fourth performance in Minneapolis. From there we will skip around the Midwest performing in Sioux City, Omaha, Lincoln and Kansas City before returning to Chicago for two weeks. I'm told those Chicago dates are already selling. Andrew placed the announcement in last week's paper." Herman paused to let that information assimilate while he sipped his coffee.

"Eva, then I have a surprise. We are going to play two weeks in San Francisco. A fellow magician that I have been in contact with has invited us out to share a stage with him. What do you think of that?"

"It sounds fantastic," she offered tentatively. "He must be very good if you are willing to share a stage with him. You've never done that before in the time we have been together." She raised that profound statement of fact simply, rather nonchalantly.

"This man is a great talent. He has some unusual illusions that I may be able to learn from him." A rushed explanation, that did not go unnoticed by Eva.

"But more about that another time. I have the confirmed reservations for our little trip." His eyes twinkled as he waved the papers in front of her. "We will be taking the honeymoon coach to Toronto and Niagara Falls-the honeymoon capital of the world. We will have a suite in the Royale York Hotel with daily trips to the falls, Indian Reservations and anywhere else our hearts desire. Any poor slob can stay in a honeymoon bungalow by the falls, but we will be treated like royalty, in accordance with our standing as the reigning King and Queen of Magic."

"Oh darling, you do have a way with words. It all sounds so wonderful," Eva gushed, suddenly overwhelmed with sensations.

It was at that moment that Herman brought forth his piece de resistance. "After a week in Toronto we will board the Empire Limited. We have tickets for the parlour car with its two hundred forty degree view for our final destination in New York City."

"Oh, Daddy, that is fantastic." This time she did leave her seat and throw her arms around his neck, showering him in kisses. Reminiscent of the emotion she used to display when they first met and just as genuine.

Herman concluded simply while fending off kisses, "We will

stay there for a week and see the sights. Besides there are some powerful people with whom I have been in correspondence. We will finally have the opportunity to meet, and I can show off my Queen in the process."

Eva continued hugging him 'so we mix a little business with pleasure. That was his way. Still we would have three whole weeks on honeymoon before time to get back to work.'

The marvelous thing about Toronto was that it was a foreign city that had all the flavor of a Midwest metropolis. Eva wondered why they had never played there. She would have Herman put it on the itinerary. The air was clean; the restaurants served liquor upon request. The Seagram's Company had a powerful influence over the Canadian government. In fact, they were more powerful than ever owing to the smuggling of Canadian whiskey into the States. Some rumors had it that old man Seagram himself bankrolled the temperance lobby in a brilliant entrepreneurial move which left him with a virtual monopoly of product. However, Eva soon realized that the best part of traveling through Canada was not being looked upon as if one were an insect or a fish out of water. An undesirable that did not know her place. For a child of the south, used to that feeling, every day of her life, the remediation of this powerful negative stimuli was emancipating indeed. The clean crisp air of Canada was truly freeing indeed! She could now, truly for the first time, understand and empathize with his talk of equality for all.

Black Jack sensed this new enlightenment enliven her being. "You feel it too, don't you? The free air of Canada. Here you can walk down the street without people looking at you like you don't belong. Like you don't realize that you have overstepped your position, your station in life. As long as you are successful and have money, you are accepted as equals."

"Why haven't we ever played here?" Eva wondered aloud. Clutching tightly to her man's arm as they strolled the thoroughfare, trolley cars clanging in the background.

"I don't really know, perhaps because I was so conditioned to seek out black audiences that I never considered how truly different it could be up here. You never realize how completely conditioned you have been by society, by politicians, until you witness something like this. It genuinely is a seminal event."

"That's true," echoed Eva. "It's like living your life submerged underwater until one day you emerge and find the reality ten times better than you ever dreamed."

Their honeymoon in Canada was the best time in the young woman's life. It also marked the beginning of her political awareness and activism. Until now, the speeches her fiancé made in private were just part of the dance, part of his illusions to control men's mind for whatever nefarious economic purpose he deemed necessary.

Now she could clearly see the grand vision, having seen the template. The truly 'modern world' with equality and justice, equal justice and access, for all. They were no longer words, vague promises, they were actionable. She would relate these revelations to others on their visit to New York City.

"My, what a grand view," she exclaimed, emerging from Grand Central Station in the heart of mid town Manhattan, the heart of the capitalist world. There was a building boom going on everywhere around them. The frenzied activity took one's breath away. Toronto seemed like a distant province in comparison, still the memory lingered favorably.

"The ride in on the parlour car did not do it justice facing, as it were, away from the city. Perhaps they should have backed the train into the city. I will have to speak to the engineer about that," Herman joked. "Let's get a cab." He looked about again, taking it all in. "Yes, New York City, just like I pictured it, with even more grandeur than Chicago." Then with a burst of emotion, yelled at the top of his voice, "Hey, Big Apple, Black Jack Herman has arrived." The passersby paid him scant attention as they scurried along their appointed rounds. Eva laughed generously.

After a bit of difficulty, they secured a cab and traveled uptown to the Amsterdam Hotel and another honeymoon suite. The hotel, located as it was on the edge of Harlem's burgeoning cultural mecca, was the perfect base of operations for him to hold conferences with those prominent people with whom he had been keeping correspondence.

That night at dinner, he introduced Eva to some of the most powerful black businessmen in New York. "Gentlemen, I would like you to meet my partner, the charming Eva." Eva blushed demurely and curtsied.

One prominent voice jeered, "Save the theatricals. You're not on the stage now. This is a dinner party, not the Savoy." A chorus of laughter followed.

"Gentlemen, gentlemen, some civility please for my Lady. She is a child of the south, who during our stay in Toronto has had an epiphany. Honey, tell them in your own words what you came to realize."

Eva rose and, unaccustomed though she was to public speaking, spoke to this group of the words closest to her heart. "Gentlemen, as the Maestro indicated I grew up in the south. The Deep South." She let the words sink in for emphasis. "Until this past week in Canada, I have never completely believed that people of color could coexist with Caucasians in peace and harmony on an equal basis. I don't know how it is out here in the East. But I have toured extensively the Midwest and the South. In the Midwest we were tolerated, especially well the further north we went. But as we traveled south, we were despised, even loathed, because we did not conform to preconceived stereotypes. Because we dared to hold our heads up and comport ourselves as decent human beings. Until now, I never believed it could be any other way." She finished that last sentence with increased emphasis, to a standing ovation from the dinner guests.

The next night she repeated her speech to a man introduced as General Marcus Garvey. She could immediately tell she was preaching to the choir.

"In the main we can't live with them," concluded General Garvey to the small dinner gathering. Witness what Caucasians do when they conquer a new territory. They transform it into a copy of homeland without concern for the consequences of their actions." He paused to puff his cigar into brilliance. "With capricious disregard for the indigenous species and populations. These Caucasians, do you know that stands for the Cacus Mountains in Russia? These tribes, we call them now countries, are descendants of the barbaric hordes that ravaged Rome over fifteen hundred years ago," he concluded smugly. The crowd was silenced by this scholarly inculcation. Not Herman.

"The problem goes deeper than that. What they can't have, they despoil. Like the belligerent child who is unwilling to share or play fairly. Do you know your Roman history?" Black Jack looked around the room to quizzical faces. "When the Romans could not conquer a territory, they burned the crops, salted the fields and the wells. Their answer was that if we can't have it, nobody will.

Then there is the whole slavery issue. From time immemorial, the victors in a conflict have always taken the losers as slaves. Read your Bible, from the Jews on down, everybody took everybody else as slaves. Why should it be any different now?" Black Jack had posed the question of the hour. General Garvey interjected, "He's right. Even Jesus himself did not criticize the taking of slaves. He only espoused that they should be treated with respect." He finished that ground shaking statement to cries of "He's right" and "Here, Here." Thusly emboldened, he embarked on the central tenant of his thesis "It is impossible to conclude that the situation can materially change in the decades ahead. Look what the Caucasians have done to the American Indians. After their property was seized, they were forcibly resettled to camps in the Midwest." Garvey paused to make sure he had everyone's rapt attention, and then delivered the punch line. "Guess what? Irony of ironies. The land on which they had been resettled under the Auspicles of the Bureau of Indian Affairs; the organization established to paternalistically watch over them, that land was found to be sitting on vast pools of oil. Enough to make these tribes the richest entities in the country. But are these tribes rich?"

"No. No, they were robbed," a chorus of diners insisted.

"That's right. They were resettled again. This time to barren rocks. Politicians were paid off by powerful forces intent on seizing the oil. They were called 'The Robber Barrons,'" Garvey concluded fiercely. "Captains of industry."

Black Jack broke in above the crowd, "I am surely glad that there is no Bureau of African American Affairs." The crowd burst into laughter. Herman continued in a more serious vein. "In order to achieve anything meaningful, we need organization and coordination of tactics to operate as one cohesive unit. I have seen how the mob operates in Chicago. How they conquer a territory, control it. Integrate their resources to maximize profit. We can do the same economically if we all work together. I tell you truthfully that the mob, their day will come to a swift end. While ours is just beginning to dawn. We can be free and independent if we control our own destiny. If we control our destiny we will have the power. That's the missing key, the key to success!"

The speeches and some would say, rabble rousing, continued late into the evening. More meetings were held on subsequent days all with the same purpose, to formalize lines of communication and foster the building of a network of economic cooperation. Garvey assured Herman that his talents and gift for oratory would be well received in New York. Black Jack promised to spread Garvey's message in his travels. They both agreed to work for the shared goal of black self-determination.

It was time to leave. Black Jack apologized, but insisted that his magic troupe must have time to practice if they were to be at peak performance on their next tour. Eva too, who had delighted in such sights as seeing the Atlantic Ocean at Coney Island and traveling to the Statue of Liberty, was also longing for home. She knew all too well that the show would have to continue. The road beckoned Black Jack.

Riding on the Twentieth Century Limited back to Chicago, Herman had time to think. They could not secure a sleeper car berth for the overnight journey, so he and Eva had to sit in coach for the duration. As the train left Pennsylvania and Eva dozed on his shoulder, his thoughts turned to Washington D.C. and his experiences there.

He smiled when he thought of the Turkish Ambassador who still wrote to him every so often. Entreaties to perform at one gala event or another that would showcase his talent. In each reply, Black Jack sent his regrets. In his most eloquent response, he commented on a more commodious venue to express his talents:

'Sir, what I would deeply like to do, what is closest to my heart is to perform for the entire city of Washington, dignitaries and all, at the foot of the Lincoln Memorial. Alas, for while Lincoln emancipated the slaves over fifty years ago, we have become ensnared in a socio-economic plot more pervasive and pernicious than slavery itself. Until I can perform in Washington D.C. for all of the people, all of the time, Sir I have to respectfully decline.'

Black Jack decided to send a copy of this response in his next correspondence with Mr. Garvey.

VII
Phoenix

The abbreviated summer 'Voodoo Twenty-Two Tour' saw more action behind the curtain and off the stage than usual. Andrew, their new stage manager, had taken full advantage of his position as Black Jack's brother to become a little major domo. As he now oversaw every aspect of the production, he took it upon himself to over manage every decision. Moreover, his curt manner and incendiary personality had everyone on edge. Behind his back most of the troupe called him the 'little tyrant.' In short, he was officious in his business dealings and oafish in nature.

Pleas to Black Jack about this petty dictator fell on deaf ears. "I have given him the responsibility for keeping the show running smoothly," he stated flatly. "I have also encharged him with supervision over the distillation and bottling of the health tonic and keeping track of the mail order correspondence. I know he has a lot on his shoulders, but I think he can handle the load." As Black Jack's patience for mundane problems waned, he formulated a simple disclaimer which he would carte blanche, "He's running the show now. Deal with it."

As had become their habit when not on stage, Herman and Deborah spent a lot of time together in consultations. When not in meetings or practicing his routines, Black Jack's head was buried in any one of a number of books on the occult. Eva glanced through them one night before bed, Hypnotism and Hypnotic Suggestion, The New Occultism, Voodoo Practices of the Omadi Women, Unleashing Your Hidden Mental Powers, there were others. She leafed through one. A grizzly picture caught her eye, a drawing of a man submerging an obviously entranced woman in a vat of water. He was holding her by the hair, wet and matted, obviously she had been dunked several times and was gasping for air. Her eyes unblinking stared straight ahead, the blank stare of a zombie. Shuddering, she slammed the book shut and vowed not to inquire any further. Eva simply refused to contemplate on the direction he was heading despite the results of her findings. Ignoring pleadings from within her mind.

Secretly she daren't even admit this to herself; she <u>was</u> becoming distressed with his obsession with the occult. 'The stage show was already a success,' she reasoned. 'Why did he need to keep studying these texts for? What dark secrets was he researching?' Another question surfaced. 'What part did Madame Deborah play in this puzzle? If her talent was God given, as Herman had once asserted, what could she possibly be teaching?' All of these questions preyed on her mind, began to burden her soul. She vowed not to let it distract her performance or color the relationship with her partner.

Eva kept confidences with Lilly, the only friend to whom she could turn. In fact, while they had always been close, since that first voodoo ceremony, which seemed like years ago, they were now closer than ever. Lilly occasionally joked that since they had been 'indoctrinated' they were now 'voodoo sisters.'

They had in point of fact a lot in common. Both young women in their twenties, who were now more or less equal in station. There was a certain hierarchy involved in the act. Herman was supreme. With the addition of Deborah, Lilly had been demoted from her position as Black Jack's confidant. At the same time, Eva, now an accomplished professional, was approaching equal footing with the seasoned veteran. Thankfully, the girls who used to be roommates still enjoyed one another's company. Perhaps even more now that they no longer lived together. A case of distance making the heart grow fonder, or more accurately, personal space providing a buffer against over familiarity.

One afternoon during make-up, Lilly confided to Eva, "After we finish with the show in San Fran, I'm going to follow your example. Maybe settle down with one of my 'sugar daddies.' You know I've had my offers."

"You mean you are going to leave the show?" Eva asked incredulously.

"Honey, haven't you heard? After this tour Herman is thinking of revamping the act. Going in a new direction. Haven't you noticed how he and Deborah are always huddling together?" asked Lilly, begging the question. Then deciding not to wait for a response, she delivered the coup de grace. "Besides, Andrew told me. He said the magic and sleight-of-hand were mostly out. Professor Herman was going to concentrate on the powers of the mind. You know that mind over matter stuff."

To Eva this news was like a bolt of lightning out of a clear blue sky, unexpected and unwelcomed. She tried to shrug it off in front of her friend. "Well, as the saying goes, the lover is always the last to know." There was a savagery in her voice that belied the nonchalance of her words. Deep inside this news panicked her, sickened her stomach.

Although Eva would like to know more she daren't broach the subject with Herman who, once again, was becoming aloof and implacable. Eva, now a seasoned veteran of touring with him, had seen these irascible moods before. Usually this behavior could be ascribed to the 'rigors of the road.' This time somehow everything was different. He had given up control over the day to day operation of the show, not something a person like him with a 'hands on' mentality would do easily. He spent most of his free time with Deborah practicing only God knows what. Then there were all of those books. Eva struggled for understanding. If she were not in love, engaged, she might fear that she too would be ostracized. But 'she was promised,' Eva felt comforted by that thought. All appearances confirmed Lilly's information that Herman was going to transform himself, his show, into she knew not what. She did know for certain that he would tell her when he was ready, and only then.

Black Jack would only talk about one thing-their performances in San Francisco. Sharing the stage with the great Professor Maharajah. He couldn't wait to get to San Francisco; you'd think it was the promised land of milk and honey to hear him talk. While he spoke expectantly, he would provide no further details, just a faraway look in his eyes. This unnerved the young woman more than anything else, the change in her man and her inability to share his vision.

Initially the locality, the beautiful surroundings, did a lot to allay her concerns. The golden city by the bay was a marvelous mecca rising around verdant hills. Building was going on everywhere and the small metropolis, much smaller than New York or Chicago, was bustling with activity and prosperity. It had all the trappings of a boom town drunken with opulence. San Fran truly resembled those fabled cities paved with streets of gold, Babylon, Imperial Rome. It was also the epitome of the prosperous American city as seen through the eyes of immigrating Europeans. Eva had met many of them in her travels. They spoke often of America as that 'shining city on the hill.'

Here they were again by the hundreds and thousands engaging in gleeful commerence, happy and secure in their new homeland. That was the heart of it, not just the buildings. 'My but they were impressive.' She and Herman had taken a carriage ride up Nob Hill when they first arrived. 'The mansions!' One reminded her of the Turkish Embassy. Her mind harkened back to those halcyon days. What opulence, what grandeur, here it was replicated.

Far more than the bricks and mortar, the gold and copper, there was an indomitable spirit, an esprit' de corps. A shared manifest destiny that could not be ripped from these people by fire, flood or earthquake. Eva had read about the great San Francisco earthquake, most school children had. Yet, here and now, fifteen years later, there was no evidence of its aftermath. It was as if this city, broken but not beaten, had risen of its own devices and reclaimed the birthright growing bigger and stronger in the process. This air of confidence was infectious, invigorating and as palpable as the evening's fog rolling in off the bay. The image of the shining city invincible, the embodiment of the Greek legend of the Phoenix, rising from the ashes stronger and more resilient. This spirit of reawakening would comfort her, be her stalwart in the arduous times ahead.

Eva wished they could stay there forever. There was a new area going up across the bay called Oakland. It had small town charm combined with beautiful views and clement weather. 'The perfect place to raise a family,' she thought.

Black Jack, as she knew all too well, had other plans on his agenda; other manifest destinies calling to him. Eva had all too reluctantly realized that when you belong to a powerful man, you become a slave to his whims and desires. Your place in the history books would be by his side. Now that was enough for most days, most women. Just once in a great while you get a glimpse of something different, something safe and compelling, outside of the maelstrom. Sometimes, just a small wish that this cup might pass from your lips.

It finally dawned on her that San Francisco evoked the feelings that she first had in Toronto. A nice place to live where you were judged more for character and content rather than color. A place where no matter how cliquish, after all different ethnicities would naturally prefer the pleasure of their own company. Many could speak barely a world of English. They were all more or less on equal footing. Unlike the eastern United States where the vested interest lay entrenched for centuries, in San Francisco there truly seemed to be opportunity for all.

The trolleys ran right past the fairgrounds with their clang-clanging. After a few days, Eva realized their routes so regular, their stewards so competent; you could set your watch by them. Too bad they couldn't work them into the show. And what a show it was. The crowds flocked to their pavilion to see the two great masters of mind control, Professor Maharajah the Hindu Hypnotist and Black Jack Herman Master of Voodoo and Magic. The combined performance lasted a solid two hours. First Professor Maharajah, by virtue of his senior status within the magical community, performed various illusions expected of a Hindu 'fakir' including the charming of a six foot python. Then Herman would take the stage with his voodoo revue. Foregoing the typical magical exploits until the finale, Herman and Deborah concentrated on putting the assistants through their paces.

For the final third of the show, the Professor joined Black Jack on stage and assisted with the sawing in half, et cetera. The two magicians updated Herman's levitation trick with Professor Maharajah causing the suspended subject to disappear in mid-air within an explosion of smoke. Obviously, upstaging the startled Black Jack to howls of laughter from the crowd. Of course, this had been pre-arranged and practiced exhaustively by the duo prior to their debut.

For the finale, Lilly and Eva would lock the Great Professor into a milk can; the same type employed by Houdini himself, and then partition him off from the audience to occlude his escape. The Professor took great pains to emphasize that this device was of the same type used by the Great Houdini, lest the significance of the demonstration be lost on the crowd. After his triumphant emergence from this prison at center stage, both companies joined him to take their bows amid thunderous ovations. They performed two shows every day except Sunday.

The atmosphere of the combined entourage seemed constantly charged with electricity or maybe it was the San Francisco air. Whatever the cause, the girls had rarely seen Herman this energized. He was full of life and emotion, a broad grin now creased his usually granite demeanor.

Herman was actually enamored of his fellow magician. Eva had never seen him so excited about another performer. The Professor also was apparently quite taken with Black Jack's talents. Andrew, noticing the young girl's discomfort, in a rare gesture of compassion confided that the only man BJ was ever close to before was the great Prince Herman. Madame Deborah confirmed this clue when she observed that "He must have been much the same with his first mentor when he was just starting out. Before he was beaten down and hardened by the slings and arrows of outrageous fortune." To Eva it didn't matter, weather or new companions, she was glad to have the man she fell in love with returned to her.

Not that they spent much time together. When not on stage or rehearsing, Herman and Professor Maharajah would tour the fairgrounds or take on Chinatown. Often returning after many hours and in more than slightly inebriated condition. Eschewing hard spirits the Professor advised that, "The imbibing of wine was more 'natural' and healthful to the constitution." Besides in this burgeoning new European community, they found great wines were cheap and easy to come by despite any ordinances to the contrary, so the two of them would drink the local produce by the bottle while swapping stories and pouring over diagrams. Herman was ever the eager student.

Finally, on Sunday morning after the second week of performances, Herman was to witness the fabled trick that he had been promised. That Saturday night's performance was to have been their last, but because of the extraordinary demand, they had agreed to hold the revue over for one more week. The entire troupe celebrated their good fortune until late into the evening. When Herman arose early Sunday morn, he was able to dress and slip out without disturbing Eva.

Catching a trolley just coming up the hill, he arrived to meet his new mentor at the appointed time, just across the street from the fairgrounds. The mists were beginning to evaporate in the early light of the newly risen sun. The promise of a memorable day hung in the late summer air.

The Maharajah was there waiting for him in a small truck with three companions, two men and a woman. He was dressed in his usual white sultan's costume sans hat, which must be there somewhere inside the truck. 'Man, he never breaks from his character,' thought Herman, ever the student. After hugs and salutations, Black Jack joined his elder and the woman in the cab. The two men rode in the back of the truck with the wooden box and the shovels.

Herman sitting behind the wheel started the truck and turned it into the road heading uphill toward their predetermined destination. The young woman sat in the middle between the two master magicians. Herman had spoken to her briefly upon his entrance. No need to carry on casual conversation. Everyone knew their place in today's performance.

After the rickety truck had climbed Army straining and groaning under Herman's shifting of the gears passing the Castro, they could see their target looming ahead of them. Thrust above the surrounding hills in unparalleled prominence was the twin peaks. The towering twosome that dominated the San Francisco skyscape. More than capstones to the indigenous peoples of the area, they were the harbour of great magical powers. The perfect place to perform their trick.

The destination, a small valley between the towers moved ever closer. Herman anxiously quickened the vehicles pace as the truck left the road and approached the site of highest spiritual significance. Professor Maharajah began his preamble. "Until now you have been studying and practicing your craft in a half fashion. Today I will demonstrate what you have only read in books. Teaching you to replicate my performance and incorporate it into your act. Remember this is no illusion. This is the true power of mind over matter." The truck ground to a halt. They had reached their appointed destination.

The two men in the back hopped down from their perch. The Professor reacquired his turban and stepped onto the grounds searching with his eyes presumably for the optimum location. The young woman stayed seated in the front, barely moving.

The venerable professor walked for a few paces kicking at the ground with his feet, testing the soil. He stopped almost equidistant between the two towers and brushed away a pile of rocks with his feet. "Boys, over here," he cried loudly. The two accomplices grabbed their shovels and raced to the spot indicated by his beck and call. At once, they began digging with purpose.

Herman, who had been stretching his legs and watching the sunny daybreak overhead, felt his pulse quicken. He rejoined the group to once again immerse himself in his mentor's tutelage. Professor Maharajah began instructions as he neared, "The first thing you must do is find a well drained soil with a light loam. Heavy clay soils are a nuisance to dig and remove. Today we will have to deal with a lot more rocks than I would like, but this makes for the perfect location." The young men working swiftly were already standing in a hole up to their knees.

Black Jack watching them was suddenly pained with feelings of remorse, misgivings for the intended star of the demonstration. "What about her?" he inquired, motioning toward the waiting girl in the truck with his jaw. Had he been overcome by a strange burst of compassion? Maybe it was the air after all.

"Oh, she'll be fine." The other man brushed off any notion of a cause for concern. "I have her now in a light stupor. When we are ready to begin, I will put her completely under. Don't worry. She will have nothing but pleasant dreams. I've done this with her several times before. She is very receptive. The only reason I put her in a stupor now is to keep her from thinking about it on the ride up and all. You know, it preys on the mind. In her world we are going out for a Sunday picnic lunch."

Herman winced, but said nothing.

The Professor continued, "I cannot reiterate this often enough. For the 'event' to work properly, you must use a subject who is very receptive to hypnotism. You know some people are resistant and others will only go into a light trance. It wouldn't do to have someone wake up in the middle of the demonstration. Being buried alive is no fun if you are conscious," he smiled knowingly at Herman. "Once they are down there, it takes a while for exhumation. There's no way to speed up the process."

Black Jack nodded with understanding. He already knew which of his girls would make the better subject.

The boys were having trouble with a rocky layer they encountered slightly below the waistline. Herman returned from the truck with a pickaxe as per their request. Briefly he stopped to view the young lady sitting quietly in the front seat. She barely moved, but smiled in recognition of his features. They had shared the same stage for the past two weeks. If all went well, they would once again have that pleasure the forth coming week. There it was again, that pang of concern for their intended.

For purposes of this demonstration, a full six foot depth would not be required. The axe wielding duo had prepared the soil to a depth of four feet. More than enough to cover their victim. Black

Jack's fears were assuaged by the knowledge that in case something awry occurred, they wouldn't have that far down to go to get her out. He was understandably nervous. This was his first time.

Black Jack's professor was speaking again, "Of course, for a genuine 'buried alive' demonstration you need to go down the full six feet. The crowd required that authenticity. Not that it really matters, eh?" He jostled Herman who was somewhat stupefied by the aggregation of events.

The assistants had assiduously left the freshly prepared soil and now returned from the truck with the wooden box propped upon their shoulders. The Professor excused himself and returned with the star of the demonstration on one arm. Black Jack, the showman used to being in control, now played the unfamiliar role of audience. He could feel the anticipation coursing through his veins. He was both elated and nervous at the same time. Until now, he had not even considered the possibility of someone stopping by and interrupting their plans. 'What if they were spied upon and the police summoned?' Who would believe they were merely practicing a magic trick without a permit? The usually stoic performer was anxious.

The Maharajah interposed on his thoughts, "Now watch me closely. To hypnotize deeply, completely, you must stare long and hard into the eyes. Gloria," he called in a deep commanding voice. "You will listen to my voice and obey."

"I will obey," came the monotone response.

"You are tired. You will lay back and go to sleep. It has been a long day in the hot sun. You want to sleep, someplace cool and dark." He paused to gage her comprehension. "Here is your bed. Lie down. Go to sleep."

"I am very tired." The comely young woman stepped into the box and lay down as if in her bed. She closed her eyes.

The Professor uttered the final instruction, "Good night. Pleasant dreams."

The grave diggers covered the coffin gently, screwing the top shut, and then proceeded to maneuver the box to the edge of the precipice where they gently lowered the unconscious girl into her cool dark room for four hours of rest. Gingerly the young men gathered their shovels and covered the girl, completely filling the hole. Further as commanded, they smoothed around the area covering any evidence of their crime from chance passersby.

Herman, the audience of one, could barely believe his eyes. Here was no illusion, but the genuine article. He stood staring at the patch of ground where the hole had been. The entire event had taken not more than twenty minutes from the time the young lady had left the truck.

Herman's mentor approached and placed a hand on his shoulder, speaking to him in fatherly tones in order to allay any latent fears in the younger man's mind. "Don't worry, she has hours of air. When you are this deeply under, you take maybe five breaths a minute. Relax, let's have some brunch. The boys have packed a mean picnic basket."

So it was that they brunched and lounged close by keeping a taut eye on their experiment. Black Jack, his once indefatigable spirit now indelibly altered, smoked a cigar pensively towards the end of the drama.

Finally it was over. The young men worked as if demonically possessed to unearth the captive, their buried treasure. Once the top was cleared, no further exhumation was necessary. The screws were undone at feverish pace, and the top was removed revealing the sleeping girl. She seemed so peaceful in fact, that at first Black Jack thought she might have expired during her ordeal.

The Maharajah knelt down beside her and gently patted her on the face. "Gloria, this is your control. Hear my voice. It is time to wake up and go home. The picnic is over. Wake up slowly now. Do you hear me?"

"Yes," slowly the voice came through stuffy lips. Herman visibly relaxed. She rose like the phoenix, alive again. The 'experiment', it was an experiment in his mind anyway, had been a success.

Gloria, now sitting up and still in a light stupor, was being helped out of the box by the young men attending.

The Professor admonished his pupil. "You see, didn't I tell you? Everything worked out as planned. Before she fully awakes, I will reinforce her post hypnotic suggestion that we were at a picnic today. She will be perfectly content with that illusion and her mind won't inquire further. That's how it always goes."

He turned to hasten the young lads at their tasks. "Hurry up boys, will you? We want this place cleared so we can get out of here before we wear out our welcome." He felt sure the twin peaks would keep their secrets.

On the ride back down the hill Professor Maharajah promised Black Jack, "After our engagement is finished we will perform this trick one more time. I want to make absolutely sure that you get it right the first time."

Their engagement at the state fair ended not with a bang, but with a whimper. All of the fireworks came afterward. Actually, their combined performance concluded to thunderous ovations for the entire cast. Red roses all around for the female performers. Each standing onstage holding a bouquet of a dozen roses bowing to the herald.

The female assistants truly resembled beauty queens, what with those tight outfits glittering in the spotlight. The two magicians extraordinaire continued to use outstretched arms to encourage the crowd, fanning their exuberance. It really was a magnificent sight; the combined entourage taking curtain calls until the crowd exhausted.

The backstage celebration began with champagne overflowing like Vesuvius, with women running and screaming in laughter. Men chased with bottles uncorked, apparently with the aim of drowning their prey in sudsy bubbles. The merrymaking retired to a local restaurant which the troupe inhabited until the wee hours of the morning.

The next afternoon after everything was packed away, after everyone was semi-sober, Herman and Deborah sat down with Eva and explained to her just how events were destined to proceed. That's when the fireworks began.

"Then it is true. Everything I've heard is true. You two are planning to break up the show." There were tears in her eyes and rage in her voice as Eva confronted the pair. "Why at the height of success would you want to dismantle our organization? It doesn't make any sense." Eva stopped to collect her composure and order her thoughts. 'So this day had finally come,' she thought. In an instant she decided to lash out at Deborah. "I suppose this is your doing. You two have been working for months to build up his ability to read people, to manipulate crowds. Don't think I haven't looked into all of those books that litter my bedroom." Herman winced. Madame Deborah tried to soothe her fellow performer who obviously had been left out in the dark for too long. "Honey, it isn't like that at all. BJ, like so many good magicians, just wants to take his talents to the next level. To redefine his craft and continually upgrade his performance. To present the best possible show. You know that magic is a constantly evolving art form. How many times has he upgraded his show in the years that you have been with him? This is just one more incarnation."

"We have never dismissed the entire act before. Besides, we still have so many places we could demonstrate our current performance. How about a west coast tour?" Eva rationalized in exasperation.

"It's time, Eva," Black Jack stated with a profundity and surety of one in touch with his own destiny and the other riddles of life. He continued, beginning to fill in the missing pieces of the mosaic. "The people with whom I correspond in New York contacted me before we left for San Francisco. They feel that the time is right to bring our performance to the big city. I should have told you earlier, but I wanted it to be a surprise. I hoped it would be a pleasant one," he concluded with a touch of regret in his voice, mingled with disappointment.

Eva argued, still not understanding his meaning. "Well, that is great news. Something that you don't keep from your lover. But why not take the whole troupe? They haven't seen the show back east. We could tour New England, maybe Canada as well. You remember what a fine town Toronto is. How we so enjoyed it on our honeymoon."

"My dear, you don't understand. The times are changing, and we must change right along with them. We can't be slaves to the past. I can't explain everything to you at once and you are right, I should have confided in you sooner. It's just that while I had the expert in the science at my disposal, I threw myself into her confidence to the exclusion of everything else. Don't worry, baby, it won't happen again." Black Jack sounded sincerely apologetic.

Deborah too, launched her reassurances, "Don't worry, Eva. I am not going to New York. My place is in Chicago. I know that just as certainly as I know that your place is forever by Herman's side."

Eva was stunned into speechlessness by the other woman's sudden burst of candor, clairvoyance.

Black Jack continued elucidating his plans for Eva's benefit. "Darling, my friends, some of them you met on our 'honeymoon', have advised me that in their opinion the time is ripe for change. The economy is booming all over the country and causes, like our rights movement, are gaining supporters daily. Since women won the right to vote, many feel newly emboldened.

Our people in New York have suggested that I come and give a series of lectures. Talk about the various areas of the country and the conditions I have witnessed. We have witnessed.

I have been huddled with Deborah in order to divine some of her talent. It can be learned you know. You have to look into people's hearts, their very souls, and if you listen closely enough the answers will be whispered to you out of thin air. Just like magic. It really is an incredible talent. You'll see. After all, you will be right there with me on stage. I want all eyes focused on you. That will give me the time to listen for my muse or whatever. As always, you will be on stage to mesmerize the crowd. There, doesn't that make you feel better?"

"Well, I guess a little." Eva sounded slightly contrite, if not totally convinced and forgiving.

"That's my girl," Black Jack soothed. "Now, there's just one more trick that you need to learn to help me in my quest to become the greatest showman of all time."

It was there and then the real fireworks erupted.

VIII
Phoenix Rising

Eva was in a quandary. Her mind couldn't believe what it had heard. What they were asking her to do. 'Were they serious? Did they actually expect her to agree to something so abhorrent?' Panic crept up her throat threatening to choke her senseless. Somewhere in the distance a bell was tolling. She couldn't connect it with the trolleys. Couched in utter astonishment she shrieked, "You want me to do what?"

Black Jack repeated simply, matter-of-factly, "The trick is called 'buried alive.' We hypnotize you, place you in a box and cover you with dirt for a period of time. Then we bring you back. It is a show stopping sensation." Better to not go into all of the details at one time. Let her adjust to the idea he reasoned. Truth was he could not force her to do anything foreign to her will or anything that would break the bonds of trust and love that they shared. She must be guided into accepting the proposition. To this end he would have to eliminate any shadow of fear within the young woman. Magnify her love for him to the point that she was willing to place her very life itself in his hands. This would be the magic trick he would have to perform behind the scenes. The crux of his dilemma.

He would have to profess his love for her, passionately, repeatedly, vehemently. Convince her that above all else, he held her love, her safety and fidelity predominate. After all, since they had met was there any question of his even looking at another woman? 'Of course not!' Did they both not believe that they were star crossed lovers, their union preordained? Well, this was part of it then. He, the great showman and she, she was his subject extraordinaire. This new demonstration of mental prowess would make her a star in her own right and place this dynamic duo on a par with the Great Houdini himself.

This was the significance of Professor Maharajah's escape from the milk can. By successfully duplicating an escape performed by the greatest magician of all time, he brought the 'Great One' down a peg to just slightly below the clouds, elevating himself in the process. The 'buried alive' trick was another attempt to balance the scales. Something that even Houdini had never attempted. Of course, one needed the right assistant, the right partner. Also one needed to be prepared for the repercussions from the public for the performance of such a shocking demonstration. Eva was the perfect partner. Black Jack knew that in his bones. As for any adverse consequences from the performance of the trick, the hell with it.

When at anytime in his life had he, Black Jack Herman, shied away from controversy? In his younger days, had he not courted chaos? Why should it be any different now then, at the top of his game, on the verge of being greater and more famous than few in history dared to dream? This demonstration of his mental powers, prowess would be the lynchpin in his repertoire. If they believed in him, they would follow his advice and if they followed his advice, then he could mold them. Shape the face of the future.

Herman finished ruminating and a conscious thought occurred. 'Professor Maharajah!' It was he after all who was the teacher of the trick. It was logical that he would be the one to allay the fears of his star. To convince her that this demonstration was absolutely essential to the furtherment of her lover's career. Convince her of the unequivocal truth that she was an integral part of his success. Assure her that no harm would come to her. Most of all, present to her the fact that this was part of her manifest destiny.

Armed with new enlightenment on how to proceed down

this difficult path, Black Jack turned to Deborah and said simply, "Would you go and find our esteemed professor? Ask him to step in here for a minute." After she had left the dressing room, Black Jack, that imposing figure of a man in granite, began speaking to his love in softer seductive tones, reminiscing on their first meeting.

"Eva, you remember when we first met in New Orleans so long ago? After you had left your parents home. You were so alive, so awestruck, filled with joy and wonder, so trusting. It is inevitable that you will lose much of that wonderment after you see how the tricks are performed. How the public is conned. That is just one of the reasons that magicians constantly have to upgrade their act. Not only to preserve the novelty factor, but to stay one step ahead of the critics and cynics who are constantly trying to unmask our illusions. It is not enough for them that the public knows the tricks are fake. These inquisitors must break that unspoken bond between the magician and his audience. You'll remember I spoke of that during your early tutorial. The age old bond between magician and audience. The hope we provide that there is something more outside of the realm of observability. These debunkers live to discredit us and elevate themselves in the process. You know that yourself now that once a trick is revealed, it is no more use to anyone. Once the mystery is dispelled, the audience denies the 'magic.'" He paused.

"Honey," he continued in pleading tones. "We are on the verge of breaking that boundary, of going beyond the art of illusion and delving into the science of the mind. This is the future of performance drama. Not parlor tricks, but the powers of the mind over matter. Eventually, over life itself. What we have only played at heretofore, we will now honestly perpetrate on the public. We will be pioneers on the vanguard of this new art form. Houdini was the first to embrace and demonstrate the power a fully developed mind can have over one's self and surroundings. We, you and I along with a few others, will follow him and in the process be transformed into legends." Herman paused to catch his breath and assess the effect of his sermon on the audience of one. He truly hoped she would see this for what it was, a soul sharing. A meeting of the minds that he had not attempted for far too long in their relationship.

"Darling, I need you to remember back to those early days of our association. How strong our adoration, how solidly we built those bonds of love. I need you to look inside yourself now and reconnect with those feelings. To remember how much I love you. To place your faith and trust fully in me."

Although she was outwardly silent, the whirring in her mind continued unceasingly. 'Yes she loved this man with all of her heart, but he had been strange lately.' So prepossed with the occult. Did he really love her or was she simply a means to an end. 'He had loved Wanda once.' Strange she hadn't thought of her in a long time. But that statement, from wherever it came was so true. 'Would he discard her when her time was through? Abandon her for another? Never!' She dismissed the idle doubt. Although she had been a child when she fell in love, a neophyte in the ways of the world, she was certain that what they shared together was something special, rare and distinct.

What was it that Madame Deborah had told her all those many months ago? 'Every rose has thorns.' She smiled sardonically to herself. 'Well this was certainly one of those occasions.' But she did say that she and Black Jack were meant to be together. Never in their history together had Eva known Deborah to prevaricate. In fact, instead of calling her clairvoyant, she should simply be referred to as a truth-teller. Yes, she would trust this oracle, but to a point. She needed confirmation from a higher power this time. Silently she clasped her hands together and bowed her head slightly while Herman continued to prattle. Sitting there in her chair she secretly launched a prayer shooting forth into the heavens-a flare indicating a vessel in distress.

'Dear Lord, God above, tell me should follow this man I love. Please be kind and show me a sign. I only wish to do the will of thine.'

It was precisely at this moment that Deborah reemerged into the dressing room. The Professor tagging behind her.

"So I see you have been discussing the demonstration. Eva, you trust your man, don't you? Trust him to look out for your welfare and keep you from harm," the authoritative fatherly figure cross-examined. The Professor had a talent of focusing on the crux of any situation with crystal clarity.

"I suppose that I do," Eva ventured dubiously. Uncertain as to whether this man was the answer to her prayer.

"Then have faith in me. I am the teacher of this particular demonstration of mental prowess. I have performed it many times with great success. I have taught your Herman how to perform the feat, and now I am going to teach you."

He walked over to where she was sitting and tilted her head skyward so that his eyes could gaze down into hers. "You will learn to relax and enjoy a greater contentedness than you have ever known before. You are filled with joy and elation. When you hear my voice or that of your man, you will know that you are perfectly safe and will surrender complete control. Do you understand?"

"Yes." The long, drawn out answer emerged from the mouth of Herman's protégée.

"Good. You are a wonderful and understanding person." The Maharajah paused. "Now hear me, Eva. I will tell you the secret of the trick, and you will teach it to yourself. When you hear the control voice tell you to go to sleep, you will put yourself into a trance so deep, your bodily functions will slow down to a fraction of normalcy. Your mind, your wonderful mind, will slow your autonomic responses down to a small fraction of regular. Your breath will become but a whisper." He paused again to let the enormity of the instruction permeate her unconscious mind. "You will in no way be harmed by this condition. Instead your body will take this time to strengthen itself, repair itself, and cleanse itself. Do you hear me in the depths of your unconscious?"

Another long drawn out affirmative from the seated woman, clearly entranced. But this was different from when Herman had put her under. Her conscious was present and participating in this ceremony. In fact, she suddenly felt as if she were many people combined within the one. An entire audience witnessing and participating in this drama. They understood, were calmed, by the knowledge and most importantly, they were willing.

She, the part that was most distinctly Eva, regretted that from this vantage point she seemed submerged under water. Looking out at these three figures peering into her, two men and a woman, she recognized them instantly. Emoted strong feelings for two of them; felt calmed by the presence of the third. She just wished it wasn't so difficult for her to communicate with them from her world. To express, nay to share, with them the joy she was feeling at this moment.

Outside, in what passes for the real world, the three conspirators peered inward trying to gauge the progress of their protégée. Deborah and Herman, remaining skeptical, were unsure of the Maharajah's mental manipulations.

"I have put her in a light preparatory trance, not unlike the one you saw me perform on Gloria," the Professor advised. "While not fully conscious, she is not fully under either. So watch what you say. As you have heard, she has been instructed as to what is expected of her and how to internally prepare her body. As she is trusting of you Black Jack then by rote, she accepts my authority over her as her control. If she did not, her mind would have rebelled and shaken off this suggestive state. As it stands, her acceptance of the hypnotism signals that the majority of her mind has acquiesced and consented to the performance."

"The majority of her mind?" said Black Jack querulously.

"There is a theory among psychiatrists and hypnotists that the mind of an individual is actually honeycombed with a plethora of personalities. Some studies cite the observance of multi-personality disorders as proof of the 'community of consciousnesses' within the human mind. But we don't have time for a discussion on Rationalistic Pantheism right now. Since she is receptive, when do you want to do this?"

Herman needn't have looked at his watch. He already knew it was too late today. He was just stalling for time. "Like we did last time. Early in the morning," he said finally.

"Very well. Early tomorrow morning it is. I will have the boys pack a table and some chairs. We'll make it a picnic."

Professor Maharajah ceased conversation and returned to bend over Eva, who with her many personalities, had been observing the discourse.

"Eva," he spoke distinctly and directly to her, face to face.

"Yes, I'm here," she responded after a moment. Her dominant

personality having had time to swim to the surface and bridge the gap to the outer universe.

"Eva, I'm going to release you. Command you to release yourself from your reverie. You will remember everything that has transpired this afternoon, and your acceptance as evidenced by your cooperation. Do you understand?"

Eva nodded. The word "yes" was clearly audible.

The Professor concluded, "You will rejoin our company now." Forcefully he clapped his hands together in front of her face.

Eva, her various personalities suddenly reincorporated, looked up at them. There was a discernable sparkle in her eyes that bespoke clarity and consciousness. It hadn't been there a moment earlier. In her confused state, Eva tried to speak and rise from her seat at approximately the same time. She accomplished neither and fainted dead away instead.

Black Jack rushed the chair and cradled her in his strong arms to prevent her from falling to the floor, to protect her. His love for her suddenly manifest in an overwhelming paternal urge. A desire to protect her from all harm.

Madame Deborah, the oracle, had not foreseen the event. She gasped in shock and dismay.

To Professor Maharajah Hypnotist Supreme, there was no cause for concern. He stated as much flatly to allay the concerns of his partners. "Not to worry. This sometimes happens to first timers upon reanimation and emersion into the conscious world. After a few minutes she will be fine. In a couple of hours, she will feel as right as rain."

But Herman wondered to himself now suddenly protective of his trusting young love, how will she feel tomorrow morning, then afternoon and how about all the tomorrows to come? He winced mentally at the ordeal he was asking her to undergo. That he himself was prepared to put her through. Black Jack, his namesake dominant personality, deeply regretted this decision, but it had to be done. There was no going back.

The next morning the fog broke early. A warm wind coming up from the central valley encouraged the wisps of moisture to take flight out to sea. The warm air and clear sky above the rising sun promised a San Francisco day with temperatures above the normal for the advent of fall. Promised temperatures above normal for most days in the seaside city. It would be the perfect day for a picnic.

Eva awoke from a sound sleep with a curious notion floating to the surface. She rolled over in bed and addressed her lover, who was already awake lying there in silence contemplating her.

"Daddy, are we going on a picnic today?" There was that coquettish voice, that trusting nature. She was his little girl again.

"Yes, baby, we are going on a picnic today. We are going to have a wonderful time," he monotoned remorsefully. 'Better get out of bed and get the day over with.' He was glum. His thoughts were glum. He hated himself. 'The show must go on,' from what depths of his being did that hellish voice stem.

They arose, dressed and had a light repast. Just tea, cakes and jam. Nothing too heavy to unsettle the stomach, to cause any gastronomic distress. Once he put her in the ground, he wouldn't be able to look after her, care for her. This had to go right the first time. They were all at the mercy of Professor Maharajah, trusting his expertise, his competence. 'You see, he's not putting his wife underground,' one of his rogue personalities taunted him. Perhaps the one that loved Eva the most, urging a sense of caution. 'I don't even know if he is married,' Herman responded. Maybe he was once. Maybe he did once. Who knows? He never talks about himself. He seems one-dimensional, perfection of craft his only goal. Black Jack knew this secret. Great discipline was required if you wanted to stay on top, continue to be one of the best.

It was just about then that Deborah rang up on the telephone. She would join them on their trek up the hill in a few moments. Now the bad news, Lilly had refused to join. She had stated flatly to Deborah that she would have no part in the proceedings. "Sorry to be the bearer of the bad news BJ, but that's how it stands."

"Very well. See you soon," Black Jack barked into the receiver and hung up savagely. 'So the rats have begun to desert the ship,' his mind peppered. I won't tell Eva. Let her concentrate on her illusion. Save all her strength for the ordeal ahead. She would need it.'

As before, they were waiting for the trolley car to take them to their rendezvous with the Professor at the fail-grounds. With frightening precision, the trolley turned onto their street at the junction below and emerged from the shadows just in time for them to board. Three solitary figures entered and took seats in the middle. Neither looking nor interacting with the sparsely populated coach early that Monday morn. Two of them had a lot on their mind; the third had surprisingly little.

Disembarking with many of the passengers at the fairgrounds, they were greeted warmly from across the street by their companions.

"Great day for a picnic. Looks like fine weather," shouted the Professor eager to maintain the charade, both inwardly for his cohorts and outwardly to the world.

"Yes, yes, a little warm for September," Herman said crossing the road. Deborah and Eva in tow.

"Nonsense," came the reply. "Nothing better than a warm, dry September day." Black Jack realized that the assurances no matter how superficial were beneficial and welcomed indeed. Deborah smiled thinly, with her arm around Eva, who was beginning to look lost.

The Maharajah continued in conversational tones, "I've borrowed a car for you three. One of my boys will drive you. When we get there you and Deborah can start setting up the table and chairs for our picnic. The boys will get right to work. For this demonstration, we will go down the full six feet." Receiving the confirmation from the glint in the other man's eyes, he continued in hushed tones. "Better leave her in the backseat until we are ready."

In an instant, Black Jack caught his secret. That's how he dealt with it. He depersonalized the event. Dehumanized the assistant performing the stunt. Relegated her to the status of an object to be used. Nothing more. In that same instant, he surmised that if Professor Maharajah had ever been married, he certainly was not still wed.

The twin peaks were waiting for them. The position of their previous experience still visibly outlined in the rocky soil of the narrow valley. They parked the truck in front of their area of operation to obscure observation from chance. Herman and Deborah set up table and chairs as requested under neighboring trees. It was a little early in the day for a picnic,' Herman's subconscious nagged. 'What they really resembled was a band of gypsies up to mischief-making.' Which was essentially what they were. He sincerely hoped that no one passing by in the distance would take serious notice. He could envision the unpleasant legal entanglements.

Eva continued to sit in the backseat of the automobile, apparently not a care in the world.

Deborah noticed it first, pointing it out to Herman. "Look BJ, she seems to be talking to herself." Indeed, Eva was engaged in what looked like quite an animated conversation.

In an instant Deborah concluded, "I will go and sit with her. You get the Professor."

Arriving at the auto, she entered the back seat and sought to comfort her companion. "Honey, is everything all right?"

"I don't know. I feel weird inside somehow. Something is about to happen, and I don't like it." Eva burst forth with that last powerfully. Somewhere deep inside, she knew.

Deborah wrapped her arms around Eva to offer solace, comfort, security. She held her tightly as a mother would with her chin to the top of the younger woman's head. "Do you know what, hun? I'm going to give you a reading. Would you like that?"

"Un huh," Eva's cathartic response.

Deborah, who had never lied to Eva, indeed who held her craft in such high regard that she virtually never lied to anyone about the visions that she glimpsed, would not do so today either. "Eva, you will arise like the phoenix- spreading your wings, beautiful and incessant. Do not fear the ending of things, for these events are truly the beginnings of our journey." Deborah loosened her grip to look her charge in the eye and soothe with a, "There isn't that better? Nothing to worry about."

Eva remained silent with a glazed, distant look in her eyes.

Black Jack arrived with Professor Maharajah at his heels. "The post hypnotic suggestion is breaking down. That happens sometimes. It's all right. We are ready for her now anyway." The

Professor sounded quite complacent in his expert diagnosis of the patient's condition.

The trio extricated Eva from the car and headed her over toward the occluded side of the truck, away from the potential for prying eyes. The box lay next to the graveside, open and waiting.

Herman was speaking with the Professor; Deborah had Eva by the hand, soothing.

Suddenly sanity broke through and Eva bucked. Instantly the magicians were upon her, holding her solidly within their grasp.

"Daddy, I can't do this," she screamed, balking at the thought of going into the enclosed box.

Professor Maharajah turned her to face him and spoke roughly to gain her attention, calm her fears before they became uncontrollable. "Look at me." He held her tightly, his fingers taut above her elbows. "I said look at me." Fearfully, her gaze rose to meet his cold stare. "Now there is nothing to be afraid of ever again. Do you understand?"

"Yes," meekly his subject mewed.

"Now, concentrate. Look only at my eyes. Nowhere else." His voice was hard, insistent, demanding. She was compelled by his power of will to do his bidding.

She stared deeply into his iris' becoming mesmerized within the bottomless dark pools. They held at once, everything and nothing at all. An entire universe in his eyes. Consciousness expired. Her trance-induced body fell limp. Black Jack, who was holding her shoulders from behind, felt the extra weight and knew that she was truly under.

Professor Maharajah spoke to her slowly and in a deep voice. "Repeat after me. I am your control."

"You are my control," Eva monotoned.

"Listen to me, child. You will live a long and prosperous life. Do you hear me?" her interrogator bellowed.

"Yes, I will live a long and prosperous life." Eva repeated apparently without meaning, but somewhere deep within, the statement and its affirmation struck a distinct chord.

"You will perform this trick without fear. Nothing can hurt you. Do you understand?"

"Yes. Nothing can hurt me," repeated Eva, this time with some semblance of confidence.

The Professor was satisfied. "Very good. Now when you hear my voice again, we will be ready to begin." The Professor motioned instructions to his assistants not wishing to speak or lighten his grip on the girl for fear of breaking the spell.

"Eva, you will now go to sleep. When you awaken, you will feel refreshed and with an elation that you have not felt since you were a child. This will be a very deep sleep. Do you understand? You must obey your control."

"Yes, a deep sleep. Good night." And upon the completion of her answer, Eva's head fell sideways. For all intents and purposes, she was dead to the world.

Gently, ever so gently, they lowered her into the waiting box. Herman touched her cheek tenderly with the back of his ring hand before the assistants quickly screwed the lid into place. He helped them to maneuver and position the box in its waiting receptacle.

Deborah bore the true demeanor of a mourner. Somber and pensive with her hands clasped together below her waist. Her head angling down toward the grave as the box rapidly disappeared below the dirt shoveled in by assistants, now experts in their work. When the hole was completely filled, rocks were strewn over the area in attempt to obscure the evidence.

Afterward when the job was done, it was barely mid-morning. Still too early for a proper picnic, but never mind, one had to play the part. The show must go on and all that.

Shovels were stowed behind the seat in the cab of the truck until needed in another four hours. Picnic lunch was brought out and the table set. However, no one had an appetite for much of anything, including conversation. Herman smoked cigars pensively for the duration. While Deborah sipped coffee and picked at a cold plate, Eva slumbered entombed.

The sun continued its arduous journey across the sky, taking an eternity to reach the apex that signaled the noon hour. Herman mused as he chewed on the end of his second cigar that the old fellow in the chariot that pulled the sun across the sky must have a broken wheel. It was certainly an excruciatingly long journey. Made all the more so because his baby was interred alive in a patch of dirt alongside him. "How much longer," he inquired brusquely of his mentor, the great hypnotist,

"About an hour and a half," came the unemotional response. "Don't worry. If my girl can do four hours, so can your Eva. I have personally seen yogi's entrance themselves, slowing their heartbeat down to ten, twenty beats per minute and stay in that condition for four days!"

"But they have years of training, mental discipline," countered Herman.

"Correct," agreed the Professor. "Four hours is enough for a novice. Eventually with training and practice, you can increase the duration to six hours without concern for her health or safety."

Somehow this candid conversation relaxed the worried magician. Imagine him and Eva practicing this demonstration, honing their craft. The image was pleasing to him somehow.

Deborah continued to say nothing, do nothing, but pick at her snack abstractedly. Sympathetic vibrations carried by some ethereal transport now bound the two women together. Madame Deborah could now sense the others essence. She was comforted by the knowledge that at least Herman's protégé was at peace. She reassured with her mind that it would be over soon.

Finally, it was. The Professor checking his pocket watch instructed his lads to "get the shovels" and "get to work."

The exhumation process proceeded rapidly. By the time the coffin lid was uncovered, that was enough for Black Jack. "Let's get her out of there," he cried, charging the box screwdrivers in hand.

When they had her sitting up in the box surrounded by upturned dirt, the Professor commanded, "Eva, wake up. The picnic is over. You have played your part well. After a long hot day in the sun you will sleep well tonight. In the morning you will awaken feeling refreshed and elated. Do you hear me?"

"Yes, Professor. I am very tired. I need to sleep," she muttered feebly.

Herman turned to Deborah and mouthed with finality, "Help me get her up, and let's get out of here." The three of them moved to the car and rapidly departed.

IX
White Lies

The next morning, the beginning of another beautiful late summer's day, cast a pall over the Herman household. Eva had awoken feeling refreshed and famished just as the good Professor had predicted. Outwardly there was no difference in the young woman, not that anyone could tell. Still Black Jack felt that something was amiss. The gaiety that had once surrounded their San Francisco sojourn was gone forever. He had to pay the price.

Every good magician knows about the price paid to the piper, paid to the gods of necromancy or whomever. Every new trick, illusion came with a price attached. A payment in exchange for the knowledge and expertise required for the performance. The acquirer did not always know in advance what the price would be. Only that he would recognize it when it manifest.

Black Jack initially sensed that something about Eva was different. She was colder somehow, aloof and distant. Almost as if she had taken on a philosophical persona. She would get these far away looks in her eyes and stare off into the distance. His little girl was gone. So this was the price he had to pay for the promised power and fame that the demonstration would provide. 'It had better be worth it,' his mind chided. 'I'll make it worth it for both of us,' came the dogged reply to the doubting elements within his persona. The one thing that bothered him the most was the uncertainty over what price Eva had paid. He doubted that she would ever be able to tell him what she left behind in San Francisco, up on that hill.

Lilly was the first of several visitors that day. She came around about noon with hot soup. "How's our patient doing?" she shouted to Herman as she entered the small apartment the couple had rented for their stay in the bay area.

Black Jack glowered at her, but technically could do no more since the performers and crew were on notice that the road show in its current form was being disbanded. "She's just fine, still a little weak but that's to be expected. I'll go and get her." Apparently he had been brooding, an unfamiliar habit. His shoulders still slumped; he left to fetch his starlet.

"Oh, hey honey. How are you feeling today?" Lilly greeted the couple, mostly Eva, with effervescence. Herman had returned with Eva solidly within his grasp. His arms clutched her shoulders supporting, directing her steps. Almost half again as tall and though not more than ten years apart in age, they somehow now fully resembled a father and daughter instead of a loving couple.

"Oh, I feel just fine." Eva told a white lie. "We really had some day yesterday. They called it a picnic. You should have been there." Her weary smile stretched her face, thinly disguising the ordeal she had undergone. Lilly wondered if Eva felt as uncomfortable as she looked.

"I just couldn't, honey. Look, I brought you some soup. Just the thing for when you break a fast," replied Lilly earnestly wishing to change the subject.

"Oh, thanks. I've had breakfast already. I'll have some later. I'm sure it's good. You always took such good care of me."

Now it was Herman's turn to feel uncomfortable. "I'll leave you ladies alone to chat. I've got to run out for a couple of hours and see to the shipping arrangements. Andrew's got the bills of lading fouled up again." He stopped to grab a hat and some fresh cigars before heading for the door. Pausing, he couldn't resist one final attempt at bravado. "You take good care of her, Lil."

She waved him out the door without further comment. Turning

to Eva, who was sitting on the couch next to her, she hugged Eva long and hard. "I'm so sorry. I'm so sorry," she repeated over and over into the other's ear, tears streaming down her face. Suddenly she pulled back, afraid that she might crush Eva in her fragile condition and regarded her maternally.

Eva, appearing none the worse for wear, began comforting her friend. "Don't worry. It's a good thing you didn't come. That would have made it all the harder. You know how emotional you get. Besides, Deborah was there, and she comforted me when the time came. She really is very empathetic." Lilly relaxed visibly while Eva continued. "At first, I was okay. Professor Maharajah had given me some sort of post hypnotic suggestion that I was going to a picnic. I felt very lightheaded, but elated. I guess I even imagined people milling about and children playing. You know like at a church social." Lilly nodded listening attentively. "Then reality intruded and I heard voices saying, 'You know what they are gonna do to ya? They're gonna put you into the ground. Bury you alive.' I argued with them. Then Deborah appeared and said some kind things to me, told me everything was going to be all right. I relaxed, felt warm inside. You know, contented.

Soon after, the men came to get me, Black Jack and that Professor. He grabbed me and spun me around to look at him. The last thing I remember was staring into his eyes, those dark bottomless pits. The next thing I knew the voices were telling me it's all over, time to go home and sleep." Eva finished abruptly, looking sheepishly at Lilly.

For long minutes, Lilly sat flabbergasted, her mouth open, unsure of what to say or do next. Then she just gushed with overflowing emotion. "Oh honey, when I found out just what they wanted to do, I couldn't have any part of it, couldn't stand to...witness." Her voice broke, words failed her.

"You know they didn't even ask me if I would perform the trick. They wanted you. Herman said you were more receptive and that Professor Maharajah," Lilly said his name with derisive emphasis, "He agreed that you were better suited due to your smaller build. You are about the same size as his assistant Gloria. Rumor has it that they performed a sample demonstration on her. Black Jack wanted to see the trick performed on someone else before he risked using you."

"Oh, he did! That's so sweet," Eva interrupted with a sudden burst of feeling.

Lilly continued undeterred. She had come not to praise this man, who had until recently been her employer and confidant, but to destroy him in Eva's eyes. "No, it's not sweet. It's despicable what they did to you. Not at all like the fun and games we had around the apartment in Chicago. That was just a harmless light trance, and we were never out for long. Nobody ever got hurt. Just a little embarrassed is all. And the 'Voodoo Tour.' That was all just a big joke. A con game we played on the audience. There was no danger involved.

But this...this is out of bounds. It goes beyond all rhyme and reason. It is dangerous and deplorable." Lilly stopped there, not wishing to overtly jinx Eva by insinuating that she might come to harm by continuing this type of performance. Show folk are very superstitious people.

Lilly was satisfied that she had made her position clear and then Eva could make up her mind for herself. Unspoken in her postpartum protestations was her fear of Black Jack and possible reprisals. She could not have spoken earlier lest she queer the rabbit from the trap and spoil the hunter's fun. She could voice her opinion now that the rabbit was already ensnared and leave with a clear conscious.

Eva understood perfectly, knowing the nature of the beast. She was grateful that anyone spoke up at all on her behalf. 'Risking the consequences of meddling in matters which they could not possibly understand,' that would be Black Jack talking, his words in her head. Strange that she could sense his thoughts more clearly now. Afterward, a lot of things were becoming clearer to her. Take her feelings for the man; they seemed to be evolving from awestruck puppy love to dogged devotion. She now possessed an unflappable determination that she would stand by his side forever and share his glory. She couldn't put her finger on why and when this profound change had occurred. She guessed maybe she was just maturing.

Anyway she was glad that Lilly had come over to express her concerns, and she told her so in no uncertain terms. Assuring her that while a little tired, she was fine and had accepted the new direction the act was taking and her role in the drama. "Black Jack knows best," she reasoned.

Lilly took this opening to indicate that, now that "things had changed," if it was okay, she would head on back to Chicago on her own. Maybe set up housekeeping with some lucky paramour.

"You know it's high time I got on with my life, left the road behind. Settle down with some man and raise a family. Isn't that the great American dream?"

Eva inquired sincerely, "I thought you were looking for Mr. Right?"

Lilly, with a hint of the charm reminiscent of their early days together and a glint of mischief in her eye, replied, "Honey, they're all Mr. Right when those lights go out." Both girls giggled like sisters.

So Eva released Lilly from her obligations and sent her on her way, promising to call upon her when the couple returned to their Chicago apartment. "We'll go shopping when I get back," she promised. "And of course we will have you over for the holidays. Why we'll have plenty of times together."

They both knew it wasn't true. It is just the sort of thing that you tell friends upon parting. The little white lies that soften the pangs of separation. That mitigate the reality of the ending of things.

After Lilly left, Eva went to the kitchen and examined the soup, the parting gift from her friend. It smelled good. Beef broth, she thought, filled with the aroma of garlic. She could see peas and carrots floating in the sea of brown. She tasted with an index finger. Umm, salty. Her body craved salt. She knew what that meant.

However delectable, she was too tired to eat right then. Her stomach groaned at the concept of containing food. She grasped a half a glass of water from the kitchen faucet, that was all she could stand, and went back to the bedroom to await Black Jack. She suddenly felt very tired and alone.

The berth on the Twentieth Century Limited was just the same size it had been on their journey to California. Now however, it was uncomfortably small and confining, especially when the two of them were there together. The tiny bathroom was a nightmare. She couldn't even go in unless the door was left open. So when she had to go, she bade Herman to leave the compartment so that she might have her privacy. He gingerly complied without hesitation or comment. In fact, she began to notice in him a deference to her needs and desires. At least their new 'mature' relationship was beginning to have its perks. She would have to ruminate on exactly how to exercise this new found power she had over him. 'Was it not said that turnabout was fair play?'

As a consequence of her growing claustrophobia, she spent a lot of time in the parlor car on their homeward trip. Sometimes with Herman, others alone, with a magazine in her lap unread, staring out as the rocky mountain ranges receded into the background. Not admiring the purplish majestic mountains but just staring past those cold, ice covered tops, lost in thought. Somewhere deep inside, she knew that instead of lamenting the past, what she had lost, she needed to embrace the future and the endless possibilities outstretched before her. It would take just a little longer to come to grips with the situation.

Late in the evening on the second night, after the train had left the mountains of Colorado for the flat grain covered plains below, Eva awoke in a pool of sweat. Perhaps it was the downward motion of the train that set off this particular vexation. Perhaps just another in a series of bad dreams, she had four so far in the week since the 'event.' Upon waking in the bottom bunk, she completely forgot that they were traveling by train. To awake from a nightmare where having been buried alive unconscious, you revive to find dirt pouring in all around, smothering and suffocating you as the coffin fills to the brim, only to find that you are still in a metal coffin struggling for your survival. That was too much for her mind to process in those first brief moments of consciousness. She started kicking and screaming, scratching wildly at the metal slab above her head that supported the upper berth.

Herman jumped down in an instant, his being awakened in mid night by her screaming and crying was becoming routine. However, this time no matter how hard he tried, she would not go back to sleep in that room. Ringing for the porter, George was his name, he paid the man twenty dollars to help him move her blankets and pillows to the parlor car where Black Jack sat and cradled her until after dawn's early light had broken across the receding mountain tops and they could hear the stewards setting up for breakfast in the dining car adjacent. She had been dozing fitfully in his arms until at this last she was awakened gently by his voice. "Come on, baby. Let's get you cleaned up and get some breakfast into you. By tonight we will be home."

Home was not what Eva had in mind, at least not their home. By the time the train pulled into Union Station, she had decided to exercise her newfound power.

Announcing simply that she wanted to go to St. Louis and see her parents' new home, Eva instructed the porter to hold her bags for the next train south.

Black Jack, far from objecting, agreed heartily that this would be a marvelous diversion for her. "Yes, go home and see your folks. Stay in the new home that your efforts have purchased for them. Stay for a week or more. While you are gone, I will get the apartment up and running. Don't worry about me; I have plenty to do here. You go and have a good time," he said jovially.

"I don't know how long I will be gone," she replied icily. "Maybe a couple of weeks. Maybe longer."

She was in luck. The evening train to St. Louis would be boarding in just over an hour. This gave her time to send a telegram to her folks. She kept it short and succinct: Keep the light on- arriving tonight- Eva. 'There, that will keep them from being too surprised when I show up. Hope I don't startle them too much,' she thought to herself. Right now her mind realized she was the best company she could keep and her advice to herself- get out from under all of the competing influences. Get off the merry-go-round for a while. 'Get out of town and away from Black Jack!' She desperately wanted a drink; she settled for a coke.

Emotionally, Eva didn't know if she could ever forgive him for what he had done to her. If he really loved her, cared for her, how could he let that awful man into her mind? Ugrech! Sitting there in the coach, the clickety-clack of the wheels over rails, thundering below, Eva could still feel his alien tendrils coursing their way through her thoughts. He had done something to her, left suggestions, changed her somehow. She couldn't identify how. Eva only knew that she was not the same. Would never be the same again.

If Herman was watching over her, protecting her, why didn't he say something? Stop the procedure? Maybe the manipulations were too subtle, unobservable to the naked eye. Professor Maharajah was a master of hypnotism while Black Jack was only a novice. Maybe there was no way to stop him from performing mind twisting machination. She continued to search her feelings. A chorus of personalities assisted her in her efforts. There <u>was</u> something deep down out of reach, just out of focus.

She resigned herself to her fate, shoulders slumping forward slightly. Unconsciously she stiffened the muscles of her lower back, lest she fall completely off of the bouncing coach seat.

Eva continued the process of rationalization and repair within her being. She knew Black Jack still loved her as much as ever. Look at the way he was caring for her, doted on her. He was like a recalcitrant little boy. He let his ego and ambition get in the way and now he was sorry that things had gotten out of hand. Well, it had happened before, but he had never asked this much of her, so taken advantage of her trusting nature. No matter that they were lovers, there were boundaries and they must be respected!

Eva decided that she would eventually forgive him. 'Was there ever any doubt? Was there ever any choice?' But before she did bestow upon him the tender mercy of her forgiveness; she would make him sweat and pay. 'Yes,' all the voices agreed she would make him pay. Maybe a month in the country with her parents would show him. 'Serve him right if she stayed more than a month! 'The grinding of gears and the concurrent slowing of wheels brought Eva back to the outside world. In less than three hours from the eight o'clock departure the train, the City of New Orleans, was pulling into St. Louis. My, but her parents would be surprised to see her. 'What would she tell them? How could she downplay her impromptu visit? It was a good thing she had purchased presents for everybody in San Francisco.'

Black Jack and Carl arrived home to a dark, deserted apartment. "Ah, home at last," Herman exclaimed as he cast off outer garments, throwing them carelessly onto the first available chair.

"Drop those bags anywhere. Relax and take a load off. It has been a long journey, and the first thing I need is a good stiff drink. How about you, Carl?"

"That sounds like a fine idea, sir," he said depositing Herman's suitcases in a corner.

"Here we go my man, scotch rocks. I've found half a bottle of the good stuff. After we finish this why don't we go out and get something to eat? Wasn't that railroad food the worst?" Black Jack inquired semi-rhetorically while handing his chauffer/bodyguard a tumbler of whiskey.

"It wasn't too bad this trip. I've 'had worse," Carl offered, sipping his drink.

"You're right there," said Herman, downing his drink in one large gulp. "Ah, that's better. I guess we both have had worse in our time together, eh?"

"You know it. Some nights we were so hungry we could eat the scraps off one of those tables. If we could get it." Carl laughed heartily while Black Jack refilled both their glasses.

"Well anyway, I feel like a nice thick steak smothered in onions, with potatoes swimming in gravy. Are you with me?" Black Jack was beginning to feel more like himself as he contemplated a boys night out.

"I'll be right behind you all the way," Carl assented. "Oh, just remember the railroad said they will deliver the trunks early in the morning."

"Shit, why do they have to be so damn prompt?" Herman rankled. Then another thought, "I wonder if Andrew has arrived yet with our props?"

"He should be back. Didn't his train leave the day before ours?" Carl ventured tentatively, sipping his second scotch.

"What do you think of him?" Black Jack demanded suddenly. "I mean, how is he handling the show?"

"Well, boss," the big man began diplomatically. "Anybody filling your shoes will have to take some time to adjust, us to him and vice versa. He does a fine job getting the show off on time. He's just a little hard on the whip," Carl finished earnestly.

"I know. I know. You know that he's my brother and some time back we got into a spate of trouble, and he bailed me out. I sorta owe him. You understand."

"Don't worry, sir, we all understood. Besides, you have bigger things on your mind. The elevation of the act and all," Carl commiserated.

"Very perceptive of you, my lad." Black Jack was slightly tipsy. He had been off the hard stuff since the first week in San Fran. "I have to keep focusing on the big picture. Gotta get ready for the big show in the big town. New York. Ever been there?" Black Jack was in a rollickingly good mood now.

"No, sir. But I hear it is fantastic. Bigger than Chicago." Carl was warming to the unaccustomed comradery.

"Bigger and better, Carl. Bigger and better," pouring the last of the scotch into his glass Black Jack announced. "I'm getting hungry. Let's get after that food."

The two men, upon reaching the garage and locating their cars, were in for a big surprise. The limo and the roadster were in a forlorn state of disrepair. The limousine was sitting on four flattened tires. One headlight was shattered. The roadster, looking like a wounded animal, was flat in the front. The broad white walls clearly displaying puncture marks where the air was liberated.

They approached the vehicles with a sense of shock and incredulity. Black Jack stood by the roadster, his baby, with hand on the front grill in a comforting gesture.

"All four are punctured over here." Carl shouted his report none too discretely.

"Who could have done this to me? Don't they know who I am?" Black Jack exploded, yelling wildly.

"Well, sir, they can't be fixed tonight. I'll have to stop by the store and purchase some new tires in the morning," Carl said, shaking his head in disgust.

Black Jack, no longer hungry, was furious. He would find the person or persons with the unmitigated gall to mess with his things.

With the temerity to try and muck up his life. And he would make them pay for this outrage. Pay double.

Carl could see the other's seething rage and attempted to coerce him. "It's probably just kids. Better to just forget the whole incident. Let's go back upstairs and have another drink. I know you've got some more booze stashed somewhere. While you do that I'll raid the kitchen and rustle us up something to eat. Let it go. Tomorrow is another day." The big man had to almost forcibly drag the magician away from the cars. But he did manage to get his boss back upstairs. By the hardest.

The anger over the incident subsided the next couple of days. However, the feeling of violation remained. Black Jack was first and foremost clearly possessive of his personnel and belongings, and he harbored the idea that this vandalism was not some random act, but personal upfrontery. Not something soon to be forgotten.

The tasks at hand occupied his mind as he proceeded to put his house in order. Andrew had arrived and warehoused the props as ordered. He was woefully behind in his correspondence pertaining to the mail order business, but that was understandable given the daily demands of the road.' Black Jack would help his brother smooth out kinks and delays, show him the ropes. After which he'd check on the wife and kids.

Carl had done yeoman's work on the vehicles, including tune ups on both. All in one days time. That man was worth his weight in gold.

The maid had been in and the digs were once more habitable. 'Did they really leave it in such a state of disarray?' Well, never mind. The rooms were now in acceptable condition to greet Eva. 'Wonder when she would decide to return?' his mind queried. It had been over a week with only one phone call to say that she had arrived safely. Better let her have her space. She couldn't stay away forever. She <u>had</u> to return. Professor Maharajah said so: 'She will never leave you,' he promised.

Black Jack believed that to be true, trusted in the amazing skill of the man. Truth be known, was in awe of him. The only man alive that he could say that about and only the second man that he had ever met in his lifetime. Sorry as he was, after the fact, of what he had put her through, he still celebrated the result. She would never completely leave him. Eva, in return, would have his undying devotion.

Towards the end of their fourth day back in Chicago, Mr. Entolleni himself, showed up with their liquor order.

"Hey, boss, you made it back. How was your trip? Pleasant, I trust." The man was as dapper and self-effacing as his men.

"Yes, we were successful in our endeavors." Black Jack kept details to a minimum. He had long ago made up his mind to separate himself from these gentlemen (i.e. thugs) as much as possible.

"Great, glad to hear it. Businessmen like us need to keep expanding our endeavors. Isn't that right?" The dapper dandy didn't wait for an answer. "Of course, a man of the world like you knows that." He was full of himself and started to babble. "I admire you, you know? A man like yourself, rising above your disparities to stake a claim on stardom and fame. Taking a grab at the good life.

I like that. I'm doing just like you, expanding, reaching into new enterprises. We've gone from merchandising to entertainment to security work. Now I'm into personal security. Anybody bothers you instantly has a beef with me. And let me tell you, I settle a beef promptly." He looked Black Jack squarely in the eye to transport his meaning. The subtlety did not go unnoticed.

"If anybody messes with you, your people, your vehicles," he paused ever so slightly. "Why I'll take care of it. All for one low monthly fee."

Herman sensed he had just been given a sales pitch and smiled inwardly. He also understood now why his possessions had been disturbed. "I see. Thanks for the info. I have a bodyguard who takes good care of me and mine. But I will give it some thought. Now what do I owe you for your delivery? The usual?"

"Afraid not, boss. Due to circumstances beyond our control and increased competition from rival business organizations, the price has increased another twenty percent." A somewhat smug reply.

Black Jack paid the price gladly and watched the man leave. 'Good riddance!' he thought to himself after the nuisance had disappeared. If only they could make this supply last until time to head for New York in January. These people were getting too bold for comfort.

"What's the matter, child? Eva's mother was speaking. She had come out onto the porch to comfort her daughter who was sitting on the porch swing staring aimlessly into the night. A position she had occupied after dinner every night for the last week since her arrival.

"Oh, Mother." Eva finally broke down. "I have seen the evil that men do. The rich and the powerful, been inundated by the immensity of their crimes. I feel lost and soiled. I've gotten to the point that I'm not sure who I am anymore. Please don't tell Daddy, he wouldn't understand. I'm afraid he would disown me and never speak to me again." Eva sounded as if she was sobbing. She wanted to cry, but the tears wouldn't come.

"Oh, dear, don't worry. I would never tell your father. Wives do have some secrets they keep from their husbands." She winked at her daughter with a smirk. A vain attempt to cheer her.

"Oh, why did I do it? Why was I so headstrong?" Eva threw herself into her mother's arms.

"There, there honey. We all make mistakes, stumble sometimes. The only thing we can do is pick ourselves up and move forward. You need to search your feelings and then ask the Lord for guidance. After all, He will never let you get into a hole so big that He can't help you out again." An ironic choice of phrases on her part. Eva had never mentioned the cause of her current dilemma. "Even if you make a misstep, God can make a plan to have it come out for the better. For the enhancement of the common good."

She was stroking her daughter's long hair. Eva's face, buried in her mother's shoulder, had apparently remembered how to cry. She sobbed softly as her mother continued.

"Do you love this man? I mean, truly love him? Do anything for him as I would for your father?"

"Yes, I guess," came the meek reply from the little girl clutching her mother tightly.

"Then when you go back to him, as I know you will, tell him you will be his partner and work with him. Not his servant or a puppet who performs on command."

'How much did she know?' A wild itinerant thought crossed Eva's mind. She calmed herself, let the initial anxiety flow through and dissipate.

Her mother was still speaking, "If you work with him and trust in the Lord, then everything will work out. He will find a way to exercise you for His plans."

"Okay, Mother," Eva moaned into the other's shoulder.

"After all, I know BJ loves you. Look at the way he humbled himself before your father. I watched him. It is very hard for a proud man who had made his way in the world to demonstrate such subservience." Eva sat up to face her mother.

"Yes, you are quite right. That was very hard for him to do. I was so proud of him. He genuinely meant every word. I know him well enough to tell you that was not an act." Eva was wiping the tear stains from her face. Drying her eyes. It wouldn't do for the whole family to see her in her sorrows.

"You see, dear. Even your heart tells you that he loves you. He would never let anyone hurt you. I think he would even die for you. I have no doubt he would kill for you."

Eva looked her mother squarely in the eye and asked, "Mother, what makes you so smart?"

The instant reply, "Twenty five years of living with your father, honey. It's been on-the-job training since day one."

They both laughed softly together sitting there on the porch swing in the warm evening air.

Two weeks later, Black Jack called for her on the telephone. "Hey, babe. How are you doing?"

"I'm fine I guess," Eva coyly conveyed into the receiver.

"Hope you're well rested. In a couple of months it will be time to go to New York."

"Yes, I know." Her tone was noncommittal.

"I'm gonna send Carl with the limo to pick you up."

"I'll be ready," she avowed and placed the receiver back in its cradle.

Two days later, Carl arrived with the limo to reclaim Herman's pride and joy.

X
Pursuit of Happiness

Eva walked along Fifth Avenue in New York City. The cold, cloudy January day was turning to snow. As large puffy flakes descended from the low ceiling to settle upon the scurrying crowds, Eva cinched the mink coat around her neck to ward off the chill. It was a damp cold that crept into the bones and numbed the senses, not completely unlike Chicago, but different somehow. For one, there was no wind accompanying this onslaught as was so often the case in Chicago when the northern winds came off Lake Michigan and blew through you as if you were made of paper, transparent. The cold in this city gripped you tightly in its clutches and squeezed. Held you tightly in its grasp and became your innermost confidant. Eva feared that if she didn't get out of the cold, it would squeeze the living daylights out of her.

But where to go? She was tired of the shops, still brightly adorned with Christmas decorations and overpriced clothing. She tired of the prying eyes of the patrons, their curious glances. The cynical looks of the salesgirls surreptitiously following her every move as if she were about to pilfer a pocketbook or perhaps a bottle of expensive perfume. Even dressed as she was in her full length mink, Herman's Christmas present to her, she stood apart from the primped ladies of high society.

153

One salesgirl even asked if she was there to pick up a package. Eva smiled charitably at the young woman of about the same age, but did not correct her. 'She must think I'm the maid, having borrowed my mistress' coat to run an errand.' Then another thought, 'If it were not for Black Jack, she probably would be somebody's maid on an errand.'

No, she did not want to go back into those shops. The shopping excursion had been Herman's idea to get her out of the apartment. "Carl, take her downtown. Let her pick out some of the latest New York fashions." Then turning to Eva, "Darling, I want you to look your best while we are here. The crème de la crème of black society will be introduced to us over the next few weeks-including the first woman millionaire. We don't want to look like country bumpkins." Eva knew he exaggerated. They were always clothed in the finest garments wherever they went. He must want her gainfully occupied while he attended to business. So she would go see the shops, sample their offerings and take in the sights. One thing he had said stuck with her, intrigued her, 'Imagine the first woman millionaire was African-American.'

So now here she was several hours later having seen the shops and the sales help, et cetera. Walking along the street, still too early to return home, with the sky a darkening grey and snow beginning to stick to the sidewalk. In fact Eva had no intention of returning just yet. She continued to proceed in a direction away from Carl and the waiting limo. Looking for she knew not what. Eva was beginning to shiver insider her mink coat as the grip of the deepening cold tightened around her. A malevolent evil that constricted her breath which would burst forth form her being in small puffs. Clearly visible gasses that hung in midair momentarily until disintegrated by the continuing onslaught of falling snowflakes.

She was uncertain of her next move until she saw the rising edifice of the cathedral as it disappeared into the low hanging gloom. She would go inside the church and seek warmth. It was only after she was inside St. Patrick's Cathedral that she decided to seek forgiveness.

'Forgive me Father, for I have sinned.'' Having entered the confessional and seated herself, Eva began with the traditional opening. While not actually a Catholic, she was familiar with the trappings and after all she reasoned, 'It's the same God.'

"How long has it been since your last confession, my child?" the voice behind the screen inquired politely.

"Well, I've never confessed before. I am not actually a Catholic. I was born and raised Baptist. I was outside on the avenue, cold and tired, when I saw the church. It was only after entering that I realized how overwhelmed I have become by recent events."

"That's all right, my child. You just continue at your own pace. Unburden yourself. Let it all out." The priest's voice from the other compartment was soothing and strengthening.

All of a sudden, the dam burst and Eva poured out her heart to this closeted voice, an abject stranger. "Father, I have sinned. I have allowed powerful men to do terrible things to me." She paused to let the solemnity of her revelation reverberate through the booth. Never realizing that the priest, especially in this part of town, had probably heard this line many times before. Eva continued, filling the silence between them with her fears. "I am afraid that I have lost my faith. The faith that I grew up with as a child."

Eva was weeping softly now. She was sure that it showed in the delivery of her next line, her most secret fear. "Father, I am afraid that the things they ask me to do shall result in my demise. What shall I do? I am promised to a powerful man who believes that he is on the verge of greatness, on the verge of changing the course of human events here in America. His intensity, his devotion to his dream, sometimes it scares me. I think if things go badly it will destroy both of us." Tears flowed copiously down her cheeks. It was good to let it out.

"There, there, my daughter, do not despair. Place your fears and your faith in the bosom of the Lord. He will guide you and protect you from all evil," came the seemingly mechanical response. It did not satisfy her.

Eva, still sniffling and teary-eyed decided to tell him the rest of her story so that he could clearly see her plight. As she concluded the sordid tale, she explained, "So you see Father, I can never leave him, and I am afraid that if I stay terrible things will continue."

After a considered silence, the voice from the other side of the screen comforted. "Have no fear my child, for as the Bible says, 'He through faith is righteous shall live.' The priest paused to let the momentum of those words sink in and soothe the young woman. Then he began again, "Remember in Galatians 3 verse 9, 'So then those who are men of faith are blessed with Abraham who had faith.'" Before concluding, another verse came to him which seemed to apply particularly to this young woman in peril. "In another verse, my daughter, Paul seems to speak directly to you: 'Having begun with the Spirit, are you now ending with the flesh? Did you experience so many things in vain?-If it really is in vain.' That is your answer. The one you have come seeking. Never lose faith in yourself or your part of God's plan. Thus, just as Abraham believed in God and was rewarded, so shall you be also. Do not fear losing your faith-your moral compass is strong. Now go and let the love and warmth of God surround you and protect you."

Rejuvenated by her conference, Eva left feeling becalmed and warmed by his words. She no longer felt the external chill despite the steadily increasing snow and now biting wind that was marching an army of snowflakes down Fifth Avenue.

The month's engagement at Liberty Hall, Marcus Garvey's imposing structure in Harlem, began the same way each evening. A message of felicitations and congratulations by Marcus Garvey to Professor Herman and in response, Herman's salutations to his host and the audience.

General Garvey, as he was known to his friends, was never at a loss for words. "Professor Herman, I want to assure you that our welcome to you is warm and heartfelt. We hope you will enjoy our city and that the friendships made here will grow and deepen. This community welcomes you with open arms. We are indeed very grateful that you are here."

Professor Herman reciprocated with heartfelt emotion. "I am deeply honored by General Garvey's invitation extended to me to address you this evening. I have pleasant memories of my visit almost a year ago with my lovely assistant, Eva. The expressions of intellectual concern about our current direction and lack of progress, except in the most ephemeral and transitory matters. The intelligent conversation from our business leaders concerning their frustrated attempts to obtain capital to expand their enterprises. Even here in the financial capital of the country. All the while, well-financed interlopers carve up our markets among themselves, exporting our hard earned capital out of our community. Leaving us not impoverished, but neither advancing.

There seems to be a ceiling through which despite our best efforts, we are unable to break through. We are allowed the honor of being workers, but denied the dignity of ownership. The critical step that would allow us as businessmen, to control the flow of capital, redirecting it for projects that would benefit the entire community. In short, we need to become better organized in order to foster minority development."

General Garvey, beaming to the audience, "See? Didn't I tell you he is a fluent speaker? A man of extraordinary vitality and vision? In coming to know him through correspondence, I have come to admire his penetrating insight into the complexities of the interracial situation. He is indeed a man with the most remarkable mental powers of perception and persuasion. Furthermore, he has always performed his arduous illusions with a sense of seriousness and responsibility to his art form that few practicing professionals demonstrate. He comports himself with a feeling for the gravity of his craft. Also, his cognizance of the issues involved in social change in these modern times deserves your rapt attention."

With a final handshake, General Garvey left Herman alone at center stage to mesmerize the crowd.

"Wow!" Herman exclaimed. "Now that I have recovered from the General's generous introduction, I would like to begin with a ceremonious singing of 'America, the Beautiful.' I would now ask that you rise and sing that song to the President of the United States. Sing loudly to remind him that this is our country also. That we have inalienable rights for the equal pursuit of happiness guaranteed by Mr. Lincoln and ratified by Congress.

For those of you like me that can never remember the words, you can follow along on the screen over the stage. Now if you will all please stand. Maestro, if you please." Professor Herman led the audience in song.

After singing the anthem, the crowd quite invigorated was

ready for anything. It was at this point that Herman would usually tease, "Now how about a little magic?" The crowd already standing would naturally burst into ovation. This was Eva's cue to appear pushing a table containing various props onto the stage.

"Ladies and gentlemen, I am pleased to introduce to you my lovely assistant, Eva." Herman continued his well worn preamble born through years of practice. His comfort on stage with his possessions, his audience, showed. He truly was never more alive than when he was performing.

The professor began his performance with a little trick he called, 'The chicken or the egg.' Moving to the table, he placed his wand on the top hat sitting upright. "I would like to begin with a little philosophy question that has intrigued scholars over the centuries." Herman began, facing the audience with Eva standing attentively to one side. "Evolution theorists have presented us with an interesting question. Which came first, the chicken," He raises the hat to expose a full grown hen, only to lower it quickly and raise it once more evidencing a solitary white egg, "Or the egg?" The audience gasps.

"Creationism would have us believe that the chicken," he raises the hat again exposing the clucker, "Came first. Evolution would suggest the egg." Herman raises the hat once more then replaces it over the oval object. "Alas, we may never know for sure. Personally, I enjoy both fried chicken and scrambled eggs. I don't really care which came first." Professor Herman raised the hat one final time and displayed a plate of fried chicken and eggs to the audience, to the receipt of howls of laughter and thunderous applause. Herman would perform a few more standard magic tricks but kept the routine short. He did not want the crowd's attention to wane. After all, they had come to see 'Professor Herman Mentalist,' to be moved and swayed by his deeper more powerful secrets of mind control.

After the initial tricks were concluded and assistants had removed the trappings, Herman ordered the stage lights dimmed and a spotlight for center stage. Eva, who was standing center left, was again presented to the audience. "The lovely Eva will now help me demonstrate one of my most famous illusions which I learned from an East Indian Mahatma many years ago, the illusion of the lady floating in midair. To be properly performed, the subject must first be put into a deep trance." Black Jack stared into his lover's eyes and prepared to put her into a trance. By this time, all that was needed was a presaged hypnotic suggestion, the one that was conceived by Professor Maharajah in San Francisco using a secret code word. Of course, they had to put on a show for the crowd, turn the whole affair into a long, drawn out process. It was show business.

"Eva, look deeply into my eyes. You are growing tired. Your eyelids are heavy. You are falling under my spell." The professor continued for a few moments longer with drawn out hand movements and verbalizations. She swayed too and fro to his ministrations. Finally pronouncing, "There, it is done." Professor Herman would invite two or three women onstage to verify for the audience that indeed, Eva was entranced. Herman offered them a couple of dull pins with which to poke her and observe her reactions, or lack thereof.

All the while, other female assistants brought the levitation table onstage and waited dutifully for commands. Herman bid Eva to lie down on the table while the assistants covered her with a cloth. To a drum roll from the orchestra and conjuring verses from Herman, the spotlight narrowed its focus squarely on the table which seemed to rise into the air right on cue. The two lovely assistants then proceeded at Herman's urging to pass a golden hoop around the table top which hovered in midair. Thus proving 'no strings attached.' One woman would escort the hoop halfway, passing to the other assistant who would complete the journey. Herman would continue to hold the table suspended in space until he feigned tiredness and allowed the top of the table to float gently back into place.

Then to the cheering of the crowd, he bent over and revived his sleeping beauty. She sat up and momentarily stood up, joining Herman to receive the thunderous ovation of the standing crowd.

Now for the piéce de resistance, the moment many had come for, Professor Herman would seat himself in the chair provided by one of his girls who would then join her companion, scurrying about in the audience distributing and collecting little slips of paper containing the questions from the patrons. In many cases, no mere trivialities, the hopes and prayers of lives in torment were scribbled on those small scraps of paper. The crowd murmured with obvious anxiety and anticipation. Herman let them mutter amongst themselves until the fishbowls full of dreams and desires were delivered to the front of the stage. Retrieved by Eva, they were placed by his feet. She resumed her position standing dutifully by his side as he called the audience to order.

Beginning with all due solemnity, he proceeded as Madam Deborah had instructed, calling out each first name after reading the question and requiring the patron to stand.

By the end of the first week, word had spread of his 'marvelous dexterity' in handling questions of all types, from job loss to the prospect of marriage or divorce. Audience participants were amazed at his confidence in instantly handling complex issues. As with Madame Deborah's performances, many people would come just for the chance to have their question answered; many more would come just to be in his presence. They packed the hall night after night, a feat only accomplished by one other, Marcus Garvey himself.

So the crowds would come night after night and watch in awe, Herman sitting while Eva stood by his side-taking questions from the audience, up to one hundred a night. Many had never seen anything like this, the organized mayhem of Herman's attractive assistants scurrying about collecting slips of paper while the beautiful Eva, his masterpiece, stood center stage with her man in the spotlight.

She was his shill, attracting the audience's attention, while he read and figured out the best possible response to the customer's query. In the minute that he took for each question, searching for the author's true intent, the attention of the audience was split between the garish Eva and the standing writer of that particular quandary. This allowed Herman to search his psyche for the answer that would satisfy and form the response in a way that would provide the crowd with the greatest entertainment. It was certainly magic of the highest order. Having studied Madame Deborah for several years, he was able to copy her style and adroitly replicate her performances. The presence of Eva, her shining sensuality, deflected too close a scrutiny.

At the closing of each show, Professor Herman would leave the crowd with a little reminder of his political agenda. A small remunerative to carry with them until the next time they returned to Liberty Hall to see him perform. Many in the audience would do just that, returning over and over just to hear him speak.

"I would like to thank you all for coming," Herman would begin to the groans of the crowd, realizing with certainty that the question and answer segment had ended. Now standing he would continue, "I would just like to remind you that you cannot buy happiness. You cannot go to the local grocery and purchase a pound as you would flour. But since happiness comes from within, you can secure a measure of contentment by your own acts, and at the same time help your fellow man.

You can do this by supporting your local minority owned business and by purchasing products produced by minority owned manufacturers. They in turn will donate a portion of their profits to help the local minority economy and help the residents lift themselves out of impoverishment.

In closing, I would like to paraphrase the words of the great Abraham Lincoln who in a memorable address said: 'The world will little note, nor long remember what we say here, but hopefully it will never forget what we do here.' Thank you for coming. Good night." Herman would take Eva by the hand and leave the stage. Deigning not to return despite loud ovations and catcalls. As his mentor Prince Herman had advised, "Always leave them wanting more."

Exhorting the public every night, he continued the private pronouncements of his passions during the day- his passion for the advancement of colored peoples. In the third week of his tenure at Liberty Hall, Mr. Garvey hosted a celebratory luncheon at the headquarters of his Universal Negro Improvement Association. As both Master of Ceremonies and Chairman of the organization, General Garvey had the great pleasure of introducing the entertainer of the hour, who by now needed no introduction to anyone. "He is a great American with faith in the American people and in the democratic process. His conviction and steadfastness show through everything he has done and written. Witness how every night he raises his voice against bigotry and hatred." General Garvey was interrupted by cheers. "Here, here," came the cries from the audience, sporadic clapping evidenced their delight.

General Garvey continued raising his voice to assure everyone could hear over the growing din. "In both his public and private life, he continues to demonstrate a deep and abiding feeling for our people whose opportunities have been limited by cruel conditions imposed upon us by circumstances currently outside our control." He paused to catch his breath and continued in more conversational tones now that the crowd of businessmen had quieted.

"He feels as we all do that we must stand united and vigilant, to continue to organize and support business and political leaders who will make sure our voice is heard." General Garvey was having trouble being heard once again over the exuberance of the crowd. He redoubled his efforts to reach his conclusion. "He feels as we all do that only through universal suffrage can we redirect this country onto its professed tract, justice and equality for all. Without further ado I present to you Professor Black Jack Herman!" General Garvey had to shout to be heard over the roaring approval of the assembly.

Professor Herman rose from his seated position on the dais and joined Marcus Garvey at the podium, beginning with a handshake that culminated in a warm embrace. But before he could acknowledge that generous testimonial with salutations of his own. General Garvey had one more duty to dispense as chairman of UNIA; one more bombshell to drop. Facing the attendees with an arm arched to drape across Herman's shoulder he joyfully announced, "My dear Professor, your stay with us has been marvelous. Each night you perform to sold out houses, standing room only. Therefore, it is with great pleasure that we request that you hold over your sensational performance for another month!"

As if on cue the businessmen, those that were not already on their feet, rose and the entire crowd applauded enthusiastically. The cries of 'Speech, Speech" echoed along with the tinkling of water glasses in adoration.

Professor Herman, ever the consummate showman, let the crowd roar for long moments before motioning them quiet with outstretched arms. That small task accomplished, he began his greeting. "It is my privilege to be here today and bring warm felicitations to the Universal Negro Improvement Association with its dedicated mission of liberty and freedom for all."

Herman paused for the anticipated applause and then resumed his speech. "We believe liberty to be the secret of happiness and courage to be the foundation of liberty. We believe that freedom to think as you will and speak as you think are indispensable, that without free speech and assembly slavery would reassert itself in short order. Just as a perverse economic slavery has taken hold in many parts of this country.

Without public discourse and the freewheeling exchange of ideas, the populace is easily cowed into a state of submission by politicians and industrialists intent on keeping us subservient and ignorant of our Constitutional rights. Leaving us living in a constant state of fear and anxiety." The audience was so quiet that you could hear a whisper if anyone were bold enough to be that impolite.

Herman continued succinctly, "Furthermore, we believe that fear breeds hate and that hatred further separates us from the rest of society. It works both ways: fear of us separates blacks from whites and hatred by us further alienates us from the mainstream and from each other. This also blinds us from the fact that only through unity can we obtain freedom from the second class citizenship of separate but equal." The crowded auditorium rose in unison with thundering ovation. Herman paused, letting them voice their approval while he satiated his thirst. Finally he calmed them with a joke. "Gentlemen, gentlemen, I find it interesting that in my travels foreigners of color are treated with the same courtesy and dignity as Caucasians. They have unrestricted range of travel and access. No matter how dark their skin color, they are treated with respect. Only us Americans are treated as second class citizens. Is it any wonder then that so many of my fellow magicians claim citizenship to those mystical far off Eastern lands?" Herman's anecdote was received with uproarious laughter.

"In conclusion gentlemen, I tell you with certainty that bad laws must be broken and rewritten. The Ladies Temperance Movement has given us the template. Just look at their successes; women have won the right to vote and men have lost the right to drink in public (hoots of laughter). If we wish to assert our rights, we must follow their example." Professor Herman concluded earnestly to shouted accolades from the crowd.

That afternoon Herman bounded through the front door of their apartment shouting for his lover, "Eva. Eva, where are you?"

"I'm in here, honey. What's the matter?" came the sleepy reply from the bedroom. She had been napping in preparation for the evening's performance.

Black Jack broke into the bedroom, larger than life. Eva could see he was happy, actually smiling, a rare occurrence. Hints of joy resonated in his voice, "We've been held over for another month. People have been writing in for tickets from as far away as Albany, Philadelphia and Baltimore. Garvey told me so at lunch." He swept her out of bed and carried her around the room overcome with elation.

"Darling, that is wonderful news. Now put me down. I need my beauty rest if I am to be at my peak for tonight's performance," she only half-scolded.

She was delighted by their good fortune and made that fact known with her eyes, despite her pretense of ill humor at being rudely awakened. Eva was especially happy for Herman who had wanted for so long to be accepted by this city, its people and the organization which he hoped would change the face of America.

Black Jack aka Professor Herman, was much too excited to rest before the evening's performance. He sat in the living room which looked out over a small park and the Harlem River to Yankee Stadium, which was under construction on the other side. Lost in thought, he smoked one of his cigars in the dwindling afternoon light.

Eventually he fell into a light reverie, reminisces of his last conversation with Madame Deborah before embarking on this current venture. He had sat down with her in their official 'reading room', something told him perhaps for the last time. "Deborah, you are more than just a trusted confidant and respected fellow performer. I truly believe that you have a gift in this area. Tell me how I will fare in New York."

The room was shrouded in silence, the scent of jasmine incense hung heavily in the air. Deborah looked out into space, or was it inward into herself, and then began to speak. "There are new beginnings within new beginnings," she began slowly, reverently. "I can see your resurrection to heights only dreamed of by most men. Your fame will be without parallel. Your riches will be multiplied tenfold. But remember that life, like-the show, must go on." As was Deborah's way indeed, the way of most mystics, she mixed a note of caution in with the herald of glad tidings and the promise of fortunes to come.

A warning to the recipient to temper enthusiasm with caution, joy with prudence. It was also an homage to the muse that provided her sight. The spirit guide that lifted the veil of tears. Black Jack had been satisfied. He had received the confirmation that he wanted, needed in point of fact. He had come to New York armed with the knowledge that he was unstoppable, that his show would be a smashing success. That his manifest destiny was about to come to focus.

And so it came to pass that events began to unfold just as Madame Deborah's foresight predicted. Word of Professor Herman's Magical Mental Performance spread like wildfire throughout the African-American community. Audience members came from far and wide to seek his advice, witness his fame. In two short months, his notoriety blossomed into cult status.

Eva took the priest's advice and continued to have faith in herself, in her mentor and in the Lord. She continued to believe that this was all part of God's plan in which her role was indispensable and would produce positive aspects. Herman's faith in himself and his destiny never wavered. With his success in New York now assured, he continued to build strength on top of strength, planning a sensational new performance that he would take on the road throughout New England beginning in the summer. He had left the crowds wanting more and shortly, he would deliver.

The couple and Carl stayed in New York that spring practicing the act that would change the course of magic forever. As usual it was Eva that had to assume the precarious position, her position in the show. By now she had resolved herself to the repugnance of lying in bed in the spare bedroom for hours, twice a week, hypnotized and hardly breathing preparing for her portrayal in the 'Woman Buried Alive' demonstration. Eva no longer had the nightmares, having had her faith strengthened by her visit to the Cathedral. Curiously she had not been back although she wanted to on several occasions. Still, she carried with her, buried in her bosom, the priest's words. 'He who has faith is righteous-and shall live.' Consequently, she no longer feared the immersion into that dark underworld. Eva viewed her performance as part of God's greater plan, too immense and complex for her to comprehend. She derived satisfaction from the knowledge that in some small way she was helping to advance the cause of righteousness. She felt confident that this line of reasoning would help to mollify her parent's concern. She still wrote them and like a good daughter, she told her mother everything.

So twice a week, she would let Herman entrance her while lying on the bed and then command her subconscious to take only five breaths per minute. Unbeknownst to her, after her transference into another worldly state, he would attach a mirror to a flexible rod placed just above her mouth to register her breaths.

Now while the initial tests had lasted for four hours that was many months ago and under the supervision and expertise of Professor Maharajah. Herman was warned that even the Hindu priests themselves dare not exceed the six hour limit without constant practice. Black Jack loved Eva deeply and never wanted any regrettable, preventable misfortune to befall her. But, he also had an innate sense of showmanship and knowledge of how to structure the act to obtain the maximum effect on the crowds. In his estimation, to bury a woman six feet under for six hours at a time would be a show stopping event that no one would even dare attempt. All he had to do was to transform his-baby into a Hindu Holy man.

Black Jack was not being blasphemous or ridiculous to his way of thinking, but simply pragmatic. To safely perform the trick, it was not really an illusion, all that was required was persistence and practice. After all if the holy men of the East could do it, then so could he- by replication and repetition, teach it to others. Just to be on the safe side, he figured that before the first actual performance he would have a couple of dress rehearsals-just in case.

Carl, who had not been with the select few for the rehearsals in San Francisco, was at first agog with the notion that the woman he had come to know and respect over the last few years would be subjected to such unthinkable treatment. He had realized long ago that he had been wrong about her- she was the one. He had watched attentively rather enjoyably as the neophyte had turned into a consummate professional capable of handling anything Herman could conceive and performing resplendently. She was the proverbial phoenix, a true show woman.

Carl, in his long association with Black Jack had seen a great many things, but now living as he was in the third bedroom, brought him into closer quarters with the peculiarities that marked the modern couple's romance. He had stumbled upon Eva sleeping on the bed in the spare room quite accidentally one afternoon. Thinking he had heard a noise, while passing the cracked door, he peered in. Startled, he began to excuse himself then he noticed the-mirror. Moving closer to investigate, the young performer was not moving at all, barely breathing. He could count her aspirations as the escaping gasses graced the mirror. 'Two, three, four, five...' He checked his watch almost a full minute had past. 'What sort of madness was this?' he thought, his mind wildly alarmed. When he questioned the boss,' he was instructed to forget everything he saw and forbade to tell anyone ever.

"She is practicing for a new and sensational trick that we learned last summer while we were in San Francisco," Herman informed the chauffeur. "Don't tell anyone about it. We don't want someone stealing our thunder," Herman advised in all seriousness. Carl assured that of course, he would keep the confidence. Yet he could not help but to feel sorry for the young woman whom he had secretly grown to love.

In the interim, construction proceeded on the ball park across the river outside their living room window. In those intervening months, between Herman's smashing success at Liberty Hall and the planned sensational summer tour, Black Jack, aka 'The Professor,' practiced his magic and continued to push his political manifesto.

Herman made appearances at meetings and dinners at Mr. Garvey's behest. He would perform a few simple tricks. Everyone expected that of course. Then he would settle into an oratory on the pressing problems of the day. The economy was booming, running well on all cylinders. Real estate speculation was running rampant. Ever since the end of the Great War five years before, waves of immigration fleeing the repression of the south had flooded the city, indeed most northern cities with plentiful cheap labor. The ensuing boom in manufacturing and construction had left a bifurcated economy where the rich got richer and the poor were left running in place. Constantly held hostage to the next wave of newcomers who would do the same job for less money. It was the best of times for some.

Organizations like Garvey's, repeated attempts to unionize labor had been met with violent reprisals against both the agents advocating change and their hopeful followers. Anyone foolish enough to dream of a better life and act upon that desire. Examples had been made. Of course the police turned a blind eye to the sporadic outbreaks of violence. Some rumors had it that the 'bully boys' hired by managements for union busting duty were in reality off duty cops. No one doubted the allegations. This was the dark and ugly underside of the booming modern society. The same ugly secrets responsible for building the pyramids over four thousand years earlier. There is truly nothing new under the sun. There must always be an underclass for the proletariat to prosper.

General Garvey's organization believed, hoped, that having a celebrity like Mr. Herman in their midst would help gain supporters among the local black businessmen who were beginning to shy away from the cause, becoming content with a portion of the increased growth and prosperity that was bestowed on the region. 'Why compete when you could complete?' went one of the sayings among minority businessmen. Fill the niche markets with products or services that the large, less-specialized companies had ignored or overlooked. Trouble was that if you became too successful in your endeavors, someone would come knocking on your door.

Lately in the past year or so, a new group of bully boys had arrived on the scene. As in Chicago, a group had organized and branched out from their initial endeavors to dominate other markets and fields of service. While less flamboyant in their expressions of deadly violence than their Chicago cousins, they were thoroughly venal. Under their stewardship, the level of violence had risen to the occasional fire bombing of union activists' headquarters. As usual, the police never had any suspects and though everyone knew their name, no one dared to speak it.

Black Jack was happy to accompany Mr. Garvey to his various meetings, standing next to him at the podium, expressing his grand vision to the crowd or pressing the flesh at local business luncheons. It enhanced his standing within the community to be seen with a minority leader of such growing international stature as Marcus Garvey. Not that he needed further enhancement. After his recent string of hit performances in Harlem, the mere mention of his name was enough to draw crowds. The two of them could bank on that. As any great performer knows, you transform yourself, your act to continually mesmerize your audience. They did just that, Garvey and Herman. Played to each other's strengths and in the process, swept the crowds up in their enthusiasm. He certainly had become as he once bragged to Eva, "The Performer of the Hour." He had become that and much more.

When he was not out speechmaking, Black Jack was busy fulfilling the demand for personal consultations. General Garvey had rented him a small room in the headquarters building for the purpose of entertaining 'guests.' As was his practice in the many major metropolitan areas in which he had traveled, the clientele was kept to a select grouping. They were advised to remain discreet and were scheduled for regular one-on-one consultations with the Professor. These business leaders and ladies would constitute his entourage and the core of his sphere of influence, which would grow slowly over time as he became one of the focal points of the black intelligentsia in the most powerful city in the United States.

Keeping all of those plates spinning in mid-air was a time

consuming task, but Black Jack relished presiding over his growing business empire. He delegated the correspondence with Andrew, who was still in Chicago, to Eva, who nowadays rarely accompanied him on speaking engagements. The book sales and magic tricks by mail were still doing well. However the sales of tonic were slumping, presumably since he was not on the road hawking that item. Black Jack rationalized that sales of his soft drink would improve once he got back on the road that summer. 'I wonder if I should have Eva drink half a bottle before I put her under the ground,' he pondered. Deciding to table the question until after completion of the first 'dress rehearsal' which was still more than a month away.

She was coming along well in her breathing exercises, able to maintain her breathing for over five hours in steady rhythms before becoming erratic. Carl was now encharged to supervise her progress and tasked with recording her breaths per minute, once every fifteen minutes after the first hour. Every ten minutes after the fourth hour. At which time, he was not to leave her side under any circumstances. In case of emergencies he had been given the control word to bring her out of the trance, should her breathing become erratic or labored. As a consequence, he grew very devoted to her, protective of her welfare and safety. Eva, in her catatonic condition, knew nothing of this fidelity.

One day the chauffeur was given a curious order. "Carl, I want you to go rent a truck and tonight when nobody is around, go out and secure four sheets of plywood, the type they use for flooring. You should be able to get it from one of the construction sites. Don't let anyone see you bring it back. You will also have to pick up some tools: saw, hammer, nails. I've got a little job for you."

"Just as you say, boss" came the smart reply from the chauffeur who through long association was used to taking orders and not asking questions. He arrived with truck around six and then waited until long after midnight to complete his nefarious task. As luck would have it, he had decided to take the bridge across the Harlem River into the Bronx and drive past Yankee Stadium.

On his first circuit he noticed some despoiled sheets of plywood sitting out apart from the rest of the construction supplies that were padlocked behind a chain link fence. Obviously these were being discarded because of some small flaw. No one would mind them missing. Quickly, he looked around. 'Good, no security guards,' he thought. Stopping the truck, he hopped out and hurriedly threw the wooden sheets into the rear bed of the pick up, dashing off before anyone was the wiser.

Not one to press his luck, Carl decided to buy the tools way up in the Bronx the next morning after he dropped the wood back at the apartment before dawn. No one would know him up in the Bronx. He could buy the tools and the sawhorses, somehow he knew he would need sawhorses, and be back long before noon. He could get everything upstairs and no one would be any the wiser.

The usually unflappable assistant was pensive on the drive back from the Bronx. He had remained stoic during his many travels while under Black Jack's employ. But he simply dreaded what was coming next, and he hated himself for being part of this conspiracy. He genuinely hoped Herman knew what he was doing.

The spare room was transformed into a carpentry workshop. The bed had been dismantled and placed in one corner smothered under three sheets of plywood stacked sideways. Black Jack was despairingly examining the merchandise one board at a time. "Is this the best you could find? Look at these cracks, and that one has a large knot."

"Hey boss, free is free," the big man began and then thinking better of himself decided to moderate his tone. "Don't worry, I can cut around those. It will be good enough for your purpose."

"Don't you presume to tell me my business," the boss responded curtly. "I want this to be a proper dress rehearsal, not a slipshod operation."

"Hey, you've seen me build a stage from scraps we found in a junk yard. You know I can build this tight enough to keep out the dirt. I worry about her too, y'know. We won't let anything happen. She'll be all right." Carl's words, kind as they were, provided cold comfort to Herman. They failed; 'to neither mollify his demeanor nor remove the scowl from his face.

"All right, she's going to be out of the house all afternoon getting her hair done and primping. We have a dinner to attend this evening. I want this thing finished today before she gets back. You have the specifications, now get to it."

"Yes, sir." Carl resisted the urge to salute. "Your wish is my command." He worked all afternoon sawing and hammering, aiding and abetting in the crime that he felt they were perpetrating upon Eva.

Andrew had been summoned to New York to confer, ostensibly about the mail order enterprise. In truth, Black Jack had summoned his brother because he needed another confidant, an aide de camp as it were.

While Black Jack glorified in the friendships he had made since his arrival nearly five months ago, he was not ready to trust any of Garvey's men, even General Garvey himself, with the secrets of his proposed show stopper. Herman's instincts as a magician ran too deep. There was an old line amongst magicians about never trusting anyone outside of the business and, absolutely never trust anyone within the business. While taken by many as something of a joke, there were relatively few exceptions to that rule.

Advising Andrew cryptically to 'quietly slip out of town,' his brother had provided changes of post office box numbers to relay to the Chicago office. Andrew, knowing well Black Jack's ways, had a feeling that he would not soon return.

Carl met Andrew at Grand Central Station upon his arrival and ferried him uptown to the apartment for dinner with Black Jack and Eva. While the meeting was pleasant, Andrew could pry no information out of the chauffeur except that, "Things are going fine here in New York. But I suppose you already know that from your correspondence." Was it Andrew's imagination or had the big man lost the joviality he had once possessed? If indeed, he had ever possessed any at all.

The dinner went well. Black Jack had one of the assistants from his show work as a serving girl for the evening. She and her companion would work the card parties and dinners that Herman had begun having on weekends. It was a long apartment with rather large rooms. There was even a little nook graced with an upright piano. Herman and his mistress had become quite the mainstay of the Harlemite social circle in a few short months.

"You've got a fine place here, brother. Congratulations, you've taken New York by storm just like you planned," applauded Andrew after receiving the grand tour.

"The best is yet to come, dear brother. That's why you're here. I need your help," advised Black Jack brandishing a bottle of brandy and filling his brother's glass.

Eva, who was looking a little pale, had been quite subdued all during dinner. She chose that propitious moment to announce her exit. "Honey, I think I'll go and lie down. I've been feeling quite tired all day."

Andrew misspoke, through innocence, of the drama that had been unfolding while he was in Chicago. "I'm sorry you're not feeling well. I hope that you're not coming down with something. Seems like everyone's sick in Chicago."

Eva smiled thinly. "No, it's all right. I will be fine. I just need my beauty sleep. Glad to see you again, Andrew. I'm sure we will be seeing a lot more of you now that you're here." That duty dispensed, Eva rose slowly, still gracefully, and pecked Herman on the forehead as she made her way out of the room.

After a pregnant pause in the wake of Eva's passing, Black Jack suggested to his brother that they take their brandies down to the living room and watch the boats as they passed down the river in the twilight of early evening.

"First off, let me tell you little brother that I've rented an apartment for you and Carl half a dozen blocks from here. Just down that hill." Black Jack pointed southeast outside the window. His brother followed with a glance. Black Jack continued, "It is two bedrooms, of course, a little smaller than ours. There is a garage nearby where we can park the limo. I'm getting tired of coming out in the morning to find kids hanging all over the hood. Besides, I don't like having the neighbors apprised of my comings and goings. I need to retain my aura of inscrutability. You know me, Black Jack Herman, Man of Mystery." He had lit a cigar as he spoke, standing in the window with one foot up upon the sill. Blowing smoke through the raised sash, he casually followed its journey.

"That sounds fine. So I take it that this will be our base of operation from now on?"

"Exactly." Black Jack sent another puff of smoke out the window and on its journey.

"Well, I kinda expected that when you sent me those change of address forms for the lock boxes. At least that's what I told Deborah when I saw her night before last."

"You saw her?" Black Jack's foot abruptly came off the sill. He turned and sat down in the window box. "How is she? Damn, I've been meaning to call her but I've been so busy."

"She looked fine. She has a small clientele and she likes it that way. She keeps a low profile, you know." Black Jack nodded.

Andrew continued, "She must have known you weren't coming back. She redecorated the apartment. Real light and airy, got rid of all the voodoo stuff."

"She did? Didn't her clients, my clients, object?"

"Naw, she thinks most people like it better. She still has the reading room with the blackened windows. You know, the chair and table in the center. But even there she took out your alter and the skull. She gave me a tour before I left. She insisted."

"She knew you would tell me," Black Jack concluded. "Did she say anything else?"

"Not really," Andrew racked his brain. "Except to tell you not to worry, that she could take care of herself."

"Good, good," Black Jack mused. "I've got enough to worry about around here preparing the new show."

"Is that why everyone around here seems so subdued and uptight?" asked Andrew in a moment's clarity. "What's the big deal anyway? What is this sensational new show stopper that you have been alluding to?"

Without another word, Black Jack finished his drink and put his cigar out in the empty glass. Rising from the window box, he motioned for his brother to follow him down the hall to the spare bedroom.

Andrew tagged along nonchalantly. His curiosity growing as he approached the door which Black Jack had waited to open until his brother's arrival. There it was sitting in the middle of the floor. The dominant object in the room. The plywood coffin which Carl had made to specification. Andrew's jaw dropped and words escaped him.

XI
Woman Buried Alive

"We've found the perfect spot," Andrew exclaimed bursting through the front door of Herman's residence followed closely behind by Carl. "It is a virgin field hidden by some woods just off the highway north of Scarsdale. The dirt is soft and crumbly. We dug a couple of small test holes." He was obviously elated by this discovery, his contribution to their little caper.

"Did you see anyone else around?" Black Jack asked cautiously, mindful of his warnings from Professor Maharajah.

"No, it was quiet the whole time. There is a small dirt road that passes through the woods to the field. You can barely see the highway through the woods." Carl confirmed Andrew's opinion that this could possibly be the location for which they searched.

Black Jack remained dubious. "How long were you there? We will need absolute privacy for at least six hours."

"How about we have a practice session? A dry run?" said Andrew falling in love- with the brilliance and simplicity of the suggestion as the words left his lips.

Black Jack and Carl looked at each other and smiled. It was settled. They would have a dry run of the dress rehearsal.

The next Sunday Andrew, Carl and Black Jack escorted the two assistants from the New York show on a picnic in the woods upstate. The girls, very effervescent and giggly, were glad to get out of the city for the day. They were also delighted to be in the company of such handsome brothers. As they had worked for Black Jack for five months, like most women in his company that long, they had become quite enamored. It had been decided early in the planning that Eva would remain at home. Black Jack had arranged for some of the wives from Mr. Garvey's organization to call upon her around lunch. Eva continued to become introverted, 'keeping her own counsel' as Black Jack called it. No point upsetting her unnecessarily or give her mental images on which to linger. Black Jack had always been a person who just went out and did things with as little aforethought as possible. "Just go out and conquer your obstacles," he would advise to clients both on stage and in his readings. It was one of the hallmarks of his philosophy, just go and do, figure it out along the way.

The relaxing picnic in the countryside that afternoon passed without incident. The sporadic motorists passed by with nary a notice. Carl was right; from the highway they were practically invisible. In mid-afternoon, a young man approached down the road herding half a dozen cows. At first the picnickers were afraid that he intended to bring them into this pasture for grazing, but he kept right on down the road herding his charges to one side with a long stick. The girls thought they were so cute.

The girls thought the location was cute. They thought the company was cute, and oh those 'cute cars' rolling down the highway. They thoroughly enjoyed the fried chicken and biscuits, the lemonade and potato salad. In fact they were having so much fun that it was decided not to spoil their outing by revealing the real reason for the occasion. Upon their arrival back in Manhattan that evening, the decision was finalized; next Sunday was go for the dress rehearsal.

The intrepid little band set out about 10 A.M. in two vehicles. Black Jack drove the limo populated by the three women, two of whom had been informed of what the other already knew.

They were all appropriately somber. Andrew accompanied Carl in the rented truck which carried a wooden box hidden under a waterproof tarpaulin. Three shovels were hidden behind the seats in the cab.

A sense of déjà-vu overwhelmed Black Jack. This scenario was eerily similar to the last time this trick was performed back in September in San Francisco. Other than Eva, who sat stoically being comforted by Charmainge, one of the assistants. Black Jack was the only other participant in that event supervised by Professor Maharajah. 'He had to get this right,' his mind nagged. There should be no problems he assured himself. All the proper precautions had been observed. They had practiced Eva's hibernation for over six hours in the apartment with the lid sealed. That meant there was enough air inside to comfortably sustain his protégée. 'Why am I worrying?' he chastised himself. 'Madame Deborah has peered into the future and assured my success!' What were her words again? 'Within resurrections there would be resurrections.' No wait. 'Within new beginnings there would be new beginnings.' No matter, it meant the same thing. She was obviously talking about Eva 'rising resplendently.' Wasn't that the council she had given to his lover in San Francisco, according to her own account of the event? Then no matter, their success was already a foregone conclusion. Black Jack ceased his ruminations and continued to follow Andrew and Carl on the hour's journey to their selected location.

The girls in the back seat became more somber with each passing mile. By the time they reached the destination and turned off the highway, tracks on the faces of the young ladies revealed that they had been crying.

Eva sat upright in the back seat, resolute and unmoved. Her strength came from years of practice in dealing-with Herman's schemes and from higher powers of other dominions. She was actually smiling serenely. This dismayed the girls further. They wondered aloud if she was not losing her mind. Eva comforted them by saying simply, "Everyone has a part to play in the plan. Don't worry, I will be fine." The women, younger than Eva, looked at each other in amazement at her fortitude in the-face of this seemingly overwhelming ordeal.

As events were preplanned, the men began their tasks with

vigor. They would quickly dig the hole to the prescribed depth, and then preposition the box beside the orifice. Black Jack would fetch Eva from the car and put her into a deep trance, encouraging her into the enclosure. The lid would be sealed tight to prevent leakage of dirt. Finally, the three of them would-lower the box containing BJ's pride and joy into the hold using ropes to assure a smooth descent, and quickly cover it to ground level. A large oversized picnic blanket would be procured from trunk of the limo and placed over the gravesite. Then they would literally sit around above Eva's sub-terrain location whiling away the hours until the examination.

In their planning they had not anticipated the reactions of the starlets upon viewing Eva's entrancement and entombment. In each young woman's mind it was she who was placed in that precarious position. They moped around morbidly for the next couple of hours. The other thing the planners of this little outing had failed to anticipate was the arrival of a bus load of churchgoers out for a Sunday afternoon picnic on this first week of June.

The somber sojourn had progressed about two hours when a bus loaded with gospel singing parishioners turned decidedly onto the dirt road headed right for their pasture. The quick thinking magician, ever the showman, sprang into action. "Damn! They're coming this way. Places everybody, we have to make this look like a happy-go-lucky Sunday afternoon picnic." He yelled at the girls who had been moping standoffishly, full of concern for their submerged sister. "Okay, girls, fix your faces. You have to start acting happy and gay as of now. If this goes badly, there will: be trouble aplenty," he warned tersely.

The bus pulled up to the group and the pastor emerged, a rather large and jovial fellow. "Hello friends, see you're having a picnic. Mind if we share your field?"

"Why, of course not." Black Jack said with outstretched hand. "We have been by here several times in passing and often remarked what a nice place for a picnic. We thought, my brothers and I, how nice it would be to get our girlfriends out of the city."

"Yes, indeed. The Lord truly has made a fine day to sit back and celebrate the idyllic nature of our existence." The reverend concurred philosophically. Then added, "We want you to feel free to share our bounty."

"Thank you very much. You are too kind," Black Jack rejoined.

"Not at all. Our faith requires, nay demands, that we provide charity for all who grace our presence. Besides our female parishioners have been cooking since Friday night. We certainly have-some month watering delicacies for you to sample. Just give us a few minutes to get set up."

Carl and Andrew both looked in a bit of a quandary. The girls had been shushed into silence. Only Black Jack seemed master of the situation. "Well, everybody, until these nice folks leave, we will have to play like happy campers. So everyone smile and act like you're having a good time." He didn't have to tell them again.

The afternoon passed pleasantly enough. Part of the time they forgot the reason they had come and the woman slumbering six feet below the pasture. They learned that the reverend's flock belonged to a local church and that one of the parishioner's family owned the land on which they were spending an idyllic afternoon. A vow of charity forbade them from turning away strangers. They also learned that the summer picnics were a monthly occurrence which the church members looked forward to with great anticipation.

There was ample food for member and guest alike. Also there were games for the children and informal excursions into the woods for the adults. The Herman party however politely remained close to their blanket after returning with samples of the wonderful smorgasbord.

The reverend learned from them that Andrew was working construction upstate and had met them there to be with his girlfriend for the afternoon. Black Jack, he introduced himself as Ben, had rented the limo and the driver for the day to impress the ladies. Too bad Carl had not come in uniform, an oversight. The reverend, guessing that he had received only part of the story, never questioned the veracity. Returning to his flock, he left the couples and their driver to their own devices.

During the fifth hour of Eva's submergence, the couples decided to take a walk in the woods leaving Carl to stand vigil. "Will these people ever leave?" Black Jack asked the heavens above just as soon as they were out of earshot. Upon returning to the campsite, their eyes-were greeted with the sight of women packing up and men loading items onto the bus. "Hallelujah!" he swore under his breath. "They are finally leaving." He checked his watch. It had been more than six hours. It would probably take them another half an hour to get gone.

The June sun had moved decidedly into the western sky as the busload of picnickers moved down the dirt road toward the highway. They all waved fervently with broad smiles and 'so longs!' Before departing the pastor had taken Black Jack aside, er Ben, and told him. "I can see that you want to be alone. God be with you."

"Get the shovels," BJ shouted as the bus turned onto the highway. "Ladies, get that blanket out of the way." It was nearly six o'clock, almost a full seven hours since they had seen Eva alive last. "Dig!" he cried. "Dig with everything you've got." Black Jack had grabbed a shovel and was digging wildly, throwing dirt over his shoulder. In fact, the three men were all digging wildly in discord with one another, heedless as to the size of the hole they were creating. It took an eternity to reach the four foot level where a shovel blade scraped against plywood coffin. The young women clutched together for support with pain stricken expressions, squealed releasing anxiety at the recognition of the sound, the sound of the shovel striking Eva's repository.

Black Jack was now on his knees wiping away the dirt with his hands trying to find the screws to free his beloved. Carl and Andrew were still removing dirt from the periphery in order to fully expose the wooden box. The coffin cleared, Andrew suddenly joined his brother and the two men worked feverishly with screwdrivers to release Eva.

Carl lifted off the top and there she was, pallid and quivering. Black Jack pressed an ear to her mouth. Her breath was shallow and erratic. "Eva! Eva, can you hear me? This is your control. Time to wake up!" He shouted the code word. No immediate response. "Darling, it's me. Black Jack! I love you!" The last was blurted out before his conscious could censor the emotion. It didn't matter. Right now in his universe there was just the two of them.

Far from reviving, her body underwent an outbreak of

convulsions. Black Jack was at a loss to explain or modify her reaction to the exposure to fresh air and sunlight. He gently slapped her face, called her name.

Nothing was working. Eva remained unconscious; her body jerking to spasms. Finally, Carl pushed past the two kneeling brothers and pressed his lips to the prone beauty. He blew into her mouth.

The others were aghast. They had never seen this type of resuscitation. However, desperate times called for desperate measures. No one attempted to stop him. For once in his life, Black Jack was helpless in a crisis.

Once again, Carl breathed in deeply and exhaled into Eva's mouth. This time he got a response. She coughed, then took a deep breath on her own, and then another. The four of them staring at Eva and Carl could clearly see that she was beginning to come around.

Black Jack pushed Carl out of the way. "Eva, can you hear me? It's Black Jack. Come back to us, honey." A feeble arm lifted. A cold hand touched his arm. A garbled sentence passed through thin pursed lips, unintelligible.

"Baby, what is it? I couldn't understand you."

"Take me home," she repeated coherently. The hand caressing his arm collapsed, too tired to continue the effort.

"Yes, of course. Right away. Carl, help me get her out of here." BJ was frantic. The big man swept her up in his arms and stood up. Andrew and his brother scrambled up the incline and prepared to relieve Carl. Eva was placed gently on the back seat of the limo, her head supported by Charmaigne's lap. Black Jack and the other girl, Marsha, jumped into the front seat and fired up the auto. His parting words, appropriately brief. "Let's get the hell outta here." They sped off down the dirt road and onto the highway leaving Andrew and Carl to clean up the mess.

"She'll be fine." The doctor levied a welcome prognosis. "I've given her something to help her get some rest. In a couple of days she should be as good as new. Poor thing, she was totally exhausted. What did you say you were doing again?"

"We were practicing a new stunt for the show," Black Jack reiterated bashfully. "I guess we got a little carried away."

"I guess you did at that," came the sharp castigation. This little lady here has all the symptoms of oxygen deprivation. Her pulse was very shallow, but is getting stronger. You weren't deep sea diving, were you?"

"I don't know what you mean, doctor."

"Don't play innocent with me. I have seen those water tanks you magicians submerse yourselves into, trying to be the longest to hold your breath. What's it all for anyway?" scoffed the doctor.

"It's all to thrill the crowd." Black Jack had accepted the bait. "They live through us vicariously. We provide excitement to their hum drum lives. A fascination for their senses."

"Half the time people come to see you make a mistake. They hope you guys will screw up badly, maybe kill yourselves. Then they can tell their friends that they were there witnessing the event. Makes 'em feel like big men. Makes them feel that they bested the great magician so-and-so, that they were smarter than you. In the end it's just not worth it. The terrible price you pay for perfectly performing a stunt of endurance is that you must perform perfectly every time or you risk paying the ultimate price. Whatever happened to the days when you just pulled rabbits out of hats?" he asked rhetorically. "I know, I know, not sensational enough."

Black Jack, rarely speechless, nevertheless demurred to the professional presiding over his baby's recovery. Perhaps a little contrition would go a long way in pacifying the family physician.

"You're absolutely right, doctor. We in the Brotherhood of Magic often let our egos get out of control in our zest to outdo one another. Innocent bystanders are sometimes hurt, maimed or worse." He let those last syllables drift off in lowered voice in lieu of formal apology.

"Hell man, it's not me you should be apologizing to, it's your assistant. These women must love you idiots very much to go through with these crazy stunts. Whatever it was." The doctor had put away his stethoscope and closed his bag. He indicated that there was nothing more to do now. Time was her ally.

As they neared the front door of the apartment, the doctor

turned to offer one more piece of advice. "IF she is not on her feet and regained her strength in a couple of days, call me. One more thing, no more practice for at least two weeks."

"Yes, doctor. Thank you very much, doctor."

Returning to the master bedroom he regarded his passion's pride. Her dark eyes sunk deep within their sockets accentuated the circles below. She lay in the bed weakly regarding him.

"Doctor says no practice for two weeks. As of now, you are on vacation. Weather's getting warmer. Maybe we should go to the beach for a few days. The sun and salt air will do you good."

"But what about the show? July fourth is just a month away. All of our plans are already in motion." The strength in Eva's voice belied her physical condition.

"No honey, you come first. Taking care of you is what's best for the show," he said tenderly.

The week at the beach was just what the doctor would have ordered had he thought of it. Within days of Eva's recovery, Carl drove the couple to a little bungalow in Asbury Park just steps from the seashore. Daily Herman and Eva would take tong walks down by the shore line, deeply inhaling the salt air. Therapeutic in theory, this bonding of the couple and the sea, reminiscent of their stay in Norfolk years ago, once again brought them closer together.

The long walks, the handholding, the deep stares into one another's eyes, Eva could feel it, she was falling for this man all over again. He doted upon her. Suddenly, it was all about her needs and desires. Their passion, once rekindled, bloomed in the June nights. The couple's ecstasy rose to fill a void left too long dormant. It was a magical ten days. Realizing how much she missed this intimacy, the closeness between them, Eva thought back to when she last felt this way. It wasn't hard. Her mind went right back to that seminal event in San Francisco ten months earlier. Once again, she realized what she had left in San Francisco. Secretly, she vowed to get it back.

Destiny had taken a holiday, but the show must go on. On their last night by the ocean, Black Jack had a local restaurant whip up a special celebration. For dessert, the chief and staff wheeled in a vanilla iced cake with the words 'Happy Anniversary Darling' written in flowery red lettering.

She had completely forgotten-it had been a year since their 'honeymoon' in Toronto. She thought it seemed so much longer. Tears welled in her eyes.

Black Jack read the words to her on bended knee at the side of the table to the enjoyment of the restaurant staff.

Then he added a little twist of his own. "Darling, I will always love you. Please stay with me forever." Startled, she looked down. There he was on one knee holding an open jewelry case containing a diamond bracelet. Somewhere deep within herself that little girl spoke out a resounding affirmative. "Yes darling, yes. I'll love you forever."

The couple arrived back at their apartment in New York City ready for the arduous summer tour ahead. A stack of messages from Andrew greeted Herman on his arrival-everything from trivial concerns about costumes and billboards to inquiries from Mr. Garvey's group about this sensational new show stopper they had heard about.

"Damn!" Black Jack swore under his breath as he read that last. 'Wonder how they found out.' He read the attached communiqué. Seems they wanted to distance themselves from him should the trick turn out badly. He laughed out loud. He would do them one better-he would publicly disavow any ties to the Garvey organization before the show, per their request. After the successful completion of the event, they would be clamoring to reassociate themselves. He would make them sorry they ever crossed him.

All that remained was one more in house test of Eva's ability. For this last test, Carl was instructed to install a glass window in the lid so that Eva's reactions could be observed continually. If anything were to go wrong, they could stop the experiment and cancel the engagement. Black Jack swore that he would not go on without her. A noble sentiment, but hardly practical. As Andrew pointed out, "The crowds will be coming to see you, to hear you speak. If you disappoint them, it may be tougher to get bookings in the future."

"I don't care." Black Jack was adamant. "If my baby's not ready to perform, then neither will I."

Carl and Herman sat over the box regarding Eva's progress apprehensively, charting her breaths through the glass window. Occasionally, questioning their observations. "Did she just twitch?" Herman.

"No, I don't think so. She looks perfectly peaceful." Carl.

Andrew would pop his head into the spare room every half hour or so with an obsequious, "How's she doing?"

Eva, for her part, remained the picture of contentment, utterly oblivious to the consternation of the two characters praying over her. It was the end of June, only one week before the scheduled big event. Their last chance to get it right.

One hour, two hours, three, four, the time passed at an agonizing pace. The two men would get up, stretch, walk around, and switch places. Never taking eyes from their precious performer for more than a minute. During the fifth hour, Black Jack could swear he saw a sneeze and feared that she was beginning to breathe erratically.

Carl, with his keen powers of observation, could not confirm. Indeed, the little mirror by her mouth only registered regular breaths. There it was three...four... five. 'Was that a minute?' Check the watch. 'Good, another minute passed- no problems.'

Nearly the end of the trial and Herman was antsy. He had to forcefully contain his anxiety. 'How are you going to get through the performance when you can't make it through the rehearsal?' he ridiculed himself, his mind jabbing him with fears and doubts. 'How long will it take her to stand? How would it look if she collapses on stage? What was the name of that first magician to utter those fateful words "Is there a doctor in the house?" Forcefully, he shut everything down and concentrated on the present.

"How long, Carl?" veritably growling at his companion.

"Just a few minutes now, Mr. Herman. Everything looks fine. Nothing to worry about," Carl soothed.

"Six hours in three, two, one. Mark!" shouted Carl.

Black Jack was already on the screws. The bodyguard joined him, swiftly liberating the lid. As they worked Black Jack decided on show day to begin the exhumation process before time expired.

At the end of the final hour, they wanted to revive her right away. The audience had gotten theirs. No sense taking any more chances than necessary.

"Eva, this is your control. Come out of your trance now!" Herman commanded loudly.

Andrew had peeked his head around the corner of the doorway, having heard the commotion. He peered at the scene open-mouthed.

"Eva, darling. Time to wake up!" Black Jack coaxed.

A low groan emanated from the wooden box followed by, "How did I do?" in a hoarse whisper.

"Fine, honey. Just fine. Carl, help me get her up."

They raised her fragile body and placed her in a waiting chair to check her pulse.

"Strong and regular," signaled Carl with more than a modicum of relief in his voice.

"Strong and regular."

After a few moments, Black Jack picked up his baby and carried her down to the master bedroom. "You rest here a while, hon. Daddy's got to go make preparations."

'Daddy' had to go and pour himself a stiff drink. He poured one for Carl too and headed back to the small room where the other man was still straightening up.

"Here you go. You've really earned this today. I'll bet this has been one of the longest days of your life."

"You can say that again," Carl said as he gulped at the drink.

"Well you had better get used to it. They are going to get a lot longer from now on," Black Jack quipped.

The sun, a fiery ball, was glaring in the east. Hot sun rising, nothing hotter than the fourth of July in New Jersey. The infant science of predicting the weather had called for a clear and sunny day with a high ceiling and visibility to twenty five miles. It was beginning to look like they would be right on target. The perfect day for a carnival.

Of course, it was no mere carnival that Black Jack had chosen to debut his sensational new feat of endurance. The Independence Day Jubilee Aviation, Carnival and Athletic Meet in Hasbrook

Heights was easily the largest event in northern New Jersey that summer. Thousands of people would be attending this day long gala. It was the perfect venue to begin the new tour.

As they were setting up on stage early that morning, Herman bragged to his younger

brother. "It's sheer genius I tell you Andrew. Sheer genius."

"What's that?"

"The location I've picked out. It cost a few dollars extra." He winked knowingly. "But it is worth it to be right in the middle of the crowds traversing from the sports complex to the aviation show. In the morning the crowds will be moving toward the athletic events- that's when we entomb Eva and put on a little show. In the afternoon, the crowds will be over at the air show. Now get this, for the finale I have paid one of the stunt pilots to land right on top of the spot where Eva is sequestered. After the morning's performance ends at noon, we will secure a giant cloth with a bull's-eye painted on it over her location. An adjacent sign will inform the public to return for the spectacular climax at 4 P.M."

"But we won't be digging her out until almost five o'clock." Andrew puzzled, and then he got it. "Oh, I see. You want time to sell them merchandise."

"Exactly," Black Jack smiled that devilish grin. "People won't buy much in the morning because they have to carry it around all day. And of course, after the event is successfully completed," he crossed his fingers behind his back, "People will be anxious to leave. While they are waiting for the sensational climax to the sky show, they will be milling about. That's when you and the girls go into overdrive, hawking all these goodies," Black Jack concluded lifting another case of health tonic onto the stage.

"Very smart, brother. Very smart. Just like the old days." Andrew was duly impressed.

"Hey, the more things change.. -You know it's the same old game to success."

By now the crowds were beginning to file past to see the early sports matches. Herman's assistants, scantily clad of course, were standing on either side of the stage yelling to passersby, reminding them to come back and see their show beginning at 10 A.M. The onlookers could hardly forget, the attractive women were but mere bookends to the giant sign that dominated the rear of the stage reading: Black Jack Herman Presents Woman Buried Alive.

The show began promptly at ten. Black Jack appeared in a puff of smoke on stage. His two curvaceous assistants in puffs of smoke amongst the audience members. The men got a good look at their assets in those short costumes as they wiggled their way onto the stage. The actors performed some standard tricks, staples from the magician's repertoire including the woman sawed in half. But the crowd was petulant; they wanted more. They were anxious to see the event promised on the billboard, scheduled to begin at eleven. With sporadic shouts and catcalls, the audience made known their desires.

"Patience, patience," Black Jack chided. "We still have a little time before the scheduled demonstration." He knew the crowds would be anxiously awaiting the promised event, that they would balk at the tired old routines. Nevertheless, he had them right where he wanted them. Time to launch into his political manifesto.

"Ladies and gentlemen, I'm glad you have come today to see the sights and witness events extraordinaire. It is to commemorate the accomplishments of our forefathers that we gather here today. To celebrate the successful resolution of their struggles. But their work is not done. There is something else to be done, and it is up to you to do it. I'm referring to voting. I urge you not to overlook the need to elect the right men to state and local offices. I believe most deeply that the roots of good government in this country lie in clean, honest local and state officers. Too many times we only concern ourselves with electing representatives to national office. In which case, we overlook the possibility of electing officials with the ability to liberalize our local jurisdictions.

We-want clean and effective government all the way from the local level right up the ladder to Washington. We want people who will be responsive to our concerns, fight for our rights. The only way we can achieve this is to vote as a cohesive unit on Election Day."

There was a small smattering of applause. The crowds had come to see the trick.

Herman, undeterred, continued, "Yes, we must vote and continue to vote as a bloc for candidates of our choice. Unintimidated by violence or threats of job loss from the parties behind the current status quo. The party bosses who are determined to keep us running in place, our progress retarded, doing the jobs they deem appropriate for us." Black jack paused for breath and raised his voice to convey further emphasis. "All the while they dictate the terms and conditions of our very existence.

This forfeiture of the right to self-determination on our part cannot continue to stand. Therefore, be grateful for your heritage. Be proud and aware of the benefits the Constitution confers on you. If we work together to elect the right politicians, we can prevail upon them to eradicate this mandated separate equality which has us shackled.

In conclusion, pray to God for the continuance of those rights as spelled out in the phrase 'All men are created equal.' As we work tirelessly for these rights to be extended to everyone in a truly inclusive society as espoused by our founding fathers in the statement: 'We the people.' "

Not waiting to gauge the tenor of the crowd to his sermon, BJ launched his fireworks. "Now, who wants to see something that they've never seen before?" The crowd yelled wildly with excitement. It was ten forty-five.

Carl and the limo containing the star performer were just pulling up to the side of the stage. Eva garnered all eyes as she emerged wearing a white flowing gown, and with the assistance of her chauffeur, approached the stage climbing the steps one at a time. Her hand clutched the white wooden railing for support. It was all very theatrical, but also very true. Her long months of practice had left her muscles weak and flaccid.

"Ladies and gentlemen, I'd like to present my lovely assistant, Eva." Herman began with the usual banter while raising her right arm skyward. The crowd signaled their hearty approval. There was bloodlust in the air.

The consummate entertainer sensed that the crowd was close to being out of control. He waited long minutes until they quieted.

"May I have your attention please?" Once quieted, he was able to command their attention.

"Secrets from the Tibetan holy men have been conferred upon me in my quest to uncover all the knowledge of the ancients in order to reveal the mental powers that were prominently practiced by priests and emperors of long ago.

This demonstration will showcase the most cherished secret of those Buddhist monks, the ability to slow one's heartbeat and respiration down so low as to hardly register. To accomplish this task takes fantastic powers of control and autohypnosis. We will go one better today and perform a feat only a few of the high priests are able to replicate. We will hypnotize a willing subject and entomb her for six hours in an airtight container."

The showman paused to let his words wash over the crowd. "At the end of the air show we will resurrect her, whereupon I will bring her out of her trance and reveal her to be safe and sound." Black Jack finished with his usual flair and offered assurances to the squeamish in the crowd.

They were chomping at the bit, pressing forward to obtain the best view of the coming spectacle. Black Jack threw a smoke bomb stage left and in its wake a mahogany silk-lined coffin appeared on stage.

The crowd yelled and cheered. They were so loud that Herman had to shout to be overheard.

"Eva, are you ready?" He smiled reassuringly at her.

"Yes," a small voice barely audible on stage over the crowd.

"Then let's begin. Look deeply into my eyes. You will have no fear. You will shut out everything but the sound of my voice. The crowds are gone. The sunny day is gone. It is just you and I, and I am your control"

"You are my control," she repeated, already under.

The members of the audience shushed one another, afraid of missing something important. Some hoping to vicariously usurp some of his power, such was human nature.

Eyelids now closed, Eva relied on Herman to guide her steps. He walked her over to the casket sitting upright, and bade her to enter.

When she was settled comfortably and in full view of the audience, he instructed her to go into her hibernative state.

"Go to sleep now, darling," he said sweetly to her. "Go into a deep sleep and I will wake you in several hours. Goodbye." Eva lay motionless as he closed the lid and turned to the audience. "Ladies and gentlemen, the show will conclude in the adjacent lot." Black Jack pointed with outstretched arm and right on cue a large truck was moved, revealing a deep hole with shovels sticking upright from a pile of dirt.

"I will need the assistance of several strong gentlemen from the audience. Who wants to volunteer?" More than a dozen hands sprouted from the crowd. Black Jack picked six. Once assembled, they carried Eva's performance chamber down from the stage and over to the edge of the precipice. She was then lowered by professionals using ropes and a good-sized block and tackle. The contents safely intact, the pit was quickly filled until it was level with the surrounding earth.

The crowd cordoned behind a metal barricade had been hushed by the event they just witnessed. A few with cameras captured the moment for posterity.

Black Jack had them in the palm of his hand and he knew it. He relished the sensation. Men envied him. Women wanted him. Even if there were those gawkers that doubted him, he never doubted himself. As men in the background spread the large cloth with the bulls-eye on it and secured the four corners with stakes pounded into the ground. Black Jack teased the crowd. "Have a nice day, folks. Go out and see the attractions. Enjoy the fairgrounds. Don't forget to come back here at four o'clock for the show stopping end to our spectacular demonstration."

The crowd applauded heartily, enthusiastically, but somewhat apprehensively as well. Many didn't know what they should be feeling and lingered uncertainly. Some stayed with the aim of keeping the trick 'honest.'

It did not matter to Herman, he and his staffers disappeared from the scene leaving only Carl, a silent sentinel, seated in the limo adjacent to the stage, waiting and watching. He never left his post.

Towards two in the afternoon a group of pigeons, pregnant with peanuts and pretzels from the carnival stands, landed on the cloth looking for a place to rest. Carl emerged from the limo, his first time during the vigil, and quickly coaxed the birds into leaving. In addition to the aviarists, there was a small crowd milling about, perhaps two dozen in all, spectators waiting for the conclusion of the stunt one way or another. It probably didn't matter to most.

About three-thirty, Black Jack arrived looking positively electrified. The girls accompanied him and brought Carl some food, samples from the midway.

"How's she doing?" BJ asked, conscious of the incongruity of the question.

"Just fine. Boss" a somber reply. "Everything's going just fine."

"Good. That's what I like to hear, positive attitude. Girls, you better go and set things up. Get ready to sell your wares," Black Jack joked. "Don't worry, Carl. She _is_ just fine. It won't be long now."

Indeed it was not long until Andrew and his crew showed up and began selling merchandise. The renewed activity around the magician's site, combined with the rapidly concluding air show, encouraged the audiences return. Everyone wanted to have the best possible vantage point for the unearthing. It was now after four in the afternoon and the merchandisers were doing brisk business. Everyone wanted a piece of memorabilia just in case the stunt failed.

Herman and the girls took the stage about four thirty, smiling and waving to the crowd that was growing thicker by the minute.

"Everyone, may I have your attention please?" Black Jack needed no megaphone to address the crowd. They stood about in quiet anticipation. "The air show is about to conclude and I caution you not to stand too close to the bulls-eye where my darling associate is entombed. Our special guest will be dropping in any minute, and he may be a little off in his logistics." The crowds moved back substantively, but reluctantly.

Minutes later a biplane, a two-seater, did a loop to loop far overhead from where the crowd had gathered. While the plane was upside down on the second revolution, the passenger fell from the rear seat. The gathering oohed and aahed; this event momentarily distracting their attention. Heads were riveted skyward, fingers pointing. The figure began to plunge, then suddenly a parachute opened and the descent slowed. The aviator was gently gliding, falling right toward them.

"Don't worry, folks. That is our special guest, and he is right on time." Black Jack and the girls clapped encouraging the crowds to do likewise.

Slowly, adroitly, the practiced parachutist made his way through the clear skies to the looming objective below, landing just as planned within feet of the center.

"Ladies and Gentlemen, I'd like to introduce Lieutenant Julian, our special guest. The lieutenant is an aviator supreme and hero of the Great War in Europe. Let's give him a hand. He never misses his mark." While the crowd was celebrating loudly, Black Jack seethed at Andrew. "Okay, show's over. Let's get that thing out of the way and dig her up."

Quieting the audience with his outstretched arms, he was heard to say, "And now the time has come for the culmination of the event that everyone has been waiting for all day, the triumphant return of my partner. Witness the truly incredible results of mind over matter."

With the end of this exclamation, Black Jack left the stage and rushed over to where the men had already begun the exhumation. The crowds followed as far as they could, packed tightly into the metal barricade. The spectators in front were beginning to regret their decision to be first in line as the crowds moved in behind them, relentlessly pushing. It was four-fifty.

The box was unearthed, raised and stood slowly upright on the ground. There was a hush of anticipation from the crowd as Herman, for once in his life ignoring the audience, opened the lid and peered inside. The following minutes equaled an eternity.

Black Jack spoke into the box softly, then louder for the bystanders to hear. "Eva, arise. Open the door! You are now to awake from your slumber and join us once more." Nothing happened immediately and the crowd stirred, murmured. Herman called Carl over to assist him. Just in case? The chauffeur joined him and conferred, then looked into the coffin. It was all a theatric- a play.

Designed to give Eva the time she needed to recover and step out to the amazement and adoration of the crowd which went wild at her emergence. The consummate show woman waved to her fans and received a kiss on the cheek from her doting paramour before being assisted to the limo by her chauffeur.

"There you have it, friends." Black Jack was beside himself with joviality. "The secrets of the Tibetan monks displayed for your viewing pleasure. Tell your friends, tell your family. You'll not see anything like it anywhere else. Buy some souvenirs to commemorate the event. Andrew and the girls will be here for another hour. My associate and I are going home. It has been a rather long day." Black Jack disappeared into the limo beside the reclining Eva and the limo sped off presumably toward Manhattan.

As they turned out of the Fairgrounds, Herman held his weakened lover to buoy her from the bouncing of the limo as the ground underneath changed from dirt to pavement. He held her face with one hand and looked into her tired eyes. "Honey, you were incredible," he said tenderly.

She was too tired to fashion a response.

Eva recovered her strength in a few short days. A true testament to her indomitable spirit, the essence of the phoenix that dwelled deep within. The first two days she had her meals in bed. From this vantage point she could see her man running up and down the hall excitedly when he was at home. There had been little time for lengthy conversation that first week of July. Nevertheless, Eva knew the signs. Her demonstration, that 'consummate feat of endurance' as one of the papers she read had called it, was an unqualified success.

Privately she said a prayer of thanks to God for giving her the courage and strength to undergo the ordeal. Publicly in an interview conducted in her living room, she thanked Herman for his constant coaching and training. Madame Deborah for the emotional support during those 'first dark days' as she put it, resisting temptation to go into further detail. Finally, she thanked her parents for their rigid Christian upbringing. She went on to say that yes, she would perform the feat again, probably several more times that summer. No, she wasn't quite sure when and where.

Black Jack was in charge of the itinerary. The interviewer asked the final pressing question. "What would you say to other women who were contemplating trying to beat your record?"

"Don't," Eva replied seriously. "I did not attempt this feat of endurance to set records. In fact, I'm not sure any record has been set. I only wanted to help further the career of Mr. Herman. To aid him in his quest. That of being the greatest African American magician in history." Eva would have ended the conversation there, but something urged her to issue a word of caution to any would-be copycats.

"Just one more thing I'd like to say to all of the ladies out there. Consider carefully before you contemplate attempting any death-defying acts. There is always a price to pay, and it might cost you your life."

"That sounds like good advice. Thank you. Miss Eva. I believe we have enough." The reporter put down her pad and shook Eva's hand.

Black Jack showed up later in the afternoon grinning from ear to ear. He was carrying another bunch of roses, which he promptly gave to the new housekeeper who was there ostensibly to wait on Eva's beck and call. "You really are sensational. Do you know that?" He regarded Eva with such a look as she had rarely seen before. Something akin to awe and worship.

She was still sitting in the living room two hours after the interview concluded. She had been idly looking out the window. A crowd was gathered at the ballpark across the river. Apparently, a game was on. Eva had never been to a ballgame like normal people. She feared that she would never be normal again.

Herman was still speaking, "We are confirmed at several state fairs here in New England. I think a couple of them secretly wanted to wait and see our performance in New Jersey before they gave the go ahead. You know, try as we might, I don't think we'll ever top that show unless we bring a stunt pilot along with us. Honey, you should have seen the crowd's reaction when that Lieutenant floated down to land on top of you. Right on target!"

"A real show stopper, I'll bet," Eva concurred, stealing his thunder. She was growing tired, soon dinner and then bed. "How many more times will you want me to do this, Herman? I told the lady reporter three or four times."

"That's all, baby. That's all," he soothed. "And only at the largest venues. Those state fairs I mentioned. Otherwise, I'll have Marsha and Charmainge run through a stable of old tricks and go back to being 'Professor Herman, Mentalist- Solver of Problems.' Y'know like we did at the Liberty. All you have to do is stand by me looking radiant," He added meekly. "That is if you feel up to it. After all, you are a star in your own right now. People will come out just to see that 'Buried Alive Girl' in person."

"I could manage that," she said, looking introspectively. "Yes, I am a star in my own right, aren't I?"

As Black Jack had promised, the stunt would only be performed a limited number of times. He could see that it was wearing on her health, tearing her down. Herman hadn't stopped to consider that by relying on Madame Deborah's prophecy that he was pressing his luck. She hadn't told him how many times to attempt the feat. And of course, she would not give him direct instruction; provide a blueprint for his actions. That's not how the gift worked. He knew better than that. When one had a fifty percent chance or even a thirty percent chance, you took a shot. But to guide someone through the course of future events, you could only suggest and encourage action. She had told him so. This was one of the secrets she imparted. Therefore, he was a success because he had willed it to be and worked hard to make it come true. The same internal forces put him on top would indicate to him when to stop. Of this, he was sure.

So the merry little band of entertainers toured the northeast that summer playing the 'Mentalist' act in the smaller venues that were interspersed between the large show stopping 'events' performed only at those selected locations where the audience could number up to one thousand.

Word had spread throughout the countryside aided by advertisements Black Jack had placed in local papers. The routine was the same in the first two demonstrations. First, a few simple illusions followed by Herman's political dialogue. Then Eva would be presented to the crowd, always to thunderous applause. Eva entombed was committed to her test of endurance. Not having a stuntman to parachute to a spectacular landing, Black Jack borrowed first a lion, and then a tiger for the second demonstration. Staked over Eva's subterranean location, the animal was a constant reminder of an 'event' in progress, tantalizingly promising of a fantastic conclusion.

In Nashua, New Hampshire in the middle of August the rain poured in from the Green Mountains for days before the scheduled event, forcing Black Jack to cancel Eva's part of the act. Instead, after an expanded magic act, Herman sat down with Eva by his side to answer questions.

The show went reasonably well, but the crowds were not quite as large. They did not stick around as long nor buy as much merchandise as usual. This disappointment was Herman's first indication that he was too far afield from his home base, and that the crowds were becoming more demanding. Their sense of danger jaded by the onslaught of events in this modern life, these modern times. He heard the doctor's voice in his mind 'Half of those people only show up in case you fail. They want to be the ones to say they were there when something went wrong. Tell their friends they beat you.'

Black Jack, ever the savvy entertainer, placed heavy reliance on his sixth sense. It was now clearly telling him that they had taken this act about as far as possible. 'Once more' he promised the muse. 'One more time and that will be all!' He had to perform for Mr. Lincoln.

XII

Baltimore

It was a crisp October morn. A hint of the previous night's frost still hung in the air. A harbinger of the cool weather that would soon invade Baltimore from the western mountains. The rising sun had been greeted by clear azure blue skies. Sunlight reflected off of gaily colored leaves that were just beginning to turn golden. The clear skies bode well for the day's performance and at this latitude; the sunny day would prove warmer than San Francisco in summer.

Black Jack reminisced about those three weeks just over a year ago and the correspondence that had lead to that momentous meeting and the conveyance of the trick that changed his career. Propelled him from the ranks of just another black magician to superstardom. 'Changed them' his mind chided. He could never mitigate Eva's contribution; he would be lost without her. He must never forget that fact and always let her know just how much she meant to him. Perhaps one day he could properly reward her for all of her love and devotion. Adequately repay her for all of the hardships she had borne on his behalf. And she bore them so well, quietly, unprotesting, very workman-like in her approach. Nowadays, more methodical than ever before. Suddenly he missed her effervescence, her joie de vie, the way she used to call him Daddy. But...

Herman had satisfied himself with the Baltimore location for his last 'Woman Buried Alive' performance. His magical prowess was simply no match for the Washingtonian bureaucracy. Nothing could be promised before the following spring, and even then obtaining the proper permits was dubious. He had gotten that feeling from a compilation of several telephone interviews. 'This is the nation's capital. Theatrical events of this nature were simply not done here.'

So he had been able to secure a pasture owned by a chicken farmer just north of Baltimore. Having advertised the event in Black-American newspapers from Philadelphia to Richmond, he was certain of a large turnout. Herman smiled wryly to himself. That poor farmer didn't know what he was in for. Never mind, he had been well paid for the use of his land. Black Jack suspected that the price had gone up when he heard the magician's name. Perhaps he, Herman, should have hired a white lawyer as agent. Too late for that now. Andrew and Carl had been sent down two weeks ago with a crew to erect a stage and prepare the venue for their star performer.

Eva and the girls had accompanied Black Jack on the four hour train ride two days previous. The trip, pleasant, but uneventful for seasoned veterans like Eva and her beau, was nothing short of a busman's holiday for the two neophytes who had never traveled this far on a train before. Much of their travels that summer had been by cramped auto with limited breaks to stand and stretch. Here they could roam the train peering at one thing or another, gawking at unfamiliar sights or rivers passing far below. Eva saw them running through the coach for the third time and wondered if she was ever that naïve. Eva couldn't imagine her and her sister ever behaving in such an infantile fashion. Not that these two were related, which made their actions all the more egregious. She didn't dwell on it, focusing instead on her sister. Eva hadn't talked to her family for quite some time. She sincerely wished that they were doing well. There would be time enough soon to catch up. The holidays were coming. A good time to go home, rest and regroup.

Black Jack would undoubtedly be going home to be with his family, 'his wife.' Eva bit her lip at the thought and decided resolutely to go home and be with her family for a while. After this trick, one more performance. Black Jack had promised this was the last time. When she looked into those deep brown eyes awash with ruby red, she could refuse him nothing. 'But just what was his fascination with Mr. Lincoln anyway?' No answers from her mind. Instead, the two of them sat there in silence as the scenery sailed by watching the two assistants making fools of themselves.

At the hotel check-in, she signed the registry Mrs. Herman, as was their custom. Especially in the south as unwed couples were not only frowned upon, but in many cases, expressly forbidden. The two starlets, who bunked together, received a room across the hall from the Hermans'.

When Eva remarked about the queer looks they received from the front desk attendant, Herman quipped, "Clearly they haven't had a lot of show business professionals staying here." That was two days before the scheduled event. The city was already a buzz with anticipation. After a quick conference with Carl and Andrew, Herman departed with his female entourage determined to show them a good time on their first night in the new town.

"How about some seafood tonight, ladies? Can't come to Baltimore without sampling the best of what Maryland has to offer," Herman offered affably, once again enjoying his role as tour guide. They all agreed that was a wonderful idea, so Carl was engaged to drive them to one of the minority owned restaurants that dotted the north side of town.

Eva was escorted in on Herman's arm, as was her place and custom. Carl brought up the rear with a woman on each side. The group was seated next to a couple wearing lobster bibs and swacking with mallets at large reddish crabs. Pieces of shell and fleshy innards sprayed everywhere, miraculously not reaching their table.

The young starlets could not contain their dismay in having to witness such a disgusting scene. "I'm not eating that," Marsha complained quite vociferously, looking to her comrade in arms for confirmation.

"Relax, girls, relax. What the natives lack in sophistication, they make up for in Epicurean delights. We will order the crab patties. All of the taste without the fuss and muss. Now, how does that sound?" He talked to them as if children. The girls looked at each other and decided that would be okay.

"Waiter," Herman bellowed as soon as the man came into view. "What are they eating?" He pointed to the next table.

"Why those are the Miles River hard crabs. Would you like those?"

"Yes, but made up as crab cakes. Give us some blue crab cakes also. Your white marlin, is it fresh?"

"Yes, sir, caught fresh this afternoon."

"Very good. For the main course we will have marlin fillets all around. In the meantime, give us some oysters on the half shell for appetizers."

As usual, Black Jack was right. The meal turned out to be an Epicurean's delight. The crab cakes meaty and flavorful, browned to perfection in a seasoned butter sauce. The fish fillet also sautéed, was light and flake, served with hush puppies and harvest fresh sweet corn.

Everyone commented on how well the food was prepared, and Carl, the last to finish, continued until he got his fill.

"You better slow down, old man. Only so much fish in the sea," Herman jibed him. The girls giggled.

Eva, who had been quiet through most of the dinner, rose to his defense. "Don't let them kid you, Carl. You go ahead and enjoy your meal. That's what God put the food on the earth for, to be enjoyed. Her defense of the chauffeur did not go unnoticed by Black Jack, who scrunched his eyelids together and wrinkled his nose in response.

After dinner, it was time for entertainment. At least, so said the boss. Eva begged off indicating that she was worn out from travel and needed to gather her strength for the big show two days hence forward. "Honey, you go and have some fun. Let off a little steam. I'm going back to the room. I need my rest."

"Okay, okay. You go back to the hotel. Carl will drive you. Meanwhile, the girls and I will knock over a couple of jazz joints.

I've heard tell of a couple of places that serve that Blue Blazes, Maryland corn liquor, you know 'moonshine.' Would you like to try that, girls?"

"Sure, Mr. Herman, that sounds fine," they replied in unison.

So it was that Carl escorted Miss Eva back to the hotel for her beauty rest and Black Jack took off with the girls to revel in the nightlife.

"Are you all right, Eva?" Carl inquired as they prepared to begin their journey.

She roused out of her contemplative state to assuage the man's concerns. "No, I'm fine, Carl, nothing to worry about. Seems like only yesterday I was the one headed out to enjoy the nightlife. Now I'm too tired to do anything but sleep. I think I've gotten old before my time. What happened to me?" A rhetorical question. They both knew the answer.

"Don't worry. He still loves you every bit as much as he did yesterday, perhaps more. He is beholden to you even more than you are to him. Without you, well I don't know where we would be. You are something special, Eva, a real show stopper."

"Thank you, Carl. That means so much coming from you. Now let's get your show stopper back to her bed so she can prepare for her big finale."

Later that evening, Eva was awoken from a sound sleep by the noises of a couple wildly copulating somewhere down the hall.

"Oh yes, do it Daddy. Harder, harder. That's right. Ohhh! Give it to me!" A woman's voice echoed down the corridor, full of reckless abandon.

Eva, only half awake, turned her head restlessly to the other side of the pillow and resumed her slumbers. Before she lapsed into unconsciousness, she realized that Herman's place was empty.

Sometime later she awoke to another vignette. Black Jack, having obviously returned, was showering. She could hear the water rushing, steam escaped through the cracked door as did a stream of light from the single bulb. She could not tell what time it was. She only had the notion that it was late. Feigning sleep as he came to bed, jostling the mattress upon his entry, Eva remained motionless with eyes closed. She lay there for some time using her hearing and the tendrils of her mind to reach out and scrutinize the condition of her man as he tried to sleep.

When she awoke the next morning in the full light of day, he was gone, probably attending to preparations for tomorrow's scheduled event. His impression in the sheets was so light as to be almost nonexistent. She hardly believed he had been in bed at all. Had she dreamed his presence? 'No.' Eva shook her head. It was not merely a case of wishful thinking. He had been there. His scent lingered on the sheets. 'Scrubbed fresh,' her innermost voice reported. 'Yes, he had been there and now he's gone. He left his scent to carry on.'

She rose ruefully and complained to that inner voice, I don't know what's going on anymore. He treats me like I was some sort of precious china doll. 'Is it me, or is it him?' No reply from the aforementioned voice. Alone once again, she dressed and prepared to go down to the dining room and have breakfast by herself.

Around noon while she was sitting in the hotel lobby reading the local tabloid, Carl burst through the double doors apparently looking for her.

"Good morning. Miss Eva. How are you feeling today? Mr. Herman sent me with a message." The big man was nearly out of breath.

"I'm fine, Carl. I wish everyone would stop tip-toeing around me," Eva responded somewhat tersely, regretting the words as soon as they had left her lips. "I'm sorry, hon. You said he sent a message?"

"Yes, he said for you to get all dolled up this evening. That he was going to introduce you to some important businessmen."

"That probably means he will be up all night playing cards." Her voice was tinged with irony. Then another thought, "Tell me this, after you dropped me off did you go back and pick him up?"

"No, ma'am. He told me to take the rest of the night off. I was really glad too because Andrew and I have been working really hard to get the site ready for your performance," said Carl in his usual good natured way. Eva was sure he genuinely cared for her. It was comforting somehow.

She patted him on one of his bulging biceps. "I'm sure you have. How's it looking by the way?"

"Really swell. We've built a stage and cleared the field next to it for your performance. We've borrowed some animals from a local zoo. There is going to be an elephant this time! And a lot of local vendors have paid a fee to sell their wares during the day. Black Jack says we will have a really big crowd since the weather looks like it's going to cooperate." The big man was overflowing with enthusiasm. Too bad it didn't rub of on Eva.

"Sounds great. Is everybody out there now?"

"Why, yes. I ferried them out to the farm early this morning right after breakfast. Black Jack said you were still asleep." Carl said that last almost apologetically.

"That's fine. When you see him tell him I will be ready. What time was it again?"

"Oh, I'm sorry. I forgot to tell you, six o'clock."

"Six o'clock it is then," she replied returning to her newspaper.

"Gentlemen, I'd like to present to you Mademoiselle Eva," Black Jack bellowed as he entered the room with his show stopper on the arm. While not the grand ballroom of a four star hotel, but merely the private dining room of a local restaurant, his entry had the same effect.

There she was bejeweled and dazzling in a near floor length ruby red gown, that 'Buried Alive' woman everyone was waiting to meet. As any good con man knows when an item becomes inaccessible it becomes even more mysterious and desirable. Thus was the case with Eva. Now that she was a star in her own right, her infrequent appearances made her presence all the more coveted.

Black Jack would show her off, introduce her to the dignitaries and then have her leave feigning tiredness in preparation for the big event, which was close to the truth. Let the starlets flatter and cajole, tantalize the men while they played cards. Eva was too good for that now. She was a star, his star performer.

So it was that after a dinner of laughter and levity Herman begged off for Eva and sent her back to the hotel to rest despite a chorus of groans from the assembly.

"Don't worry, gentlemen. Don't worry. Black Jack has something up his sleeve," he said with a chuckle. Sure enough when Carl came to fetch Eva, he brought the two starlets, appropriately attired of course. Eva took one look at their skimpy outfits and said, "You boys have fun. But not too much fun," she cautioned. "I expect to see each and every one of you bright and early in the morning." With that, she and Carl made their way out through the front of the restaurant leaving the men to their night of frivolity.

On show days, the mornings came early. Eva arose to find Black Jack already shaving in the bathroom. It was just after dawn and again she could hardly tell from the condition of the sheets whether he had slept or not. She decided not, with little evidence to support either proposition.

Urgency gripped her and she rushed the commode pushing her way past her lathered partner in the process. There was no modesty in their relationship. Besides, these hotel bathrooms had obviously been made for one occupant at a time.

"Are you ready? Going to be a glorious day." Black Jack's way of greeting his lover instead of 'Hello, darling. How are you this morning?'

"Ready as I'll ever be," the automatic response. Then the cross-examination, "You're sure that this is the last one? The last time I will have to undergo this ordeal?"

"Darling, yes, a thousand times over. Never again." Herman's eyes met hers to prove his sincerity.

"Fine," Eva's acquiesance. Her mind rankled 'Until he can think of some other way to torture you.'

"I'm thinking of going home after the show." She was in the shower now, her hair wrapped in a bun to prevent its getting wet. No good lying around all day with wet hair. You could catch your death. 'The ground would be cold today despite the warm sun up above.' Involuntarily, she shuddered.

"Yes, we will all be leaving after the show. I've booked passage for us to New York day after tomorrow." Black Jack had finished shaving and was working on his pencil thin mustache.

"No, I mean I'm going home to St. Louis for the holidays right after the show," the unequivocal response from behind the curtain.

Herman fell silent, not knowing her mind, leaving Eva free to elucidate the logic of her argument. "After all you'll be going home to Chicago soon. How long since you've seen your kids now? Ten months?" She was spot on. "And your wife." The latter comment cut through the curtain between like a knife. "I just figured since you don't need me in New York or at parties anymore that I would take some well deserved time off with my family. Give you some time to figure out your next move." There she had completed her task, finally gotten out the words that had been burning within her breast for some time. There was rank silence from the other side of the curtain.

Then as the commode flushed, a solitary "Very well" as Herman exited the bathroom, leaving Eva alone with her thoughts.

He was fully dressed when she emerged, straightening his white bow tie in the mirror.

"Here, let me help you with that." She always did his ties. Black Jack turned dutifully and stood straight up like a little boy as Eva straightened his tie, her open robe revealing a slim toned figure and pouty breasts. In an instant he grabbed her to him, her gleaming nakedness crushed against soft cotton as he kissed her deeply, passionately.

After momentary interlude she backed away brusquely, pushing him away with her arms. "Now none of that. There isn't time. Besides we can't have the Great Black Jack Herman appearing with his suit mussed."

"There was a time when that wouldn't matter." Touché, Black Jack had cut her to the quick.

Ignoring the comment, she grabbed her nylons and plopped down on the bed preparing to dress.

"How did the poker game go last night? Were there any big winners?" She had successfully transmuted the conversation.

"Just one. Some chicken farmer who lives just outside of town." Herman grabbed his top hat and cane.

"What a lucky man." Eva smiled a wide, knowing grin.

"The girls looked awfully pretty last night."

"Yes, they were at their glowing best. Don't worry. I let them tease, but there is no pleasing. We don't want to get that kind of reputation. Just leave them high and horny."

Herman smirked and his whole face became a scowl bisected by shiny white teeth.

"I know, always leave them wanting more." Eva, finished with the stockings, was reaching for her garter belt.

"All righty honey. I'm off." Black Jack was suddenly ebullient. The start of the show was drawing near. His blood was beginning to quicken. "Let's have a great show. I love you."

"I love you too," came the dutiful reply.

"Aw honey, don't be like that. Give us a kiss for luck." Herman bent down and his mouth covered hers once more. "That's better now. Put on a smile and get all of those negative thoughts out of your head. Everything will be better next year. I promise. Just concentrate on today."

"Okay." She mustered a smile. 'Just one more day,' Eva told herself.

"That's better. I'll tell Carl you'll be ready in half an hour. Love ya. Bye." And he was out the door.

Eva relaxed visibly after his departure. She luxuriated in the little time she had left to be alone with her thoughts. The couple enrapt in coital bliss the other night was preying on her mind.

There is an old saying that 'if anything can go wrong, it will.' Some call it Murphy's Law. While not everything was going wrong, there was enough askew to give a sober man pause. Not Black Jack with his devil may care attitude and belief in his predetermined manifest destiny. Something in every show was bound to go wrong. They would just plow right ahead. There was too much money riding on this event to do anything else. And plow ahead they must.

Traffic was backed up for four miles as a tour bus trying to negotiate the turn onto the farm road had run into a ditch and cracked an axel.

Herman, Andrew and the girls came rambling up the wrong side of the road honking all the way to clear their path. Stranded motorists had abandoned their vehicles becoming pedestrians and creating further confusion.

"Andrew, take us up to the stage and then bring the truck back and get this bus outta here. They're gonna hold up the show," the older brother barked.

"Right. I'm on it. I'll take a couple of guards and pull it off the road." Andrew thrust the gearshift into first and stormed up the dusty dirt road to the stage.

As soon as their precious merchandise was unloaded, Andrew and security guards departed to relieve the congested roadway that was preventing the suckers, er patrons, from completing their journey.

"Well, at least the stage looks to be in good shape," said Herman with hands on hips talking to no one in particular. The two young women were the only others in attendance.

"Where do you want these, Daddy?" asked Marsha, holding a box of Black Jack's simple magic tricks for kids.

"Put those over there," he pointed, "in the booth closest to the stage. The health tonic goes in the booth next to it." "Okey dokey," she replied and wiggled her way across the stage.

The October sun was rising rapidly as the vendors began to arrive to set up shop. Evidently the congestion was clearing. Herman looked at his pocket watch. It had stopped. 'Must have forgotten to wind it.' Anyway, he figured it was well past eight. Standing on the stage he could see the 'tin lizzies' beginning to file into the parking lot.

The long dirt road ran slightly uphill from the main highway. On one side was the chicken farm. On the other, a vacant pasture which for this occasion had been turned into a carnival town. An outlet in the barbed wire fence had been made to accommodate parking. The ditch corresponding had been filled. There was a guard on duty to take the ten dollars per car admission, hundred dollars per bus. The fees didn't end there, however. Once you entered carnival town, you had to pay for everything.

The stage in all of its grandeur was situated on the top of the gentle sloping hill. Two booths on the left side nearer the road housed the magician's merchandise. Eva's performance theatre was on the right. Next to that cleared patch of dirt, space was provided for a petting zoo populated with a whole host of tamed animals including a bear, foxes, two llamas, a camel and an odd assortment of cows, sheep and chickens. There was also a very friendly donkey and an elephant appropriately named Jumbo.

Stretching down the far side of the lot, a series of booths had been constructed at no small expense to the operator, where all manner of items would be hawked to an eager public. Everything from Maryland's finest seafood to barbeque ribs and chicken. All the ingredients required for a nice Sunday afternoon picnic in the country, including cotton candy. There were also a handful of booths dedicated to tests of skill and chance. Black Jack had wanted enough activities to keep the crowds from getting restless while waiting for the grand finale. He had even decided to add a second show reviving some of his Voodoo Tour illusions.

It was now nearly nine-thirty. Herman had gotten his watch started with a couple twists of the knob and a hard bare-knuckled rap. Nothing wanted to work right this morning. The parking lot was beginning to fill nicely, containing over a hundred cars with a smattering of busses stacked to one side. The pasture was certified for one thousand people by the county commissioner. Herman had paid dearly for the certificate. It could probably hold fifteen hundred paying customers, if not more. What he didn't realize until later was that once traffic began to back up, people started parking by the side of the road and on adjacent lands. Sneaking onto the property by hopping the fence behind the concession stands.

The show went on as planned. Promptly at ten, Black Jack took the stage in a puff of smoke. Looking downhill, as he was, he could see over the heads of the crowd to the parking lot where a considerable number were still filing out of their autos. No matter the show always started on time.

"Good morning. Welcome to our extravaganza. Has anyone seen my two lovely assistants?" he asked jovially. Actually, he could see them scurrying into their proper places. There it was, one puff of smoke and then the other from either side of the crowd.

"Here we are. Black Jack," they cried in unison.

"You had better get up here right away. We have a show to do," he scolded good naturedly. The performance was half an hour old when Herman surreptitiously checked his watch; he had just finished sawing Marsha in half and still no sign of Eva and Carl. Time to launch into his speech.

Everywhere he traveled. Black Jack spread a similar message, one of solidarity and the exercise of political and economic strength. He was more than halfway finished and still no sign of his show stopping entertainer. "We do not have to succumb to a regime of separate but equal, but should instead focus on a society of separate but better. Better opportunities for our working men and women. Better schooling for the younger generation with an emphasis on higher education as a means of climbing the economic ladder of success.

If we support black owned businesses and merchants, together we will work effectively to help keep our economy vigorous and expanding. Assuring better jobs, better living conditions and a better future for all our people." Herman was nearly finished with his oratory. While the crowd was politely attentive, he knew they were waiting to see Eva. So was he.

'There! There was the limo!' Black Jack saw them racing up the dirt road and he hastened his conclusion. "Remember we must look to the future while never forgetting the past. In order to become truly prosperous, we must become a society of owners and savers investing in the potential of one another. When we have to do business with other races, be sure to choose those individuals and corporations that have clearly demonstrated they take our interests into consideration.

Thank you for your kind attention. Hopefully, I have given you something not only to think about, but to act upon. Now, who wants to see something they've never seen before?" The crowd roared as Herman turned to see the limo arrive at the side of the stage.

"You're late," Black Jack hissed to Eva as she ascended to the platform.

"Car trouble," Eva replied tersely through clenched teeth.

"Never mind. Let's go. Andrew has everything ready." Herman turned back to the crowd and raised the arm of the woman buried alive. As usual, the crowd roared approval and pressed forward to mob the stage, eager to witness what they had only heard through rumor.

Andrew prepositioned the coffin and on Herman's signal, the exploding smoke bomb, it rose onto the stage. The raucous cacophony quickly subsided as Black Jack and Eva went into their dance.

Just before Herman issued the magic words, he asked under his breath, "Eva, if you still love me, trust me. This is the last time."

"I trust you." she replied somberly, tilting her head backward to stare into those deep brown eyes. The ruby swirl seemed to go around and around. It was done.

The volunteers carried her entombed body to the pit where she would begin her test of endurance. So far everything was going according to script.

For a time, the crowd milled about uncertain as to their next move. Many began to avail themselves of the recreations offered. Others simply spread blankets and camped out with boxed lunches, prepared to wait until the next show.

The first sign of trouble began in the petting zoo when Jumbo decided she would rather sit in the fresh dirt next door than in the pasture with the other creatures. Bounding away from her handlers, she decided that early afternoon would be the perfect time for a roll in the cool dirt.

"Hey, Black Jack, the elephant's gone wild. She's rolling over and over right where we placed Eva." Andrew's voice bordered hysteria.

"What the hell," Herman emerged from the tent where he had been resting, sans tie and jacket. Running across the pasture to the spot where the elephant luxuriated. Black Jack accosted the trainer.

"Get that thing out of here. Are you crazy?"

"I'm trying. She has got a mind of her own. There must be bugs or something in the grass causing her to itch. This is her way of scratching." The trainer was clearly exasperated.

Black Jack grabbed him around the collar and shouted, "I don't care about that. I'll kill it if I have to. She's endangering the life of my star." He was livid and on the borderline. Just then Andrew and Carl caught up and pulled him off the trainer.

"This isn't helping. You're drawing a crowd," hissed Andrew. "Relax. It will be all right." Indeed as the elephant rolled about using its trunk to throw dirt over her back, the crowd thickened, not wishing to miss a moment of the unscripted drama.

The trainer, now filled with the fear of God, returned with a bullwhip and began exhorting the animal. Long minutes later while Carl and Andrew restrained Black Jack, Jumbo reluctantly returned to the adjacent pasture. There she was chained until her trailer could be summoned to take her back to the zoo.

"Nothing to see here, folks. Everything's all right. Enjoy your afternoon. Next show in an hour and a half." A now becalmed Black Jack was trying to put a glad spin on the occurrence. While he could hide his apprehension, he couldn't help staring at the indentation in the ground right over Eva's location.

"Come on, BJ. Let's go get a drink. She'll be all right. At least she's in a sturdy container. Not like that plywood box we used in those practice sessions." Carl encouraged.

"But you don't understand. I promised her this would be the last time. She trusts me. I can't let anything happen to her now." Black Jack, clearly beside himself with anguish, was nearly in tears.

"Relax, everything will be fine. Get some rest. Remember you promised to put on the voodoo show at two, and like you always say, the show must go on."

But the show did not go on. The weather saw to that. Within an hour the clear blue sky became overcast and grey. Wisps of ice cold air circulated through the encampment, spooking the animals and unsettling the guests. Out toward the western mountains a dark black line appeared on the horizon. All signs pointed to a powerful storm in the making. Odds were it would arrive before the scheduled two o'clock show.

"Herman, what are we going to do? That looks like one big mother headed this way." Even as Andrew spoke, a clearly defined black amorphous blob was looming closer and closer. The high cirrus had blocked the warming rays of the sun causing a corresponding drop in temperature of at least fifteen degrees.

"Nothing for now. Maybe it will blow over and move out to sea. But let's get those animals caged just in case. Last thing we need are any more rampaging critters."

Ten minutes later, the wind picked up creating swirling dust devils in the parking lot and the adjacent dirt road, overturning blankets and generally causing anything not tied down to undergo a frenzy of activity. Black Jack decided to address the crowd. "Just a little inclement weather, folks. Nothing to be concerned about. Most likely, the approaching storm will blow right past us. Just in case, we suggest that for now you return to your cars and busses. But don't you go anywhere. Just as soon as this little inconvenience blows by, the girls and I will be back to entertain you. And of course, you'll want to be around for the fantastic completion of Eva's test of endurance."

As he spoke, the crowds had already begun scurrying toward the parking lot, abandoning many discardables to the will of the wind. Those hundreds that snuck over the fence to see the show huddled around the concession stands which began to take on the appearance of an overcrowded shantytown. As the first large drops of wind driven rain started to fall, the open pasture had been completely abandoned. The clear sunny day had given way to wind driven rain, the crackle of lightening and the resounding accompanying boom.

Far from blowing over, the torrent stalled and strengthened over the conclave, most likely fueled by moist offshore currents. Long rivulets formed as gravity encouraged the overflow from the sky downhill in ever faster currents. The little road that separated them from the chicken farm was fast becoming a babbling brook. A small pond formed in the indentation that was Eva's grave.

The trio of men looked out-the tent flap. From their location behind the stage they could see naught but the curtain of rain. They couldn't see the cars beginning to leave or the hordes in the shantytown abandoning en masse over the fence as lightening cackled overhead.

"How long are we gonna wait, BJ? How long before we go and get her outta there?" It was Carl that spoke first.

There was a long silence interspersed with flashes of bright light as BJ consulted his muse. "We will wait another half hour. She's only been down there three hours. She should be all right. If the rain doesn't stop by then, we will cancel the rest of the show."

"If the rain doesn't stop by then, the show will cancel itself." said his brother more right than he realized. Already the parking lot was half empty.

In the ensuing half hour, the fury of wind, thunder and lightening subsided, but the rain kept up a steady downpour. Without any further word to the remaining vestiges of the scattered crowd, the promoters decided to unearth their star performer.

First, a small makeshift tent was erected over the site and the pond drained. Six strong men with long shovels went to work on the now saturated, impacted dirt that had been Jumbo's playground. It took an agonizingly long time.

The flurry of activity did not go unnoticed and even in the pouring rain, a crowd gathered around the barricade anxiously awaiting the outcome. Most didn't care if it had been four hours or six; they just wanted to see the successful resolution of the event that they would tell their grandchildren about. They wanted to see Eva emerge from the tent safe and sound.

The diggers had proceeded past the four foot level when Black Jack ordered them into silence. He had heard something. Perhaps it was a psychic connection with Eva, perhaps it was love, but he knew what he heard, the faint staccato of a woman screaming. Eva was awake-and trying to get out.

"Faster, men. Dig faster," he suddenly shouted trying to perform mental calculations. If she was awake then she would be expending oxygen at a rapid rate. She was running out of air. Moreover, the corresponding build up in carbon dioxide would soon begin to poison her, accentuating mental trauma she must have experienced when she awoke entombed. Black Jack couldn't be sure just when she revived from the trance, but he'd bet it had something to do with that damn elephant.

The men were nearly upon her now. Obviously, she heard them digging. They too could now hear her screaming and banging.

"Well, at least we know she's alive and all right." Carl tried unsuccessfully to comfort his boss.

"Yes, but she's been down there too long. She's running out of air. Listen to her, she's hysterical." Herman sounded near the edge of a breakdown himself.

Finally, the lid to the coffin was uncovered. Herman slid down the muddy slope into the open grave. He wanted to be the first person she saw when they opened the crypt.

There she was in her white performance gown gasping and choking on the fresh air, too rich in oxygen for her body to immediately process. She saw him leaning down over her and reached for him. Instead of hugging him in loving embrace, she beat him with balled fists about his head and chest.

"I hate you. I hate you," she wailed over and over in uncontrollable rage.

He grabbed her and held her close, her balled fists pounding a tune into his back. "I know, honey. I know. Let it all out. That's my girl. Shh! It will be all right now. Never again, I promise. Never again." Black Jack slowly managed to absorb her rage and transmute her hatred back into love.

As Eva began to breathe regularly, she began to compose herself and form coherent sentences. "Do you know how long I've been awake? It seemed like hours. There was this pounding noise above my head and a sound like everything was crushing down around me. At first I called out but when there was no response, I panicked, started kicking and screaming. Then my mind told me to relax. Maybe if I went into a light sleep I would use less air. Since I didn't know how long I had been down, there was no way of knowing how much time was left.

Later I awoke to what sounded like thunder, and I knew something must be wrong. I lay there for a long time trying not to breathe. I was hoping you were coming to get me, but my mind was going wild with crazy images. I didn't think I would make it out alive." Eva sobbed into his shoulders.

He let her have a good long cry, and then it suddenly occurred to him that there must be people outside the tent awaiting her triumphant reappearance.

"Quick, Andrew, take a look outside. How many people are out there?" BJ instructed, the showman in him returning.

"Must be a couple hundred just standing there in the pouring rain, waiting and watching," came the prompt report.

"Okay, here's what we do. Carl, you get the limo. Park it next to the tent. Eva, you will just have to take a couple of steps, wave to the crowd and then disappear into the auto. You can do that, can't you?"

"Sure, I can manage that," she said thoughtfully, her color returning.

"Oh, and one more thing. When you emerge from the tent, take a drink of the tonic for me, baby." He smiled at her.

"Anything for the show, Daddy," she responded with bitter sarcasm.

"Okay, everybody. Let's go. Guys, help me get her out of here."

The flurry of activity heightened the anticipation of the crowd. They packed tightly into the barricade and murmured amongst themselves.

The limo pulled up alongside the tent and Carl emerged to walk over and open the flap. The pouring rain had remitted to a heavy shower.

All at once, there she was. A vision of loveliness in white surrounded by dark brown and grey. She was waving to the crowd. They responded with jubilation uncharacteristic of people standing in a muddy field for almost an hour. A palpable sense of relief spread through the audience.

Now Black Jack was by her side encouraging her to drink some of his tonic to help her regain her strength. She tilted the bottle up to her lips and then walked unaided to the limo. A final wave before vanishing into the back seat.

"There you have it, folks." Black Jack was speaking. The crowds were cheering. Even the rain showed indications of subsiding. Things were looking up.

"Thank you for coming. Andrew and the girls will be here to help you purchase memorabilia of this once in a lifetime event..." The noise of the remaining attendees drowned out Herman's summation.

As the limo exited the rear entrance to the pasture Eva, reclining her length upon the back seat, had one simple request. "Carl, take me home."

"Relax, honey. Remember we have train tickets for the day after tomorrow," Herman interjected.

"No. I want to go to my home in St. Louis," she insisted. The strength of her voice belied her overall physical condition. "And I want Carl to take me now!" She repeated the command with extra emphasis. "Carl, I want you to take me, St. Louis, now!"

"Yes, mistress," the big man replied with gusto.

XIII
Through the Looking Glass

Of course Carl did not drive Eva all the way to St. Louis. After stopping briefly at the hotel, just long enough for Eva to pack her bags, he drove her to the Washington D.C. station where she could catch the evening's train to Chicago.

Eva arrived in the city of big shoulders before noon, plenty of time to transfer onto a train heading for St. Louis and parts south. Early afternoon she stood on the steps of the home her hard work played such a large part in purchasing. Unannounced as she was, Eva had forgotten to send a telegram; the family knew something was amiss.

"How long are you here for this time? Or have you decided to give up that man for good?" her father inquired brusquely upon finding his wayward daughter swinging on the porch in the early twilight.

His wife, upon hearing the commotion, came out and interceded on her daughter's behalf. "Charles, don't treat her like a child. She is a grown woman involved in complex relationships. Life is a lot more complicated now than when we grew up."

"Don't make excuses for these show folk. They live jaded lives with warped values. You can't tell me everybody in Chicago and

New York acts that way. The answer is very simple. What Eva needs is to find a man of her own and be done with this philanderer."

"Stop it both of you," Eva shrieked in exasperation. "I didn't come here to be argued over. You're both right. I'm not a child anymore, and I do need a man of my own. But right now I'm wrapped up in a complex relationship which I can't seem to get out of. Not now anyway. At least now I have a claim to fame. I am that 'Buried Alive Woman.' That's got to count for something. People will pay money just to see me. Black Jack said so."

"And you' ll never have to perform that awful stunt again. Right, honey?" Eva's mother encouraged, seeking to reassure her husband.

"Right," Eva said adamantly with a touch of vehemence. "I told him so before I left. From now on, he is to put me on a pedestal. No more daredevil stunts."

"I still say you should leave him for good, but you two have your own ideas. Far be it from me to argue with two women. Honey, is my dinner on the stove?"

"And where else would it be after all these years?" his wife chided.

"Good. I'm going in and leave you two to your own devices." Noisily the burly man stomped into the house.

After he was out of earshot, Eva continued with her mother. "I know he's right. Mom, but he doesn't understand. I can't leave him. Not ever! The best I can do is get away for a short time."

"Is it that you love him too much, honey?"

"It's more than that, Mother. It's like we are tied together as soul mates. That's the best way I can describe it." She decided not to say anymore.

Changing the subject, her mother asked, "So how long can you stay this time? Through the holidays?"

"Yes, I'll be here for a good long time," Eva said firmly.

"Hello. Honey, is that you? It's Lilly. Happy New Year." The voice squeaked through the receiver. "I've been trying to contact you, but I couldn't find the number. Finally I called Black Jack's and they gave it to me."

"Yes, yes. He called here a couple of times before Christmas, but I'm not ready to talk to him yet," Eva replied, still exasperated at the mere mention of his name.

"No, I'm not calling for him." (Pause) "Then he hasn't told you yet?"

Eva could sense the trepidation in the other's voice. She had to end the suspense. "Tell me what?" she demanded.

"Honey, Deborah's dead." (Another pause) "Hello? Hello? Are you there? Eva?"

Eva had dropped the receiver in the wake of this shocking news. It swung listlessly on the cord tethered to its wall mount in the hallway.

So many questions: 'When did it happen? How' And then the whys. Most importantly 'Why didn't Herman himself call her with the news?'

It happened days ago, just after the beginning of the New Year. Deborah was running to catch a bus. The streets of Chicago had been slickened by an overnight snow and <u>apparently</u> she slipped, stumbling into traffic. Fortunately, they said that her expiring was almost instantaneous."

Ruled an accident by the police who questioned the truck driver involved, no charges would be preferred and the incident marked closed.

Lilly continued with her duties as informant, "Honey, because Deborah had no next of kin and the apartment was empty, Wanda got the call. Apparently it was well known that Black Jack and Deborah shared a close association, Wanda called Andrew. Apparently, Black Jack was out of town."

"That's odd," said Eva out loud before she could stifle her reaction. 'Was he not home with the wife and kids over the holidays?'

"Anyway, the funeral is tomorrow afternoon. You had better come quickly if you want to say your goodbyes. You can stay with me in my extra room. It will be just like old times. Besides, Andrew says don't go to the apartment. At least that's what he told me, although he didn't say why. I have the feeling that something strange is going on here. Everybody's acting so weird!" Lilly had pinpointed the what, while she couldn't fathom the why.

"All right, I'll come. I owe her that much. It's too late for me to catch a train this evening. I have to pack and all. Tomorrow morning, first thing. I promise. Probably be there by noon. Look for me."

After she hung up she realized that she had been conversing as if she were sending a telegram instead of talking to a live person. Obviously, she had been caught up in the emotion of this unexpected and unwelcome news. 'Helluva way to start a new year.' She would have to tell her folks at dinner that she was leaving for Chicago. They would understand.

The cold wind whipped the scarves around the well-protected heads of the mourners. Bodies shivered and fur-lined collars were turned up in protest to the gale. A bitter chill presided over the early afternoon graveside service which was sparsely attended. Black Jack was there with his wife and family, along with a smattering of Deborah's loyal clientele. The most prominent members of her flock stayed away preferring to maintain anonymity. They were represented by wreaths of flowers of which there were aplenty, most with, but some without cards. There was even a gorgeous wreath expressing the condolences of Mr. Entolleni to wit: 'Deepest sadness on the tragic loss of your partner.' Herman paid particular attention to that message and purloined the card for future reference.

After the tasteful non-denominational service had acquitted itself, many of the mourners adjourned to a local south side restaurant for a brief celebration of her life. As per Deborah's wishes, it was a dry proceeding.

"You would think that being a clairvoyant and all that she would have been able to foresee her misstep and avoided the accident altogether," postulated Lilly. She and Eva had taken a small table close to one end of the side walls. As far away as possible from the constant mayhem surrounding Herman and his entourage.

Not far enough away to be invisible. He and Eva had exchanged glances, hard looks, at the burial. Now again sharp daggers shot between, usually when no one else was looking. Eva knew she would have to deal with him sooner or later.

"Maybe she did see the event. Maybe long ago. She told me in San Francisco that she 'knew' her place was in Chicago. That's why she was not coming with us to New York. Maybe she knew then. Maybe there was no way to avoid this outcome."

"Ooh, spooky," teased Lilly.

"Maybe this, maybe that." Neither woman turned. They both knew that deep booming voice all too well. "Maybe the alternative was too horrible to contemplate. Did you two geniuses think of that? Maybe Deborah took the easy way out." Black Jack had appropriated a chair from another table and sat down facing the two women. Before continuing the conversation, he removed a silver flask from his breast pocket and after liberating the cap poured a generous amount into his glass. It was obvious that he had been drinking for some time.

"Do you ladies have any idea what is going on here?" he growled while the women looked at each other dumbfounded. "It's war!" He cursed under his breath. Having successfully startled them, he finished his drink in one gulp and then poured another while they sat speechless.

"So you think I'm crazy." He produced the condolence card from his pocket. "Read this-deepest sadness on the loss of your partner. Ha! It was those bastards. They murdered her."

"Herman, keep your voice down. People will hear you. Besides you don't know what you're talking about," Lilly challenged.

"Oh, don't I? The last thing Deborah said to me was not to worry about her, that she could take care of herself. That I had enough to do worrying about Eva and the show." Incredibly, he was close to tears.

"What you ladies don't know, what I never told you, was that after we came back from San Francisco I was visited-by this man." He pointed angrily at the card. "He told me of how they were getting into the personal security business. He said that they could protect us and exact retribution if 'anything happened' to my personnel or property."

The women stared at him open-mouthed. Then Lilly began the cross-examination, "But you don't know that. You don't have any proof."

"Open your eyes. You live here. You read the papers. This sort of thing is happening everyday," BJ barked. "Besides, the man showed up right after we arrived and found the vandalized vehicles." Both women looked at him in confusion.

"See, see, that's another thing you ladies know nothing about. The very night we arrived and Eva went straight to St. Louis, we found the cars, tires slashed and all. If you don't believe me, ask Carl." The girls looked across the restaurant to another table where the big man was attempting a simple magic trick. They decided to take Herman's word.

"So I know what I'm talking about. Remember I know people and these snakes were up to no good from day one. I just wish we could have gotten out of here before trouble erupted."

Inadvertently, Black Jack had dropped a bomb shell. Realizing his faux paux, he let loose with the other. "Anyway, if it's a war they want then that's what they will get. I suggest you two ladies keep your heads down."

"Black Jack, what are you talking about?" Eva deciding to speak hoped-that her calming tone would persuade Herman to cut through all the melodrama and tell them straight up what was going on.

Lilly interrupted, "Hold on. What do you mean 'You wish you could have gotten out of here.' You mean you're moving?"

Black Jack answered indirectly, "We're just speeding up the schedule a little, that's all. After the reception we received in New York, Eva can tell you, the die was cast. The most important people in the country, for our purposes, live in Harlem. Culture, finance, manufacturing, all the expertise, all of the creativity. The cauldron is boiling hot and overflowing with potential. I decided when I sent for Andrew last spring that my headquarters should be in New York. That's when Andrew gave me the message from Deborah that it was all right." BJ, his mouth now dry, stopped to pour another drink.

Suddenly, a light went off in Lilly's brain, the realization of-what he was saying was just beginning to dawn upon her. She was livid. Lilly rose swiftly. The chair fell backward as she sprung to her feet. Flattening her right palm, she brought her hand violently into contact with his face, knocking the glass to the floor with a resounding crescendo.

"You rat! " Lilly bellowed loudly for the whole place to-hear. "You hung us out to dry. We're not pawns in your little power play. We are people. People with rights not to have our lives put into peril. You filthy rat bastard."

Black Jack, while taken aback, was rarely at a loss for words. He replied displaying the coldly calculating disposition of his will, "Deborah did not think you would be in danger or she would have told me."

"You don't know that for certain. Nobody does. You can't trust her opinion. She's dead." Lilly crying, now clearly fear-stricken, stormed out of the restaurant leaving overturned chairs in her wake.

Eva, taking charge, rose to go comfort her friend. "I'll go and talk to her. Calm her down."

"Tell her she can come to New York; share that big apartment with you. I've bought a townhouse for the family." Herman was just full of surprises.

"I'll deal with you later. I haven't decided whether I will go to New York or not," Eva said savagely.

"Suit yourself, but if you stay here be mindful of what I've said. Keep your head down. Plans are already in the works. Tell Lilly," he instructed dourly.

"Oh, you men are the worst. I think you're all wicked." With that, Eva stormed off to find her friend.

Eva did not catch up to her fleeing ex-partner until she reached the apartment. Once there, she had to repeatedly bang on the door to gain entry.

"Lilly, it's me. Open up."

Finally, the door opened a crack. The chain lock fully extended, a teary-eyed face peered forth. Eyeliner streaking each cheek gave the usually gregarious young woman a sad clown look, understandable given recent revelations. "I thought maybe it was a goon squad come to finish the job." She sobbed between inhalations that bordered on hiccups.

"Open the door, silly. It's only me." Eva suddenly recalled those lines had been used by the other to comfort her in a time of personal crisis. A tempest in the teapot by comparison. She marveled on how far they had come, and know Deborah was dead. 'What had she told Herman? Life like the show must go on. Yes, she knew.' Eva was certain of that fact now.

Slowly the chain was removed and the police lock adjusted. Eva was granted permission to enter.

"Come on, let's get you cleaned up and then get some alcohol into you. That's the ticket.

Everything looks better when you're half-crocked. Besides, we didn't have a proper wake for our departed sister."

"That damn man. He knew and he didn't say a word to anyone, did he?" She looked to Eva for confirmation.

"Honey, he couldn't 'know,' he could suppose. Only Deborah could know for sure and she made no attempt to move out of harm's way. Perhaps she was offering herself as the sacrificial lamb. You know, paying the price for all of us." Eva talked as she scrubbed Lilly's face clean, washing away the fear and trepidation, leaving her clean scrubbed-and ready to face the world again. Eva concluded with a thought designed to comfort and allay further fears, "Certainly if she thought something bad was going to happen to you, she would have told someone, right?"

"I suppose, but what if that something were to come after? I mean, she couldn't see after, could she?" still sniffing, Lilly asked the unanswerable question.

"That's why Black Jack advised us to keep our heads down," Eva replied with vigor. A plan rapidly generating in her mind. "He sounded as if reprisals were already in the works." She sat Lilly at the kitchen table.

While Lilly slowly quieted her sobbing, Eva searched the cabinets for the hidden bottle of scotch. She presented scotch, soda and two glasses of ice along with her plan of action. "Tell me now, is there anything keeping you here?"

"No," Lilly had to slowly drag the confirmation out of her depths, unwilling to share the secret even with her closest friend. "My latest 'sugar daddy' went back to his wife just before the holidays."

Eva winced with silent understanding. "Then why don't you come back to New York with me?" Eva handed her the solution to their problem along with three fingers of scotch.

"I don't know. What's in New York besides Herman?" Lilly spat his name.

"Why everything. I've got a lovely apartment overlooking the river. It's high up on the hill. There's plenty for us to do. Why we don't even have to see him." Eva, having warmed to –the idea, was now speaking elatedly. "Come-on, it will be like old times. We'll-be roomies again."

After a couple of drinks Lilly was persuaded that this would be making the best of a bad situation. The conversation inevitably, unavoidably, turned to Deborah.

"You know, she really was a great gal. The only one who could put BJ in his place," said Lilly refilling her glass for the third time.

"She's the one that hung that moniker on him. Remember the first time she called him that? How his eyes flared, but he said nothing." Eva laughed.

Lilly picked up the chorus, "We'll have to call him that from now on just to keep him in his place. She raised her glass. "Here's to BJ, the scoundrel who got us into this mess in the first place."

"To BJ," Eva chimed. Glasses clinked.

The women had been sitting there for over an hour reacquainting with each other's company while the liquor warmed their bellies. Suddenly there was a knock on the door.

"Shh!" cautioned Lilly. "Don't make a sound."

There was another knock. The girls remained silent.

Finally, "C'mon, open the door. It's Carl. I know you're in there. I heard you laughing."

Slowly the door opened. Lilly looked out. Carl could see Eva standing behind her holding the mop as if it were a baseball bat. Her makeshift weapon.

"Don't you two look a sight. Don't worry, it's only me. Have you two been drinking? Man, this place reeks." Carl had swiftly entered and relocked the door.

"What are you doing here? What do you want?" Lilly, slightly inebriated, was spoiling for a fight.

"Black Jack sent me. I'm here to get you packed and outta here tonight."

"What?" The two women in unison stared in disbelief.

"Herman doesn't want to take anymore chances. He wants you both on a train this evening. His plan is already in motion. It is going down even as we speak." Carl's tone was no nonsense. The two women knew better than to argue, their very lives may be at stake.

Hurriedly, Eva and Lilly began to throw her things into suitcases.

"Take only what you absolutely need. We may be able to come back for the rest later," the big man advised.

Lilly's 'necessities,' including books, pictures and clothing, filled three suitcases. She also insisted upon taking the record player and its collection. Eva had the two bags she had brought from St. Louis.

As they were about to depart, Eva asked, "Wait a minute. What about Herman and his family?"

"They've already boarded a train for New York. He sent me back for you two."

Eva and Lilly exchanged knowing glances upon receipt of that tidbit of news.

The three of them loaded with suitcases and boxes piled into the waiting cab and sped off into the night for Union Station. Fear has an amazingly sobering affect. Soon the young women had revived from all but the slightest effects of alcoholic haze.

Lilly was continually looking over her shoulder to see if any of the lights behind were following them. She was convinced that at any moment they would be tommy-gunned out of existence.

Eva, less fearful and more circumspect, was begging to be apprised of the situation.

"Shh! Not here," Carl countered. "Wait till we get to the station."

By the time they reached their destination, it was past ten. Black Jack's train for New York had left nearly two hours earlier.

"Not much leaving this late, ladies," he consoled. "The only thing I could get was three tickets to Kansas City. Guess we will have to stay the night in the train station once we get there."

"And then what?" snapped Lilly, now completely sober, anger replacing fear.

"Why we will work our way to New York, of course."

"Of course," replied Lilly sardonically.

Eva thought about going to St. Louis, but she kept that thought to herself.

When they had boarded the train for Kansas City, found an empty railcar and were well ensconced, Eva proceeded to drag the plan out of Carl.

"Well you see it's like this," he began hesitantly. "When BJ heard the news," the two women could see Deborah's legacy at work already. They smiled. "He took it real bad. Then he vowed to get even. He swore 'If they want to play the protection racket, then it's them that'll need the protecting.' Unfortunately, he couldn't find anyone who would help him take on those gangs. He had wanted to fire bomb their offices, you see." Carl paused to let the women realize the scope of the deliberations that had taken place and the seriousness of these discussions. "Anyway, it was one of Andrew's guys that came up with a solution that satisfied Herman's lust for vengeance and yet left no finger pointing back at us. After all, we are magicians, not murderers. We can't continue to perform and constantly be on the lookout for vendettas. It took a while to drill this into his head." Carl paused, and they exchanged knowing glances.

"Go on. Get on with it." Eva was growing impatient.

"What's happening tonight?" implored Lilly.

"As I said, one of Andrew's guys, Washington Irving? No, that's not right. Washington something came up with the idea to mark them but leave us blameless. So they staked out the headquarters, a hotel in Skokie, and timed the shift changes for the guards. Tonight he will sneak down the coal chute into the basement. When everybody is asleep, he will put red dye into the water heater. In the morning when the first guys take a shower, wash their face, whatever, their skin will be indelibly stained red. They will be marked with Deborah's blood."

"Is that it?" screamed Lilly. "Is that the best you big men could come up with? A childish prank? Why don't you just blow up the building?"

"You can't," Carl replied somberly. "They are like roaches. They will always come back. No matter how many you kill, they will always come back. If you did that, you would be signing your own death warrant."

There was silence.

Then Carl uttered one final sentence. "Black Jack knew you would feel this way Lilly, so he told me to tell you that 'Karma would catch up with them.'"

"That's it, karma." Lilly was incredulous.

"That's all there ever is," Carl replied and the subject was closed.

Washington Reeves never knew Madame Deborah. He often heard stories about her spoken in hushed revered tones. She was clairvoyant, soothsayer, collective conscious of them all.

He had become infatuated with Black Jack's ideals, personality, at the meetings in Garvey's hall a year earlier. Impressed with the idea of combating the tyrannical powers that controlled their lives with unity and demonstrations of defiance; he hung around the UNIA offices performing odd jobs and seeking the opportunity to prove his worth.

Andrew had hired him for several jobs and, fascinated with his alacrity and personal devotion, found him a permanent position on his staff. Mr. Reeves in six short months had become Andrew's number one choice when something had to be done in a hurry.

Here he was crouching in the dark waiting to strike a blow against the tyrannical forces that were driving his mentors out of Chicago. Against those that had murdered their spiritual leader. He could prove his worth this evening and solidify his position as Andrew's right hand man with the successful accomplishment of the plan he conceived.

Alert now, blood coursing, his moment was approaching fast. The guards at the front door would walk down the stairs and around the building, to be replaced by two new guards from inside the building. He had just a minute to cross the street, open the coal chute and slide into the basement.

Landing in the coal bin, his eyes took a few minutes to adjust to the pitch dark. Afterward, he made his way to the boiler room and performed his nefarious task. It was a small punking to be sure, not the dramatic countermeasure some senior voices advocated. But one which would keep them from getting their hands dirty. Reeves chuckled to himself at the irony. He sincerely hoped that a good many of them would have hands and more stained blood red, stained crimson with the blood of the woman they so cruelly cut down as if she were a dog in the street. Imagine the callousness of these monsters with their capricious disregard for human life.

There, it was done. The liquid poured into the valve and the petcock was opened, red concentrate mixed with hot circulating water deep within the bowels of the boiler. All he had to do now was pick the lock on the rear door and flee across the vacant lot to the rear. No one would be the wiser.

Too bad he couldn't hang around until morning and watch the fun. There were sure to be fireworks aplenty. However, there was safety in discretion, providing valor to fight another day. He left as soon as the coast was clear, making his way to Union Station for the first train out of town.

XIV
City Life

There was no mention of any sort of unusual event surrounding a hotel in Skokie in the Chicago papers the next couple of days. He was not surprised. The organization boys would not want it to get out that they had been 'skunked.' Black Jack had called a source and a week's worth of news was mailed to his post office box in New York.

No sense in giving out his new address to anyone in Chicago just yet. There would be time for that later. Better now to lay low. Concentrate on his new business associations in Harlem.

Besides, planning a dinner for all of his new friends and neighbors, outfitting the house just the way he wanted it to be. Just the way he always dreamed it would be. This was his current and most enjoyable preoccupation.

For once Black Jack was a sponge. Actually for the third time in his life. The previous two were under the tutelage of great magicians. This time Herman was endeavoring to learn from the greatest entrepreneurs in African American society.

Once again, ever the chameleon, Herman would transform himself and his show. This time the 'show' was transmorphed into Black Jack Enterprises. His interests would run the gamut from publishing his books and games to the merchandising of his health tonic and beauty aids. The latter would be displayed in stores alongside Madame Walker's hair care products. Tentatively, Wanda would be in charge of that.

By copying the successes of his neighbors, Herman was sure that his wealth would soon multiply. In fact, he was determined to go them one better by capitalizing on their fears and insecurities. He remembered well the old axiom- the more you had, the more you had to lose.

To that end, he outfitted the center room on the first floor with all of the modern gadgets he could find. This would certainly be a séance room supreme. Already he was receiving inquiries about instruction from beyond; there were certain business negotiations of a sensitive nature. 'Could he take a look at the situation and offer advice?'

This room, located as it were at the center of the house, would become the lynchpin of his allure, his business dealings. It was the area of expertise that he brought to the party, his talent for legerdemain, his 'mentalist' powers; they placed him squarely above his elitist peers. His bag of tricks would continue to inspire awe and generate the impression that certainty could be gleaned from the beyond, conquering the uncertainty of this fast-paced modern world. Of course Herman now had an even greater edge; he had a former partner on the other side.

"Well ladies, how did you like the grand tour?" A smugly smiling BJ was overjoyed to be impressing these two ladies of long acquaintance.

"It is simply a fantastic place," Eva was genuinely gushing, not mindful of how much her performances contributed to Herman's new estate.

"Looks like you've made it, BJ." Lilly was a bit somber and stingy with her congratulations this cold February day. She had made it plainly clear that she considered his actions as playing fast and loose with her life. Inwardly, she doubted that she would ever forgive him.

"Thank you both for your sincere expressions. I feel that there is a lot of all of us in this place, a culmination of all our hard work and efforts. I am determined to make it one of the nicest homes on the block." BJ was certainly the most impressed of this gathering of three.

As the mid-winter afternoon drew to a close, the two women made their excuses and prepared to leave. Lilly, who had vowed never to work for Herman again, had secured a waitressing job at a local restaurant. Her expression of urgency was genuine. She had to get to work. Eva's anxiousness stemmed from her desire not to run into Wanda upon the latter's return from the shops.

"See you again, boss," shouted Lilly who was already heading down the street with Eva in tow.

But it was Black Jack: who would have the parting shot. "Eva, we are having a party Saturday night for some of the neighbors. I told them you would be there. See you at six."

"Whatever you say, BJ. I'll be there," said Eva with a hint of resignation.

On the way home, the two women huddled together to fight off the cold. Lilly castigated her roommate, "Why don't you tell that bum where to go? If I were you, I wouldn't have anything more to do with him."

"You don't understand. It's not that simple. Besides, you saw those houses; there is a lot of money to be had here. If we stay close to him then we can get our share," Eva reasoned.

"Now you're talking, sister. Hurry up. I don't want to be late for work." They hurried along the fifteen block trek to their abode, both to get Lilly to work and to get out of the cold.

The affair that Saturday evening was opulent beyond all reason. Crystal chandeliers newly hung, blazed gloriously illuminating the grand dining room with the equivalent of hundreds of candles per square foot. Herman had spared no expense in providing a smorgasbord of exotic delights. Sumptuous appetizers filled several tables lining the periphery of the large room.

Chairs were set up in semicircle facing the entrance to the dining room. Obviously a show of some sort was planned.

Carl, for this evening playing the part of butler, stood in white tie and tails at the front door and announced the arriving guests. "Mr. A. Phillip Randolph and his wife, Mr. James Magus and wife." The list went on and on.

Herman and Wanda greeted each party, cajoling them over cocktails until the dinner hour.

One of the last to arrive, owing to her penchant for dramatic entrances, was Miss Alelia Walker, daughter of Madame C.J. Walker, the sponsor of Black Jack's new line of beauty products.

"Now that everyone has arrived, I would like to welcome you to dinner and a show," Herman addressed his roomful of Harlem's elite. "First, before dinner we will have a short show. I would like to introduce to everyone Eva, that 'Woman Buried Alive.'" There was a smattering of polite applause. Eva suddenly appeared in a cloud of smoke to stand beside Black Jack in the doorway to the grand dining room. She wore a ruby red, scooped neck, floor length gown with short puffy sleeves. Her hair, done up for the occasion, was garnished with a diamond tiara Herman had purchased just for the dinner party. Her standard diamond necklace adorned the space above her breast.

On cue she sneezed, a polite achoo. "Oh my dear, I hope you are not coming down with a cold. Here, take my handkerchief." Black Jack pulled the cloth from his breast pocket. It kept coming and coming. Eva grabbed the white linen, producing an even greater surplus of material. Finally help arrived in the form of Marsha, dressed in a skimpy maid's uniform. She produced a pair of scissors and solved the problem with a quick snip. After Eva playfully dabbed her nose, Marsha returned to the kitchen with the volume of material.

"Well, that didn't go well, did it?" Black Jack said as he straightened his hanky, restoring it to the proper position. "You know; my dear, you look lovely. Doesn't she look lovely, folks?" Robust applause. "What you need is a bouquet to go with your outfit." Instead of flowers, she was handed a magic wand instead. "Sorry, my mistake," Herman teased.

"Oh, I know what to do with this." She struck the wand against the banister behind her and presto, flowers.

Next Marsha appeared in the doorway pushing a small table covered with a white cloth. The two women stood back leaving Herman center stage. "I hope, ladies and gentlemen, that you are enjoying the appetizers. It seems the staff neglected to provide finger bowls. I think I can find one around here." He reached around behind his back searching for something inside his jacket. "Yes, here we go. One big enough for everyone." Black Jack produced a fishbowl instead, complete with several darting goldfish.

"No, this won't do at all." He placed the bowl on the table and tried again. This time, "Crystal ball? No, I wanted finger bowls. Marsha, this must be the wrong coat. Help me get this off."

"Sure, Daddy," came the coquettish reply from the scantily clad assistant.

The young woman's tonal qualities and her emphasis on the word 'Daddy' struck a chord in Eva's mind. An instant comparison was made to a certain carnal cacophony in Baltimore. The true professional that she was, Eva never flinched a muscle as her mind arrived at a positive comparison. She would file the information away.

Meanwhile, Herman had put his top hat upside down on the table and now Marsha was helping him out of his coat, pulling it inside out in the process.

She had wrested the sleeves from his arms and was now holding the garment in both hands as he turned to face her. "Okay, let's try one more time." BJ produced a wand magically in his right hand and began waving it over the limp coat while mumbling magic words.

"We are looking for finger bowls. Viola." He grabbed the coat out of her hands to reveal...another fishbowl. The attentive audience laughed and applauded with approval.

As prearranged, the cook made an appearance and whispered into Marsha's ear. She in turn stood on tippy toes to whisper into Black Jack's.

"I'm sorry to report, folks, that the cook says there will be a slight delay in dinner. It seems that one of the main dishes, the rabbit fricassee, is missing a couple of rabbits."

Just then, the young woman looked into the magician's hat. Becoming very animated, she pulled on his vest tail and began pointing.

"What the... So there's where you've been hiding." Herman pulls one, then another plump bunny from the hat and passes them to Marsha amid resounding applause.

"Thank you. Thank you so much. Glad you enjoyed our little show. Now, who has a question for Professor Herman, Mentalist Supreme?"

Hands thrust in the air. A chair for Herman was provided. As Marsha scurried about removing the previous props, Eva remained stoic, standing with her right hand on the chair as 'The Professor' began his routine.

"How will the stocks fare? This year will they continue to go higher?" Mr. Magus asked. The crowd murmured.

"Stocks. Since they represent the companies that make up the economy and the economy is booming, stocks should continue to do well." The 'Professor' had struck out in his first attempt.

"You sound just like my broker," the man chided.

"So you want more?" Professor Herman challenged, pretending to put himself into a trance. "Invest in things that will last, not relics of the past. If you invest without care, your profits will multiply out of thin air." Professor Herman opened his eyes and addressed his client, "How was that? Better?"

"Yes, thank you very much, profits from thin air." Mr. Magus, a wealthy manufacturer, was wiping his brow elatedly, convinced that the spirits had shown him the path to prosperity.

Herman took a few more questions from the guests. Alelia Walker asked the most interesting question. With a twinkle in her eye, she asked Herman, "What will the hairstyles be like a year from now?"

"Why, my dear, I continue to see the fashions calling for both long, luxurious hair and lots of curls. So tell your manager to make sure to run the plants overtime." A chorus of laughter and applause accompanied this last, as BJ announced that dinner would now be served.

"Ladies and gentlemen, I can see the tables are now prepared and the cook has signaled that dinner is ready. So if you can please find your place cards on the table, we will begin shortly."

Eva found that she was hosting a table full of middle-aged couples all from Harlem's Striver's Row, but none of the notable celebrities. She soon realized that she had drawn the third table in the hierarchy; the first two presided over by Black Jack and Miss Walker. She consoled herself that this was the position that Deborah would have probably occupied and comported herself accordingly.

"What does it feel like to be buried alive?" one of the wives asked. This was of course the most common question she received. Lately she had tired of this line of inquiry, usually changing the subject. For tonight's gala however, she would entertain the notion.

"It's not as difficult as you might imagine," she began politely. "For me it is just like going to sleep, a deep sleep. When you wake up, it is all over. It is very tiring. I had to practice a lot in preparation. Also, as you can imagine, the event is quite strenuous on the body. Once or twice I woke up and I was chilled to the bone."

"Why, you poor dear," a condescending condolence.

"Will you be performing another such demonstration?" Another spouse asked the second most frequently asked question.

"Not on your life," Eva's crisp reply. "I'm sorry; I don't mean to be discourteous. It's just that we have moved on from daredevil stunts to concentrate on the powers of the mind. Remember what Professor Herman said while entranced, 'Do not dwell on relics of the past.' We will give our permission to anyone willing to attempt or update the trick as part of their performance. As for us, and I think: I speak for both of us now, we will never attempt that stunt again."

The dinner went exceedingly well, and Eva was grateful that from the positioning of her chair that she had neither a view of Herman or Wanda.

Before she left, she was able to pull Marsha aside into the hall closet for a little cross-examination.

"I know you and BJ were together in Baltimore before the show. I heard you; hell the whole floor heard you. I just want to know one thing, over Christmas was it you he was with?"

Marsha, shocked that she had been found out, made no attempt to deny the accusation. Steadfastly denying any hanky-panky over the holidays, she fingered her friend. "It was Charmaigne. She went with him on a business trip,"

"You're not lying to me, are you? Where is she now?"

"She's back at the boarding house where we live. She hasn't been feeling well for the last few weeks. Throwing up and stuff. Maybe she's got a bug," Marsha surmised.

Eva thought that maybe she had come down with something else. Eva was able to exit without having to converse with Wanda, small consolation given the news of the evening, that Black Jack was double dipping with both of his apprentices.

In the taxi home, she thought of Wanda and wondered why the woman wanted to hang on to him so. 'Wasn't it obvious? Just look at all those new trappings. She now had everything her material heart could desire.' The real question was why did she, Eva, love him so. It maybe true that she couldn't leave him until he released her from his spell, but why did she love him? She couldn't answer.

A month passed winter into spring. Activity across the river from the girls' apartment at the newly furbished ballpark quickened. Obviously preparations for a new season were underway. From their front window, they could see it all. The room across the hall from Lilly's, the one that had once been Eva's practice chamber, became the sewing room, Eva's new hobby. Lilly was too busy to entertain a hobby between working two jobs and enjoying the company of gentlemen callers. It was a good thing the apartment was long and had an "L" shape. Still the occasional odd moan wafted down the corridor, but Eva could now turn up her radio as a countermeasure.

She thought about that line Black Jack had uttered at the party, 'Money out of thin air.' Well that was what radio was all about, broadcasting over the air waves. Maybe he was on to something after all. Maybe she would get a job, earn some extra money for investing. Wasn't that what all of the 'thoroughly moderns' were doing? It was beginning to dawn on her that if Herman could afford this new townhouse, maybe the significance of her contributions had been understated.

"It was karma," Black Jack extolled the virtues of his philosophy. "You just have to wait and let karma lend a hand." He had burst into the girls' place early one Sunday morning, unable to contain the good news.

Waving a Chicago Tribune, "Here it is, ladies, hot off the presses." Sure enough, splashed across the front page, 'Konetti killed in drive by shooting.' The accompanying picture showed a bullet-ridden roadster with a well dressed figure, apparently Mr. Konetti, slumped over the wheel.

Herman was beaming. "See if I leave these guys to their own devices, they will 'take care of' each other." He blithely used the mob's colloquialism for murder.

"That's still not the big boss, the one who ordered the 'hit' on Deborah," retorted Lilly, desirous of stealing his thunder.

"Don't worry, he will get his. Time will tell." Black Jack was not to be denied his victory.

"Anyway Mr. 'Prestidigitator,' Mr. 'Mentalist Supreme,' where were you last week for Eva's birthday?" questioned Lilly regaining the upper hand.

"Oh, babe, has that come already? I'm really sorry. I was wrapped up with Andrew and mail order business. We've got to get the response time down to four to six weeks, especially with the tonic. We are shipping in cans now, no more bottles. The returns were killing the profit margin."

"Oh, the travails of the business mogul," mocked Lilly.

Black Jack took this last jab as a personal affront. "Hey, we sweated and struggled to get to where we are now in the center of everything. If you don't want to participate, don't you try to belittle others who relish their victories."

"It's just that your victories revolve around you. I don't see the rest of us getting rich off of our hard labor."

"So, is that the way you feel too, Eva?" BJ interrogated.

"Please leave me out of this," said Eva, finally looking up from the Chicago paper. She had read every line twice to confirm the untimely demise of the dapper dandy who had haunted their lives for over three years. "You two argue more than my parents. Lilly, you've told him how you feel, that he made his fortune on our backs. As for me, I'm satisfied with the present situation," she lied.

"Well ladies, I just wanted to give you two the good news. I didn't mean to cause an argument. Eva honey, I'm sorry about your birthday. I'll make it up to you. Enjoy the rest of your day." With that, he was off.

Eva decided that it was time to have a serious talk with her roommate. "Why do you do that, Lil? Start a fight with him every time? Don't yon think he's broken up enough about Deborah, or is there something more? Are you upset with the way he is treating me?"

"It's a damn shame and you know it. If you hadn't put your life at risk, he wouldn't be where he is today."

"You don't know that for sure," barked Eva with uncharacteristic acrimony. "You didn't see him perform at that hall downtown. That was his shining moment. He did that for two solid months to packed houses. That's what the people wanted, still want. You should see the wealthy patrons at his parties. They all want to peer under the veil. That's all him, he and Deborah. My performances last summer were just the icing on the cake."

Before Lilly could get a word in, Eva concluded, "Remember this, will you? Whatever Deborah taught him, she did so willingly, knowingly. Never forget that she had a great talent and was in control of her destiny. You don't have to take up her cause or mine."

Lilly, speechless for once, had been cut to the quick by Eva's harsh words, no matter how true.

After a period of silence at the breakfast table, Eva continued with a final thought, "You know Black Jack's good news does mean one thing. Nobody will be out gunning for us. You can go back to Chicago if you want."

"I'll think it over," was Lilly's only reply.

There after, the girls stayed out of each other's way, pretty much for the rest of the day. The rest of the spring passed quietly with the exception of the ballparks across the river and down at the end of the block. When both teams were playing home games at the same time, the neighborhood took on a carnival atmosphere. You could hang out your front window on those warm spring afternoons and hear the roar of the crowds. Their volume would indicate the flow of the game. The crowds naturally cheered more when the home team was winning.

Lilly, Eva and their dates had taken in a couple of games sitting in the bleachers. No matter that the ball parks were in their community, they were segregated to certain sections. She soon tired of the sport, it was too confusing. And it took too long. Also, she resented being shoved into centerfield far away from all the action. She had been initially attracted by the noise of the crowds. Curiously, she missed the touring, standing center stage, the cheering crowds. She secretly longed for the life on the road and the nightlife of gin, jazz clubs and Black Jack.

Black Jack had no time for touring that summer. He was too busy building his empire. Eva would participate in the occasional demonstration at dinner parties. He insisted that she be present for his mind reading performances, claiming she was his muse. These typically were performed after Herman and Marsha's parlor tricks. Charmaigne having returned home pregnant.

Neither would Lilly last out the summer. Her constant melancholy and growing estrangement from her roommate dictated her eventual return to the town she loved.

Speaking of love, Black Jack's conjugal visits dwindled down to a precious few. Granted Eva was required to work his social gatherings and the infrequent stage performance; she also made the appointments for his fortune telling sessions. But other than professionally, their paths rarely crossed, let alone commingled. Like Wanda, Eva knew well Herman's sexual appetite and if not she or the wife on the receiving end, and she seriously doubted the latter, Eva surmised with whom and how often.

What had Lilly told her once in a previous life, "Don't let any other woman get him the way you did." Well, she had failed at that. He was onto something new and exciting. 'Always for the show,' her mind mocked her. She began to believe that was just an excuse for his roving eye.

Eva, still young, attractive, could still be fun, go out for a night on the town. Trouble was few asked. Almost nine months since the last time she performed that hideous stunt and she felt great. In fact, better than ever! She was stained, stained with the scent of Black Jack Herman.

As his star, no other man would touch her. Strange since as his starlet, everyone coveted her.

She was in no man's land. Not the wife and only a part-time mistress. Washed up at age twenty-four. Maybe it was the ring. She still wore it for some unknown reason. That's it, 'Take off that damn ring,' her mind coaxed. Then the men would flock to her. Get down off that pedestal and let the men see a truly modern woman. Yes, she would show the world there was still a lot of life in the old girl.

Eva took the ring and threw it into the back of her stocking drawer. She would be a kept woman no more.

Summer faded into fall. Lilly was gone and so were the baseball players from up the block and across the river. The carnival atmosphere ceased and the apartment surrendered to silent solitude. There was still no one to fill the void in her life.

As the leaves turned, Herman planned another gala event. This one to celebrate the birthday of Miss Walker. The two had become very close in the months since they became neighbors. It had been a good year.

After the failure in Baltimore, it was a failure in his mind, even though financially it was a huge success, the businessman in Herman realized it was time to give up the allure of the road for the security and acclaim derived from being the toast of the town, the celebrity maximus of Harlem. He had arrived. There was no greater position to which to aspire. Nothing left but to settle back into his townhouse in New York City as the titular head of black culture and weave his influence on the minds of the most successful and progressive thinkers in African American society.

He began to practice that age old maximum, 'Love thy neighbor.' Under the pretense of business consultations, Herman kept constant company with the young heiress whose company was producing a line of beauty care products under his moniker.

Outwardly, the couple had become close business associates. Always in each other's homes or circulating in the posh establishments of polite society. Secretly, they had become passionate lovers. To the many women that knew him, who were well versed with his philandering, this assignation was to be expected. This time he was doing it for love and money. Wanda for one could not confirm her suspicions, dared not inquire too closely. Wanda was getting a beauty care line to manage in return.

The script for this gala followed the same pattern as the others Herman hosted. Cocktails followed by a brief magic show. Then Professor Herman would show off his mental powers channeling the wisdom of the ages. He had eschewed the practice of hypnotism on his wealthy patrons, at least in public gatherings such as parties. However, what happened in his séance room stayed there and was never spoken of in public.

Still he would pretend to entrance himself when answering a most difficult question. As when one of the gentlemen, pleased with his past pronunciations on stocks, wondered if his run of profits would continue. "We have been advising that if you invest without a care, profits will come out of the air," said the 'Professor' with one hand upturned to his forehead. "Atwater, Kent, CBS, all of these will continue to march to their zenith." The crowd murmured excitedly. "Also, we advised not to invest in the relics of the past. For steamship lines, the die was cast. Titanic tragedy, ten years ago, left so many aghast. The radio we think is the one that lasts," he concluded cryptically.

So many in attendance had lost so much investing in the Black Steamship Lines of Marcus Garvey. They secretly hoped for a reversal of fortune. No one had lost more than the Walker's but it hardly made a dent in their immense fortune. There she was, little Alelia, the birthday girl, sitting in the front row thoroughly enjoying the show, swept up by the charm of this great man.

"Could you explain your last comment a little further?" The same gentleman pestered, angling for more free advice.

"Well, it occurs to me that the head of the radio company was once a young telegrapher who was responsible for taking many of the last messages from the rich and powerful on the sinking Titanic. The relic of the past. He now heads a company that pulls profits out of the air, which we think will last. Any more advice on this subject can be handled in a private consultation. Now, any more questions before we continue the celebration of our guest of honor?" Black Jack winked at Alelia. She beamed in return.

Once again the question was asked, "Will you ever again put on the Buried Alive demonstration?" Eva, standing at her usual station wearing a floor length pearl satin gown, winced.

"Ladies and gentlemen, I would like to put this rumor to rest. We have renounced the daredevil daring do. The bloodlust of the crowds was just too overwhelming. I prefer to concentrate on the study of Black Magic and the mystique of the mind, wherein lies true mystery and magic.

Let others do death defying stunts to further their reputation as performance artists. Like that actor who crawls all over the outside of buildings, hanging upside down in perilous positions. The greatest power is that of mind over matter."

After a sumptuous dinner which culminated with a beautiful birthday cake wheeled into the dining room by the staff, guests prepared to leave for the jazz club and the evening's entertainment. Eva was paired with an older gentleman who had arrived unescorted.

As they stood outside Herman's residence, she could see Herman at the front of the line escorting Miss Walker in her flaming red gown.

She cringed inside, realizing how far she had fallen. Neither wife nor concubine, assistant or harlot, all of those positions had been filled by others. Eva was just personal secretary and seat filler. A beautiful doll to be taken off of the shelf and played with if so desired. Just another face in the entourage. That would have to do. She would have to adjust to the new reality. Suddenly she felt very alone in this crowd in New York City. Like a fish out of water.

Unbeknownst to the evening's revelers, there was trouble brewing in the entourage. The government's war against Mr. Garvey and his associates had been a smashing success. Now convicted, he would soon be going to jail. Black Jack had managed to escape scrutiny, owing to his brief association. However, in light of his initial accomplishment, J. Edgar Hoover stepped up his campaign to surveil and discredit black leaders who were outspoken and flamboyantly urging African Americans to unionize and stand up for their rights. Mr. Hoover believed the rabble rousers to be agents of Communists; wittingly or unwittingly at best, tools of the devil at worst.

Thus it came to pass that he put one of the two Black American FBI agents in his employ to the task of uncovering information about Black Jack that could be used to discredit, hopefully convict him, in a court of law, of un-American activities.

After a time, one of the agents was able to slip into, infiltrate, the circle of black intelligentsia in Harlem and become a trusted member of Herman's entourage. From his coveted position, he would bear witness to all of the goings on within Black Jack's enterprise.

XV
Crimes of the Heart

With the advent of the holidays Herman began paying more attention to his long neglected star. Eva, feeling that there must be an ulterior motive, nevertheless did not question her good fortune. Like a raging bull he engorged her, lifting her time and time again to the heights of ecstasy. Echoes of their passion coursed through the large apartment which had remained silent for far too long.

Not only were there the clandestine encounters, but now here she was on his arm in the local clubs where the vainglorious gathered and reveled. She mused. Imagine us rubbing elbows with the 'hoy floy." They were an item again; a couple, that's all that mattered. And then after the evening's entertainment, it was back to her apartment where he would ravish her like a man possessed until the wee hours of the morning. It was all too good to be true. Then came the request that would burst her bubble.

"Honey, after you spend the holidays with your folks in St. Louis, I want you to go back to Chicago and open an apartment. It has been too long since I have been there to visit with our associates. We need to reacquaint ourselves with the powerful people of black society in the Midwest. I don't want them to think that Black Jack has abandoned them altogether. After you get things set up, I will be out there every couple of months to host parties, provide consultations and the like. It will be our time to be together." He had that gleam in his eye, the one that women could not refuse.

"Sure, baby, that sounds fine. I think I was getting tired of New York anyway." While she was only half fibbing, her feelings were genuinely hurt. Did he have so little regard for her that he felt the need to use one of his routines? Wined and dined her, made love to her, then the smarmy look and the request that she move back to Chicago. She felt cheapened. Didn't he know she would do anything just for the asking? She didn't know him at all anymore. Yet, she would do his bidding. This and more. Anything for the man she loved. Were they not 'star- crossed?'

Andrew had found the perfect place and furnished it appropriately as befitted the stature of the great Black Jack Herman. When Eva arrived from St. Louis she found her new home waiting for her.

"Here you go, sweetheart, move in condition." He was unusually chipper as he turned the key in the front door lock.

Eva marveled. The rooms were huge. The walls gave off a creamy glow. The scent of fresh paint hung in the air. This turnkey affair was completely decorated, furniture, tapestries, even shelves filled with books.

Eva stepped into the kitchen and found pots and pans, dishes and utensils all stowed in their respective cupboards. Everything the modern housewife could want except...

"You are now the executive in charge of Herman Enterprises West. How do you like it?"

"Why, it's beautiful," Eva gasped. Suddenly tired of subterfuge, "What's going on here? Why all of a sudden was I shunted back to Chicago?"

"You want the real reason?" Andrew scuffed the toes of his shoes against the wooden floor then regarded their soles. "Wanda was tired of having you around with your 'constant upfrontery.' Her phrase, not mine."

"What? I hardly ever ran into her. When I do it's just polite conversation," Eva exasperated. "Oh, this is too much."

"I agree with you, kid. But you know how she gets. She kept up a ruckus until BJ finally had to do something," he commiserated, seemingly with genuine affection.

"I just don't get it."

"I think I do. You know she's always been jealous of you, considers you her greatest threat. After all, you are BJ's star performer and always will be." Andrew winked and then continued in confidential tones. "You know that there has been a lot going on in that house in our first year in New York. Most of it Wanda had no control over. Maybe she felt that if she got rid of you, it would be a victory sort of."

"A small victory indeed," came Eva's appraisal.

"Why that scheming little..."Eva stopped short. No use in casting further aspersions. What's done was done.

"Anyway, Black Jack has a special job for you in addition to your clerical duties, the handling of the Midwest mail order requests and such," Andrew continued amicably.

"And that is?" Eva queried dubiously.

"He wants you to write his autobiography."

Eva, alone again in the big city, decided to reach out to her best friend, her only friend.

With Black Jack out of the picture and Lilly once again familiar turf, she was more than amenable. Their first meeting in more than eight months took place in Eva's apartment on a cold February day.

"So what have you been doing with yourself?" Lilly inquired, casually inspecting the living room.

"I've taken this time to do some reading, study ancient philosophies. Andrew provided quite a library." Eva's hand waved at the bookcase on the far wall. "Did you know Socrates always used to answer a question with a question? He began what is known as the Socratic method of learning."

"By questioning instead of thinking you know everything."

"Exactly. In fact, he was so dedicated to the search for truth that instead of telling falsehoods, he drank poison and died," Eva authoritiated.

"On purpose? You're kidding."

"No, I'm not. He had a great influence on his pupils, Plato and

Aristotle. Plato gave us the allegory of the shadows on the cave wall, which Shakespeare turned into the players on the stage."

"Now Shakespeare, I've heard of that cat. Didn't he say the show must go on?"

"No, that is Black Jack's. Shakespeare said the play is the only thing that there is."

"So I guess this guy Socrates would be the sort of anti-magician," theorized Lilly.

"Not necessarily, as long as you were truthful in the presentation of your craft. If you let the audience know you were performing an illusion then they have the option of trying to figure it out or sitting back and enjoying the show," instructed Eva.

"I see and not pretend that you are in touch with other-worldly spirits or have mystical powers and can see the future." reproached Lilly.

"Sound like anyone you know?" asked Eva with a wink of her eye. They giggled like little girls, as best friends should.

"And he's still at it," Eva confided. "Andrew just told me this the other day. Remember his assistant Charmaigne?"

"The one he got pregnant last winter?"

"Right. Well she showed up with a five month old baby girl named Louise for Herman to raise, and she just left."

"What! You're kidding," Lilly was stupefied. "What did BJ do with the child?"

"He gave her to Wanda to take care of, told everyone that this was their new daughter. Now get this: When some smart-alecky reporter asked him where the child had come from, Black Jack claimed he produced her out of thin air with his handkerchief." Eva delivered her punch line with aplomb. "Now what do you think of that?"

"Same old BJ. Socrates would not be amused," laughed Lilly.

"The thing is I really wonder sometimes if he doesn't believe the things he says." Eva pondered in a more serious vein.

"I guess we will never know." said Lilly. "So, you're really going to write this great autobiography? That sounds exciting."

"Haven't started yet, still waiting for 'the great one' to make his appearance, and technically I will just organize his dictation.

He has hired a professional writer to put it all together. But it does sound exciting," smiled Eva.

"It should, thousands of people will read this over the years, maybe tens of thousands and you will always know that you had a hand in it," said Lilly with pomposity.

"Stop it now, you're making me nervous," teased Eva.

Black Jack finally arrived unannounced one winter afternoon. Eva, returning from the shops with her bag of groceries, saw him exit the taxi as she rounded the corner. Had he been waiting for her? He would have his own key, of course. Andrew would have seen to that. This was his dramatic entrance, sheer theatrics. It was the showman in him.

For an instant the fight or flight instinct took hold. Eva stopped, hesitated, and then her legs marched her to him. They kissed on the street. Not a passionate lover's kiss, but the sedate affectionate peck of two people long in the other's employ. Herman, always the gentlemen, took her package in one hand, whisking her into the building with his free arm. Black Jack and Eva saved their most impassioned kisses for the privacy of their abode.

Herman, who was never at a loss for words when onstage in front of huge crowds, was having difficulties with the dictation to his audience of one.

"Let's see, I was born in a log cabin.' No wait, that's not right." Black Jack scratched his brow and grimaced.

"What's the matter, BJ?" Eva had stopped writing and looked up from her pad, almost devoid of scribbles after an hour of attempts.

"It's hard to make it both believable and interesting sometimes. Put this down instead: I was born between the crack of lightening and the roar of thunder. My mother screamed at the top of her lungs, and it was done. She looked down and said 'Thank God, it's a son.'

I was a smart lad and drove my parents crazy before it was done. I started talking at the age of one. How does that sound, Eva?"

"Believable, if a little boastful. Sounds just like you, baby." She smiled.

"Very well: Realizing that there was hardly nothing I couldn't do, I began to practice magic at the age of two. I would collect chicken eggs with my mother, who soon realized that I could make them disappear at will. Then I showed her that I could make them return with just a wave of my hand. After her initial shock and fright, my mother would clap and congratulate me on my performances. What a great son she would exclaim! The pride and delight, it showed in her face, as I practiced my Legerdemain."

Herman paused to gather his thoughts and catch his breath as he paced the room during his oration. "By the age of three, I could make a basket of eggs disappear or double in size depending upon my whim. My father was afraid of me. People told him that I was touched by the devil, must be a voodoo child. It got so bad that he began to deny I was his son.

He would go away for weeks at a time and then come back, beat my mother. I remember her hollering from the bedroom all the time. After my mother had Andrew, my father took off for good. By the time I was five, I was the man of the house."

"Honey, maybe there was another reason they were hollering. BJ, maybe you are your father's son after all." Eva smiled at him and winked. There was a gleam in her eye.

The dictation continued for days on end with Eva recording the details of his childhood upbringing, splashed with sensationalism. No matter how fantastic, she dutifully recorded his claims. Like how he caused a lightening bolt" to strike a tree and provide all of the kindling they would need for winter.

"The bolt hit on my command and the wood was piled up at my feet ready to use." Parts sounded more like the tall tales of Paul Bunyan than actual history.

However, many parts smacked of harsh realities that sounded all too true. How he left school at age ten to get a job and earn money when his mother became ill with the diphtheria.

How working at the lunch counter would provide enough food to take home to the family, as the boss let him take the scraps. How after his mom died and they couldn't afford the rent, they stayed in the back of a neighbor's barn for two years.

Most of all, the truth of the storey revolved around "The Prince' as Black Jack called him. The man that rescued him from the mundane and showed him a glimpse of the eternal, showed him how to glimpse into men's minds, use the power of illusion to inflate their fears, satiate their desires. Once you understood how to, it was easy. Everybody was the same deep down. These were the secrets that con men and magicians understood, that within several different archetypes of being, there were always in roads into the soul. Highways of desire that could be exploited for fun and profit. To a poor boy with few talents, the practical knowledge of how to proceed with productions, potions and the like gave him a huge net with which to troll for prosperity.

Eva soon realized that these secrets could only be hinted at and never given away. At all costs, never given away. The very essence of magic relied on maintaining the mystique, the aura of infallibility; the inscrutable nature of the magician must be maintained. The tall tales served their purpose, to entertain and disinform.

Eva however, had glimpsed under the curtain, seen the whole story of the little boy growing up all too soon. Relying on no one until this man came along and stayed just long enough before passing to deliver to Herman the keys to the castle, the keys to success. The keys that would allow him to unlock the door to the human imagination.

Over the years he had imparted this secret to her, but she never realized it more clearly than now. Also, at just the same time came the realization of her deep love for this man. Far beyond infatuation or carnal urge, this was the deep love of long association and appreciation. A mature love born of understanding, of having walked a mile in the other's shoes. Despite his cruelty, his lasciviousness, most men had these; he genuinely cared about people, his people. Intertwined in all he did was the element of uplifting, of teaching others: 'Here look at me. If I can do it so you, too, can find a way to prosper and hold your head up. Feel better about yourself.'

His endeavors were worthy of a great man, one with a manifest destiny and she would be there to help him accomplish his tasks. Although they lost their way sometimes, they would return to the path as war weary veterans and support each other through the trials and tribulations to come. Eva was sure that their love, specifically her love for him, would carry them through whatever in the world was to come. Thus armed with her faith in the Lord and her man, she was ready for the challenges life presented.

They finished the dictations early that spring with a few rehashed, reworked magic tricks from earlier editions. 'No sense giving everything away.' Also sprinkled in were a couple of recipes for love potions. These were always in demand and while non-toxic in nature, they were also dubious in effect.

During the interim of their collaboration, this new apartment took on all the charm of their old love nest and more. Without all of the voodoo trappings scattered about, except in Herman's séance room which Andrew had made to specifications. "It helps me read people," he once confided to Eva. "Keeps them off their balance, constantly on guard. This allows me to clearly see what is in their hearts. Armed with this information, I can give them what they need or what they desire, which many times is essentially the opposite."

Eva remembered well his penchant for the use of prevarication, misdirection in peering into a man's soul. This and surprise were a magician's favorite tools. She was resolute that these secrets and others would never find their way into any book. His use of voodoo and mysticism for example. Let the reader imagine what they will, each owing to the darkness within their own souls.

Their parties were subdued this season in Chicago. While their new bootlegger provided top shelf goods, his infrequent shipments from Cincinnati made conservation a watchword. Besides Eva vowed that there would be no 'highlife' while Herman was in New York. Her mission here was to help this great man accomplish the goals he had set. Her only desire to effectually represent Herman Enterprises in the most professional manner possible.

After Black Jack returned to New York, Eva busied herself editing her dictations and handling the correspondence of the mail order business. She and Lilly communicated often and went out occasionally on 'girls nights' when Lilly was not otherwise engaged.

Spring was in full bloom in Chicago when it began to dawn on Eva that something wasn't right.

"I can't believe it Lil, but I've got all of the signs. I feel irritable all of the time. I'm bloated and I can't keep anything down, especially in the morning."

"You're right, sounds like the signs." came Lilly's dour appraisal through the receiver. "Have you skipped?"

"That's just it, I don't know for sure. I've never been terribly regular, all of the stress of performing. I've had one while he was here, but that's been over six weeks now." Eva's voice sounded close to tears.

"That's it. I'm coming right over. Nurse Lilly to the rescue. You know I always take good care of you."

An hour later Lilly was knocking on Eva's door, a pot of hot soup in her hands.

"What's that? Oh, I couldn't eat anything."

"Relax, its chicken broth. You just sip it. Here, come and sit down." Lilly, beginning to mother her younger friend, brought a shawl from the bedroom to wrap around Eva.

"How could this happen to me? I can't understand. We were being careful and all." Eva, shocked as the realization of her pregnancy hit home, sat there with hands on her head ignoring the cup of soup before her.

"Here honey, drink some of this. It will make you feel better," said Lilly.

"You know we've had relations for so many years, I deluded myself into thinking that I couldn't conceive." said a dumbfounded Eva.

"Honey, that's why I use the Coke-a-Cola treatment-every time-just to be safe." Lilly lifted Eva's chin. She could see the line of tears flowing down her face. Then a soothing thought, "You know, you should be happy. You are bearing his child. The two of you will have a baby between you to bind you together."

"Not like this. I didn't want it to happen like this, just as if I were another of his impregnated assistants. I wanted it to be special. We were to be wed, but that witch Wanda wouldn't let him go. Now she has had me banished to Chicago."

"What?" Lilly's mouth dropped. "Is that the real reason you're back here?"

"Yeah," cried Eva sniffling, tears really flowing.

"Well then if that's all you mean to him then maybe you should leave him for good, like your father advised. That would teach him a lesson," raged Lilly, getting her Irish up.

It was then that Eva dropped the other bombshell, her secret shame. There was no point in holding back with pretenses any longer. "But I can't leave him," she sobbed. "I can't ever leave him. He saw to that. Black Jack had that Professor Maharajah implant a post-hypnotic spell or suggestion or whatever you call it on me. He told me I can't ever completely leave Herman. 'That our destinies are entwined forever.' I've searched my mind. I know it's there deep down where I can't get at it. Try as I might, I can never be completely free of Black Jack." Eva, exhausted, buried her head in folded arms on the table top and wept.

"This is diabolical," Lilly was newly enraged. "I would have never believed he would go to such lengths to hold on to his star performer. I've got a good mind to go to New York, march into that mansion and tell that man off in front of all his new friends. Make him change his plans."

"No Lilly, don't. You can't." Eva looked up. Her teary face now fear-stricken. He only did it because in his own way he was afraid of losing me. He told me so. It's part of our being 'star-crossed.' Also, now we have the baby to consider."

"Poppycock."

"Besides, only Professor Maharajah can remove the spell. He is one of the greatest hypnotists of all time."

"Then I know what we have to do," Lilly said firmly.

The Federal Bureau of Investigation agent in Black Jack's entourage had been quite busy observing and cataloguing the events in the Herman household in Harlem. He had seen the lavish parties, the post midnight revelries that lasted until dawn. The informal caucusing amongst the high and mighty of Harlem's intelligentsia and the curious goings on in the secret room. As his job required, he noted dates, times, names and where available, snippets of conversation.

He had listened to public and private speeches, mostly innocuous pronouncements about how the Constitution applied to everyone equally. How if blacks acted in concert, just as women did when they won the right to vote, then they could achieve their goals, earn the right to a better life. No Communistic leanings here. No Bolshevik agenda, other than the emphasis on unionization as a tool for the betterment of quality of life. Privately, the young man agreed with many of the precepts espoused by Black Jack in his performances. Publicly, he was just doing his job. Was it any wonder that the contradiction was tearing him apart, causing him to drink to excess? He just hoped that Mr. Hoover would be happy with his report and get him the hell out of there.

J. Edgar Hoover, fresh from his imprisonment of Marcus Garvey in February in the Federal Penitentiary at Atlanta, far from his power base, was ready to attack the next head of the hydra. He took what little information he had on Mr. Herman to the Department of Justice. Outraged when his requests for indictments were turned down, he developed an alternate plan. He would coerce an attack from the state level.

"Mr. Mayor, do you know that there is a hive of malcontents up in Harlem plotting insurrections?" So went the line of conversation.

"Why Mr. Hoover, this is the twenties. People are not plotting anything anymore. They are too busy having fun and making money." The jovial rejoinder.

"Sir, I have eyes inside one of the ringleader's organization. We have definite proof of conspiracies afoot. If you act now, you can nip it in the bud. Cut off the head of the snake."

"I thought you did that when you convicted that foreigner Garvey," insisted the mayor.

"Our information is that another almost as eloquent in speech and more daringly cunning is about to take the reigns of UNIA. We don't have enough to prosecute at the federal level, but my source can provide enough for you to cool his heels awhile upstate. 'Steal his thunder.' Isn't that a phrase those show folk are so fond of?" said Hoover craftily.

There was a gasp from the other end of the line. "Certainly you don't mean..."

"None other," J. Edgar's unequivocal reply.

"But...are you sure? What about riots?" The mayor was desperately looking for an escape from this trap.

"Don't worry, he won't make any trouble. If you need to, the Governor can call out the National Guard. If we act quickly we can arrange this quietly, before the opposition has time to mount a campaign."

There was silence at the other end of the line.

J. Edgar continued in a tough, thug-like voice, "Remember you owe me. That little bit of trouble with the girl in Jersey, crossing over state lines."

"But she said she was eighteen!" the exasperated cry through the receiver. He was hooked. Then the resignation. "What exactly do you want me to do?"

"Have the District Attorney swear out a charge and tell the police captain in Harlem to go pick him up. We will provide you with the documentation forthwith."

The police broke into the Herman residence early one morning dragging Black Jack out half-dressed in front of his wife, children and gawking neighbors. Thrown into a cell, he was kept incommunicado until his arraignment nearly a week after the arrest.

There he was facing the judge in the pants, t-shirt and slippers he had worn when arrested. The indignity of his being seen like this in public unshaven and unkempt was part of the plot to break his spirits. It did not work.

Andrew was there with their lawyer, Wanda with the children.

The Assistant District Attorney handling the case was reading the charge. His heinous crime, the one for which a denial of bail requested, fortunetelling. This was the full scope of the charges against him and the culmination of nearly a year's work by an agent of the FBI.

Bail initially denied was eventually set at the considerable sum of twenty thousand dollars. The house in Harlem was put up as collateral against unlawful flight to avoid prosecution.

At the trial, incontrovertible evidence was provided by a star FBI witness whose identity was nevertheless kept confidential because of ongoing criminal investigations. There were dates, time and witnesses who were protected from prosecution if they participated in the charade.

A friend of the court brief was filed, written by J. Edgar Hoover himself on Department of Justice stationary. Combined with the incriminating documents, the state had an airtight case.

Considering that this was the first offense of a model citizen, it was odd that he was given the rather lengthy sentence of one year in Sing Sing, the upstate penitentiary. This despite the many character witnesses who testified on his behalf and pleas to the court for leniency.

Thus the heavy hand of the government came down hard on Black Jack Herman. It was supposed to be a message to others not to incite minorities to desire unobtainable solutions. In this respect, the promise of the modern life could not transcend the reality of second class citizenship. Imagine in this, the best of times, the very specter of economic isolation and physical annihilation still resided at their doorsteps.

"Hello, Eva. I just wanted you to hear it from me first and not have to read it in the papers. The judge gave him one year in Sing Sing." It was Andrew's duty to deliver the bad news.

"Oh, God, that's horrible. When does he have to go?" asked Eva.

"They've taken him already. We will appeal, but it doesn't look good. They really came down hard on us." said Andrew dejectedly.

"It's just; I had wanted to talk to him before...y'know."

"Well he said to tell you that the 'show must go on.' We will get through this and be bigger than ever. You just keep doing your job and the time will pass before you know it," the pragmatist advised.

What Andrew did not know, could not know, was that the young woman on the other end of the line, four months pregnant, had never told the father about his latest child. In the whirlwind in which they had been caught up, Eva had never found the right time to tell Black Jack she was having his baby.

It was a difficult summer for Eva. The current Chicago heat wave through which all of the populace was sweltering was but one of her problems. Her pregnancy was becoming most unusual. Instead of gaining weight as most women do, Eva, it was apparent, was losing weight in her face and limbs white her breasts and belly appeared engorged. To the casual observer she resembled a skeleton smuggling a bowling ball. Far from the healthy glow most women engendered, Eva's skin took on a sallow, waxy texture. Dark circles formed under her eyes. In the current heat wave constant perspiration matted her hair, her clothes. Even the ephemeral gauze-like numbers stuck to her skin stretched to the limit around her middle and hanging limply everywhere else. She looked almost as awful as she felt.

Lilly, her only friend and constant companion, had moved into the apartment to help Eva take care of Herman's enterprises and look after her little sister' as she had begun calling her. The name stuck. "Little sis, I'm going out to the grocery. Is there anything else you can think of? I want to get an early start. The temperature is supposed to be in the nineties again."

"No, nothing else. I don't have much of an appetite, can't hold much down. Do remember the Epsom salts. I will have to soak my feet again tonight."

"Right, it's on the list. Ok, I'm off." Lilly, with that announcement, slung her shopping bag over her shoulder and exited the apartment making sure the door locked securely behind her. It was no small occurrence for Lilly to go out onto the streets. The violent crime wave had increased precipitously in the year since she returned. True, much of that violence, gang related, was white on white and happened in other parts of town. However, Lilly could not shake the premonition of being tommy-gunned in the streets while walking, like so many innocent bystanders. She read the papers, listened to the radio; there had been drive-by shootings all over town. And now the slew of bank robberies, violent shootouts with police, could occur at almost any intersection.

Moreover, the streets in their neighborhood seemed meaner, dark and dirty, neglected. A spillover from the heightened violence around. This was no illusion. When more police were needed to control mob related activities, the resultant shift in manpower had to come from somewhere. You had to watch your step when walking these mean streets day or night.

At night, of course, Lilly would be in the company of a gentleman and they would be riding to and from the clubs. Even the clubs were not immune to their share of trouble. The occasional turnout from the police anxious to show an ever inquirious press that the law of the land was being upheld especially in an election year. Funny how those rousts always seemed to occur in minority neighborhoods mused Lilly. Anyway 'better to spend a few hours in jail than be gunned down in the streets.' Yes, she definitely still preferred the nights. Especially now as the summer sun was arcing its way above the buildings to obliterate the canyon of shadows, heating the concrete and asphalt to temperatures more suitable for cooking than walking. She would have to hurry.

Hastening her return before the sun reached its zenith; Lilly was back in little over an hour with summer melons and juices for Eva and soda and tonic water for herself.

"Honey, I bought a bunch of lemons. They were on sale. Thought I would make a big pitcher of lemonade. Wouldn't that be nice?"

"Yes, that sounds fine, cold lemonade on a hot summer's day. You can put some gin in yours," Eva chided.

"I intend to," the confident reply. "You could to if you didn't believe in that silly superstition about not drinking while pregnant."

"It is not silly. It is not an old wives tale. My mother insists it is a fact. She reminds me not to drink or eat sugar every time we talk on the phone. Of course she also says not to look at anyone ugly or the baby may come out that way." Eva re-hung her head. Her shoulders slumped forward as she wrapped arms around her knees sitting sideways on the sofa, resuming her semi- fetal position. Too tired to laugh at her own joke, she looked as uncomfortable as a summer's day was long.

After a glass of ice chilled lemonade had relieved temporarily Eva's distress, replenished her being, Lilly attempted to distract with a little news of the day.

"Look here what I found in the paper. 'Egyptian holy man defies death. Seals himself in waterproof coffin, submerged in lake for over an hour. 'How about that, honey? They are performing your trick."

"It's not my trick. Besides if he wants to perform a death defying trick, let him try having a baby," Eva said somberly from her position on the couch. Truth be told she tired of carrying this boulder around within. She would happily go into delivery mode at any moment.

"Baby, I know you feel bad. I was trying to cheer you up. Get your mind off your problems. You see, your legacy lives on. You will always be that buried alive lady."

"That was not my intention. I was just trying to help the man I loved and look where it's gotten us. He's in jail and I feel imprisoned myself. We have both been overcome by events too powerful for us to control." Eva's head disappeared between her arms and legs. Lilly thought she could hear the sounds of soft weeping emanating from the couch.

"Don't be like that, little sis. You and Black Jack will arise like that bird. What is it? The phoenix. The two of you will soar to new heights greater than ever."

Suddenly another thought, she would try a different tact to comfort her friend. "Honey, just think how bad Herman is having it. Here is a man who is used to writing his own ticket, having his own way. He is on top of the world one minute and incarcerated the next. Now he is locked into a prison cell, told when to eat, sleep, and work. He has been a free bird all his life. It must be intolerable for him. But you know what? I'll bet he's giving those guards hell," Lilly chuckled. They both knew that she had his character described perfectly.

Eva raised her shrunken head and evinced a thin smile.

Herman was giving them hell. Performing tricks for his fellow inmates, performing pranks on the guards. Holding fortune telling sessions at all hours of the night. He was certainly a king holding court, given the royal treatment. Other than a couple of notorious murderers, there was no greater celebrity in Sing Sing.

While Eva had only Lilly on which to rely, Black Jack had the whole entourage to provide support. Andrew made the biweekly sojourn to apprise him in person of business operations and the ongoing appeal process. "While our petition for a new trial was denied, which we expected by the way they railroaded you, our lawyer is more hopeful that the appellate level may throw out the verdict because you were not able to face your accuser. That's one of the basic precepts in modern jurisprudence, the right to face your accuser."

"I know that. I've been doing a little reading in the months since I got here. The State claims that since participants in the ceremony testified against me, they don't have to provide the original complainant, citing safety and confidentiality issues relating to his work," Herman concluded authoritatively.

"And ongoing investigations whatever they are." reminded Andrew.

"Right. Thing is we are going to have to be a lot more careful in our public dealings from now on. I sure would like to know who this special agent is. You stay on top of this. Question everybody." Black Jack commanded.

"Will do. Did I mention the letter writing campaign we have started? We are asking everybody in Harlem and your mail order clients across the country to write the Governor of New York and ask him to pardon you for your crimes in recognition of all the works you have done for the public good."

"I think that's what got me locked up in the first place, my do-gooding for the public. What did that fellow call it? 'Rabble rousing'? It was a message. I was an example to anyone who would stand up for African American rights, that they would be slapped down hard.

Anyway the only letter I'm interested in right now is one from Eva. Why haven't I heard from her more than the one time since my incarceration?"

"I don't know. She can't be that busy with the mail order business. The editing of your dictation was completed and sent to the ghost writer a couple of months ago. By the way, the new book should be out this fall."

"Looks like it will be out before I will," Black Jack exclaimed dourly.

"Hey, look on the bright side. Since you've been in the papers with the court case and now jail, your popularity is greater than ever. We're having a tremendous demand for all the mail order products, especially your books."

"I'm so happy for you," Black Jack shot back sarcastically. "I want you to get on the phone and talk to Eva. Find out what's going on. I have the feeling that something terrible is happening to her and she's suffering in silence. You know how she gets. Go to Chicago if you have to, but I want answers the next time I see you." Black Jack was adamant. Andrew knew better than to dismiss his brother's intuitions. They had proved surprisingly accurate all too often in the past.

"Eva, are you all right? Is there anything you need?" Andrew's voice squeaked through nervously with a hint of urgency.

Eva, hair matted, disheveled, sweat pouring down her face, lied. Her thin frail voice, the true testimony to her condition, "No, I'm fine. Sure is hot here in Chicago. Guess it's hot there as well. It is summertime. Lilly's here with me helping with the paperwork. Gosh, the mail order requests are just overwhelming."

Lilly, who was in the bathroom running a tub of cool water for her little sis,' overheard snippets of conversation. "Is that Andrew? Tell him I want to speak to him." She came storming out of the bathroom.

"Now Lil, please don't..." It was no use. Eva was no match for her enraged 'big sis,' who snatched the phone from her hands.

"Let me tell you a thing or two about your brother," Lilly began screaming into the mouthpiece. "Just who in the hell does he think he is? I don't care if he is in prison. After some of the things he's done, he belongs in prison. Let him get a taste of how the rest of the world lives. What do you mean calling up here and asking her about business and she's sitting here struggling with your brother's child." Lilly's tirade was abruptly halted as Eva broke the connection.

"I wish you hadn't told him like that. I was trying to wait for a better time. I wanted to tell Herman myself, but I couldn't put it in the letter I sent to him," Eva said sheepishly.

"Better time? Do you want to wait to invite Black Jack to the baby's birthday party, 'Oh by the way honey, we're having a party

for your baby. Please pick out a nice present on your way over."'
Lilly was ranting.

"That's not fair and you know it. The man's in prison."

Lilly placed the receiver on the table instead of its cradle. She
was primed for a fight and now she would have one. "Fair?" she
shouted. "When have they ever been fair? Look what they've done
to you, to me."

A sudden wave of realization washed over Eva. "Then this is
about what they did to you?"

"You're damn right it's about what they did to me. Do you
know how long I worked with him? Sweated my ass off on that
stage? Escaped close calls in those one-horse towns we played
back then before he met you? Before Deborah, I was his confidant,
his partner. You remember?" Lilly's usually pleasing appearance
had been turned into a grotesque mask flush with emotions long
hidden. "Then suddenly everything changes. In the blink of an eye,
new voices are in control and its thanks for everything. Goodbye
and good luck. They denigrated my contribution and left me with
nothing. What's a washed up actress like me to do anyway when
the music stops and the merry-go-round ride is over? Nobody
wants a has-been."

She who had been Eva's comfort and support was now sobbing
on the younger woman's shoulder seeking comfort. "Don't cry, Lil.
You'll have me crying in a minute." Eva soothed, stroking her big
sister's hair.

"I have a feeling everything will work out. After Black Jack and
I are married you can be sure I won't forget you. We'll give you a
nice high advisory post in our organization, something befitting
your status and our long-standing relationship."

Lilly started laughing between sobs. "You're mad, do you know
that? Wanda will never give him up. He's locked in prison and
you're here in Chicago with no one to take care of you except for
me. That's the reality," scoffed Lilly.

"It doesn't matter. I don't care if what you say may be the truth
now, but I can feel it. Things will change. He will come to me and
we will be married." insisted Eva, suddenly clairvoyant. "But first I

will have to be free of him so that I can belong to him. You know what I mean?"

"Uh huh," Lilly looked at Eva through her own tear soaked eyes, beginning to believe.

"Now let's hang up the phone. I'm sure that Andrew is frantically trying to contact us. Lilly, you have put this process into motion. Now we will have to follow the path and see how it all plays out."

Almost immediately upon hanging up the receiver, the phone rang again. Eva picked it up. "Hello, Andrew. Yes, it's me. I'm sorry I hung up on you earlier. I have something for you to relay to your brother."

They say that sometimes walls have ears. If that is true, then they must also have eyes and tongues. How Wanda found out no one could say. Regardless, she was livid and determined that she was not going to take it anymore. Her husband's libido had completely run amok, two children in two years! Here she was caring for the product of one of his infidelities and there was another one on the way in Chicago. How many more had there been, would there be in the future? Moreover, he had lied to her again claiming that the affair was over. Was this the third or fourth time she had heard this chicanery. Enough was enough. Time for the ultimatum, one of them was going to go. If she left she would be taking half of their combined assets upon her departure. She enjoyed freedom of action while Black Jack was in prison unaware. Wanda would have her lawyers, something she learned from her new neighbors, prepare the documents, set up her case. When he emerged from his penance she would put it to him. The question: 'that little witch or me?' If she didn't like the answer then the hammer would fall. Wanda vowed to herself that she would make Herman's last year look like a holiday by comparison to what came next. She smiled. It was a good thing that she had someone who was looking out for her.

"So that's what happened. Andrew, I told you time and time again, I always trust my sixth sense." Black Jack guided his brother as they sat face to face across the long visiting room table. "I'll tell you this too, she is having a difficult time of it. Something is wrong with the baby. That's part of the reason she's been so quiet.

The other reason is that she is ashamed to have this child out of wedlock. She is afraid her father will disown her. He's a strong man of high principles. I'm sure she hasn't told him, maybe not even her mother. You say Lilly is with her? Well that's good. She needs somebody. I just wish I could be there with her."

"But BJ, how could you two ever be married? You know Wanda will never give you a divorce. You've tried half a dozen times. Remember that tirade of hers about hell freezing over?"

"Old son," Black Jack never called his brother by this name from their broken childhood together. "A stay in a place like this makes a man realize just what is important in life. You never realize what you can give up and still retain your dignity until everything is ripped away from you. Andrew, there are few enough things in this life to make pleasurable the passage of time. When you find one you must fight for it with all of your might, defending it against all intrusions. Among these are love and liberty, which when combined together conclude the pursuit for happiness. The two together supercede the desire for material wealth.

"Wow, BJ, that's deep. You should be a politician."

"I am dear brother, I am." BJ chuckled.

The letter writing campaign, one of the tools employed by the disenfranchised to occasionally remind those in power of the potential power of the ballot box, was having a positive affect.

After ninety days of letters flooding into the governor's office not only from New Yorkers, but supporters from across the nation, it was decided that the continued publicity surrounding Herman's incarceration would do more harm than good. Building him up to be a martyr in the eyes of the general public, to exalt rather than admonish.

Thus it came to pass that Governor Alfred E. Smith, man of the people, would in his benevolence commute the year's sentence to six months. In consideration for the time served, Black Jack would be home for the holidays.

Anyone who thought the Great Black Jack Herman would be subdued or recalcitrant at the ceremony surrounding his release obviously did not know him well. He used the event of his press conference to further build his mystique in the eyes of his legions of followers. "They couldn't hold me," he boasted to the throngs of supporters who showed up at Grand Central Station to herald his release. As reporters scribbled nervously, Black Jack surrounded by his family and smiling entourage,' ironically this would be his last happy family scene, addressed the members of the press. "Ladies and gentlemen, seven times they locked me up and seven times I let myself out. I gave them hell, so they gave up and finally let me go." he boasted to the crowd.

While his boast of opening jail cells was clearly reminiscent of a stunt Houdini had performed decades before and an attempt to evoke a comparison, the latter was all too true. He had given everyone involved in his incarceration fits.

"You can see that iron bars could not hold the Great Black Jack. In order to avoid embarrassment, they had to let me go. Imagine how it would have looked if I was home carving the Christmas turkey when I was supposed to be in prison upstate. Who would be the turkey then?" Black Jack and his entourage behind the podium were beside themselves with laughter.

The crowds applauded. The crowds approved. The crowds did not inquire too closely. They needed heroes, leaders who would speak out for their rights, for their livelihoods. Fact was each day their very survival was becoming less consequential. As the torrent of immigrants flooding into New York and fanning out across the country threatened to take all unskilled jobs away from the black man. In short order, they would surely be the skeletons at the feast. Some even spoke of a great reverse migration back to the agricultural fields of the south. A virtual return to slavery. For any rational mind, such a surrender to subjugation for generations to come was too horrible to contemplate. Such was the need for saviors among the panicky populace in the wake of Mr. Garvey's departure. Everyone was looking for the next Black Moses.

While Black Jack held some pretensions toward that throne, his immediate attention was concentrated on his family, more succinctly on the love of his life, Eva.

By now everyone in the household knew the story of how the pregnancy had gone horribly wrong. Lilly had kept Andrew constantly updated. He in his turn advised Black Jack biweekly up to and including the forced labor just before Halloween. "The doctor's advised the procedure to protect the health of the mother. BJ, they say Eva is horribly thin and in great pain. Lilly says she hardly gets out of bed anymore."

Black Jack, still unaccustomed to this new state of affairs, was listening to Andrew with two fingers pressed to his temple bracing for the worst.

"When she delivered, they found that the child had been draining the life out of the mother," Andrew said rapidly, the best way to deliver bad news.

"So it was..." began BJ in hushed tones.

"Stillborn," Andrew finished the sentence.

Herman longed to be with her at that moment, offer her solace and comfort for the blessing they had lost. Their punishment for the crimes they committed. 'No, better not to think that way, it was unproductive.' Guilt is a wasted emotion that the weak use to retard their resolve. Strength was the hallmark of survivors, overcome all obstacles, rise resilient and refreshed. This was their modus operandi.

He had to get out of Sing Sing, go to her. How she had suffered in silence. It was most inconceivable. According to Andrew, the pain was unbearable. He had to go to her, just one obstacle in his way.

"So your crimes have come to the light of day again." Wanda started in on him as the limo left the press conference at Grand Central.

"Oh, let up woman, would you? Eva's almost lost her life," he growled in response.

"And now I suppose you will want to go to her. Take care of your delicate flower. Well, I won't have it," Wanda retorted. Battle lines had been drawn.

However, prison had not so cowed Herman that he would be dictated to in his own home. Upon arrival at the mansion, he began to pack and make preparations for his trip to Chicago.

The rapidly estranging couple continued to snipe down corridors and up stairs, in full view of a dozen or so family and staff members.

Black Jack emptied the wall safe in his office of all contents and bellowed for Andrew to get him a ticket on the evening's train to Chicago.

"If you leave this house tonight, don't bother coming back. I will have an injunction slapped on you by morning," Wanda yelled, venom fully flowing. She had been waiting for this moment for a long time.

"You should know by now that I don't respond well to ultimatums. Remember I still have a few things on you as well," Herman cautioned.

"If you decide to move against me, you had better pack your bags because it will be you who will be gone." He promised.

"You can't threaten me. I've raised your children, taken care of your bastards, I am entitled to half and I will get my due. I'm not afraid of you, Mr. Black Magic Man. Ha!"

"Enough," he yelled in a voice loud enough to crumble the walls of Jericho. "Let that be your last word. You have cursed yourself. You will get what's coming. But you won't get my house," his grisly prophecy. "Be gone by the time I return. I don't want to see you here again." Black Jack said that last with the cold finality of someone contemplating a murder.

All who heard this icy tirade thought it better that Wanda not test the limits of his patience.

Eva spent Christmas in a convalescent home; the best Black Jack's money could buy. He would visit her daily bringing presents and flowers. Pushing her in a wheelchair to the solarium to sit by her side for hours. Alternately ordering the nurses and staff about as if he owned the place and performing demonstrations of magic for the patients. In short, he was himself at his best and worst and Eva loved him all the more for it. She was the center of his universe again. She would be his bride at last. Scherazade arisen! They would rebuild their broken lives. Together they would be bigger and better than ever, soaring to new heights on the wings of their love.

XVI
Whirlwind

Herman's time in jail had only multiplied his fame and the demand for his services. Touring the Midwest in the spring of 1926, he played to packed houses. He and Lilly were held over everywhere they went turning away dozens each night.

The crowds wanted to witness his fantastic mental powers, hear him lecture on freedom and equality, comment on the problems of the day.

Among the tricks they reprised, the popular chicken and egg trick, which was concluded with a little social commentary.

"Thank you ladies and gentlemen for your applause, but far from being an esoteric concept these days, the religious zealots down in Tennessee are trying to put a schoolteacher in jail for teaching his students that man evolved from lower species, for espousing the scientific theory of evolution proposed by a man named Darwin. The bigots want to teach that the Bible is the literal truth, the only truth."

Black Jack paused and raised his voice so that all could hear him clearly. "I want all of you to realize that this is just another attempt to relegate the black race to the status of second class citizenry. Who among you knows your Bible?" A couple dozen hands went up in the audience. "Then you will remember that after the flood there were no black people. We didn't make it on to the ark, if indeed we existed at all." The crowd was stone silent waiting for the punch line. Many already knew what was coming.

"After the flood," Black Jack repeated for emphasis, "What happened?" Someone would always shout out Noah got drunk. "That's right; Noah got drunk and cursed his grandson who went on to populate all of the colored lands from Africa and Asia." Herman paused and a slip of paper appeared in his right hand accompanied by a small puff of smoke. He continued, reading the paper in revered tones, "Cursed be Canaan, a slave of slaves shall he be to his brothers."

Black Jack always stopped to regard the crowd at this point. There was usually quite a bit of consternation, neighbor talking to neighbor. Some in the audience displayed visible signs of distress.

"Listen to me, folks. This is their ultimate agenda. This unholy alliance of church and state is designed to keep you as second class citizens or worse." He would let this sink in for a minute before continuing. "This has been the religious justification for slavery for hundreds, heck thousands, of years. That it was ordained by the literal word of the Bible. That's why they want to teach creationism over evolution. When we unmask their hidden agenda we find they seek Biblical authority for their continued subjugation.

That is why we have millions of men and women marching around in sheets today causing mayhem. A pseudo-religious army spouting hatred and sponsoring terror, denigrating the American flag and desecrating the cross."

Black Jack had made his point, now he would deliver one more bombshell, a feel good piece of gospel for the audience to take home with them, warm their souls through the long nights. "Ladies and gentlemen, those voices that speak with hidden agenda don't tell you the whole truth, the rest of the story." More smoke, another piece of paper appears in his hand. "This is the true reason they wish to subjugate us, they are afraid. Afraid of our power within. Afraid of once and future kings. People rarely talk about Nimrod. He was born of that line cursed by Noah, but refused to be a slave. Here it is, the literal truth of the Bible 'Nimrod; he was the first on earth to be a mighty man. He was a mighty hunter before the Lord;

therefore it is said, Like Nimrod a mighty hunter before the Lord.' The passage also goes on to say how he founded Babel. Even the little Sunday school children know that the Tower of Babel was the tallest building in the world at that time. So you see that we have had a glorious past and I foresee a glorious future. While I cannot as yet discern how this trial of science vs. religion will turn out. I have faith that men of sound mind will exercise good judgment or in short order the zealots will have us believing that the sun revolves around the earth as we did, not five hundred years ago. But remember their true agenda is to support a two-tier system that perpetuates a nation of haves and have-nots. Thank you for coming. See you next time. Don't forget to buy my books and memorabilia on sale at the rear of the theater."

Next morning there was the obligatory phone call to Chicago. "Good morning, babe. Did I wake you?"

"No, I've been up for a couple of hours. How did the show go last night?" asked Eva.

"Great, honey, just great. We played to another packed house. They wanted to hold us over, but that would make us late arriving in Cincinnati. So we just couldn't stay in Cleveland any longer. Theater manager was disappointed, says his business has rarely been this good. I tell you it's been that way all over the Midwest. Simply fantastic."

"How's Lilly holding up? It has been several years since she has been on tour," asked Eva. "You know, she is a real trooper. Once you are a star performer, you never really lose that talent. She can't wait to get to Cincinnati and replenish our supply. We ran out of gin in Michigan," confided Herman.

"Now you watch those martinis. I don't want to hear of you two going on a bender and winding up in the drunk tank." Eva chided.

"No ma'am! Don't worry; we'll be on our best behavior. See you in a couple of weeks. I love you. Bye" Black Jack had not asked her how she was feeling. He knew she wouldn't tell him if she was experiencing pain.

"Love you too, honey. Can't wait to see you." Eva cradled the receiver in her arms long after the call was finished.

Eva had routine daily duties with which to keep busy during her recuperation. In addition, she had her weekly phone call to Andrew to advise him on the status of mail order requests. He in turn would advise her on events surrounding Wanda's departure. "Yes, this time's for certain. She's got most of her things moved out of the house including all of the living room furniture. I don't know where she is going to put it all. Probably in storage now."

"Let her, everything that is not nailed down. She'll probably take it anyway," came Eva's contemptuous retort. While uncharacteristically bitter, Eva was tired of this other woman who had made her life miserable since the day they first met.

She, Eva, had finally won out but at a terrible price. It was time to put the past behind and focus on the future. Her future with Black Jack, the only man she had ever loved. Just one more thing she needed to do. Lilly provided the key in a clandestine call from Cincinnati.

"Hi honey, it's me. I finally found out the information you wanted. Someone from one of the other acts here knows of, has a friend, who is touring with him. Says they will be at the Starlight Lounge in New York City for the next two weeks before taking their show on the road. Honey, it looks like you will have to go to New York. Can you manage that on your own?" Lilly's doubts were echoed in Eva's mind but her resolve held firm.

"I'll have to. I have no choice. There can be nothing between us if I am to return to New York and live with BJ in that house as his woman. Don't worry about me, Lil. Its taxi cabs and trains there and back. It will be a straight trip, no detours. I could be there and back in three days with plenty of time to spare before you guys return. I'll tell the maid that I am going to St. Louis for a few days to visit my folks. That way if the subject ever comes up, I won't have to completely lie. Just fib a bit you know, a little white lie."

"Girl, you've gotten so good at subterfuge, it's scary," chided Lilly good naturedly.

"Well it must be the company I keep." (giggle) "Anyway, let me go. I will make the arrangements now. See you when you get back." Eva almost whispered the last sentence into the receiver suddenly afraid of being overheard.

"I'd better go too. Goodbye honey and good luck." Lilly cut the connection.

Eva roused herself from the bedroom just long enough to make sure the maid was out of earshot. She returned to the phone and hurriedly made the arrangements that would take her out of town the following weekend. In less than half an hour, everything was set. Her itinerary laid out including a ticket for the Saturday night show at the Starlight Lounge. As part of her plan, she would wait and leave after Black Jack's next call informing him of her intention to visit with her mother. This would allay any suspicions on his part. She desperately did not want him to know anything of her task. But she had to be free of his undue influence over her in order to be able to completely, voluntarily give herself to him. On some level she feared he would not understand the logic behind her desire. Also and most importantly, Eva wanted it to be her little secret.

She arrived in New York City on a beautiful spring evening. The trees were a full bloom of greenery. Seems they celebrated the season a little earlier than those of Chicago. It was a Friday evening and the city was bustling with activity. Ignoring the call of the nightlife, truth be told she was still in no condition to revel, she entered a cab and was whisked to a large hotel on Harlem's outskirts. 'Good, I made it,' she congratulated upon falling backward into her bed. If she did this right, no one would be the wiser. Eva had no doubt that she could avoid Andrew and his cronies. They never frequented hotels and rarely attended magic shows. 'Right now,' she closed her eyes to concentrate. 'Right now they were serving drinks in the lounge across from the living room, entertaining some young ladies, making preparations, what clubs would they hit tonight.' She knew them, knew them all too well with their penchant for parties and wild women. Especially that Washington character, Eva shivered involuntarily. For some reason he gave her the creeps.

Yes, she would be all right. Her mind assured she would be able to remain incognito and accomplish her task if she just kept a low profile. To that end, she decided to take her meals in the room and upon exiting, wear the little hat with the black veil that covered her face. Anyway she had nearly twenty hours to rest and gather thoughts before time for her rendezvous.

The concierge had obtained her transportation for the evening. Her ticket was confirmed and waiting for her at the box office. It was show time.

"Driver, just one detour if we can," Eva requested meekly. "If you will please drive down 136th Street and then we can take the Third Avenue Bridge."

"Anything you want, missus. It's your party. The man at the hotel paid me to take you anywhere you want to go and stay with you till whenever," the cabbie informed her by way of the rear view mirror as he pulled away from the curb and into the dense Saturday evening traffic.

There they were, traveling east on 136th Street. The mansions appeared huddled together, one fading into another. Many guarded by wrought iron bars and trellis, especially here. The haves had to be guarded from the have-nots.

"Slow down, driver, but don't stop." Eva slumped down in the back seat. Just her eye line remained above the horizon of the rear door's window.

"I understand, ma'am," the cabby's deadpanned reply. The vehicle slowed down perceptively as it approached a residence with several very fancy cars parked outside. It was obvious from the look of the place, lights in the windows splashing out onto the sidewalk, that activity percolated inside. Perhaps a party was in progress. 'Look, look there,' her mind urged. There were the two roadsters, one halfway up on the sidewalk. One sedan was there, another missing. 'When the cat's away,' her mind pestered. Wanda must have taken her limo. Eva idly wondered if she was still there. Probably not, having moved so much of the furniture, at least according to Andrew. Eva sincerely hoped she could trust him.

It was over. The taxi had eased its way past the only flurry of activity on the block and the driver was speaking to her again.

"Do you want me to go around again? It will only take a minute."

No, she had seen all that she needed to, cared to, witness. "No, we had better go on to our destination. I have an appointment to keep in the Bronx."

In truth she had no prearranged meeting planned. Professor Maharajah did not even know that she would be in attendance. In fact, they had never laid eyes upon one another again since that episode in San Francisco almost four years ago. Eva's plan was to approach him after his performance, backstage away from prying eyes and beg him to reverse his dastardly deed. One way or another, Eva was resolved to force him to dig deep down into her mind and rip out, tear asunder, the bonds that held her to Herman. If necessary she would use the twenty-two caliber she now carried in her purse for protection.

The Professor, as befitting the star of the show, would be the last entertainer to perform. Thus Eva need not worry about arriving on time. She did not wish to see the whole show, but also did not wish to make too dramatic an entrance. Here of all places, someone might recognize her. She was after all a star of some renown. As luck would have it, she was seated at a small table to one side of the stage. Couched in the semi-darkness of shadows, she could see clearly but not be seen from the stage.

Eva sat quietly through a ventriloquist's act which her entrance had bisected and clapped politely as a couple of showmen, apparently husband and wife from their billing, put a group of trained dogs through their paces. Another team performed some card tricks intertwined with relatively simple attempts at mental telepathy including questions from the audience. It was all very pleasant.

Then came time for the star of the show to make his appearance. Boy did he ever. In a plume of smoke, the great hypnotist and four female assistants materialized on stage simultaneously. Wow! Enough to take your breath away. Eva was glad she was not sitting any closer. She was sure the people at the front tables were overwhelmed as the stage was suddenly transformed and stage lights glared brightly.

Eva could feel electricity buzzing through the air as audience members gave their rapt attention to the seasoned performer who commanded the stage.

"Good evening. I am Professor Maharajah Hypnotist Supreme

and while I guarantee not to hypnotize you, the audience, many of my illusions will confound and astound you." Eva, who indeed gave her rapt attention to his performance, was glad somehow that he hadn't changed perceptibly in the four years since their first meeting.

She found herself genuinely enjoying the show to the point of forgetting her original mission. Eva clapped heartily at the conclusion of the Hindu Rope Trick. After the last of the four girls made their escape ascending skyward, the Professor disappeared in a cloud of smoke as did the rope itself moments later. As he hypnotized the girls and commanded them to perform, all the old images flooded her consciousness. Three weeks in San Francisco passed by her eyes in less than a minute. It was not a completely unpleasant experience. Seeing him again, like this, performing on stage, Eva felt certain he would relieve her of this untenable burden.

For his show stopping finale, the Professor was still doing the Escape from the Milk Can Trick made famous by the Great Harry Houdini, who was coincidently performing the same trick in his act on Broadway.

The crowd at both venues watched quietly, attentively, the silent struggles behind the curtain placed around the object of entombment at center stage. One minute, two minutes, three, four. The veteran magicians were certainly holding their respective audiences in suspense. Finally, the dull of metal hitting wooden stage floor and sounds of water splashing; the great magician Houdini/ Professor Maharajah emerged from the obscurity of the curtain to reassure nervous patrons that everything was all right. Once again, they had cheated death this day. A standing ovation was their reward. Eva too, stood and applauded the dramatic resurrection. No matter how many times she had seen the trick, it was still a spellbinding performance when performed by a master.

After the show, Eva had to announce herself to gain entry backstage. This was the first anyone knew of her arrival in the Big Apple. She found his door and knocked forcefully. It opened slowly. The great man was not alone. He peered through the door. Eva thought he looked haggard without his makeup. The lines on his face deeply ingrained, older now than on stage. It was evident that life on the road was taking a heavy toll.

"Yes, may I help you, young lady?" he peered at her though not really seeing, recognizing.

"Why Professor, it's me, Eva! We shared a stage several years ago in San Francisco. I wanted to come back and congratulate you on a marvelous performance. Do you have a minute?" A subtle command from Eva, her gambit was well played.

"Oh yes, how are you, my dear? So nice to see you again. Just let me get rid of these people," he said confidentially. "Come in, come in!" the Professor said for public consumption. "People, this is a young woman I shared the stage with some years ago. Apparently she has come a great distance to see me. Get out would you and afford us some privacy. I will talk to you later." The Maharajah, never one for subtleness, brusquely ushered the guests out of his dressing room.

"So nice to see you again, my dear. Care for a cup of tea?" He poured a little brandy as well into his cup. "Just enough to settle the nerves. The old bones you know, not what they used to be."

"No, thank you Professor," Eva responded courteously as she accepted a seat at his dressing table.

The master magician continued his preamble, "I'm sorry to hear that you two stopped touring together. But for your sake, I'm glad you stopped performing the trick. It takes a lot out of you. And he loves you so much. You know that, don't you?"

"Yes, Professor, that's why I'm here. I want you to lift the curse."

"Curse?" the old man feigned forgetfulness.

"Spell or hypnotic suggestion, whatever you want to call it. Black Jack admitted to me that he had you place a condition on me, a governor if you will, that I could run away but I was always compelled to return to him. We are going to be wed now, and I don't want anything standing between us. I want to commit to him completely of my own volition, not because some implanted thought urges me to act in a certain fashion."

"Why, my dear, you are mistaken. I have never implanted any such condition into your mind. In fact, I am very surprised that he told you. This was a charade for his benefit. He was so terribly afraid of losing you as he had lost others in his life whom he loved deeply. I put the suggestion to him one night while we were drinking, and he became so attached to the idea that well, it became our little joke."

"But Professor, I've searched my mind. I know that there is something just outside my reach, beyond the limits of my conscious mind."

"Why yes, that is true enough. But that was for your benefit to stabilize your being and always give you the stage presence and courage to perform. Above all, the suggestion was placed deeply in your unconscious to give you resiliency. That is one of the paramount talents needed by professional show people." authoritated Professor Maharajah.

Eva stared silently searching her mind for confirmation of this fantastic tale. 'Isn't that what Deborah had said to her in the reading? That she would arise with resilience? This was a most shocking and unexpected revelation.'

The Professor continued his reassurances with the autopsy of the event. "You remember how frightened you became when you awoke from your light trance and found us ready to bury you in the pit? Well, I knew you would need a little help to get you through not only that practice performance, but the real thing and the next one, and the one after that. So I placed a calming suggestion deep into your mind that you would always be strong, survive to live a long and wonderful life."

Somehow she could feel the truth of it. There was no falsehood in that statement. It was then that all of her anxieties magically disappeared.

Eva, now smiling radiantly with a confidence beyond words, had one more favor to ask.

"Dear Professor, will you hypnotize me one last time?"

With the successful resolution of her quest, Eva completed the journey and returned to Chicago early Monday morning. She would give the maid a couple more days off. That would bolster the belief that she had been visiting parents. Eva was elated. She felt newly empowered both by the words and deeds of Professor

Maharajah. What a wonderful man! She now only hoped that her body could catch up to spirit. The universe was wide open with endless possibilities beckoning to her, to them, she and her intended. She must be ready to take her place beside this great man now at the advent of his finest hour. Emboldened with the confidence of the ages, she knew it would all work out given a little more time.

In late May of '26, there was a party held in the Chicago offices of Herman Enterprises, Black Jack and Eva's apartment, to celebrate their impending nuptials.

"Here's to Black Jack who predicted that if we invest without a care, our profits would appear out of thin air," toasted Eva, still drinking lemonade.

"Profits would multiply as if out of thin air, dear." the gentle rejoinder from her husband to be.

"How so ever you like it, my dear. Either way, these modern times are turning out to be pretty sensational. First we have messages flying through the air and now people will be following them," chuckled Eva.

"It's not only broadcasters and airplanes, my Ford stock was up four points last week. Here's to Black Jack who said, 'Buy things that will last, not relics from the past,'" jubilated one of the guests.

"Here's to Black Jack." Glasses clinked.

Herman cast a chill over the crowd by reminding the group the lessons of human nature. "Remember people are always happiest when they are making money. When they start to lose, they won't think my rhymes very funny. So take your profits when all is sunny. When there is fear and dread humanity will hang its head." His little rhyme had appropriately a chilling effect. "So do you think there's trouble ahead?" one wealthy middle-aged woman asked in hushed, frightened tones.

"All I'm saying is that everything runs in cycles. Even the Bible says that to everything there is a season. The people who left Sodom early were the lucky ones. And don't be like Lot's wife; don't inquire too closely of your good fortune." The big man was unusually circumspect for such a joyous occasion. His downtrodden demeanor quelled any further attempts at over exuberance at least concerning this particular subject.

"I am a student of observation. I observe people. When they get too excited about a thing, it won't last. When everyone gets excited about the same thing, it is over. Every good magician knows when to fold up his tent and move on to the next town. The stock market is just like that. Making money is easy. The greatest trick is knowing when to get out and not look back."

Herman's rude assessment was greeted by his guests with stone silence. Many were unwilling or unable to believe that stocks would ever again experience a reversal of fortune. In this modern world weren't these 'best of times' supposed to last forever?

"Well, glad to see that you still know how to turn a ballroom into a morgue." teased Eva as she motioned for the maid to circulate with a bottle of champagne.

"Now onto a lighter subject, I too have some good news and some bad news. By now you all know that Herman and I are to be wed." Slyly she winked at Lilly. "That's the good news. The bad news is that none of you are invited."

The group let out a collective groan.

"Just kidding. But the wedding will take place in New York City in July. So...in case some of you can't make it, we will hold a small ceremony here in our apartment."

"Yeah," cheers again from the crowd along with tinkling glasses and calls for a speech.

Herman, all wrapped up in his dour mood, stood and said simply, "Everyone knows this has been a long time coming. I have been enamored ever since I first laid eyes upon...you know, her long gorgeous gams. I just hope this time we get it right."

"You had better get it right." His fiancé came over and locked elbows. "Because this time is for keeps. No rain checks, no refunds." Eva asked the group, "And why do we say that?" Chorus: "Because the show must go on!"

For once it was Eva who traveled with an entourage. Her parents and older sister had come up to Chicago for the pre-wedding celebration and rode with her to New York. Lilly, as maid of honor, was Eva's constant companion.

The wedding had turned quickly into a family affair, Andrew redecorating the townhouse before they arrived and Eva's mother and sister orchestrating the wedding planning. Andrew had wasted no time in tastefully redecorating, acquiring functional furniture upon Wanda's departure. No longer French provincial as was her penchant, these new groupings had a rather eclectic 'feel.'

Much of Andrew's inspiration came from that new design center, inspired by Gestalt Philosophy, in Lower Manhattan, the Bau Haus. It was all very avant-garde. The austere design and sharp angles reflected in his mind the essence of streamlined modern society, nothing fancy just functional. The new furniture was complimented with artwork, which celebrated his taste for the surreal.

Surprisingly, it was a big hit with many guests. In fact, one of a series of inaugural parties was in progress the night of Eva's surreptitious taxi ride.

Black Jack, a traditionalist at heart, hated most everything that had been done to the home in his absence. He wasted no time in making his feelings known to Andrew. "I don't know what you were thinking, but boy, they really saw you coming."

"Actually many of our friends quite like it. Alelia said that it embodies the spirit of modern mechanized society." As usual, Andrew wound up defending his decisions.

"I think she was being kind. That doesn't sound much like a compliment to me." BJ replied smirking. "Besides, you know her penchant for Victorian furniture, authentic English teas. You won't find any of this in her house, not even in her Dark Tower room."

"You'll see, this style will catch on all over town and we will be in the forefront of a new fashion trend." Andrew encouraged. "Everyone will say Black Jack and his fantastic vision divined the future once again."

"Ok, Ok. We will give it a try, little brother. You may be right about some of that artwork. Makes you feel like you are looking into another dimension. Just the thing for clients before I usher them into the 'reading room.' A few minutes of that," BJ pointed to a painting of a black and white square tiled floor that stretched off into infinity, "will really throw them off their guard."

"Now you're talking," Andrew said excitedly.

"Just one thing, I told Eva she could redo the bedroom. Ain't none of us gonna be happy unless she's happy."

For Eva's parents this was the trip of a lifetime. After a sightseeing tour that encompassed beaches, boating and skyscrapers being built, the women went on a shopping spree the likes of which had never been seen back in St. Louis.

If there was one thing the groom and the father of the bride agreed upon, the shopping extravaganza was out of control. Cries of 'You bought what?' and 'What do we need that for?' became common refrains around the household. The two men could do naught but surrender to the madness and hand out money, each hoping that this was a once in a lifetime celebration. It is said that shared hardship breeds comradery, so was the case with these two gentlemen who could be seen sharing a drink when Black Jack was not otherwise employed.

"You know, Charles, when I consider that it has been over a year since I was hauled out of here by the police, my little brother has really done a good job keeping everything running smoothly." Black Jack confided to his future father-in-law one afternoon.

"You really haven't been here in over a year?" asked Charles, sipping scotch.

"After I was released, I came back to pack some clothes and tell my wife we were getting a divorce. But I didn't stay. I got on a train and went to Chicago to be with your daughter." Black Jack stopped the story at that point. He was not sure how much the older gentleman knew about his daughter's 'accident.' "The point is I am really proud of my little brother. He said my incarceration brought in almost more business than they could handle. Now that I'm out and touring again, I am more famous than ever." Not an idle boast.

"What were you arrested for again? Fortune telling?" asked Charles.

"It was a frame up. They apparently had me under surveillance for some time. From the evidence presented at the trial, they had someone close to the household who documented all of the comings and goings. And after all of the time, effort and expense, the only thing that they could find to charge me with was telling fortunes without a license," Herman concluded contemptuously.

Charles asked the most pertinent question. "Did you ever find out who the informant was?"

"I told Andrew to grill the staff. Find the bastard. We now think it was one of my neighbors who has been in the house a couple of times and isn't completely comfortable with our living on the block. It just shows you how desperate the government was to get something on me," bragged Black Jack.

"You don't mean the Federal Government?" asked Charles incredulously, refilling his glass from the decanter.

"Of course. There was a brief by J. Edgar Hoover read into evidence against me saying that I had associated with known agents of communists, convicted felons. You know, he really laid it on thick."

"Have you associated with criminals?" Eva's dad sounded alarmed.

"Only Marcus Garvey. They know that, and only while he was out on bail making his appeal. They wanted him because of his lectures on freedom. Then they came after me because of my speechmaking during performances. We were tarred with the same brush. Its name is Hoover." Black Jack paused to refill his glass and gauge the affect of this conversation on his father-in-law. Then the redirect. "Do you know what Mr. Garvey's heinous crime was? Mail fraud. He had mismanaged his business and he kept asking for money, painting rosy prospects. He is one of few black men ever charged with white collar crime. His real crime was being overoptimistic and not knowing when to quit."

Another break in conversation at which time Herman clinked the older man's glass with his own and continued in a confidential comradery.

"Do you know why the government is so afraid of me? It's because I'm organized as well as eloquent. Look here, I've been away for over a year and the organization still runs efficiently-if in an admittedly avant-garde atmosphere." BJ swept one long arm through the air to acknowledge their surroundings.

"I see your point." allowed Charles. "When we first met, I

considered you a bit of a bombast. Now I see you care deeply and are capable of carrying out great deeds. Mr. Herman, you have the potential to be a great man." He held his hand out to the other.

Accepting the hand shake, Black Jack looked Charles in the eye and asked rhetorically, "Do you know what makes a man great? Overcoming great adversaries. Like the great hunter Nimrod, I go forth and do battle."

The two men continued bonding until the women came back from shopping hours later.

The wedding of Benjamin Rucker and Eva Alexander was a private, understated affair at her parents' request. Uncomfortable in the limelight and given what they considered the man's sordid past, they, read her father, did not want their baby married in a circus atmosphere. To Eva and BJ, this request for a small family ceremony in the mansion suited them just fine. Neither of them wanted a spectacle after the events of the last year.

The décor presented the next problem. Eva's father described it on first appraisal as a carnival fun house gone horribly wrong. To pacify his concerns, it was agreed that a tent would be pitched in the backyard trampling Andrew's precious herbs. This task was completed the day before the ceremony over Andrew's strenuous objections.

The backyard made a marvelous venue for the melding of family and friends. Eva was never lovelier in her floor length, flowing, pearl-shaded silk gown with faux pearls embroidered across the bodice. A matching satiny veil accompanied the outfit. While the flowing train made it difficult for her to walk, as the center of attention everyone revolved around her.

Finally after years of waiting, trying, it was done. Now, not only did she belong to him, but he to her as well. No longer the duties and obligations that she owed him, but the power and control she, his wife, could exercise. Eva remembered her promise to Lilly 'she would use tender gloves. Tender mercies. 'It was a wondrous event to be sure this July wedding.

The day after the blessed event, they left on their honeymoon. BJ had booked passage on the Trans Canadian Railways. Four days each in Montreal and Toronto. 'They could see the falls again.' delighted Eva. Followed by a trip across Canada to Vancouver.

Eva thought train travel was a wonderful way to see nature and spend time renewing each other's acquaintance. Hopefully they could recreate the magic of their first 'honeymoon' in Toronto and New York City, which now seemed over a hundred years ago. Needless to say, they had the time of their lives.

Autumn found the couple back from their Canadian honeymoon and settling into the new-old routine of running Herman's enterprise. Eva settling into her new routine of running the New York mansion.

Less than two months after their return, on the morning of All Saints Day, November first, Washington Reeves came running into the foyer with a newspaper in hand, carrying the tragic headline. The tragic news that swept around the world: 'Houdini, King of Magic, Dead at 52.'

Stunned, Eva related the news to her husband. "Apparently, he followed us to Canada where he got sick. He died seven days later in Michigan. His family still lives in Brooklyn. Says here they are bringing the body back to New York for a state funeral." Now reading from the paper, 'Business' will be closed to mark the occasion. "Honey, we should go and pay our respects."

"They don't want us there, sweetheart. Trust me, he never respected my work." BJ said bitterly.

Knowing better than to argue with her husband where the subject of magic was concerned, Eva took another approach. "Well, at least let's go and see the procession. The paper says thousands of people are expected to line the streets."

Tens of thousands turned out to view the hearse as it proceeded east from the Times Square Service towards its final destination in Queens. Black Jack and entourage camped out on a corner along the procession's route four hours before the hearse was due. Despite his usual stoic demeanor, after Houdini's body passed, he was visibly moved. "You know, babe," BJ turned to Eva. "if anything ever happened to me, I'd like to be remembered that way."

"You will, baby, you will," she soothed reassuringly, clasping her hand to his.

XVII
Through the Crystal Darkly

After Christmas the invitations went out to the annual New Year's Eve bash. Not the calendar year, but rather a party centered around the anniversary of the advent of Prohibition. This year would mark the seventh such occurrence. The seventh year since the right to acquire alcohol was repealed. Lucky seven.

Not that alcohol was hard to come by, especially here on the coast where a smuggler could pull up to any port on a dark night and unload his illegal cargo. Easy access to the Big Apple prompted American entrepreneurship. The mobs were unable to wield the iron-fisted control they enjoyed in Chicago. Moreover, the average Joe could now brew his own beer and wine thanks to completely legal make-it-yourself kits. America had adapted and moved on thanks to good old American ingenuity.

The party remained as purely a symbolic affair. A social occasion and a reason to have a gala in the middle of January, filling the lull after the major holidays. It was eagerly anticipated by Harlem socialites and religiously attended.

January in the city was a cold, snowy affair. Inclement weather did nothing to dampen spirits of the inhabitants. Business was good, the stock market was soaring and the cultural renaissance was reaching a fevered pitch. It didn't matter if the city was cold, the jazz was hot. It was the best of times.

Black Jack was standing in the midst of his living room crowded with partygoer; Jelly Roll Morton's Jazz trio played in the background animating the avant garde atmosphere. His back to the band, Herman extolled the new additions to his repertoire for the coming year. "I have hired a ghost writer to provide some colorful scripts that we will peddle on tour and through our mail order catalogue. It will be a continuing series called 'Autobiographies of Black Jack Herman.' Each year we will come out with a new episode more dramatic than the last. For the kiddies, we will debut a coloring book entitled 'Black Jack's Adventures Around the World.' I will fight Chinese dragons, demons; get into and out of all sorts of predicaments. It should be a big hit." Someone pointed out that technically the term 'autobiography' meant true history penned by one's own hand. BJ was having none of that. He was too excited about his company's new offerings.

"Andrew and Washington have come up with a new product designed to capitalize on the general public's obsession with the numbers trade," he stated proudly.

"The illegal numbers racket, how can you capitalize on that?" Miss Walker asked with genuine curiosity.

"We are going to publish a couple of booklets. One will be on lucky numbers and another on dream interpretation," BJ self-congratulated.

"What are you just gonna publish a book of numbers?" asked Alelia.

"No, far from it. The daily winning numbers are based on the results from local races. The winners from the first three races make up three winning digits. Well, it turns out that Washington is a real whiz at number combinations. We have obtained through back issues of newspapers the winning races for the past two years. He has analyzed the occurrence of winning horses, in each slot one through nine, and given us the most likely combinations. It can also be used to predict the probability of a numbers occurrence in the second and third slots once the first number is known."

"Oh, I see, you're talking about a formula. You've developed a sort of statistical probabilities on historical performance. If it works, it won't work for too long. Every year they change the jockeys around and add new horses to the mix," Alelia sounded cynical.

"We have anticipated that." Herman responded confidently. "We will update the results quarterly based on computations combining the latest results. Besides the key to our success is marketing. In all of our publications, we will include encrypted numbers embedded in the artwork. You know, hidden in the background that sort of thing.

"I have personally taken on the biblical number seven as my mantra." BJ drew the group's attention to a golden chain. Hidden beneath his vest was a large twenty four karat number seven.

"Are you over here talking shop again? BJ, give it a rest. You should be ashamed of yourself. Eva locked both of her arms around one of his in an overt gesture to drag him away from the small grouping and back to the rest of their guests. "I'm going to keep a closer eye on you." Then to the small grouping, "He really is so proud of his new ideas. Did he tell you we will be touring again?"

"No, when?" the unanimous response.

"In the spring. He will perform his mentalist act. The audiences can't seem to get enough of that. I will be by his side, just like old times." she said wistfully. "Oh, I almost forgot. We will be reprising the levitation demonstration."

The group murmured surprise and approval. Mostly approval.

Thus emboldened, Eva proceeded to let the 'cat out of the bag.' "In fact, we will preview a little demonstration for you tonight." She was beaming.

No one would have the temerity to ask her if she would ever perform the 'Buried Alive' stunt again. Not now after the Great Houdini had died less than two months after performing a variation of that trick.

Now that she had spilled the beans, she was obliged to inform the other guests. "Ladies and gentlemen, I have an announcement. May I have your attention, please? After cocktails we have a special treat for you. Black Jack and I are going to give you a sneak performance. For your pleasure, we will perform one of the demonstrations from our upcoming tour, our famous levitation illusion." Eva moved through the crowd ecstatically clapping her hands.

"It has been almost five years since we performed this one in public, hasn't it, hon?" Eva said coaching her husband.

"Yes, about that. But you know the classics; they never go out of style." Black Jack tried to sound enthusiastic, but he would much rather be talking about his new literary endeavors.

"Well, I have to go get ready," Eva gushed. "Honey, you have to entertain the guests. No more shop talk."

The cocktail hour concluded in the living room, which one of the guests commented looked like the waiting room for purgatory. At the seventh hour, the maid came in and opened the sliding doors to the dining room, which for this occasion had been transformed into a performance chamber.

In place of the dining table was a smaller surface elevated three feet off the ground, back lit to highlight its presence in the otherwise empty room.

Not a soul was surprised when Herman strode center stage and began his preamble. "It is said that the ancient Atlantians knew all of the secrets of the universe. Theirs was a society that had conquered all of the secrets of the mental manipulation of matter or what we call today magic."

In an instant, all eyes were upon him. All conversations quelled.

"The Atlantians were all powerful, but not all knowing. They did not know that hubris, greed, would tear them apart. They thought themselves beyond petty jealousies, disagreements in philosophy. Their ultimate crime, they thought they <u>were</u> gods." Herman paused, the magician's pause to heighten the drama, tease the audience.

"When their plight was incontrovertible, their fate sealed, they sent representatives of the Atlantian culture to the four corners of the earth to hide the secrets of their great knowledge so that when, they were ready, future generations might become enlightened. Perhaps they would be wise enough not to destroy themselves in the process. The Atlantians had the overwhelming desire, the unmitigated gall, to wish that the knowledge of ascended beings not fall into the black death of oblivion. Over the thousands of years that followed, those remnants of kings, what we know as ancient man discovered, practiced and returned to the state of perfection those few snippets of the divine knowledge that surfaced. The only remnants of mankind's first fall from grace. Tonight, I will demonstrate one of these powers for your viewing pleasure. Remember it is only an illusion, or is it?" Now at the top of his lungs, "Ladies and gentlemen, I present the lovely Madame Eva, my charming wife."

Polite, but enthusiastic applause accompanied Eva's arrival down the stairs to stand beside her husband. She bowed deeply to cheers and cat calls.

"By now, you all know of our stated intentions to have Eva entranced, lay on that table and using the power of illusion within my mind, convince you all that she is floating above the ground in defiance of the physical laws of gravity. Just like the cap stones to temples of the sun in that fabled ancient city." He turned Eva toward him and with the use of a golden object dangling on a chain; he put her into a trance.

"Now, if anyone here doesn't believe that my lovely assistant has been hypnotized, the illusion will not work. So at this time, I need several of you to confirm the authenticity of my powers."

Several ladies and a gentleman approached and raised her arm, waved hands in front of her eyes and even pinched her. No response.

"Ok, now that we have verified her entranced condition; EVA ACCOMPANY
ME AND PLACE YOURSELF FACE UP UPON THE TABLE."

The young bride performed the task with wooden movements, lying perfectly still.

"Now ladies and gentlemen, for those of you who have never witnessed this illusion before, I need a plethora of positive energy. You must concentrate on the woman on the table and will her body to float into the air. You must concentrate on this task with all of your might. Any negative energy will cause this trick to fail."

Encharged with their task, Herman's guests could be seen

to scrunch noses, furl brows, some unconsciously, to aid in the event.

Slowly the prone figure appeared to be rising in the flickering candlelight surrounding her body. Herman raised his extended arms, waving the one carrying the wand in orchestral fashion. Her body, in response, moved higher and higher.

Black Jack feigned exhaustion. "Alelia, take that hoop and pass it around her body." he commanded hoarsely.

His willing accomplice, caught up in the drama, hurriedly grabbed the golden hoop on the floor and passed it forward and back between Eva's body and the table below.

"Very good," BJ groaned. "Now, I will let her gently return to her resting place."

The prone figure appeared to move lower, candlelight peeking from under the body was extinguished.

"There it is, done," announced BJ, his arms outstretched, his back to the audience. There he remained until the silence in the room was overwhelmed by clapping.

Upon command, and after she had been released from her spell, Eva rose to face the audience of friends and neighbors.

"Bravo. Well done, Eva," they congratulated.

"Thank you. We are glad you enjoyed the demonstration. It is one of our favorites." she said, standing next to her husband.

Black Jack enveloped her in his arms. His massive frame threatened to swallow hers completely. An unaccustomed display of affection. "Dear guests, while the room is cleared and tables set for dining, and..." he looked down at his wife. "Eva changes back into her evening gown, we will have another round of drinks."

At this cue, the staff circulated with trays of champagne for the ladies' and highballs for the gents.

As he circulated, reveling in the adoration and approval of his peers, the calls for him to do a reading increased. Soon everyone was calling for a command performance. After a little more coaxing, he relented, condescended. This was his home and he would play the part of gracious host.

"Hey Washington, go into my office, get my crystal," BJ beckoned, pulling the young man away from table duty.

"Right away, boss." The congenial reply. Hurriedly, he disappeared, and reemerged holding an object in his hand covered in purple cloth.

"Thank you. I'll entertain them while you guys go finish up," Herman said nonchalantly.

"Ladies and gentlemen, what I do now is for entertainment purposes only. I do not claim to be in touch with any spirits from the great beyond. Nor do I claim to possess any magical or mystical powers. While I have studied astrology, no knowledge of the zodiac is required for this performance. All you need is the concentrated power of the fully cultivated mind which anyone can accomplish if he or she devotes all of their time to study and practice." A pause to catch one's breath. Then a joke. "My lawyers made me say that." The room resounded with a chorus of laughter.

"Okay on with the show. Now who wants to go first?" A flurry of hands.

"Mr. Magus." BJ picked on an old friend. "I know what you want to know. How will my stocks fare tomorrow?" He mocked his friend in jest.

"Yes, yes." the man gasped eagerly. "Will my profits continue to multiply?"

Black Jack stood in the middle of the room commanding silence with his body language. He concentrated, his body turning rigid. You could hear a whisper. Returning from the ether, he stated slowly, solemnly, "Life is long and then you die. Trees never ever grow to the sky. At the top, they never ring a bell. When it reaches the century level, you sell, sell, sell."

Mr. Magus stood before the great magician with eyes wide, hands clasped together. If he had any less strength in his limbs, he would have dropped to his knees. "Thank you, Mr. Herman. Thank you so much."

BJ interpreted his vision for the rest of the guests. "If you didn't understand the prose in my vision, I told him when his stock reaches one hundred, he should sell. Now, anyone else? Who wants to be next?"

"Ah, Mr. McCarthy, step forward and let Black Jack peer into your future."

The real estate owner-operator happily took up position across from the hulking prophet. The crystal ball danced between them held in BJ's extended hand. They dominated the center of the room.

After a long pause, Herman began, "I see your many buildings tall and proud." Black Jack hesitated. "The sunlight glints upon them, but they are empty. They have been emptied through evictions." Black Jack could not stop. It was as if the crystal was drawing the vision out of him, making it manifest. He was the conduit and no longer in control. The words poured forth placing a pall upon the joviality of the occasion. "There's no one to pay the rents. No one with any money. There are soup and bread lines, but no honey."

Eva, now in her evening gown, had rejoined the gala in the midst of his performance. She sensed that he was not in control. This happened in rare instances. Certainly this was not party talk. "Honey," She moved to the center of the room, and placed her hand on his arm, breaking the spell. She repeated, "Honey, I don't think this is particularly party talk. You're scaring the guests. Remember our nice neighbors?"

Herman, suddenly back in the present, looked around, surprised to find the room full of people.

"Ladies and gentlemen, that's all for the amazing mental powers of the prolific mind of Professor Herman. How about a hand?"

Muted applause followed the request. The once jovial attendees were disquieted and withdrawn, visibly disturbed by Herman's dramatic vision.

Later after the party, at bedtime, Eva sitting on the side of the bed chastised her husband. "What were you thinking? Do you know that you gave everyone a fright? They'll probably be talking about it for weeks."

"I'm sorry. I didn't mean to startle them. I lost control and the vision overcame me. It was like watching one of those moving pictures except it was in color. The sun was setting and there were masses of people in the streets. No lights in the buildings. The setting sun cast a pale glare on empty windows. It was as if something horrible had happened."

Eva had never heard him talk like this before. She decided to question him no further this night lest she share his dark vision.

Black Jack's vision had possessed his being, indeed permeated his very soul. It would linger and grow, robbing him of the ability to find the peace forth coming from sleep, haunting his waking hours.

In the coming weeks, Herman became more morose than Eva had ever witnessed. More introspective than even those days with Deborah five years ago when the preparations for 'Professor Herman, Mentalist' were laid. His advice to clients, publicly and privately, changed subtly at first, then overtly within weeks. He now advised saving money for a rainy day. "Look around you and enjoy the things you have. Cherish your family, friends, be aware that in an instant it can all change." The advice he imparted to a wealthy industrialist at a cocktail party in mid-February. A crowd had gathered overhearing his conversation. They eagerly pushed closer, waiting for more. After this advice, the mood turned somber.

"Now, now, Professor Herman," the hostess scolded. "I won't have any of your negative vibrations or whatever spoiling my party. Haven't you heard what the song says, In the morning, in the evening, ain't we got fun."'

Disenchantment with his new views and pronouncements grew rapidly among his neighbors. They quickly tired of this doom and gloom, stop and smell the roses because tomorrow may not come attitude. 'I remember when he used to be fun. What's the point of having a magician around if he can't be entertaining?'

Despite the public pronouncements of disdain many privately sought his council. In the inner sanctum with the darkened walls and incense burning, bad news was far more believable and acceptable. "Don't trust banks. Don't trust any institutions completely. Buy a safe, a sturdy model, siphon off some of your profits and stash them in your house. You may even want to wrap some cash in burlap and bury it in your backyard. But don't let anyone see you. We may reach a time when it becomes brother against brother. Also buy some food, dry goods, keep them stored in the basement. I can't tell yet, but there may be an interruption in the food supply."

"Thank you, Professor. Thank you very much. I'll do just what you say. How long do we have before this comes to pass?" came the cautious inquiry.

"It is hard to say. An event of this magnitude can cause a psychic shockwave that transcends many years. Time and space are curved in an ellipse. It could be just over the horizon or somewhere farther down the path. The enormity of my vision assures me that it will come to pass. Better to be safe than sorry."

"Quite true, quite true. I'll get right on it. How much do I owe you?"

"You can discuss that with my secretary on the way out. Please tell her to send in the next seeker of the truth." He could always be seen standing next to his voodoo altar for dramatic effect awaiting the entry of the next client. Business went on like this day after day as word of his dark visions spread quickly.

"I don't know what's come over him, Lil," Eva confided to her best friend in her weekly call to the Chicago office. "I've never seen him like this before. He's so somber and morose, hardly eats. You know, he hasn't made love in well, let's say over a week." Eva confided vaguely, not wishing to put too fine a point on the details of their sex life.

"That does sound serious." Lilly said half-joking. "Do you think there is anyone else?"

"No, he hasn't had time. There is a parade of patrons waiting for advice from sun up to sun down."

"I hear you. Word has spread of his dire predictions and I've got people asking for an audience. A couple of clients were so panicked that they hopped a train for NYC. Do you know when he is coming to Chicago?"

"Yes, I met them last week. No, I don't know when he will make the journey, but we will give you plenty of notice. I'll be in charge of sending out invitations to all of our preferred guests throughout the Midwest. They will want to meet with him at your place. One more tiring, do you know he's bought a five foot standing safe and had it installed in a closet in our bedroom? Only three of us have the combination. When I asked him about it, he grumbled something about 'Can't trust them banks anymore.'" Eva informed, unable to hide her considerable concern.

"Gosh, it sounds as if he is taking himself seriously. That's good enough for me, I think I'll buy a small safe and withdraw some of my savings from the bank."

"You see, now you know how easy it is for him to engender a panic. I'll talk to you next week."

Eva, tired of the uncertainty and the unsettling effect it was having on events in her home, decided to get to the heart of the matter. She would confront her husband within his lair and ferret out the truth. Between readings she barged into the inner sanctum demanding answers.

"Oh, hey babe, I was expecting you," He was standing by the altar staring down at the embers gently glowing within the fire. The scent of jasmine and wormwood filled the air. The dark room illuminated by a single bulb. Ruby red walls glowed hellishly in the pale light.

"Don't give me that. I want some answers now," she demanded.

"Suit yourself, but I was expecting you. Just check the calendar there on my desk."

For arguments sake, she looked and there on the page was 'talk with Eva.' She backed away slightly, at first refusing to believe this obvious magician's trick. Herman moved toward the desk. His large hand reached for the open Bible that was next to his crystal ball.

"I know you wanted to talk to me, ascertain whether my vision was real or if this is just another trick." He pointed to a passage on the open page and continued. "I have been reading the Book of Revelations ever since that party in January when I had the chilling vision of empty apartment houses reflecting the light of the setting sun, people milling about in the streets. Do you know what Revelations is about? It's about the end of the world, the herald of the Second Coming and the cataclysm that is to proceed. There is a passage here for you. I've underlined it, see?"

Eva looked where his long, bony fingers pointed. Picking the book up, she could now more clearly discern the message in the pale room light. The prophesy as foretold by Revelation 18:2

'Fallen, fallen is Babylon the great. It has become a dwelling place of demons." Eva, startled, continued to read, focusing on the passages BJ had underlined. 'Come out of her, my people' and finally, 'So shall her plagues come in a single day.'

Eva, familiar as she was with the Bible due to her religious upbringing, could read no more at that moment. There was a hush between them. Finally, she asked the two questions burning her mind. 'So this is what you think you saw?' and 'Where is Babylon anyway?'

"Honey, it's here! It's New York City!" the fervent reply. "Think, you know your Bible, the name of the great harlot is Babylon and over in Revelation 17, it says that the woman is seated on many waters and its inhabitants 'are peoples and multitudes and nations and tongues," he repeated for emphasis.

Replacing the Good Book on the desk, she stared him up and down, sizing him up. Hands on hips she cross-examined, "Do you realty think this is what you saw? The fall of New York City?"

"How can I be sure?" he answered earnestly, his voice full of compassion. "What I saw was a vision charged with emotion. The only way I can describe it, the sun setting on New York, the buildings vacant, dormant, dark. People in the streets milling about as in the aftermath of a great tragedy," his voice trailed off.

The room returned to silence for another quota.

It was Eva who had the next brainstorm. "Maybe Mr. Garvey had a similar inspiration. Wasn't that essentially his plan to provide a homeland in Africa so that we might come out of this place? I saw that was one of the passages you had underlined."

"The thought had occurred to me. But now it's too late for that. We must prepare to survive here. Remain steadfast throughout the fires and torments to come."

"Baby, you're scaring me in this light with the smoke, fire and brimstone behind, you sound just like the Baptist preachers of my youth. I'm sure I don't know what to do next."

"First thing we will have to do is change the message we planned to spread on our spring tour. I have already begun working on a couple of ideas." BJ opened a drawer in his desk and pulled a handful of papers covered with scribblings. Eva called out to the front desk and cancelled the rest of the afternoon's appointments.

Eva and Black Jack worked feverishly the next week to rework the tour in time to meet the late April launch. No clients were seen during the following week. The staff was in turmoil rescheduling, reworking and rehashing. A new book was to be produced and delivered to the publisher combining ancient philosophies and modern techniques of concentration. Black Jack not only wanted his followers to understand his vision, but to experience their own. The theory being that if they could feel for themselves a taste of the future, this might hasten their actions. Perhaps if enough people were alerted, the events might be forestalled, mitigated, even prevented altogether.

A growing unanimity of concern about this new direction engulfed the staff. Washington had urged Andrew to confront his brother and demand explanations. Andrew found BJ stolen away in his inner sanctum where he spent much of his days in contemplation and meditation.

"Say, bro, some of the staff wanted me to ask you if you were certain that we were taking the right path. You know, if this new direction the show was headed..."

"Wasn't far off of the beaten path of our traditional fare, even for me?" BJ finished the thought with distain.

"Well, yes. What's with all this fire and brimstone? We were afraid that it might drive people away."

"Nonsense. We will be more successful than ever," he replied, his piercing eyes went right through the other. "But fame and fortune are not important now. We have to prepare people. No longer can we just afford to rail against the system. The system is breaking down. The faults are not yet visible. They remain growing subterranean cracks. The day will come, possibly soon, that it will tear asunder. I know. I have seen it in my mind's eye." BJ suddenly looked as old as Methuselah especially in the hazy, darkly lit room. Andrew knew better than to question his older brother's judgment again.

A small birthday party for Eva preempted the beginning of the tour. Befitting the new somber mood around the mansion, it was a small reserved affair. "Thank you all for coming. We will have drinks and then dinner. After which, if we hurry, we can make it downtown in time to see the show. I believe it starts at eight. BJ is taking me, or should I say us, to the Follies of 1927. It was my idea," Eva added, like everyone couldn't have guessed. When was the last time Black Jack went to a Broadway production?

Over cocktails the guests shared light conversation in the as yet unaltered living room of Andrew's design. One gentleman made the mistake of bringing up the impending journey of Charles Lindbergh. His planned solo flight to Europe leaving from New York was quite the topic of conversation outside the Herman household. Another compounded the error by commenting that his airline stocks, which had been moving up in anticipation, would go through the roof if Lindbergh made it alive and in one piece.

"Stocks and stocks." The words burst forth from the big man. "Everywhere the talk of stocks, greed abounds. How high is enough? You had better stock up on supplies, ready cash. A bird in the hand. I've said it before and I'll say it again, when it gets to one hundred, sell!"

Eva conspicuously changed the subject.

The 'No Time for Magic Tour' set out on the road with Boston and would travel the major metropolitan centers on the east coast, winding up, as was their practice, with home base as the last venue. They played to packed houses all along the way. Black Jack was right. This new message tinged with the fear of God really appealed to the down trodden citizenry, the working class of every color and persuasion. At one point, Andrew confided to Washington, 'If we play this well in the north, think how many we will draw in the south.'

The typical performance would begin with Herman and Eva appearing on stage in a cloud of smoke. Cheering fans would stand and applaud. Black Jack would quiet them with outstretched arms and begin. "We call this the No Time for Magic Tour because we have some urgent business to accomplish, you and I. Few can truly conceive of the power," he paused for dramatic effect. "The power of the fully cultivated mind. You too can achieve wondrous mental powers if you exercise your mind along the lines I suggest in my new book. By purchasing my new book, you will be taking the first step toward unlocking hidden mental talents. Remember, I claim no supernatural talents, but I provide secrets from the Buddhist monks in the high Himalayas to encourage your powers of concentration.

A smattering of philosophies from the great thinkers of the last thousand years to cultivate your intelligence. I have even included a few chosen quotes from the Gospels of Matthew and John. These will prepare your mind for the visions I wish to impart. While it is true that Black Jack usually comes around once every seven years, in the last days time will be shortened to reward the faithful. Black Jack will return in three and a half years. On this trip, we wish to prepare you for the trials ahead, to strengthen your minds. Perhaps on the next trip, we will lead you home. Now, first, Eva and I will perform a few feats of levitation and legerdemain. And then, I will take questions from the audience for an hour and a half."

Armed with his apocalyptic vision, Herman held sway mesmerizing the crowds until the show's conclusion. In New York, Black Jack performed at Garvey's Liberty Hall. A month of sold out performances. Then the tour had to rest and recuperate before a swing through the southern circuit. These were to be the last shows of any consequence that were ever conducted in that theater. Their leader, recently deported, the organization was in disarray and running out of funds.

UNIA's demise only continued to focus attention on intelligent self-promoters like Mr. Herman, whose supporters multiplied with every appearance.

Another under surveillance was A. Phillip Randolph, who was locked in a bitter battle with the railroad oligarchs over unionization. Now while he would bear watching, Mr. Hoover was confident that the hired thugs of Mr. Perlman and others could take care of the dirty work. This magician Herman, with his new unsettling message, would require close scrutiny. Mr. Hoover was not overly concerned. He still had his two undercover agents and he had plenty of time.

XVIII
Sojourn

Black Jack tired of trying to weave his influence on the minds of the most successful and progressive thinkers in African American society, those Renaissance men in Harlem.

True the stock market break in the fall of '27, the mini-crash as it came to be known, did drive a few members back into the fold. However, the market quickly reversed in the spring of '28 causing most of Herman's neighbors to abandon their circumspect behavior and resume their profligate ways. They simply, what was the phrase, 'doubled down' on their investments. BJ remained resolute. This stark vision of a bleak future emblazoned just behind his eyes.

Trouble was, he surmised, most men were ruled by fear and: greed. They would only do so much, go so far, to change their lives, help their fellow man. Afraid of challenging the status quo, risk losing what in many cases they had worked all of their lives to acquire. Not just money, they feared loss of respect from the peerage and diminution in social standing. Only those with little or nothing to lose could afford to risk it all, take his advice and prepare for the worst. A very wise philosopher over two thousand years ago knew this axiom all too well. For the likes of Black Jack, it was a lesson learned late, but long remembered.

The poor, the down trodden, those with little hope or education, these would become his followers. While he lived with the rich and powerful, was one of them in fact and deed, they would not blindly follow his vision. To many he was still a carney barker, good for entertainment only. When his value as a magician faded, and he became this Cassandra, Harlem's elite found other more pleasurable distractions. Noah had: a similar problem. BJ would have to modify his plans accordingly.

Eva Rucker, Mrs. Herman, was having quite the opposite reaction to her husband's new status as prophet of doom. Renewing her Baptist roots she had joined the local church and taken an active roll right away. As the wife of a prominent personage you were expected, nay required, to set a certain example of charity and attendance as befitting your standing within the community. Eva had gone beyond these in her first year as a church member. Her activities included hosting fundraisers and charity drives. She would teach Sunday school and when time permitted, man the church's soup kitchen. This work, these tasks, were not performed lightly but with due reverence deriving the genuine feeling of joy that comes with the true spirit of giving.

Eva, whose faith had been renewed on that cold, snowy day over six years ago by the priest's kind words, was now spiritually ecstatic that her husband was apparently ending his own dark journey. She regarded his vision as a miracle of no small proportion. That God had worked through her husband to warn those who would listen of the coming cataclysm. In her mind the words of St. Paul merged with those of Madame Deborah 'Having begun with the spirit, are you now ending with the flesh?' and 'You will rise resplendently.' These combined to evince that she would rise resplendently within the spirit. This convinced her that it was by her example that Herman's vision would be judged. This was only fitting since who but she knew him better? If it is true that you are judged by the company that you keep, certainly you are judged most by the actions of your spouse. She smiled to herself while sitting tall in the church's wooden pew. That little piece of Aristotelian logic had just floated into her head. All of the studying she had done during her recuperation really paid off. So Eva would be that shining example providing authenticity and veracity for Herman's vision. Given how influential they had been in the past, it was Eva's fervent hope that they would wield even more influence in the future. The lives of countless numbers may depend on their heeding his warning.

The stock market took off with a vengeance in the spring of '28, something that Black Jack's neighbors never failed to remind. "Who's this Cassandra anyway?" Herman stormed in one afternoon and inquired of his wife.

"Greek prophetess of doom." Eva instructed. "Why do you ask?"

"A couple of our neighbors just greeted me with that phrase. They won't be invited to any more parties," he glowered.

"Now, baby, don't take it too hard. There will be many who fall away, won't be able to follow your vision. You know the hardships great men face. How they have to walk alone. You've had to do that most of your life, comforted Eva.

"You have a marvelous way with words. You always know just what to say to calm me down." BJ grabbed his wife and held her close undoing that apron around her waist in the process.

"Honey, I have to finish baking these brownies for the church bazaar," Eva protested.

"The brownies can wait," he said with a devilish glint in his ruby red eyes.

No matter if Black Jack was shunned and ridiculed by many of his peers, the calls for consultations came from all across the city and far beyond. While many still revolved around health, relationships or job opportunities, an increasing number came from the middle and lower middle classes who were allowed for the first time to speculate in securities using only a few of their dollars.

"Professor Herman, I know you've always said to sell at one hundred, but after I sold RCA at ninety it went straight up. The next week it began trading at one hundred twenty. I bought one hundred shares for only ten percent down. This week the stock is trading at one hundred seventy five. There was a rumor that the company would be taken over at a much higher price. My question is I've made over five thousand dollars on paper, that's more than I make in a year! My wife wants me to cash it in, but I want to hold on. What should I do?"

BJ stayed true to his vision. After staring into his crystal and observing the man's nervousness for a minute, he made his proclamation.

"Your true desire is matrimonial bliss. If that is what you wish, then you should reduce your risk. Sell half now and let the other half run, until it reaches the moon, the stars, the sun. Lock that money away for a rainy day and cherish your wife. For I can see that she is the true treasure in your life."

"Thank you, Professor. Thank you very much. That sounds like just what Solomon would say." The man shook BJ's hand profusely and left.

Herman continued to get more and more of these consultations as the spring gave way to summer. However, they were now coming more from the wife and were taking a disturbing turn. "Sir, my husband is sure that this is our time to get wealthy. All of our neighbors seem to be getting wealthy. They have new cars, are buying new furniture and fancy clothes. They told him their new found prosperity has come from 'pyramiding.' That is using the accumulated profit in their stocks to purchase more stock in the company. The theory is the higher it goes, the more you can buy. When this thing called television comes out, we will all be millionaires if we own enough shares."

"I've heard of the concept before," Professor Herman, ever the statesman, responded. True enough, this was the third fearful wife that had been in here today. Black Jack mused how funny that women were more in touch with the ethereal plane than men. Perhaps it was a small recompense for all of the suffering that they were forced to endure. If only Eve hadn't eaten that apple.'

Back to the client at hand, the woman, probably mid-thirties, who-had obviously been sobbing recently and many times since her worries began. "If you really love him and want to keep him, you must force him to follow your plan. I have often remarked how those who left Sodom early were the lucky ones and how you must never look back. Tell him you want your half of the assets in your hands now. Inform him that you don't care about getting rich, especially if it tears apart your marriage. Remember, pyramiding is a most dangerous scheme that can end in financial ruin. Have him imagine life if you were broke. Then put some of your profits in a safe in your bedroom."

No rhymes this time, only solid financial advice. Time <u>must</u> be getting short. He had more of these inquiries everyday. Also there were the glazed eyes of patrons at restaurants they frequented. 'Stingy Sam's' suddenly turned big tippers. Waitresses offering stock tips on new issues. Some hot new idea was coming out and it would make millions 'Something new. Always something new for the show.' There it was again, that rogue voice he hadn't heard in a dog's age. 'Wasn't that what he'd say about his magic act? Now the voice demonstrated the concept applied to greater society. This was all a show. This mania developing all around was a great merry-go-round like at the carnival. As with all carousels, the faster it went the less time before the end. It spun so fast now-encompassing nearly every individual, especially in the Greater Babylon. The end could come soon, next week, next month. It was surely just over the curve of the horizon. He must redouble his efforts.

"Eva," he said one morning, exhausted after depriving himself of sleep-for another night. "I find it odd that I cannot receive any refinement of my vision, precious little information. My muse has abandoned me." He sat at the kitchen table, head buried in large hands. "Every great figure through history has been given a series of signs, directions to follow. I have naught, but the one." His anguished voice broke and: trailed off.

"Don't worry, baby. Have faith." Eva comforted, never tired of saying, "Your message will come when the time is right. Doesn't the Good Book say 'He serves who also sits and waits.'?"

"But time is short. I can feel it. Heck, I can see it. This past Christmas was the most opulent and ostentatious this neighborhood has ever seen. Every neighbor had to outdo the next. New cars, new minks for the wives, the most elaborate parties. All the while mocking me for stashing my money in a safe while they made millions in the stock market. Imagine Alelia bragging about how much that broker said her company could be worth."

"She wasn't bragging, honey. She's not like that. She just said he told her if they would sell shares to the public, it could be worth twenty-five million dollars."

"That's unbelievable," Herman exasperated.

"Let's change the subject. It is 1929. Are we going to have our party? If so, I have to get the invitations out right away."

BJ pondered for a long moment, and then exploded. "Yes, we will have it. Make it the best one yet. Spend some of that cash upstairs. After which we will go on the road and preach the Gospel to my loyal followers. The absence of a message is a message indeed! It says keep doing what you're doing until I say otherwise. So I will continue to take my message to the masses. Attempt to cultivate their minds while there is still time."

An aggressive tour was embarked upon late in the winter of '29. It was not soon enough to suit BJ. Already in late February a world-wide stock slide had returned sanity to many, the fear of God to a few. But it would not last.

Government leaders all the way up to President Herbert Hoover were quick to press, reminding panicky investors that the economy was sound, the currency was sound and the business of government was business. The fears of the public were soon allayed.

Black Jack however, enjoyed a booming business which included not only blacks and whites, but a growing number of immigrants who had only recently left countries in turmoil or famine. They readily knew what it was like to lose everything and were naturally cautious. Since coming to America, they had worked hard and were fearful of losing it all once again.

Herman's presentations took on the flavor of a tent revivalist's. In fact, they used tents wherever they could. BJ wanted his message to reach the maximum possible.

Like a great firebrand, he would walk the stage preaching. "They say that the Great Babylon will meet her fate in one day. I have seen this occurrence delivered to me in a vision just two years ago."

The crowd murmured in awe.

"The men walking idly, listlessly milling in the streets after a cataclysmic event. The women and children sitting in tents, blank stares frame their grimy faces. I cannot say when, but it is soon.

The tattered rags they wear in my vision are of contemporary styling."

The crowd drew a collective breath.

"The skeptics argue that no one knows where Babylon is. If it even exists. I say the message is clear. Babylon sits on many waters. Its people are composed of many nations, ethnicities and tongues. The ancient Babylon was a wondrous city of splendid buildings and hanging gardens. The new Babylon has skyscrapers including the new Empire State and Chrysler Buildings, stated to be the tallest in the world. So now you know the new Babylon is New York with its Babelesque edifices. I tell you now as goes New York City, so goes the United States. My message is simple and clear. Don't trust banks and other institutions. Hold tight to your families and prepare your mind for the crisis to come. To that end, my books on cultivating the powers of your mind are on sale in the back for half price. This is not about making me rich, but about protecting your wealth."

After one successful engagement, Washington Reeves came up to BJ with congratulations. "You know, boss, this doomsday kick that you've been on. I've never seen anything take off and continue to grow month after month. What are you gonna come up with next?"

Black Jack looked at him, his fierce eyes blazing and said, "You'll know when I know."

The tour which had begun on the east coast continued across the Midwest until it reached Eva's home of St. Louis, shortly before the advent of summer.

"What's this? Has your husband finally discovered religion? Word has it that he's become a real firebrand," Eva's father asked upon her arrival.

"He's had a vision, Father. Actually a series of visions all centering around the same original inspiration almost two and a half years ago." Eva instructed, but did not elucidate. (Another White Lie)

"My dear," her mother began with worried tone. "Some people say he is preaching Communism. Telling people to avoid banks and store food in their homes."

"Now, Mother. Why would you listen to those naysayers? We have spoken often enough on the phone. BJ is concerned that businesses are no longer looking out for the little fellow in their rabid run for even greater profits. The Federal Government has said that they intend to neither infringe or impinge on the ability of companies to conduct the pursuit of profits however they see fit. BJ is just trying to look out for the little guy. Someone has to."

"They say he is anti-stock market," her father countered. "The stock market is supposed to be the great equalizer, allowing each to profit in accordance with his means."

"Don't let BJ hear you say that. He now thinks the stock market is a tool of the Devil." Eva hissed.

"Honey, truth be told, we've made enough money in the market to re-do the interior. Come, let me show you." Eva's mother grabbed her by the hand and they headed for the kitchen.

Sitting behind the stage the next afternoon, Eva's parents got to see Black Jack work the crowd. The stage sat high off the ground. Flowing white cloth billowed in the wind demarking the open rectangle in which Black Jack operated. Pacing back and forth, he delivered his message of Armageddon. "For every two dollars you have, take one and put it in a safe place. Bury it in a hole if you have to, but don't trust any place that's open from nine to three. If calamity comes like a thief in the night,' how can you wait for a bank to open?"

A general murmuring of agreement.

"Also, buy some staples that won't spoil and lock them away in your larder. The day is coming you'll be glad you did. Wives buy yourselves a sturdy iron skillet. That way you'll have something to hit your man with if he doesn't follow my advice." The crowd, especially women, clapped heartily.

A discord rose among the ranks. Men shouting, heckling the speaker, Moving through the crowd with reckless disregard and generally causing commotion. This was no mere ruthless rabble, but a highly organized disinformation campaign designed to disrupt and discredit this growing threat to the American way of life. A threat at least to the pocketbooks of big business, in particular big banks. These disturbances had cropped up before, following them across the Midwest. If they could cause enough commotion, the authorities would have no choice but deny Herman permits to preach. This was the real reason Eva wanted her parents on the stage, safety.

"You're a liar, you prophet of doom. Get out of town." This and less polite phrases, epithets like missiles, were hurled at the stage and against anyone who stood in their way. Words backed by fisticuffs. Herman had hired extra security, cutting into profits, all across the Midwest to handle this menace, but these bully boys never went quietly.

While the fracas unfolded, Herman tried to keep the crowds attention on the stage. "For these past many years, I have demonstrated wondrous illusions to prove the power of the cultivated mind. Now, since my visions, I come to give you a warning and to show you how to prepare your mind so that you may have visions of your own. Don't let these bullies deny you the chance to obtain enlightenment. Your very existence may depend on the information you learn here today. These dastardly thugs are in the employ of the agents of chaos that I rail against: the banks, the brokerages and the crass commercialists who push merchandise at you year after year. Beware their nefarious agents, the advertisers who tell you over and over that you can't be a real man or attractive woman or really happy unless you have their product. It's all bunk, I tell you. They only wish to rob you of your hard earned capital and keep you running in place dancing to their tune.

They are the bane of the modern era. These men," pointing to thugs, "are merely the bottom dregs of a rotten barrel. Time to wake up and claim your economic independence before they rob you of everything you have."

Clapping started like summer rain splashing on rock. It grew in intensity until the thundering ovation mimicked those summer storms that roamed the plains.

Charles turned to his daughter, who was sitting beside him, her face shining, lost in rapture. "I will admit, dear daughter. That man can really speak."

By the time the weary band arrived in Chicago, it was time for a rest. Black Jack and Eva spent Independence Day with Lilly and her husband. She had finally converted Mr. Right Now into Mr. Right.

As usual, Black Jack found something to agitate him. Holding a newspaper up for all to see, BJ sat on the couch and declared, "Look at this headline. 'Another Wild Day for Stocks.' They go up, they go down. They go around and around, faster and faster."

"What is he talking about?" asked Lilly's husband, Daniel.

"Oh, it's his philosophy that life is like a magic show, all misdirection and sleight of hand. The government and big business work together to enrich themselves at the expense of the little guy. He's afraid after this vision he had two years ago that, how did you put it, BJ?"

"The fix is in." he advised dourly, uncomfortable at being discussed in the third person while in the room.

"That's right," continued Lilly. "'The fix is in. The great European War was the opportunity to create tremendous profits for the U.S. industrialists and displace millions of workers who would emigrate to the U.S. to fill the ever growing need of the expanding manufacturing sector."

Herman decided to finish the treatise of his own creation. "The land barons of Europe, in collusion with the banks which in many cases were one and the same, were able to buy abandoned property for pennies on the dollar or franc or deutschmark or whatever.

Their American counterparts learned a valuable lesson. Now aided by a laissez faire government, they will attempt the same thing here. The stock market is just their vehicle, a means to an end. They take it up and then they get out, leaving the little guy holding the bag. It has happened before. It is a land grab, pure and simple. That is the meaning of the part of my vision with families living in tents. It is no longer about black versus white. It is rich against poor."

"You don't know that for sure," interjected Eva forcefully. "It could still be a natural disaster. The quote from Revelations also mentions mariners, ships at sea standing afar, watching the great city smoldering."

"It could be, I grant that, but my gut feeling still rests on an economic collapse brought upon us by the evil that men do.

Remember no one knows more about the evil that men do than I."
BJ was adamant.

"No argument there," both women said in unison.

Before they left Chicago for the comforts of home, BJ ordered
Lilly in the strictest terms to close any remaining bank accounts
and to keep all cash in the safe. Also, buy a gun. "You may need it
for your protection."

"Stop it, honey. Can't you see you are scaring her?" Eva
protested.

"These are scary times, my love," he said for public consumption.
Inside his head, a voice was singing 'Through the lens darkly, darkly
we go. Now back to New York and on with the show.'

"It's been over five hundred dollars a share, but right now it has
fallen back about a hundred. I don't mind. Every time it pulls back,
I buy more and then it goes up again. By the time they perfect that
television thing and get a patent on it, the stock will probably go to
a thousand!" One of BJ's neighbors bragged in a chance meeting.
What he didn't say, but what Herman heard was, 'So much for
selling at one hundred.'

"That's great," replied BJ. "Then you can buy another mansion."

The rest of the summer the stock market zigzagged in a frightful
display of vertical moves. The pundits praised the strength of the
economy and the resiliency of the marketplace. The patrons bought
every dip. A disturbing phenomenon was occurring unobserved.
Less stocks were advancing on each revival and they were failing
to eclipse their previous peaks. The average investor, convinced
of a resumption of the previous trend any day now, continued to
pour all available assets into shares awaiting the resumption of
easy money.

"They say this will be the best one ever. Mr. Herman. Someone
at the bank said that statistically the middle years of presidential
terms are often best. Nineteen thirty could be the best year yet.
What do you think?"

Black Jack would just look at the client in the throes of greed,
but reeking with the stench of fear and say sadly, "In your case my
crystal has gone dark. Only rarely has this happened. It is a bad
omen. I'm sorry; there is nothing more I can do. Tell the secretary

I said no charge." He chuckled to himself on the man's departure. If he had read his clients right, some could only be scared straight. Any other advice would be ignored.

It was like that story Eva had told him, the Greek legend of Pandora, the curious young woman who had loosed all of the evils upon the world. After the box was emptied, she looked in and found hope hiding into the bottom. Hope was the last worst evil because it prevented you from taking steps to rectify the situation. 'Well, I will wait until tomorrow and <u>hope</u> things get better.' Black Jack chuckled. It would have been better for the world if Pandora had closed the box at that point before hope could escape. Maybe she hoped that all of the other evils would return to the box. Market investors, like Pandora, waited another day only to find continued deterioration. Unfortunately, hope sprung eternal and a nation of investors continued to wait.

The requests for an audience continued to grow, but the strain on Herman's health was beginning to take its toll on the big magician. Eva, concerned that he was neither eating nor sleeping for days at a time, curtailed his meetings to three days a week. This did not deter the crowds who clamored for guidance. After a particularly nasty market break in the beginning of September, the line of seekers stretched around the block. Eva could see them from her upstairs window, waiting. 'Let them wait.' she thought contemptuously. 'We've a safe full of cash.'

"They found a psychic who says the market is going back up." Washington Reeves burst into the foyer with the newspaper in hand touting the headline. The secretaries crowded around to confirm the good news shouted in bold type from the early morning paper.

Black Jack, after carefully reading the article twice, threw the paper onto the kitchen table. "When they pressed her for longer term predictions, she was less sanguine. I have heard of her, of course. She has been right enough times to rule out random chance."

"So the doom and gloom is over, right? The economy will forge ahead like President Hoover says?" Washington asked eagerly.

"You sound like one of those people who stand outside for hours to see me." Herman growled over coffee. "You've been playing the market, boy." The verbal arrow was on the mark.

"Me? No, sir. I was just thinking of our clients and followers. Maybe they could relax. Also, I was thinking of your reputation." said Washington sheepishly.

"You let me worry about my reputation. As for those people who line up to see me, maybe they will have another chance to get out with their skins."

The stock market rebounded for a short March of days. It might have continued to go higher except for those little manila envelopes. Requests for additional funds from the brokerages flooded the mails. Many households, rich and poor, already invested to the maximum had no recourse, they sold. Rampant selling begat more selling and the U.S. markets experienced several dramatic weeks of severe declines.

Black Jack stayed inside the mansion for most of this time. Exhausted and feverish, he maintained his schedule receiving up to fifty clients per day. The requests became more plaintive, seekers of solace desperate, reeking despondency. 'If you can tell me we will have a little more time, one more rally,' they would plead. 'I can get back to even and then I'm out.' they would promise. As the weeks progressed, the pleas became more dire. I have spent so much of the profits already, new car, clothes for the wife. I don't think I can ever get even. Please look into your crystal and tell me the bankers will come to the rescue as they did back in 1907 when J. P. Morgan saved the market. Tell me the Federal Government will step in and save the day.' The response to such a request was typically, "Sell everything you have."

The dramatic declines climaxed with spectacular sell-offs late in October. By this time it was apparent that Black Jack's vision was becoming a reality. The dramatic 'crash' that was termed "Black Thursday" was followed by an even blacker Monday. This erased all hope that a return to prosperity was just around the corner, that a bottom in prices had been reached, a stable foundation from which to begin again. Panic set in and grown men, deprived of all they knew and held dear, smashed windows and plunged to their death.

A reporter from the Amsterdam News called the following day for a quote. It was well known that the great magician had been warning of an economic calamity for years. The reporter would give him a chance to boast, to castigate others for their mocking disbelief.

While the reporter received a usable quote, "They call it Black Tuesday, but White Tuesday is more like it. Our people do not have stocks or bonds to worry about losing." The rest of the conversation was ignored. Black Jack's use of the phrase 'our people' included all those regardless of color who had followed his advice and taken profits, cut losses-gone to cash entirely.

In Herman's dire drama, this was only the first step in the socio-economic breakdown. If the banks and government could not, read would not, step in and save the stocks, would they do anymore for the burgeoning manufacturing sector as it shut down? He already knew the answer.

Privately, he had begun referring to himself as the 'Good Shepherd.' The Good Shepherd watches over his flock through the long night keeping the predators at bay. Certain that the country had entered the long night, he would do what he could to save as many sheep as possible. He would hold town hall meetings for pennies per person, just enough to pay for the rental of the hall. The Good Shepherd did not shear the sheep in winter. He had his, a safe full of cash, an ample supply of guns and ammunition, a fully stocked larder in the basement enough to last for years. If in the ensuing chaos the city burned, as in the Bible, they would take to their autos, abandon the house and flee to the countryside. Perhaps Canada, it was less than a day away.

Yes, in the meantime he would hold town hall meetings where he would attempt to allay concerns, provide hope, perhaps a little levity. He could envision it in his mind's eye, being on the stage answering questions, Eva standing by his side, her place for evermore. If no further visions would develop to provide guidance, then he would remain the Good Shepherd guarding his flock as best possible while the dark forces closed in all around. For however long as required, even unto the advent of the Second Coming if that be the conclusion of his fateful vision. This, was his manifest destiny, his raison de etré.

His grand purpose, what he had trained for all of his life. Now was his time as never before. While all others lost their heads in panic, he would remain calm, a vision of sanity and certainty standing high on a rock above the sea of chaos, with Eva by his side.

How she beamed at him these days. She was truly radiant. Inner strength poured forth from the well-spring of her soul. She delighted in the accuracy of his vision, no matter how horrible the outcome. For she was fortified by the knowledge that the Lord had brought them together oh so many years ago. Brought them through the crucible of fire, battled hardened, wiser, to prepare them for exactly these days. This calamity whose foretelling had been entrusted to Black Jack and to her, the woman behind the great man.

XIX
Season of the Witch

In the spring of 1930, the President sought to soothe the nerves, calm the collective consciousness of a frazzled nation. "The country is not going into a recession. It is only a little depression." President Hoover declared in a public pronouncement. He used a new phrase to allay the concerns of a weary populace. Economists had coined the term recession decades before indicating a period of severe downturn. These were long remembered and feared because of the employment dislocation and business upheaval they ushered. The last such business disruption having occurred a decade ago when the munitions manufacturers reduced production after the Great War, while the county was temporarily overwhelmed by waves of immigrants.

Many were fearful that the government was not doing enough to help the poor unfortunates that had been left destitute by the initial wave of joblessness which swept tens of thousands into the streets. Hoover sought to defuse the mounting criticism from the press and other quarters for his decision to deny emergency assistance to help the homeless, believing that welfare would destroy the work ethic. "Prosperity was right around the corner." so the public pronouncements went. People would just have to look harder, but they could find a job if they tried. Meanwhile, he assured privately 'The business of government is business.'

"The business of the government should be the people." shouted Black Jack from the stage of one town hall meeting. "The People's Palaces should do the work of the people, for the benefit of the general populace, not just the monied few." True enough, given that five percent of the population now controlled ninety-five percent of the country's wealth.

It sounded too close to Communism to sit well with the leaders in Washington who followed Herman's journeys with jaded eye. In their mind, no matter how severe the current situation, it was imperative that no nexus develop to lead a disgruntled populace in directions they could not anticipate or control. It was no secret that J. Edgar Hoover and others feared that the Communists in Russia would use this moment to undermine the American capitalists. Heedless to the fact that they sowed the seeds of their own undoing.

"Why won't Congress take a stand? Pass legislation to redistribute the wealth and resurrect the economy?" bellowed Herman in one of his typical tirades. "These elected officials are beholden to the voters, not the robber barons whose bellies are full. If they refuse to act to mitigate the suffering, then we shall sweep them out of office on Election Day."

Black Jack continued in his ministrations. "The United States is a country that is rich beyond compare. Millions are owed to us by the European countries whom we helped in the Great War. We are today, net creditor to the world, they owe us plenty. It's time we called in our loans. Use those millions to support the newly impoverished. Recapitalize the financial system. Get the economy off its back and put people to work again. If President Hoover truly believes that people should pull themselves up by their boot steps, at least he should provide them with boots."

'Production for use' was another slogan that struck a chord with the newly disenfranchised. Especially after news reports began to surface that summer of boxcars of rotting produce sitting on side rails because the shipping companies had gone bankrupt. Growers in both the Midwest and California had enjoyed bountiful harvest that year, but because of the breakdown of the financial system, goods could not get to market. Livestock had to be slaughtered when feed became unavailable. Farmers then became the next casualties of insolvency. In true domino fashion, additional bankruptcies decreased productive capacity depriving much needed sustenance to the ever growing bread lines.

Calls for governmental intervention increased from every quarter as the vicious cycle of economic collapse: business bankruptcy, leading to bank failure, causing further collapse in the socioeconomic fabric, continued at breakneck speed.

While the Great Depression deepened around them. Black Jack and Eva tried to remain steadfast and provide some solace. The Herman's continued to provide support to the church anonymously to maintain their shelter and soup kitchen which turned away hundreds daily. Eva, for her part, had Andrew and Washington contract with local growers to truck their crops into the city so that the soup kitchen would have a continual supply of food. Herman Enterprises was temporarily closed. The town hall meetings and consultations were continued, though throngs of clients no longer darkened his door.

There was a growing disgust even among his neighbors, the ones that had survived the calamity so far. This school of thought held the idea that maybe Black Jack was the cause of all their maladies in a self-fulfilling prophecy. This orgy of doom he predicted had come true exactly because so many believed his words. The panic ensued because it was predicted in the minds of the masses. Once they obtained the predilection from this man, they acted out of fear at the first sign of trouble. Had they remained calm, the situation would have righted itself. If was a seductive theory to be sure, but one that given the enormity of the event, could not hold up to the scrutiny of examination in the light of day. Never the less, the theory had its adherents. There was a lot of pain around and a need to focus the anguish on a convenient scapegoat.

Greater Babylon did not bum nor crumble into the sea. Neither was Black Jack burned at the stake or ridden out of town on a rail. Not this time. Life went on, some semblance of life. The day to day struggle for survival for many; the pursuit of happiness for the lucky few. It was the worst of times.

Eva could hear Deborah's words echo down the corridors of time. 'Life must go on.' as she folded sheets in the women's homeless shelter. She had divided her time between the Baptist Charity for Women and Children and the soup kitchen of the local church. 'How much did Deborah know?' Eva wondered, 'How much of the future did she see?' Was she better off having fallen in front of that truck?' 'Wasn't it said that the living shall envy the dead?' 'No, of course not!' she thought resolutely. Her spirit chastising her temporary weakness. It was always better to stand there and slug it out. Take what comes and rise resilient like the Phoenix.

Besides what was she complaining about? She had everything. Daily she would look into the faces of those who had lost everything, who had no where to turn for comfort or support. She would be strong for them. That was her job as the shepherd's wife, to deliver kindness and serenity, ease their pain, if only for today.

Black Jack, continuing his town hall meetings, became witness to a disquieting observation. The social bifurcation and racial separation began to intensify wherever he went. Not inside his 'big tent,' but outside and everywhere else. Had he been so naïve as to believe that people would magically get along now that they were all poor? Far from it. Like drowning rats, each group, ethnicity, would climb on the backs of those less fortunate or on the lower rungs of the totem pole. All bent on one purpose, cognizant only of their own survival. It was survival of the fittest at its most ignominious. A very disheartening snapshot of social Darwinism.

After a particularly vicious riot just outside one of his meetings, BJ decided it time for sabbatical. He retired to the cloister of his inner sanctum and refused to see anyone, even Eva. All the while he sat and contemplated, a little voice ran through his head with a message repeated over and over. 'To thine own self be true.'

One day while deep in meditation, his right hand found an answer in the jacket pocket of his coat. He had been idly searching for something, perhaps a tissue. What he found was a scrap of paper with a message written by Eva. He immediately recognized the handwriting and remembered it as belonging to the period when she was trying to teach him the philosophy of Shakespeare back in the apartment in Chicago during her recovery.

Smiling, he opened the paper and read the little note. 'BJ, in Hamlet we can see Shakespeare's view of life that still holds true today. Where are we? What is this place we find ourselves? Answer: 'All the world's a stage. We are but actors on it' [for a short time.]

'Next, who are we?' (Write your own script.) Shakespeare says. 'The play's the thing.'

'Finally, how do we act, interact with others?' The answer: To thine own self be true. (Herman's heart leapt with the revealing of the phrase.) "And it must follow as the night the day. Thou canst not then be false to any man.'

There was an additional note about reading Hamlet's 'To be or not to be' speech. Black Jack hardly considered that at the moment. He had his answer, 'To thine own self be true.'

Reinvigorated, he became lost in thought, the contemplation of this new source of inspiration. In his mental meanderings, he twisted slightly the bard's meaning. To BJ, the phrase 'To thine own self be true.' Meant to do what you love. To do what is closest to your heart. To focus your attention on those things that had always been of the utmost priority.

Since his earliest recollections, the cause that had meant the most to him was the advancement of colored peoples. To show them how to stand up for their rights and demand the equal justice and opportunity that was theirs for the taking by birthright. He had wavered; the 'good shepherd' had taken on other flocks in a vain attempt to save them all from the fires of Armageddon. What was his repayment? They acted like mongrel hordes, packs of wild dogs, tearing into one another despite his pleadings. In effect, muddying his message and his mission. Well then, he would cut them loose.

Shake the dust off his feet. Instead he would concentrate on uplifting his people. With the government in disarray and new leaders sure to be swept in next election, perhaps this was their time to strike for equality. If they were organized then they could accentuate calls for equal treatment under the law.

Black Jack, now armed with this new direction, contemplated

Shakespeare once more. In Eva's note, she had covered the who, what and how of existence according to Hamlet, but not the why. What did her note say? Read the speech 'To be or not.' BJ was intrigued. He was hooked. He had to find out what else Hamlet had to say. Of course, Herman never had a problem with the why of existence. To gratify, to ingratiate, to prosper beyond anyone's wildest expectations. But he was curious. What would Hamlet say?

Herman remembered Eva kept that book of Shakespeare's plays on a bookshelf in the bedroom. She was the only woman he'd ever met who kept books other than romance novels in the bedroom. Storming out of his sanctum, he was able to reach the bedroom without having to engage in casual conversation. There it was on the shelf of the highboy in the corner. He got it down and leafed through the pages in the late afternoon sun.

Eva had marked many pages with underline and notation. In due course, he reached Hamlet. A particular paragraph encapsulated with brackets caught his attention. His name was in the margin with a question mark.

'Ay, that incestuous, that adulterous beast. With witchcraft of his wit, with traitorous gifts- 0 wicket wit and gifts, that have the power so to seduce- When to his shameful lust the will of my most seeming-virtuous queen.'

Black Jack closed the book with a thud. 'So that's what she really thinks of me!' He was cut to the quick, but not to anger, fore it was all too true. How he had acted, treated her and other women over the years was shameful, bordering on criminal. 'Depending on which state you were in at the time,' his mind quipped. But he had changed his vagabond ways. Surely Eva knew that he was not now that man which he had been. Nor would he ever again be that licentious adulterer as long as he remained strong-willed.

This must have been an earlier opinion of him, when she was dissatisfied unto death of him. Perhaps in the period just after she lost the baby. Black Jack vowed not to dwell further upon this deviation. It usurped his energies, distracted his focus.

He had to see what Hamlet had to say. It was an obsession with him now.

Opening the book, he strummed through the pages glancing at words until he caught sight of his mind's quest.

A strange tongue, this ancient English. Yet people revered his writings, so they dared not change a word as if it was the Bible or something. Sitting there in the bedroom, Herman tried to make sense of Hamlet's deepest thoughts. He could see it was profound, but reading it over and over, could not clearly elucidate the meaning. It only proceeded to give him a headache.

'Why can't this man just say what he means? It truly must be that the play is the thing and the audience means nothing.' BJ had never performed with such objective. To him, the love, awe, and adoration of the audience meant everything. They were the ultimate thing. To this playwright, confusion reigned supreme. Who among the audience at first grasp could say they understood what the trick was meant to be? What the man was truly saying?

Still Black Jack strived for understanding. Concentrating on the first few lines, he gleaned what he, Herman, could incorporate into his reason for being. An actionable epistle for these trying times. 'To be or not,' the character Hamlet was deciding whether to live or die. Is it better to live as a servant, a slave to fate or to 'take arms' (that part was clear enough for him) against raging injustice, attempting to right grave wrongs even at the cost of one's own life. Wasn't this what he had decided, to fight injustice at all costs? So this was the eternal question of man and not just the province of the modern day variety. Black Jack, the superb magician and orator, knew that today's problems were nothing unique. It was nice however to see it in the print of a four hundred year old text.

While BJ had already made up his mind, it would have been nice to see what Hamlet finally decided, but for the life of him he couldn't make heads or tales of the rest of the speech.

A course of action decided upon a plan was needed. 'To thine own self be true.' To BJ that meant stick with what you know. What he knew was magic and he knew it well. He was one of the best alive at his craft, but there was one better. Black Jack hadn't heard his name spoken in a long time, but he was sure that his old mentor still drew breadth. Herman counseled himself for a moment. 'Yes' he was sure the man was still alive, but it would be hard to find him. It would take time. 'Let it take time.' He would begin in the planning stages for a spectacular new show, the best yet. In it, he would cleverly incorporate his political philosophy, showing his people by words and deeds that they were meant for something greater. He would show them how to hold their heads up and realize their self worth.

BJ had an inkling that this was not the ending called for in the Bible. For one thing, this 'Depression' had dragged on for nearly two years now. The Bible had talked about the judgment coming in one day. If this was so and the current anarchy would evolve into another facet of modern society after a fashion, then he could prepare his people to take their place as equals in that post-modern world. 'Once and future kings' he would tell them while extolling the virtues of pride, persistence and resiliency. Together they would go forward and claim their place in the sun. 'Like the great hunter Nimrod. I go forth to do battle.' That sounds good, he thought. Have to work that speech into the new act.

For the holidays, Eva had decided it was time to remake the living room and downstairs to her own liking. Something a little more light and cheery with an air of hope and optimism.

"Honey, with so many unemployed can't we provide a little holiday cheer to a few lucky workmen and businesses, brighten up this house?" So her line of reasoning went. "After all, who wants to live in a dreary manor in these disastrous times?"

'That was her true intention,' BJ thought. But he heartily agreed. The place did need a touch of gaiety. He, too, tired of his brother's surrealistic vision. Hell, if you wanted to see surreal, just pull back the curtains. Look out any window. The impoverished walked the streets seeking work. There was a shanty town in Central Park. 'Yes, it would be nice to spread a little good cheer for Christmas.'

In the spring of '31, Eva's sister sent her kids out to New York for a visit. What the children did not know was that their parents could no longer find work in St. Louis and were migrating to California. They would send for the kids after they found gainful employment and a place to stay. Eva, desperately needing the distraction that children provide, had volunteered, arguing that her father's frail health could not withstand a house full of kids.

Eva was thrilled to have children around the house for a change. They breathed life into the cold, dreary atmosphere that was her existence. Now ecstatic that they had redone the interior, the new furnishings, the creamy hued walls and parquet floors, delivered a warmth and hopefulness that was sorely lacking anywhere else in the world. They would sit in the living room, just she and the children, playing games for hours. Eva honestly wished she could stay in that room with its white frilly draperies that brought in just enough light to brighten, yet still obfuscated the truth of the outside world.

This was her sanctuary and these children her legacy, her reward for all of her hard work and perilous adventures. She would make sure they remembered her. Fervently, she wished that she could stay in that idyllic scene playing with her sister's children forever. More than ever, living now with these young ones underfoot, Eva regretted that she would never be able to have one of her own.

Perhaps after the madness ended, when the world was back spinning on its axis again, she and Herman would adopt. Yes, that was a good plan. This house, as large as two of those cottages in St. Louis, needed children. The patter of little feet running upstairs, sliding across newly waxed parquet floors. Children were needed to liven this cold brick edifice, turn a mansion into a home.

Black Jack too adored these little interlopers. A new audience for his tricks, unjaded and appreciative of the simplest of gestures, especially little Louisa, the oldest, almost six now. She stared in awe at this giant who towered over her. "Come here, girl," he bellowed in a deep basso brofundo when he spied her standing in front of his consultation chamber. Too scared to flee, she approached slowly with great trepidation. "Hold out your hands." Louisa held them out in cuplike fashion as commanded.

Herman held the palms of his great hands out over hers. His fingertips and thumbs pressed together peaked in the middle like the top of a tent where his hands met. Suddenly a great deal of change flooded into the little girl's cupped palms. It filled to overflowing. When Black Jack withdrew his hands, the little girl could see over a hundred shining pennies. The weight of the coins put such a strain on her slender arms that they could hardly bear up under the load.

"There you go now. Go put that in your piggy bank and don't spend it. Okay?"

"Okay, Mr. Herman," the five year old promised. "Thank you!" she remembered to say as she ran down the hall with her treasure, seeking her mother's sister. "Aunt Eva, Aunt Eva. Look what Herman gave me!"

Most of all, Black Jack liked the way Eva was around children, soft and loving, maternalistic. Gone was the battle hardened, jaded modern woman he had made her into. His profession, these modern times, they had all conspired to rob the joie de vie and gaiety from their lives. Here with her sister's children they were like unspoiled and new, a loving family. For a brief moment, they were happy. He had never seen Eva so radiant. Maybe they could adopt some children. Keep the house full of busy bodies. Eva would like that.

The children stayed with them for nearly a year until their father, finally achieving a steady position, sent for his progeny. Sending them to California, Eva's joy left on the train with those little smiling faces. With nothing left but the stark reality of recession and daily drudgery of caring for the poor, she threw herself into her work to the exclusion of all else. Eva sincerely hoped that she had made some impression on those young lives. That her talks about putting faith in the Lord, striving for a quality education and always working for a better tomorrow were not over the capabilities of the children's understanding. 'Not little Louisa,' Eva comforted herself. Those bright eyes and attentive manner, she would remember well those lessons learned this past year.

Black Jack and his compatriots, Andrew and Washington, had worked tirelessly on the concept and planning of the new show for many months without any word from Professor Maharajah. The group had every angle figured out except the most important, how to pull off the trick.

In the spring of 1932, many months after BJ had penned the original letter describing his new trick, a correspondence arrived in the mail. 'Was pleased to receive your letter,' Professor Maharajah wrote. 'Am looking forward to seeing you in three weeks. I will call before my arrival. Professor M.'

"So he is alive." said Andrew with a trace of disbelief. He showed the letter to Washington.

"I can't wait to meet him," he beamed.

On the appointed day, Washington was dispatched to pick up the good professor. Apparently, he reeked of whiskey.

"How much do you drink, young man?" came the proper interrogation from the back seat of the limo.

"Not much. Say what's it to you?" the snide reply.

"I must tell you that I was much like yourself in my younger years. Couldn't get enough. Why the night I taught Houdini the handcuff escape I drank nearly a whole bottle of rum."

"You taught Houdini, the Great Houdini, a trick?" The young man's derisive tone clearly indicated he thought the older man a liar.

"Yes, the very one and the same. I've taught your master a trick or two in my time as well."

"Don't call him that," Washington blustered. "He's not my master."

"Oh, you have another then?" The Maharajah regarded him with suspicion.

"I don't have any master. I'm beholden to no one." he stated vehemently.

"Everyone has to serve someone. But only one master per customer. Any more causes conflicts that prey on the mind causing confusion and contradictions. As I started to say, I was like you once. Drank all of the time."

"What happened? What changed your mind?" the cynical question.

"I learned the peace that comes with meditation. The mental strength and the clarity of vision that come with the disciplines of the Eastern philosophies have a very calming nature," the Maharajah informed rather succinctly.

"I thought it was something like that. That stuff won't work for me," he scoffed.

"Well, liquor is quicker."

"What?"

"Oh, so you haven't heard that one? On the path to self-destruction, liquor is quicker," the Professor said playfully. Then in a more serious tone utilizing that piercing insight for which he was famous. "You must have a great deal on your mind to be so consumed by drink. The disbelief, the disillusionment, serving two masters is a difficult road, not for the intellectually challenged. You have to compartmentalize, to pack your guilt away in choosing one over another. It is a difficult road that few walk successfully. True mastery requires that you hide the truth even from yourself."

All the while during this continued liturgy, Washington was becoming increasingly uncomfortable, visibly so to even the untrained eye. Finally in a desperate attempt to squelch any further conversation, he shouted brusquely, "We are almost there, Professor."

"Ah, my old friend, so good to see you again." The warm embrace from the delighted host. "Thank you for coming. Welcome to my place. Come in. Come in."

"I see you've done quite well for yourself."

"Much of it thanks to your tutelage, I fear." BJ attempted modestly.

"I think far less than you give me credit for. Your success, If I am correct, came from your study and practice of those mental disciplines of which we spoke so long ago. And as I recall you had a much better teacher than I. Whatever happened to her?"

"I'm sorry to say that she had an untimely death. A traffic accident over half a decade ago," Black Jack said with remorse.

"And what of that lovely assistant you had," the Maharajah winked.

"Why, I married her."BJ beamed. "She'll be home soon. She performs charity at the local church."

"That is good news, my boy. Good news, indeed. Let's have a drink to celebrate your good fortune. I always thought you two were made for each other."

"Of course. What's your pleasure?" the gracious host inquired.

"How about a little sherry?"

The two men were still there hours later celebrating their re-acquaintance when Eva returned from church.

"Eva, is that you? Come here, I have someone for you to meet." Herman bellowed.

She arrived in the nook next to the kitchen to find the two men engaged in the most comraderous conversation, a half-empty bottle of sherry between them.

Startled and momentarily taken aback, she stood and stared, unaware that her mouth had opened.

The good professor immediately moved to her aid.

"Nice to see you, my dear. Let's see, it must be ten whole years now. How have you been?" He stood and offered his hand.

"Yes, you really gave me a startle. I remember well the last time we met. Nice to see you again, Professor. Look, I've gotten married since we last talked." She waved her ring finger for him to see.

"Yes, very nice. Deepest congratulations on your nuptials, my dear. I wish you happiness forevermore." he said before pressing his lips to her outstretched hand.

"Coming from you that means so much. So you'll be staying for dinner then?"

"Eva," Herman began resolutely, "he'll be staying for a lot longer than dinner. He has a couple of weeks free and I need his help on a new trick that I have been working on. Once we perfect it. I'm going out on the road again. This will be my greatest performance ever."

Suddenly, Eva felt weak.

"You're going on tour, again? But I thought you were through with that rabble. I thought after last time you said they were more trouble than they were worth," she exasperated.

"Quite true, but this time will be different. I'll be putting on a magic show. In these hard times everyone needs a little gaiety and magic to temporarily brighten their lives. The political manifesto will be secondary." he soothed.

"So I guess you figure the end of the world has been postponed," Eva surmised.

"I'll admit I did misinterpret my dire vision, but this economic downturn is unlike any occurrence in collective memory. You were right." Herman ceded. "When the city didn't burn a 'la Bible prophecy, I knew it couldn't be the end of the world. But honey, don't you see that's good news?" he continued. "That means we have another chance to get it right, to organize and implore for an end to this separate but equal policy. We have another chance to help people get ahead, teach them to hold their heads up with pride."

"Another chance for you to go marching off on a damn fool crusade," Eva countered. "I suppose the good professor is going with you."

"You're dead wrong, my dear," the old man spoke up for himself. "This tour, which I think is a fine idea by the way, is totally of your husband's creation. I am just here in an advisory capacity, to help him work out the few kinks in his new trick."

"And that is... "Eva attempted cross-examination.

"Before we talk about that, let me just say that the country is hurting right now with over thirteen million out of work. Men roaming the countryside looking for jobs, food or worse."

"You're really not helping here. Professor," interjected Black Jack.

"My God, woman, there is a shanty town across the street from the White House, I've seen it. Things are really horrible, and not only here, but it is spreading all over the world. People need heroes to lift up their consciousness, soothe spirits and provide the hope that tomorrow can be a brighter day."

The Professor had shamed Eva with his master's summation of events. Now he would deliver the coup de grace.

"Rightly or wrongly this great man you married has the power to sway thousands, tens of thousands, perhaps millions to his side. Provide them with hope, faith in themselves and their capabilities. When the new administration comes in next year as surely one must, we could have an army, Black Jack's army, that could march on Washington D.C. and demand equal rights and opportunities."

"Well, you've got me sold." said Eva wearily. "Now what's this new show stopping trick?"

Black Jack spoke up with no apology. "I'm going to bury myself alive for three days."

XX

Heroes

Eva, who rarely drank anymore, went to the cupboard and returning with a large glass, filled it half-full with sherry before sitting down next to the Professor. "Now, explain this to me. How is he going to do this?"

"Don't worry; he isn't really going into the ground for three days. In fact, he won't be going into the ground at all. A hidden panel in the coffin will be released just before it is lowered into the ground. Black Jack will scamper out the back while Andrew draws everyone's attention to the front of the gravesite," he glibly informed.

Black Jack continued the explanation of this charade of his own design. "We rent a gravesite. We will call it Black Jack's Private Graveyard. We put the box into the earth, cover it with dirt and leave it for three days. Washington will stand guard while Andrew and I go scouting the next stop on the tour. When it comes time for the exhumation, I sneak back in before we open the casket. Simple, right?"

Eva, now giddy from the wine, was at least glad that her husband would not be putting himself in any peril with this new stunt. But at the same time, she was disappointed. This was just a deceit, another con. Had they come so far only to resort to tricks? She made her disappointment known to both of them.

"Honey, it's not like that at all," BJ countered, seeking to justify his decisions. "These are desperate times which call for desperate measures. This is all an effort to get them to listen and take to heart my political agenda."

Professor Maharajah added, "My dear, you have undoubtedly heard of the concept the end justifies the means? Well, your husband is right. Times are desperate and Black Americans are looking for heroes. They will not inquire too closely at how the trick is done. When BJ tells them that they too have the power within them, they will believe thus raising their self-expectations. You see, what they need even more than heroes are leaders who will stand up, speak out, give them a feeling of self worth."

"So, what now? BJ is supposed to be some sort of Black Moses leading them out of bondage?"Queried Eva.

"I'll play whatever part history will have of me." Black Jack said humbly.

"You know, my dear, you really are married to a great man." the old man said in his best wizzened voice.

The Professor's conclusions proved chillingly right on the mark. In an era where the masses needed heroes, brave men who would speak out, bucking the system, their pedigrees were not too closely scrutinized, lest they turned out to be all too human. People wanted to believe, had to believe, that he could do it, return from the dead. Could he metaphysically come back to life; many hundreds did believe there was a trick to it, that he really didn't die. Even if he pretended to come back to life, then perhaps they too could have new lives. So Black Jack provided a medium of hope and escapism, no matter how transitory, from the intolerable nature of their day to day existence.

'Rebirth,' that was the title of his sermon to the audiences of the large northeast cities in the spring of 1933.

It is time for the rebirth and reawakening of the African American spirit. Time to throw off bonds of economic slavery and embrace this doctrine of the New Deal being offered by the newly elected administration. "This time we will be included in the shuffle," he promised.

"Always remember." the preamble to his summation, "We are those once and future kings. So hold your head up. Like the great hunter Nimrod, I go forth to do battle." Then he was on to the next show. Always leave them wanting more. Prince Herman would be proud to see how far he had come.

It did not matter if the venue was the northeast or the Midwest, wherever he went the crowds flocked, anxiously awaiting his arrival. The coming of this self-styled Black Moses who was going to lead them to equality. Herman's cult of personality status had been ensured by the thousands who turned out to see him perform. Some believed that he actually rose from the dead. Many more came to hear his message of hope and courage, convincing themselves through his oratory that better times were coming. Envisioning the creation of a society greater than ever conceived, daren't dreamed.

All of this had been accomplished utilizing a few simple tricks passed on by Professor Maharajah. How to put oneself into a light trance, use a rubber ball under the armpit and a tourniquet above the elbow to nullify the pulse, thereby simulating death.

Along with the theatrics, the Professor left Black Jack some good advice in the form of a riddle. "BJ, you've heard of the Legend of King Arthur, haven't you?" his mentor inquired.

"Who hasn't?"

"Well, so the story goes after all the villains were defeated and the dragons slain, Arthur turned to his Royal Sorcerer, Merlin, and asked, 'Where now in my kingdom is evil hiding?' Merlin replied simply, 'Where you least expect it, my Lord, as always.'"

Those were his parting words to the great magician. He sincerely believed there was danger lurking close by and hoped Black Jack would figure out the solution before it was too late.

Unfortunately, the two were never to meet again. Just before the start of the tour, the Professor passed away in his sleep in his bed at home.

That summer after the Midwest tour ended. Black Jack returned to New York to be with Eva, return to their life together.

The movie theaters abounded with 'talkies' of one variety or another. One that caused a great sensation was the fantastical story of a giant ape found in deepest Africa that was bewitched by the charms of a beautiful woman. Eva, after hearing so many flattering reports, was anxious to see for herself.

"They call him King Kong. He's ten times the size of the average man and very lifelike. We really should see it." She continued to wheedle and was finally able to drag him to see the picture.

Herman didn't go in for pictures much. Just another form of illusion, an opiate for the masses especially now that the economy had collapsed. 'Just like Ancient Rome, we have bread lines and circuses' he would say. Never mind that his shows similarly distracted people from the wretchedness of current conditions. His mind countered that at least he provided a little hope that things would work out. The times would get better. Those mind numbing dramas offered nothing but sheer escapism.

However, Eva's wishes prevailed. She could still work her wiles on him after all those years, and they crowded into a local theater with so many others to see the great ape. Black Jack was actually impressed, far beyond Eva's wildest expectations. He could not stop talking about the storyline. He was enthralled with the movie's message. Distinctly apart from the cinematic wizardry, which was to his mind a new form of magic destined to destroy the conjurer's tradition of live performance. If audiences could watch these fantastic stories over and over again, anything the mind could imagine, then who would go to see a live show unless there was the possibility of death, 'or the possibility of rising from the dead!'

This confirmed his opinion, the hulking monkey moving realistically on stage, that his was the only way to spread the message of revitalization. That his hope of instigating the greatest economic resurrection for his people since the Reconstruction period following the Civil War lay squarely on the mantle of his persona. 'King Kong's got nothing on me!' His mind roared, 'Like Nimrod...to battle!'

Now the storyline, that was altogether different. Far from the romantic claptrap that was exposed at the end, he could see the metaphor clearly. The crushing onslaught of civilization and the high price for nonconformity.

"Was that the way it was with us, BJ?" Eva cooed holding onto his arm tightly as they left the moving picture show surrounded on either side by the awestruck audience.

"Huh?" he responded distractedly, suddenly forced from deep thoughts back into the mundane. Clueless as to the question, let along the appropriate response.

"As the man said at the end of the picture," his wife persisted. "When we met was it 'Beauty that killed the beast?'"

"Of course, darling, he responded sincerely. "It was your beauty and charm that entrapped me and chained me to you for forever."

"Hey, don't say it like that. You make it sound like a jail sentence." Eva pouted.

"It is a sentence. Love has sentenced me to a life term-with you." He peered deeply into her eyes, but she was not falling for his charm. Not just yet.

"Without any possibility of parole." a dovish inquiry.

"Limited possibilities. Perhaps time off for good behavior."

"Hey!" Eva protested, feigning hurt.

"Just kidding. Just kidding." Herman grabbed her tightly, his arm sweeping around her waist.

As they moved with the crowd into the cool night air, he felt the need to expound upon the meaning of the movie's message. A metaphor not only of modern life, but indeed of civilization since time immemorial.

"I don't see how they could get away with putting on such a movie especially now during a depression, except they couched the true meaning with romantic nonsense."

His wife cringed. 'Here he goes again.'

"Here we have this big ape who is king of all he surveys. Remember him standing on the cliff overlooking the forest primeval?"

Eva nodded.

"They capture him, bend him to their will. When he won't cooperate and escapes, they destroy him. The analogies are clear. Take slavery, for example. There you have a direct correlation.

We came from Africa. When we step out of line, they destroy us. Even to this day, look what they did to General Garvey. He rots in Jamaica a broken man. They had that in mind for me, but I magically escaped." He clutched his wife closer as he looked up, challenging the gods.

"Look what they did to Germany after the Great War. That upstart Kaiser upset the hegemony; they crushed him and destroyed his country. Here in America people were making too much money in the twenties playing the stock market and real estate games. So the industrialists pulled the plug on the economy to regain the power they perceived to have lost. But as usual, things got out of control and went too far. Anarchy abounded.

Now to set things right, the new president, Roosevelt, had to close the banks, calling it an extended 'bank holiday.' What a clever euphemism for the carving up of distressed assets; for the robber barons to reassert dominion, to tighten their grip further. How does the song go? 'Ain't we got fun...' The rich get richer and the poor get...breadlines."

"Honey, I think you've been listening to too many of your own speeches." Eva chirped sarcastically.

"You mark my words, Eva. The time will come. The people will rise up and demand their quotient of prosperity. As Mr. Lincoln so aptly put it, 'You can't fool all of the people all of the time.'

Herman halted his speechmaking and abruptly switched gears. "Let's go and get a drink. I have a lot to think over." Eschewing the limo, he decided to walk through the dark, desolate night. Black Jack Herman had spoken.

As Eva accompanied her husband on his quest for relinquishment of sobriety stumbling on broken pavement in vain attempt to keep up, he continued his turbulent blusterings. "President Roosevelt should repeal the Twenty-First Amendment. If you don't have a job or a place to live, at least you could get a drink."

"It seems that we can't even have equality in poverty." Black Jack was addressing a group of reporters at the Cotton Club. They were all there for the announcement of the winter tour through the southern circuit. The whole company had just arrived from taking publicity photos at a mock up Black Jack's Private Graveyard in a nearby park.

"Separate but equally poor. I like that. Maybe I will entitle my next speech with that moniker." he joked with reporters.

By this time the Jitterbug had replaced the Charleston as the dance of choice among the younger generation. The jazz age was growing up. Horns and bass were merging with woodwinds in an orchestral setting called 'Big Band.' The dancers moving to this 'swing' music jumped about like Hottentots appropriately swinging their partners to and fro. A group of twenty-something's demonstrated the latest steps on stage behind Herman's press conference.

"Ah, it's great to be here in the Cotton Club." he said, briefly acknowledging the dancers. "Very nice to finally be able to enter the club as a patron."

"Mr. Herman, did you ever perform here?" one of the reporters asked.

"I would never perform in any club where black patrons were excluded." he stated firmly. "Now that we are allowed in the front door, maybe I will grace them with a performance when I return in the spring."

"Mr. Herman, Mr. Herman," another reporter cried, "The President didn't take it too kindly when you said the black man needed another forty acres and mule."

"Boys, that was just a joke somebody took out of context. I said President Lincoln promised each former slave forty acres; forty acres to farm and a mule to plow. Somebody better tell President Roosevelt that the forty acres was stolen and the mule died." Almost everyone laughed at the rehashed tale.

"There's no story there. I only meant that President Roosevelt should dish out an equal measure of prosperity to blacks and whites when he shuffles the new deal. This time we want a real deal. I'm not falling into any of your reporter's word games, I've seen King Kong. I know what happens to malcontents." This time everyone laughed. As Black Jack and associates met in November to plan the logistics of the tour, Washington Reeves suggested they use his girlfriend as new assistant.

"I didn't know you were seeing any one woman," said Andrew.

"I met her this summer. She knows show biz. I think she could be a big hit."

"What's her name?" asked BJ.

"Lulu. She's really pretty and I didn't want to leave her alone all winter, if you know what I mean." Washington smiled slyly.

"Oh, young love." said Andrew.

"Bring her around." BJ said. "I'll give her a try."

The band of performers set out on the winter tour. Lulu in tow, and met adversity and consternation everywhere they performed. Their fame had preceded them. A soon to be familiar scene was repeated all across the south.

"Boys, it's gonna cost you a lot more to perform this year," said the county sheriff smoking a fat cigar.

"But we've already paid you the standard up front fee for the site." Andrew protested.

"That was before I got wind of your new show. I hear you're drawing 'em in by the thousands. That'll call for more security, just in case." He leaned back away from the desk, cigar now in hand, and expelled a long plume of smoke.

"Pay the man what he wants." Black Jack said dispassionately.

The roll of paper bills was dropped onto the desk.

"You're lucky I'm letting you perform at all. My phone's been ringing off the hook all day! Deacons, ministers outraged. Imagine buried alive for three days. They say you're making a mockery of religion. I told 'em freedom of speech and assembly, besides don't nobody believe it but darkies."

"So you will issue the permit then?" asked Andrew curtly.

"See my secretary on the way out. She'll have your papers."

Black Jack grabbed his brother's arm and led him away without another word. When they were out of earshot he said, "When in hell you've got to give the devil his due."

Black Jack's performance was designed from the beginning to stupefy. Every facet was engineered psychologically to give the feeling that mystical powers were at work. To prove that Black Jack was larger than life, the sign over the chosen location teased 'Look! Look! Black Jack's Private Graveyard.' Crowds would come to watch the preparation. Some would stay the entire time, over three days, relishing the atmosphere-just to be in the presence of greatness.

The grave diggers would arrive the day before, prepare the site. Others in the entourage would make an appearance, wave to the crowds. Eventually and with much fanfare, Professor Herman would arrive and announce to the attendees that; using the powers of the ages, he was going to put himself into a trance so deep as to mimic death.' He would then invite the crowd to come back in three days to witness his triumphant revival. Retiring behind a moveable screen he would climb into the coffin and perform his magic.

After about ten minutes Andrew and Washington would remove the screen revealing Black Jack lying in his coffin, dead to the world. Then the fun began as the audience was invited, for five cents a piece, to come and view the graveyard and Herman up close. A few women were chosen and invited to check his pulse. Squeamishly they grasped his wrist and pulled back in revulsion. 'He must be dead. There's no pulse.'

Depending on the crowd size, which was usually quite large, Herman would have to lay there motionless for over an hour. After the last 'mourners' had filed by, the coffin was closed and screwed shut. It was during this event that Black Jack made his great escape. He would watch from the wings as the coffin was lowered into the ground and covered with dirt.

Andrew would then address the crowd, "Show's over folks. Come back in three days and witness the amazing conclusion. But before you go, you can purchase something to commemorate the event." All manner of trinkets were offered for sale including books on mind control and magic and Black Jack's special tonic which had been reformulated and bottled for this occasion.

Washington was required to stay there the whole time guarding the site. He and another of Andrew's assistants would take turns, holding vigil all night to protect against vandals or curiosity seekers bent on despoiling the trick. Both men were well armed as there were many who would like to see the end to what was considered anywhere from nonsense to blasphemy.

The intervening days passed slowly for Mr. Reeves and

accomplice while Herman and Andrew were miles away talking up their act for the next stop on the tour.

On the day of the revival the two brothers would slip back into town and take their places prior to the exhumation and revival. Once the screws had been removed, Washington's girlfriend Lulu would step up to the platform in her short costume and perform the honors.

The lid raised, she usually slapped Herman's face lightly and stood to one side while to the amazement of the crowd, he stirred, took breath and sat up! Sometimes there was clapping, but it was more usual for not a sound to be uttered. Shock and awe swept over the audience as Black Jack, with the aid of his female assistant, scrambled out of the box and onto his feet. Lulu always presented him with a bottle of tonic to drink to renew his strength after the long sleep. It was good advertising. The crowds parted without a word as he walked forth from his 'graveyard' to stroll down the block or across the compound to the stage.

After beginning with a few magic tricks, he would launch into his sermon which for this southern circuit had taken on scolding paternalistic overtones.

"You people should be ashamed of yourselves. I've seen you scraping and bowing, calling them 'Mr. Charlie' like they've got something for you. They don't have anything for you, don't you get it?" he shouted. "We're all equal, equally poor, but we are still separate. It's time you showed a little pride in yourselves. Hold your heads up, comport yourselves like you are somebody. They don't own you anymore and you don't owe them nothing. We call this tour Rebirth because it is about the rebirth of spirit, rebirth of pride, within the African American community.

"When you address them, stop saying sir. 'Anything you want sir.' Call them what they are, men. Say listen man, neither of us has got anything. Let's see if we can get something together otherwise, stay outta my way. I'm trying to get mine!" The crowds, always a packed house, howled approval by this point. Many had never heard anyone talk like that in their lives. "Remember, we are of Nimrod!" he shouted for emphasis. "We are once and future kings and beholden to no one. King Kong ain't got nothing on me!"

Black Jack had begun beating on his chest at that point of the speech in Richmond, and it really caught on with the crowds. The men all stood and beat on their chests mimicking the great ape.

Wherever he went, trouble followed, when it was not proceeding. Many magistrates were becoming concerned at the alarming reports emanating from his show. The telephone wires between state capitals were burning. "We need to discredit him in front of his audience. Convince him that he should have stayed up north where people can appreciate his type of performance." one Congressman complained.

"I hear you. If he performs down here again, there will be big trouble. I tell you what. Making a mockery of religion, next he'll be walking on water." the voice cried, "Where is the Ku Klux Klan when you need them anyway?"

The question went unanswered for a moment, but then the Congressman had a suggestion. "There's a guy we can talk to in D.C. Maybe persuade him that it would be better for everyone if that magician didn't perform his act down here anymore. Meanwhile, I'd better call the mayor of Louisville and tell him he's in for a big mess of trouble if he lets them perform that magic show."

"Well you know technically, legally, there's nothing we can do. Freedom of speech and all," the mayor apologized. "Now if you were to tell me he was inciting to riot, I could get a restraining order lickety split. You know we are a big city, not some backwoods parish. We just can't get away with shutting him down without cause. But, I'm glad you called. We'll keep an eye out for trouble." the mayor promised.

"Oh Herman, I'm so glad to hear your voice. I've been so worried. I had the most horrible dream about you." Eva confided, gushing with worry.

"Baby, the tour is going great. The crowds are bigger than we expected. I think I'm really getting through to them. Anyway, the next stop is Kentucky. After that, we move on to St. Louis. I'll meet you in Chicago as planned. Tell Lilly hello. I love you. Bye!" The receiver went dead.

The performance in Kentucky went smooth as silk. Crowds came from at least three states to see him rise from the dead. Word had spread like wildfire of this never before seen drama. Black Jack's magical prowess and his uplifting message.

During the intervening time between immersion and revival, BJ and Andrew decided to take an impromptu vacation. With St. Louis, their next stop on the tour, hundreds of miles away, for once there was no work to be done. The brothers decided to go to Cincinnati and sample some Kentucky whiskey. Checking into a hotel under assumed names, they hung out at the bar and got drunk.

"Well, little brother, we really pulled it off. We put on a show that will have them talking for years." congratulated BJ, hoisting a glass of whiskey. "Here's to you."

"No, no." Andrew protested. "Here's to you for a magical performance second to none. Only thing, I don't know how we will ever top this."

"Maybe I could run for Congress?" BJ said matter of factly.

"Say what?"

"Don't look surprised. If that guy Clayton Powell can get elected from New York, I should be a shoo-in. Don't you think?"

"But he's our representative." Andrew decried.

"Then I suppose I'll have to move. It's just a thought. Drink up!"

BJ raised the glass to his lips and smiled—the smile of satisfaction, of one who has just become one with the eternal. His manifest destiny was becoming crystal clear.

Meanwhile, the contact in D.C. had issued a verdict that would eliminate Black Jack Herman as a problem forever.

Back in Louisville, Kentucky, the crowds were anxiously awaiting the revival. The culmination of the exotic event such as audiences had never before seen.

The sign above the make-shift graveyard said: 'Black Jack's tonic is good for you.' It was a bitter irony that just as Socrates drank poison rather than prevaricate, Herman was given poison exactly because he spoke the truth.

The eyedropper, as yet unseen, contained a combination of water and bitter almond, a crude yet effective remedy. Slipped into the open bottle of tonic by surreptitious sleight of hand, the deed was done. Afterward, the skullduggery accomplished, the sinister arm faded back into the darkness.

Lulu handed the tonic to BJ. Now a soda with a few special ingredients, a most sickly-sweet black cherry flavor, cloyingly sweet, the perfect conveyance. This bottle however had a little bitterness. 'Perhaps a bad batch,' thought Black Jack. Never mind, Herman drank his potion. The show, that iconic moment, must continue.

Black Jack, fresh from his 'resurrection,' imbibed deeply. The sweet nectar flowed rapaciously as bubbles of trapped air replaced liquid in the glass bottle. This pitch sold the tonic as nothing else: 'To refresh, reinvigorate, renew'-the accompanying slogan. The price had been reduced to five cents per bottle, a 'depression' special. A bankrupt bottling company had run them off for pennies per case. But this tour was not about profit. The message was the mission. 'We are all of us equal. They are no better than us. We are all broke. Time for a new beginning. We are once and future kings!'

In an era where the masses needed heroes, people wanted to believe, had to believe, that if anyone could do it, the Great Black Jack Herman could return from the dead. If he could magically return from the dead, then perhaps they too could have new lives and escape from the intolerable nature of their day to day existence.

Lulu headed up the street twirling her baton, a good impersonation of a drum majorette. Black Jack was close behind striding confidently, head held high. The crowds followed at a respectful distance, amazed and mystified.

As they reached the theater, his hand suddenly clutched his stomach, his left foot misstepped. Momentarily shaken, he recovered and walked to the stage. He and Lulu began the act with a few simple tricks, but Herman's timing was off. The crowds could not tell, but he could. Something was wrong. Perspiration beaded upon his brow.

In the middle of the sword cabinet trick, Black Jack Herman collapsed on stage, never to revive. Washington rushed in and called for a doctor from the audience. Help didn't arrive on time, if indeed ministrations from mortal agents could have righted BJ this time.

The audience however was in a state of disbelief. They genuinely believed that this new twist was another part of the drama. What would he do this time? Would his body disappear in a poof of smoke? Perhaps he would magically reappear in mid-air with the wings of an angel. There were many theories. Of one thing the audience was certain; this 'event' would be the best one yet. They waited patiently.

As the 'show' progressed on stage, the audience stared anxiously and attentively, not wanting to miss an iota of the drama. The 'doctor' on stage had pronounced him dead. The ambulance crew had come and placed him on a stretcher. The disposition of the body was contemplated. There was no need for a morgue, no autopsy required. It was a simple case of 'acute indigestion.' The body could go straight to the funeral home. The phrase 'acute indigestion' telegraphed through the crowd. Many smiled a knowing smile. After all, who dies of 'acute indigestion'? They just knew this was all part of the new act they were privileged to witness. The crowds waited pensively for the drama to unfold.

The next episode in the drama would occur at the mortuary as Andrew released the 'body' and the ambulance drove away. The crowds scrambled after the auto, jockeying to acquire the best vantage for the presumed spectacular conclusion. This was the best performance theater ever! How long would he be out for this time, nobody knew. Would it be another three days? Whatever the length, the crowds would hold vigil.

Word spread by mouth, telephone and even telegraph that Black Jack was involved in some fantastic new trick. There was widespread talk that he had fully ascended, as only the most powerful and holy of the Hindu masters could, reaching the astral plane, it was speculated that he would return as a ball of light shining over the funeral home. Over the next twenty four hours hundreds, if not thousands, rushed to Louisville to see the conclusion.

On the morning of the day after, Andrew and Washington were amazed to find the crowds camped en mass around the home awaiting resumption of the show. The gathering stirred anxiously surmising now that Herman's accomplices had arrived perhaps the conclusion was close at hand.

They were only half wrong. Upon seeing these crowds, ever growing, Washington had a novel idea. "Say, look here, boss." he breached the subject to Andrew. "The body has been nicely prepared over night. He looks real good in fact. With those people out there just waiting for something, why don't we let them...view the body?"

"Are you crazy? Bring that mob in here? Eva will have a fit when she gets here," Andrew's shocked reply.

"When do you expect her?"

"I don't know. I haven't called her yet." Andrew confessed with a sly grin.

"Then I'll say it again. Why don't we let in a few at a time and charge them just like Herman's Private Graveyard. That's what a great show man like BJ would have done," the sly rejoinder.

"I guess that would be all right. We will charge five cents a piece to view the body." Andrew said, mentally calculating.

"Make it ten cents," Washington encouraged.

And so the bizarre odyssey of Herman's passing continued for another forty-eight hours as crowds, ever growing, waited in line to see his remains. While many believed this was still part of some elaborate trick, most merely came to pay their respects to the man who had brought them hope and courage, levity and laughter, filled them with awe and adoration over the years. A few brought pins to stick in his body to make sure he was really dead. Literally thousands of people filed past that coffin for one final look at the great man.

Even as hundreds of followers continued to pour over the hillside, Andrew and Washington figured it time to shut down the operation. The small funeral home had been overwhelmed by unaccustomed attention. No other business was possible while this spectacle continued.

Andrew broke down and called Chicago with the bad news. "Hello, Lilly. Put Eva on. Hello, Eva. Honey, I've got some bad news," he paused. These things were never easy to tell, best to just get it over. "Honey, Black Jack died on stage. Yes, we're still here in

Kentucky. Three days ago. I know, I know. It's been so hectic. I'm sorry. Look, all the preparations have been made. Meet us at the train station. Goodbye."

Andrew left Washington and Lulu with the body at the train station to await Eva's arrival.

"Everything's been taken care of. Our equipment and supplies will be freighted in a couple of days. The body will be shipped direct to Grand Central. All you have to do is wait for Eva." Andrew instructed.

"What about you?" Lulu asked.

"I have one more thing to do." Andrew replied cryptically.

After he left, Washington and Lulu decided things would be better for them if Eva did not find them attendant. Purchasing a pair of tickets they left for parts unknown. Lilly and Eva arrived at the train station to find the body minding itself. Everyone had deserted her husband. Longtime friends and sibling had vanished into thin air.

As she signed the shipping release, Eva suddenly wished that BJ hadn't fired Carl all those years ago. 'At least Carl would have stuck by BJ in his hour of need.' She shared her thoughts with Lilly.

"But Carl was in love with you." Lilly reminded. "Black Jack could never tolerate anyone around who could vie for your affection."

"You're right, you know. After Baltimore when Carl drove me to D.C. over BJ's objections, that was the turning point in their relationship." Eva agreed.

"He always has been possessive, his tricks, his vehicles, his women. I kinda think that comes from growing up with nothing, living hand to mouth. Having everyone you loved taken away, you never want to feel the pangs of loss again. That's why he hated to think of anyone taking you away." theorized Lilly.

"You're wrong there," Eva protested softly, "He felt we were star crossed right from the beginning, you know that."

"I suppose you're right." ceded Lilly.

Eva sobbed softly. "Wasn't beauty that killed the beast this time."

The two women sat in silence as the train began its forward motion down the tracks to New York.

Their arrival in Manhattan brought another surprise. After the body was sent on its way, Eva and Lilly hurried home. The staff was still off and the mansion was quiet.

Upon entering the door to the bedroom, Eva noticed the closet door askew. With great trepidation, she crossed the room to find the door to the safe similarly ajar. "Lilly, come here quick," she shouted.

"What is it?"

"Someone cleaned out the safe," Eva yelled.

"You mean you've been robbed?" Lilly asked.

"No, I don't. You couldn't get into the safe without dynamite. See there are no marks on the door. Only three people had the combination to the safe. One's dead and another is in this room." The cold truth dawning on her.

"Say, that only leaves…" It was dawning on Lilly too.

"Right, Andrew. No wonder he wasn't waiting for us." said Eva with sudden clarity.

"What a busy little bee that boy's been. First charging to view the body and now this. He must have gotten away with a fortune," said Lilly struggling to grasp this new reality.

"More than a fortune," Eva corrected. "More like two fortunes."

"You can bet that we'll never see him again. I told you I always had a funny feeling about that little major domo and his henchmen too." Lilly was seething with vehemence.

Tears started to well in Eva's eyes. She crumpled on the bed. "You don't understand. I won't have enough money to bury him now." Distraught, she buried her head in hands and lost control of her emotions.

"Wait." Lilly counseled, an idea forming. "You may not have enough cash, but I know who will. Fix your face; we have to go see a lady."

Together now refreshed and becalmed, the two women paid a visit to Madame C.J. Walker's, their long acquaintance with the Herman's had overcome the test of time.

Yes, they had heard the news. Tales had been splashed sensationally on the front page of local papers for days. The collapse on stage, the throngs in the thousands, was big news in this cultural mecca where Herman was a local hero. New York would want to say its goodbyes as well and it expected a send off that would top anything witnessed in a backwater such as Kentucky. The Madam Walker Institute, knew exactly to what protocols they were adherent in this situation. They also knew all too well what scandal would be caused if word of this sibling rivalry leaked.

In light of their longstanding close association, they would gladly see that this great man received the send off that he deserved. This his fans required, nay history required in remembrance of him.

True to her promise to Black Jack those many years ago during Houdini's procession, Eva had provided the 'state' funeral that she knew he always wanted, with a little help from her friends.

The funeral was held with great fanfare at the largest Baptist church in Harlem, which was filled to overflowing. Crowds lined the route from the church to get a last view of Herman as his hearse proceeded to Woodlawn Cemetery in the Bronx for his final disposition.

Asked for a comment, a tribute to her husband, Eva read later that she had said, "Black Jack Herman cannot die, he must continue on Earth. His mission is to solve all the ills and ailments of the poor and disadvantaged." Eva never remembered a thing.

After the funeral, the ceremonies and the celebrations were over, Lilly and Eva retired to the mansion replacing bravado with remorse,

"What will you do now? Now that the wild ride is over?" Lilly always had a way of framing the question.

"I don't know. I guess this will mean the end of Herman Enterprises. With Black Jack gone, the demand for his merchandise will certainly dry up."

"Don't be too sure. We could probably beat this horse for another couple of years." Lilly suggested.

All at once Eva lifted the weight of the world from her shoulders and cast it squarely on the ground.

"I'm tired, Lil. I can only take so much. I've had enough. This final outrage, this thievery, that's the last straw. I don't know what

I will do, but maybe it's time to bury the memory along with the body."

There was a moment of silence in the Herman kitchen before Eva continued. "You keep the money you and Daniel have in the safe in Chicago. You'll need it. God knows you've earned it. I've got enough to keep things going here for a few months. But as of now, Herman Enterprises has ceased operations." She was weary. The light, the love of her life, had gone out of her world.

"What will you do then? Go back to St. Louis?" Lilly inquired gently.

"No." A firm reply, no hesitation. "New York is my home. I guess I'll have to look for a job."

Jobs for the unskilled were not easy to come by with hundreds of applicants applying for each opening. Months later with her meager funds almost exhausted, she withdrew to her home, despondent and alone.

For days she sat crumpled in the bedroom of that empty house, deeply depressed, reliving the events that had brought her to this sad state of affairs. How everything had been lost, stolen. She would not eat and barely slept, just sitting in that big canopied bed clutching the pillows to her breast as if they were the shattered pieces of her former life. A life that slipped all the faster away from her the more tightly she clutched.

When the marshals came and broke down the front door after repeated knockings went unheeded, reality returned to her. Eva knew what they wanted. The last vestiges of her former empire, the last vestiges of her sanity.

She clutched her throat to make sure the diamond necklace, the last of her jewelry, was still there under her dress. She hadn't lost it yet. Her last connection with Black Jack, the item that identified her as his queen. How he looked at her when she wore that necklace. How they had all looked at her. She was the center of attention, a star.

But how would she keep her treasure? Already she could hear the sounds of men coming for her, up the stairs to take all of her possessions away. Wait! What was that she spied beside the bed? A porcelain chamber pot. Yes! That would do. Eva quickly undid the clasp on the necklace, her fingers moving spasmodically behind her head. It was loose in her hands. After admiring the shining item for just a second, she dropped the bauble into the porcelain receptacle. A half empty cup of stale coffee would provide the perfect cover. The liquid effectively obscured her treasure.

Short moments later, burly men broke in bearing notices, seizure of property and chattels, eviction. Their words swept over her almost unheard. Movers proceeded to dismantle the furniture and carry it away. In the midst of this perfect storm, Eva sat motionless.

The men, their tasks complete, left Eva sitting cross-legged in the midst of an empty room holding tightly to a pillow, chamber pot by her side. The eviction notice posted on the door gave her twenty four hours to vacate the premises. In the morning when she left she had only the clothes on her back and her purloined prize.

Eva made her way to the Baptist shelter at which she had so often volunteered. After a week in their care, she was able to right herself, keep her emotions in check.

Her prize, her joy, her remembrance of a life now long gone, became her only source of funds. Every so often she would pry one of the diamonds from the necklace and cautiously make her way down to the jewelry district in mid-town Manhattan. There she would exchange her memories for enough money to live- another day, week, year.

After a time, she was able to find both an apartment and a job. Once again, she had risen with resplendence as Madame Deborah promised, as Professor Maharajah avowed. To face all the challenges the modern world had to offer.

Epilogue

Now while Eva was unable to have children of her own she had a lasting effect on her nieces. As star of the stage and widow of the late lamented Black Jack Herman, her notions on honesty and fair play; her desire for righteousness above all, carried a great import with her young charges. Many would remember the time spent in the Herman's mansion for the rest of their lives.

Of these young women influenced by their Aunt Eva, two became nuns, giving their lives to God. One followed in Eva's show business tradition spending thirty years on the Broadway stage. Little Lousia, whom Eva loved so dearly, became first a model, then a nurse-and eventually, nursemaid to her aunt.

Finally, there was her brother's daughter who came to live with Eva as a teenager, after Herman's demise, sharing the depths of the Great Depression. After the next war to end all wars, she garnered top honors in achieving an MBA; thereby, embarking on a thirty year career as a stockbroker on Wall St.

Such is the legacy of Eva Rucker.

Bibliography

Belson, David. What to say and how to say it. Secaucus, N.J.: Citadel Press, 1955.

Haskin, Jim and Benson, Kathleen. Conjure Times: Black Magicians in America. New York: Walker Company, 2001.

Magus, Jim. Magical Heroes: The Lives and Legends of Great African American Magicians. Marietta, GA: Magus Enterprises, 1995.

Time Life Books. The Rise of Dictators: 1900-1945. Alexandria, VA: Time Life Books, 1987.

Printed in the United States
by Baker & Taylor Publisher Services